SHORT-CUT TO DECAY

The Case of the Sudan

Edited by

Sharif Harir & Terje Tvedt

Nordiska Afrikainstitutet, Uppsala 1994
(The Scandinavian Institute of African Studies)

Indexing terms:
Civil War
Conflicts
Economic conditions
Ethnicity
Government policy
Political development
State
Sudan

Cover: Adriaan Honcoop
Language editing: Elaine Almén
Map: Ola Bergkvist

Printed in Sweden by
Motala Grafiska AB, Motala 1994

ISBN 91-7106-346-3

Contents

THE SUDAN. *Some places and group names used in the book*

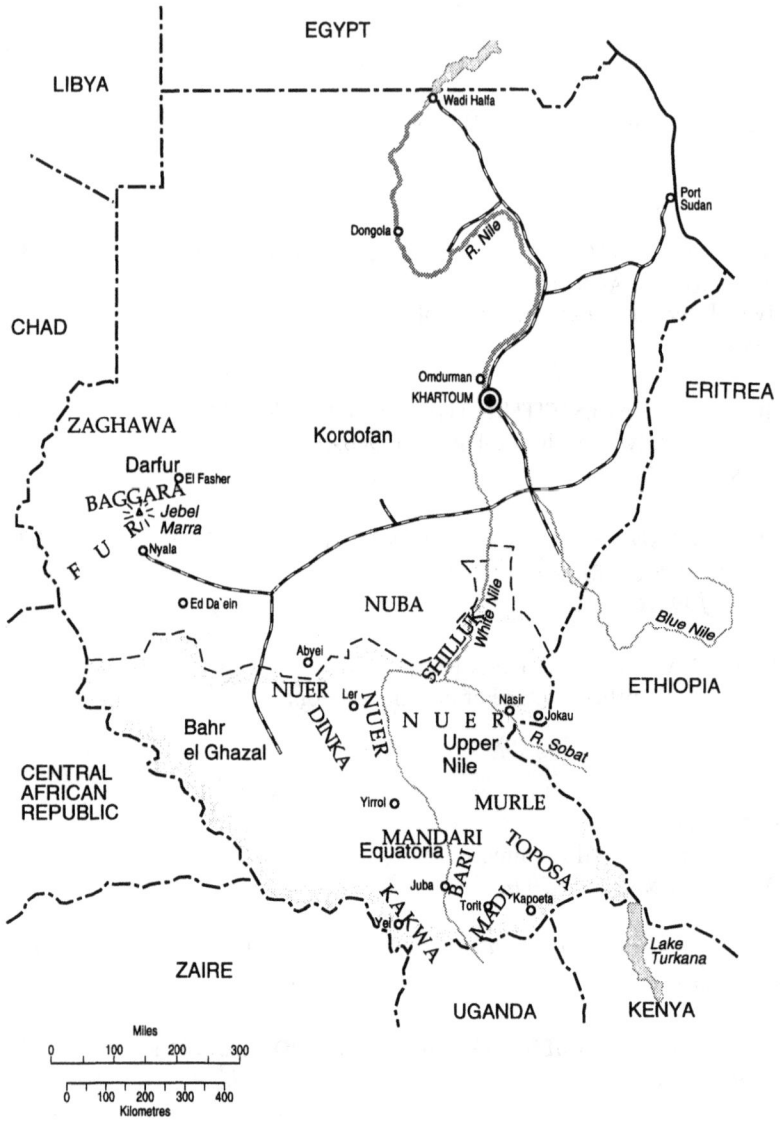

Foreword

The Addis Ababa Peace Accord of 1972 was hailed as a unique example of a negotiated peace settlement in Africa and the third world in general. It was regarded as unique not only because the leaders of the Sudan and its conflicting factions had managed to overcome their differences and opted for negotiated peace after seventeen long years of war and roaring guns, but also because it was negotiated by African partners at the peak of the cold war where every faction could easily have found allies with massive arms supplies.

Although the actual achievements of the peace accord and the concomitant political and institutional arrangements proved to have been exaggerated, the agreement showed that, even in the most intractable conflicts and provided that the political will is there, it is possible to trade guns and havoc for diplomacy and negotiations. However, the optimism which was precipitated by this "unprecedented" negotiated settlement of an intricate political conflict conducted through the means of arms, and the feelings of national unity, were soon to be eroded by a combination of what Mazrui (1986) might have called "forces of anarchy" on the one side, and "forces of tyranny" on the other. "Africa", Mazrui writes, "was torn between the forces of anarchy on the one side, in the sense of decentralized violence, and the forces of tyranny, in the sense of orchestrated centralized repression"(Mazrui 1986:20).

The spirit of the Addis Ababa Agreement was gradually but consistently undermined and eventually eroded by the same political leadership whose courage was applauded by the world when it brought about the peace settlement. Despite the fact that the Addis Ababa Agreement of 1972 had stipulated that the three provinces of the South should constitute an autonomous region with its capital at Juba, for reasons of political expediency, the President of the Sudan decreed on 1 June 1983 the division of the South into three regions. In September 1983 Islamic Sharia law was also introduced by a presidential decree which reinforced the differences between the South and the North. The civil war returned again in 1983 and it continues unabated today. The erosion of optimism and the reinforcement of animosities and the distinct possibility of national disintegration in the Sudan are apparent as never before.

It is generally accepted that there are no short cuts to development and progress. There are, however, short cuts to decay as the case of former Yugoslavia has proven and the case of the Sudan continues to demonstrate forcefully. The situation in the Sudan seems to move from bad to worse. The economy is in shambles and the country is internationally more isolated than ever. The war in the South seems to have no end—an endless cycle of repeated miseries. Centralized repression knows no limits and decentralized violence prevails over peaceful coexistence. Privatization of the state and its militarization seem to harmonize themselves in the unfolding drama of ideological bigotry and abuse of human rights. A small minority enrich themselves in the wake of the war economy while the majority have to fight for their daily bread in the camps of the displaced and urban slums.

The articles in this book, severally and collectively, address certain aspects of the processes of decay from economic, historical, political and sociological viewpoints. While the civil war in the South occupies a large space, the focus is more on the processes that are common to the country as a whole. A quick survey of these essays is in order. Douglas H. Johnson, in his article, raises the basic question: How far is the reconstruction of the Southern Sudan possible before peace is secured? He pursues this question by summarizing the scale of destruction in the rural South and in some of the towns most affected by the civil war since 1983. The amount of damage done by the New Civil War (1983–1992) has been so huge that the damage done during the First Civil War (1955–1972) pales almost into insignificance. This is due to the multiplication of the warring factions and the ideological bent this latest civil war has assumed. It has pre-empted any possibilities of development-oriented investments upon which reconstruction could be based. The prospects of rehabilitation and development before rural peace has been secured are dismal.

Terje Tvedt looks into the uniqueness of the state administration in Southern Sudan, especially after the Addis Ababa settlement. He highlights some of the problems the new post-1972 state had in rooting itself in the society as a unifying, stable force. The dominant role played by the foreign Non-Governmental Organizations (NGOs), is also analysed. Contrary to the prevalent notion that NGOs inherently play an important democratizing function in Africa by strengthening and pluralizing civil society, it is argued that NGOs may erode state authority, may "privatize" the state, without being able to strengthen the so-called civil society.

Raphael K. Badal, a political scientist and a Southerner who occupied a ministerial post in Southern Sudan (1985–86), is well placed to expose the internal political cleavages in the Southern Sudan. Conventionally, political cleavages within Southern Sudanese society, have not been a subject of interest to scholars, for the problem has generally been portrayed as South versus North. In this paper, Badal follows such cleavages through a long span of time beginning with the Juba conference of 1947, through the independence movement of the early fifties and the redivision of the South in 1983 that sparked off the Second Civil War. For Badal, these internal cleavages are as important in understanding the Sudanese problem, as the external South/North cleavages. Because, time and again, it has been splits or divisions within the ranks of Southern Sudanese political leadership or "freedom fighters" at crucial and decisive moments that have had radical impacts upon subsequent events. Vindication can be found in the split between Torit-SPLA and Nassir-SPLA in August 1990.

M.A. Mohamed Salih and Sharif Harir look into the phenomenon of tribal militias. The civil wars in the Southern Sudan have had many consequences for the Sudan. One consequence is the wide spread of decentralized violence in the South itself and in other parts of the country that lie outside the geographical South. Tribal militias tacitly supported by the government are such vehicles of decentralized violence. Originally conceived by the government as fighters by proxy, tribal militias were later elevated and given legal status by the 1989 National Popular Defence Act. The proliferation of tribal militias in this civil war does not only depress the chances of reaching a peaceful solution, but also negates the role of the government as the sole authority which possesses coercive force in conducting public affairs. It polarizes society more sharply. The chances of national disintegration are distinctly increased, especially as most of these tribal militias are sponsored by the government of the "nation" against other national groups.

Peter Woodward explores some past and present aspects of the Sudan's constitutional debate and suggests future issues. He advises against a hasty decision on a constitutional blueprint as a way to improve upon the present conflict situation. He argues that so many areas of the country are in such a condition of decay and violence that to draw up a constitutional blueprint seems inappropriate at present. Seeking consensus for a more effective constitutional structure than hitherto, is, perhaps the only way. This has to be the hope, for without it the future is bleak. By seeking consensus one develops a sense of constitutionalism, which cannot be achieved by adding new constitutional blueprints, which already abound in the annals of Sudanese political practice.

Sharif Harir demonstrates by the use of case material, how a limited conflict over natural resources can develop into a regional war of quasi-international character. The frames for this transformation are provided by the spreading civil war in the country, the ideological and material sponsoring of certain tribal militias by the government and the interests displayed by Libya and Chad as opposing regional powers. The ideological and racial cleavages between Arabs and non-Arabs which have been a constant throughout the Sudanese conflict are highlighted here in this conflict between the Fur and the Arab tribes of Dar Fur. The paper concludes, on the strength of the evidence it employs, that the Southern Sudan tragedy is likely to repeat itself in Dar Fur if necessary steps are not taken.

Karl Wohlmouth explores the economic, social and ecological aspects of the Sudan's crisis which are manifest in the large-scale human rights violations, the mass displacement of people and the increasing poverty and starvation in the country. The economic crisis escalated, he argues, at the end of the 1970s when the country abandoned its Six Year Plan and negotiated a stabilization programme with the International Monetary Fund (IMF).

However, the crisis emerged earlier and has to do with the development path chosen since independence. Decline of industrial output and capacity use, deterioration of overall growth performance and productivity, high instability of agricultural output, decreasing savings capacity and declining investment rates, were some of the observable characteristics. While the regime in power since the *coup d'état* of June 1989 has vowed to change economic policy radically, the record shows a clear contradiction between rhetoric and reality. Increasing import dependency, lack of monetary control, lack of exchange rate stability, absence of sectoral complementarity, imprudent use of public funds and reliance on deficit finance are some of the most glaring contradictions.

Most Sudanese and foreign observers would agree that the Sudan is decaying in every sphere. Sharif Harir seeks to overview the magnitude of decay and its underlying causes. It would appear that the civil war in the South, the dissipation of the nation's resources by this destructive endeavour over a long span of time and the endemic political instability have contributed to the progressive decline of the Sudanese state and the decay of its institutions. But what were the underlying causes of all these ills? This paper attempts to develop an argument around the fact that, over a long span of time, the Sudanese whether in the so-called North or South were busy attempting to make the Sudan an "appendage" to Islam, Arabism or Africanism. Rather than accepting the rich pluralism of Sudanese society, the Sudanese elites were fighting to simplify this complexity by imposing a single identity on the Sudan. The latest Islamicist takeover is just one dissipating attempt by a sector of this elite to recycle the past. Unless this vicious cycle is broken the prospects for the Sudan are bleak.

THE CONFERENCE AND ACKNOWLEDGEMENTS

This volume of essays is elaborated from some of the papers presented at a workshop entitled "A Short-Cut to Decay—The Case of the Sudan", at the University of Bergen in 1992, organised by the Centre for Development Studies. It was part of a programme on "Consequences of War/Rehabilitation of Societies after War", financially supported by the Norwegian Research Council for Sciences and Humanities. The University of Bergen has a long-standing academic interest in Sudanese history, archaeology, philosophy, anthropology and geography. A number of Sudanese scholars have visited the university and also taken their MAs and PhDs in Bergen. This conference was in the spirit of these traditions of long standing mutual cooperation. Furthermore, it was a logical follow up for a conference held during February 1989 at the Centre for Development Studies and entitled, "Management of the Crisis in the Sudan". It was attended by both leading representatives from the main political parties in the Sudan and prominent academics.

In this connection we wish to thank the Centre for Development Studies for their efficient organization of the workshop and for excellent secretarial assistance, acting director Leif Manger, and the administrative staff: Thelma Kraft, Christine Erichsen and Kristin Holst Paulsen. We also owe a debt of gratitude to the discussants from Bergen and elsewhere who made the discussion lively and the debate all the more vigorous. These are professors Gunnar Håland, Sean O'Fahey, Richard H. Pierce and associate professor Anders Bjørkelo.

Sharif Harir and Terje Tvedt

Recycling the Past in the Sudan
An Overview of Political Decay

Sharif Harir

> "The president then asked what I had been doing
> and had I seen old friends adding, to my surprise,
> "I am afraid you will find our standards have
> gone down. *The Sudan is not as efficiently and
> competently run as when you British were here!*"
> President Nimeiri to Graham Thomas of the for-
> mer Sudan service on 20 April 1972 (Thomas,
> 1990:118–121) (My emphasis).

Sudan is referred to by many scholars as representing a "microcosm of
Africa" (e.g. Abd Al-Rahim, 1985) and given its "intermediate" or "median"
position (Hassan, 1985) in Africa of different cultural worlds (e.g. Arab
Africa/African Africa, Muslim Africa/Christian Africa, Anglophone/Franco-
phone Africa etc.), changes or developments occurring in the Sudan reflect or
draw parallels from those happening in Africa in general.[1] Sudan somehow
reflects Africa and hence provides for the comparative study of African politics and society. But Sudan is also unique among African countries in the
sense that, "it is at one and the same time both 'Arab' and 'African'" (Abd
Al-Rahim, 1985:228). While the internal cultural composition of the
Sudanese population makes Sudan "a microcosm of Africa physically, culturally and ethnically", its uniqueness confronts it with its multiple political
marginality as neither African nor Arab, Muslim nor Christian (Mazrui,
1985:240). Internally this puts the Sudan in a very awkward position where
its dominant elite, mostly from the riverain Arab north, desires it to be Arab
and Muslim and its southern elite desires it to be African and de-Arabized.[2]
These two contradictory, even exclusivist, desires have been at the very heart
of the political conflict that lies in the centre of the decay of the Sudanese
state. In the continuous and relentless pursuit of making Sudan an appendage

---

[1] Sharing borders with nine African countries (Egypt, Libya, Chad, Central African
Republic, Zaire, Uganda, Kenya, Ethiopia and Eritrea) with shared communities and
"soft" borders, Sudan influences, and is influenced by, political happenings in those
countries.
[2] Because of the historical developments which gave the elite that stem from the central riverain Sudan a dominant position, it has been the case that "Arabism" as represented by this elite, gained a dominant ideological position in the recruitment of
the state elite. Africanism, though accepted as one dimension of the Sudanese identity, is played down by this elite.

to "something" Arabic, African or Islamic, both elites have failed to build "something" Sudanese as its uniqueness, expressed in being Arab and African at the same time, required. The dichotomization of the Sudanese character into either Arabic/Islamic or African/Christian lies at the root of the two and half decades of civil war that did not only impoverish the inhabitants of the Sudan but the state itself evidenced by the decay of its institutions.

By the time the startling revelation quoted above was made by Nimeiri (April 1972), the Sudan had experienced two periods of multi-party democracy and was three years into its second experiment of military rule. The only continuities which could be seen in this period of political instability were the progressive decline in the efficacy of the Sudanese state; the ever-present decay of its institutions and the civil war that accompanied the Sudan since independence in 1956. Though the war was temporarily halted by the Addis Agreement of 1972, Nimeiri's re-division of the South and his introduction of the *Sharia* laws in 1983 aborted the reconstruction and plunged the country into spiralling decay.

THE CONTEXT OF THE SUDANESE DECAY

When the 15 years of armed conflict between the Bantu and Nilotic peoples of southern Sudan and the Khartoum governments dominated by the riverain northern Sudanese elite, in which up to one million people[3] died or were displaced, was settled through negotiations in Addis Ababa in 1972, hope filled the Sudanese that reconstruction, stability and development could be achieved within the framework of a peaceful and stable political system. Given the fact that the Addis Ababa accord was one of the rare cases in which African internal conflicts were resolved by peaceful negotiations, it was an achievement not only by Sudanese standards but it was propagated as a model for solving similar conflicts in Africa and the Third World in general. The hope embodied in this achievement was that it might point the way towards a model which Africans could adopt as a way of resolving similar conflicts taking place in different parts of Africa, e.g. Eritrea/Ethiopia, Chad, Mozambique etc. Moreover, energies and funds dissipated during the conflict could be released and directed towards the tasks of reconstruction and development of the country. Rusting infrastructure and decaying institutions could be rehabilitated and reoriented towards social development and economic change. Internal and external investments could be attracted to induce production and economic recovery within a peaceful and stable atmosphere. Nation-building and the long awaited transformation of the Sudanese society could begin seriously. The introduction of a permanent constitution in 1973,

---

[3] Statistics generally and those related to war damage suffer from problems of reliability. However this figure is widely quoted see, e.g., Smock and Bentsi-Enchill (eds.) 1975.

for the first time in Sudan's history, the national reconciliation of 1977 when northern opposition groups were brought in to take part in the political process and the extension of the Southern Self-Governmental Act of 1972 to include other parts of the Sudan (1980) reinforced these hopes. International goodwill was reflected in the willingness to participate in the reconstruction process and availability of international and regional (mostly Arab) funds to aid the Sudanese development process gave substance to these hopes.

However, those hopes were short-circuited by political developments which were set in motion by the repeated undermining of the permanent constitution by Nimeiri, the then president of the republic—the very person under whose leadership both the constitution and the Addis Accord were realized. The president losing patience with due constitutional process, was moving constantly towards personal rule which depended upon presidential decrees that contradicted, and in the process undermined, the constitution and the state institutions founded upon it. Thus on 5 June 1983, the president decided to redivide the South into three regions. This was tantamount to the abrogation of the Addis Accord and the Southern Self-Government Act of 1972. While this move served both the desire on the part of the president to weaken the South and to appease some Southern political actors[4], the overwhelming rejection by the South to this policy came in the form of armed insurgency. The Sudanese People Liberation Army (SPLA) and the Sudanese People Liberation Movement (SPLM) were announced on 31st July 1983 with the clear aim of liberating the whole of the Sudan from rule by personal whim of the riverain northern elite and in order to redefine power relations in the Sudan. Nine years later, the war still rages on holding the Sudan, its economy and its future a hostage to it.

In a politically insensitive move, justified only by the political expediency of the president[5], Nimeiri introduced Islamic *Sharia* laws in September 1983 giving a religious dimension to an already escalating political conflict which was not short on causes for its perpetuation. At this point there was an already growing Northern opposition to the regime in power and with the Southern movement re-emerging, the whole of the country was thrown into a political conflict of complex dimensions.

While articulate secular elements in the Northern part of the country found some ground for political partnership with the SPLM, the generality of

---

[4] The Southern leadership at this point was divided between those who wanted the redivision of the South led, among others, by General Lagu (the man who commanded the Anyanya I until peace was negotiated in Addis Ababa in 1972) and those who were anti-redivisionists. For a vivid illustration of this polarization see Badal (in this collection). However, Nimeiri's move was not dictated only by this dichotomy. As he was moving towards the introduction of the *Sharia* laws, a unified South would have been an obstacle. Simultaneously, he would widen the domain of his patronage in the North.

[5] Mansour Khalid (1985:254–259) discusses Nimeiri's political motives behind this move towards Islam in detail.

the public in the North pressed to the ground by the daily burdens of an ailing economy, decaying state institutions and centralized repressions, revolted
against the regime on more mundane grounds relating to living conditions
rather than fighting against or for a secular or an Islamic state. In April 1985
the mass revolt which came to be known as the *Intifadha* (Arabic for sudden
upheaval) brought down Nimeiri's regime, thus bringing into focus the debate on political change in the Sudan. A one year transitional period (April
1985–April 1986) with a Transitional Military Council (TMC) to play the
role of the legislature and a civilian cabinet to play the role of the executive
were formed to oversee the passage of the Sudan to a multi-paraty democratic era. The Sudan's People Liberation Army and its political arm the
Sudan's People Liberation Movement refused to join the transitional government arguing that what happened was not a change but a continuation of
Nimeiri's May regime. This argument was based on the fact that both
General Swar El Dahab, the chairman and his colleagues in the Transitional
Military Council were in fact Nimeiri's generals. As long as they did not abrogate the so-called September laws, i.e. the Islamic *Sharia* laws introduced
by Nimeiri in September 1983, then it was doubtful whether what has taken
place was a revolution which changed a regime or a palace coup which replaced one head of a regime by another. In fact SPLA saw in the change of
the crew which took over the transitional period of 1985–86, a more subtle
move towards the consolidation of the Islamic position which the SPLA and
the liberal elements in the North were attempting to counter. Instead of carrying through the popular demands which provoked the masses to the streets
of Khartoum and were invoked by them all through the upheaval which
caused the demise of Nimeiri's personal rule, i.e. the abrogation of the
September *Sharia* laws and the trial of elements of the National Islamic Front
who were responsible for throwing the country into this political chaos, the
transitional arrangements were dominated by elements of the National
Islamic Front.[6] General Swar al Dahab, the chairman of the transitional military council, Dr. El Gazouli Dafa Allah, the transitional prime minister, and
Omer Abdel Ati, the transitional attorney general were all sympathizers of
the National Islamic Front. Thus the National Islamic Front, in some ways,
controlled and combined the legislative, executive and judiciary powers during the transitional period. While many political actors in the Sudan did not
see this aspect, SPLA did not miss it and hence its refusal to join the transitional arrangements and its insistence that the popular upheaval had been

---

[6] In fact Nimeiri saw the Islamic Front as the only potential (and probably the most
potent) opposition to his regime after the national reconciliation of 1977, and to take
the wind out of its sails Nimeiri appointed Dr. Hassan Turabi as his advisor and
later introduced the Sharia laws of 1983. Thus the Muslim Brothers were in a position to take over when Nimeiri was overthrown in 1985. But as they were counted
by the public, among those who collaborated with the outgoing regime, they contented themselves with dominating the transitional arrangements.

hijacked by the very elements against which the popular anger was directed in the first place. To the SPLA this reflected the continuation of the "self-righteous" claims which have characterized the position of the riverain based, Arabic/Islamic Sudanese power elite since independence in 1956. There is nothing new in this position as Sudan has always been perceived by this elite to be an extension either of the Arab world or the Islamic world, but not an entity of its own. The denial of Sudan as a unique entity of its own by the northern elite was later complicated by the SPLA when it over-emphasized its Africanity i.e. the fight for the authenticity of the Sudan was wrongly conducted by both parties. This multiple denial of a Sudan which is uniquely Sudanese and not an appendage to Arabism, Islamicism or Africanism lies at the root of the political problems of the "Sudan". As both the SPLA and the Transitional Military Council refused to endorse each other's proposals, the guns kept roaring in the South contributing to the mutual impoverishment of both the South and the North, exasperating in the process the economic, political and social decay of the Sudan.

In this sombre political atmosphere elections were carried out between 1–12 April 1986, where the Umma (Mahdist) party won 100 seats, the Democratic Unions Party (DUP-Khatmiya) won 67 seats and the National Islamic Front won 51 seats.[7] Diverse regional political parties were also represented in this parliament. Of the 68 southern constituencies it was possible to hold elections in 37 constituencies only. It is worth noting that these three major parties were all northern Islamic-based and Arab-dominated which leaves out the major contender in the civil war, i.e. the SPLA and the South. While the leadership of the Umma, the party of relative majority in this election, was opposed to Nimeiri's *Sharia* laws of 1983, leading to the political detention of its chairman Sadig El Mahdi, it neither commanded absolute majority nor the political will to deal decisively and resolutely with the burning issue of Sudanese politics: the revoking of September laws. The parliamentary game in the constituent assembly, between 1986 and 1989 when it was overthrown by the 30 June 1989 military *coup d'état*, was how to maintain one coalition government or the other in which the Umma provided the core and the DUP and the NIF played the variables. As unwieldy and unstable as those coalitions have been, the major issues of Sudanese politics, i.e. the question of *Sharia* and war, economic restructuring and social development were put on the back-burner. Corruption, economic mismanagement and the continuing and rapid decay of state institutions were the dominant characteristics of the third democracy in the Sudan. With the war in the

---

[7] By the time these elections were held the National Islamic Front was the best organized party. This is reflected in the enormous growth in the number of seats it was able to capture in this election compared to the 1966 elections when it won only 3 seats. In 1986 it proved to be the third major party in the Sudan and possessed the best organizational apparatus, winning 51 seats including 28 graduate constituencies.

South continuing to the order of USD 1,000,000[8] a day (not including the economic, social and human cost in the South itself), any talk of change or development was suspended and the state concentrated only on the task of survival.

To reinforce its war efforts in the South and the areas of overlap the Government resurrected tribal militias which were formed for the first time by a national Government in 1965 under the name of Home Guards.[9] Using perennial conflicts between pastoral groups, the government started providing arms to the nomadic Arab tribes in order to protect themselves against the SPLA. Those arms were used to further local ethnic wars and cattle-rustling activities to levels of brutality which were unprecedented in the histories of traditional ethnic wars. El Dien's massacre (1987), in which some 400–1,000 Dinka refugees fell to the fire power of the Baggara Arabs, is a case in point. It was an instance of an inept state, not content only with centralized repression as a means of its survival, sponsoring decentralized violence by providing arms and moral support to chosen ethnic groups against other less favoured ethnic groups. The Fur of Dar Fur were also to face a similar fate during this dark period of Sudan's history. Furthermore, the decay of state institutions and the rusting away of control mechanisms and means of legal checks led to loss of discipline among the security forces of the state. As martial law was proclaimed throughout most of this period, excesses against civilian populations in Dar Fur, the South as a theatre of war as well as in Khartoum, were commonly reported. However, the state forces committed those excesses with impunity as court cases were ruled out politically. In one case in Dar Fur in 1987 where three innocent civilians were executed by the army without trial, the investigating judge was beaten up by an angry army mob and his papers were forcibly appropriated.[10] That was the

---

[8] The enormity of this figure and the drain it has on the economy of the country can be grasped by the fact that each USD was equivalent to almost £S 100, while the external debt today stands at a mighty USD 15 billion. The costs of the war since 1986 have been estimated by General El Beshir, the chairman of the NIF-backed junta, as being over USD 6 billion, seven million head of cattle and the destruction of 80 per cent of the health and medical services (Horn of Africa Bulletin (HAB) Vol. 4, No. 2, 1992:2). In fact, the latest figure quoted by Africa Confidential (AC 31 July 1992) is the double of the figure quoted is here: USD 2 million per day which is again quoted from IMF estimates (Sudan Update, SU 9 September 1992, Vol. 3:25).

[9] In fact the use of tribal groups to fight government wars (by proxy) predates the independent Sudanese Governments to the colonial times. The Government of the Anglo–Egyptian Sudan provided arms and ammunition for both the Kababish, under the leadership of Sheikh Ali El Tom, and the Rezaiqat, under the leadership of Madibo from Kordofan and Dar Fur respectively, to harass and fight the forces of Ali Dinar: the last Sultan of Dar Fur, see Theobald (1956).

[10] This incident took place in Dar Fur when Sudan was governed by a duly elected government during the third democracy (1986–1989). The Sudanese army, like most of the African armies, is quite insensitive about the political implications of its actions and most of the time can and does act with impunity.

last anyone heard about the case. In response groups avenging these excesses proliferated in rural Dar Fur. The phenomenon came to gain the descriptive title of "armed robbery".

The war in the South, the instability and insecurity in the West and the Sahelian drought which culminated in famines in many parts during 1983–84, led to the massive displacement of population from the countryside to the urban areas. Khartoum, received the lion's share of those economically de-based nomads and traditional farmers in addition to the mass of war refugees from the South. While the west/east axis[11] of population movement in the Sudan as wage labour was accepted as normal since the target of such migrations was the relatively developed triangle of Khartoum/Kosti/ Sennar, the recent massive movement of rural population to the urban areas was looked upon in alarm and with a good reason. Unable to maintain the basic urban infrastructure, which served only about 350,000[12] before the eighties, due to the cost of the war and the general economic bankruptcy, it was a nightmare for any government to deal with the estimated six million which now made up the capital and the ever-growing slums around it. While the prevalent *modus operandi* under Nimeiri was the heavy handed approach called the *kasha*, i.e. arrest and deport, under the coalition governments of the third democracy (1986–1989), they behaved as if the problem did not exist and satisfied themselves by what they termed 'the showing of government force', traversing the streets of the capital now and then with police forces with newly acquired equipment. The problems of catering for the displaced slum populations were left for the international fraternity: the NGOs. Between 1986 and 1989 foreign NGOs undertook the responsibility abdicated by the national government and started providing water, medical and other services including the necessary food relief work. The poor of the Sudan thus subsisted on international generosity for no other good reason than that their own national government defaulted in its basic responsibilities in the pursuit of the 'higher' goals of prosenting the war. The third democracy was recycling the past history of the first two democracies, (1956–1958) and (1964–1969), during which the two dominant parties of the Umma and DUP ruled: ethnocentrism, political myopia and the self-righteousness typical of central riverain Islamic–Arabic elite.

---

[11] See the ILO report (1976). The institution of major national schemes in this triangle did not only make these areas targets of labour migration but the schemes had the effect of transforming the periphery into a cheap labour reserve, and giving the Sudanese economy its character of "dualism.

[12] Although statistics are to be taken with caution; this dramatic twenty-fold growth of the capital in two decades very much reflects the facts on the ground. Successive governments, rather than attacking the root cause, i.e. rural poverty and the destruction of the traditional economy, invariably reacted by forcibly sending back the migrants. These policies which went under the popular title *kasha* (Arabic for rounding up by the use of police) have had very little effect as the root cause remained. People returned by the first available transport.

The first casualty of recycling the past was the third democracy itself. Thus on 30 June 1989 an army coup under the leadership of Brigadier, subsequently Lt. General, Omer Hassan Ahmed Al Beshir took over the reigns of political power in the Sudan. Given the ineptitude of the party government, for the Sudanese people, it was not a question of a military takeover so much as a question of what ideological colour the generals or officers behind the takeover would have. The Sudanese people soon learned that this general was a brain-child of the National Islamic Front and that the war in the south would continue to be pursued with a greater degree of single-mindedness and religious zeal and that the question of *Sharia* would continue to haunt. As a first step towards that General Beshir and his junta decided to elevate the status of tribal militias into a legitimate national one by the creation the so-called Popular Defence Forces (PDF) under the leadership of trusted and indoctrinated, professional army officers. The contested Islamic *Sharia* laws were promulgated into the law of the land in 1991 and state institutions, including the army, were purged of all non-doctrinaire National Islamic Front or "front" members as it simply came to be known. To placate the world outside, Al Bashir also issued a pardon to include the SPLA but pressed on with his Islamic religious crusade. Mansour Khalid expressed the absurdity of this situation in the following manner

> ... the irony is not to be found in the fact that one rebel is abrogating to himself the right to pardon another rebel but also in that it is the junior rebel [Al Bashir] who is bestowing forgiveness on his senior counterpart [Garang of SPLA]. *But then the junior rebel is from the North and the presumption is clear; northern rulers, whatever the nature and origin of their legitimacy, have the right to dictate the fate of the whole nation.* (Khalid, 1990:437) (My emphasis)

The last sentence pinpoints what the Sudanese conflict is all about.

The regime of General Al Beshir did more than elevating the status of the tribal militias and pardoning of the SPLA; it dissolved political parties and trade unions under emergency laws and ruled by decrees issued by the Revolutionary Command Council (RCC) of what it termed the "revolution of national salvation". This meant the Islamization of both society and the state. Islam is the only legitimate ideology and to ensure its supremacy unprecedented repression of other opinions was embarked upon by the religious–military government in Khartoum. Sitting upon totally bankrupt administrative organs which were characterized by exhausted and decaying institutions of civil government, direct action by security and military forces as a normative way of ruling the country took the upper hand. The thousands of displaced people who populated the growing urban slums of Khartoum were the first to suffer direct military and security action when they were forcibly evacuated and their houses bulldozed. In the south the roaring guns only increased in number and intensity creating massive secondary dislocations for the population adding only graver dimensions to the miseries that have accumulated over the two and half decades of fighting and destruction,

famine and disease, stagnation and decay. In the North detention of opponents, extra-legal practices and general abuse of human rights were the hallmarks of the regime.

STATE-MAKING AND NATION-BUILDING IN THE SUDAN:
TIME PERSPECTIVE
The ethnographic present of ethnic diversity and cultural pluralism

Within the one million square miles which make the land mass of the pre-
sent-day republic of the Sudan about 570 tribes exist (Gore, 1989:269).
Across this tribal spectrum 595[13] languages are used although the Arabic
language provides a *lingua franca* (Bell, 1989). On the basis of linguistic, cultural and other ethnographic characteristics these tribes have been regrouped
together by scholars into 56 or 57 related ethnic categories. This diversity is
further reduced by the 1955–56 census by regrouping the 57 ethnic categories into eight major categories. These read as follows: Arabs 39 per cent,
Nilotic or central Southerners 20 per cent, Westerners of Dar Fur 13 per
cent, Nuba 5 per cent, Nubians 5 per cent, Eastern Southerners 5 per cent
and foreigners 7 per cent. The criteria for this reduction of diversity by classi-
fication and re-classification are not always clear and are often arbitrary.
What is relevant and sufficient here, however, is the fact that such tribal and
linguistic diversity existed within one state which aspired, like many others,
to be a nation-state.

Most of these tribal groups have a traditionally defined territory that carries their name and which, despite constant interaction with other groups,
socially reproduce themselves independent of others. Thus, while changes
stimulated by interaction with other groups within the regional and national
frameworks, those occurring due to population mobility through migration
to other parts of the country and those stemming from the influence of state
institutions and policies are constantly taking place, a considerable degree of
cultural continuity and socio-cultural resilience is maintained within individual groups. Some languages may have disappeared, as has happened among
the Berti and the Birgid of Dar Fur, but cultural traditions have shown considerable endurance over time. Arabic has replaced whatever original languages these afore-mentioned groups have had, but cultural traditions and
social organizational forms which are uniquely Berti or Birgid mark off these
two groups from their neighbours such as the Zayadia Arab camel nomads

---

[13] Abdel Magid Abdin in his book *Tarikh Al Thaga Fa Al Arabiyya Fi El Sudan*,
(History of Arabic Culture in Sudan, 1967), quotes this figure. But Bell (1989)
quoted 100 + languages. However, Mohamed Omer Beshir quoted 590 tribal groups
and 250 languages, in addition to Arabic as prevalent in the Sudan. Whether this or
that figure is the most accurate is beside the point for, even if we settled for the least
of the figures, we will get 570 tribal groups and 100 languages which is more than
enough to establish the plurality of Sudanese cultures.

or the semi-sedentary cattle breeding Missairiya. While sharing territory each of these groups reproduces its culture and society independent of the others. Even the Arabic language is not an homogenous thing. It shows considerable dialectal variations from one group to the other, e.g. Dar Fur Arabic, Juba Arabic, standard Sudanese Arabic, classical Arabic, etc., and even within one region, such as Dar Fur, there exist considerable variations of Arabic dialects.

Political and economic organization also shows considerable variation from one group to the other, e.g. pastoral, traditional farming and mixed economies. But due to the development of regional centres of power and the influences they have exerted on the hinterland, it is possible to discern regional systems which blurred the individual group boundaries to create regional systems based on consociational[14] existence. Under such arrangements while each group enjoyed considerable internal political organizational independence, a common society existed wherein all diverse groups become partners. While a degree of group clientalism and tributary status may have developed between weaker and stronger groups in such a common society, internal political hierarchies tend to make groups look like partners rather than dominant and dominated. Regional trade webs, historical linkages, marriage alliances and general webs of economic interdependence provide the socio-institutional basis of such existence.

In qualitative terms the majority of the populations in the Northern, Western and Eastern parts of the Sudan are Muslims constituting 70 per cent. Sizeable minorities which belonged to other religious creeds also existed. In the Southern part of the country the majority of the tribesmen belong to various local African religious creeds while the majority of the elite belong to various Christian denominations.[15] Even the Muslim majority is divided among different Islamic sects and brotherhoods. Major among those which link religious practice to national politics of power, are the Ansar, the Khatmiya (providing the backbone of the Umma and the DUP parties respectively) and the National Islamic Front (NIF). There is no political consensus among these groups as to what is the precise content of political Islam

---

[14] M.G. Smith (1969) defines consociation as an association of "separately constituted corporate collectivities as equal and internally autonomous partners in a common society". Quoted in Lijphart (1977:167–168). For a further illumination of consociational systems and democracies, see Lijphart, 1977.

[15] As the result of the Christian missionary educational activities during and after the colonial period most of the educated Southerners are Christians with European or biblical names. However, the majority of their co-tribesmen subscribe to various local indigenous religions. After the 1972 Addis Ababa Agreement there was a perceptible movement towards Southern authenticity reflected in the fact that some of the younger educated Southerners dropped their European names in favour of indigenous Southern ones. But one should also remember in this connection that Islam has also captured a sizable area of the Southern field of religion. For instance, the Dinka Abialang of the El Renk area are predominantly Muslim, belonging to the Ansar brotherhood.

although all three call for some type of an Islamic state. Vindication of this
lack of consensus is found in the fact that while the National Islamic Front
dominates the state today, the Ansar and the Khatmiya are leading the opposition to the *status quo*. Other Islamic brotherhoods that do not show active interest in the national power politics are the Qadriya, Mikashifiya, the
Tiganiya, the Ansar Al Sunna and a host of other minor religious associations. The point is that all these groups, each in its own right, commanded a
sizable following among the Muslim populations in the Sudan. This rich diversity within Islam in the Sudan is underscored by the lack of consensus
among these religious associations upon what makes precisely an Islamic
state. Moreover, enmity is openly traded among the three main Islamic
groups that purport to combine religious practice with the politics of power,
i.e. the Ansar, the Khatmiya and the National Islamic Front. Furthermore,
one has to bear in mind that there exist a sizable number of Muslims in the
Sudan whose view of Islam is not influenced by any one of these religious associations. Thus neither Islam nor Christianity nor African religions are homogenous entities that can cut across ethnic, tribal or linguistic groups to
provide a meaningful ideological basis for a national identity based upon any
one of these religious creeds, unless one imposes one of the multiple and
competing ideological stands or one of these diverse religious associations by
force. Likewise, no one of the ethnic groups which make up the country is
able to provide an arbiter of a common national identity except when one
aggregates them into racial groups such as the eight categories provided
above. Even in that case it is doubtful whether one is able to proceed all the
way from a racially based identity to a national identity acceptable by other
races, for in the process the dominant cultural group will appropriate and
subjugate the others.
    The Sudan seems to present a classical case of a plural society which is di-
vided by what Harry Eckstein called "segmental cleavages" (quoted in
Lijphart, 1977:3). These cleavages may be religious, ideological, linguistic,
regional, cultural racial and ethnic (tribal). Not all of these cleavages become
salient to all situations and contexts of the Sudanese political existence. Their
saliency is also very much subject to certain temporal and spacial exigencies.
For instance Arabic as a *lingua franca* in the daily social life does not become
problematic but it becomes a salient segmental cleavage in the contexts of the
formal national educational systems and in situations where its imposition
upon Southerners may carry tones of racial supremacy and subordination resulting from the association between the language and its racial vehicle, i.e.
the Arab identity. Juba Arabic is daily used and young Southerners displaced
by the war to the cities of northern Sudan use Arabic among themselves but
when imposed by *fiat* by the state, this linguistic cleavage becomes politically
and socially relevant in its problematicity. Even the 39 per cent presented
above as a category which represents the Arab identity is misleading for it
implies socio-cultural homogeneity. The Sudanese Arabs are divided into

many ethnic groups with clear cultural differences and dialectal variations. What is Arabic in the Sudan is also very diverse and a riverain Arab may have difficulties communicating with a Baggara Arab from western Sudan. Likewise a riverain Arab might look down upon a western Sudanese Baggara Arab. In fact the historical cleavage which led to the confrontation between the Khalifa Abdullahi of the Mahdiya and the riverain Ashraf involved very much the denial of worth by the Ashraf to Khalifa Abdullahi of the Taisha Baggara of western Sudan. Apart from Arabism as a racial trait and not a cultural acquisition, there existed no rationality which reduces the plurality of the Arab groups in the Sudan to a common denominator that is called Arabs. However, Arabism as a cultural acquisition is something common with many groups in the Sudan that are not racially Arabs.[16] It is only when the state elites aggregate the various Arab groups, despite their cultural diversity, into one group, that such a category assumes the role of the majority as an arbiter of a Sudanese identity worthy of being imposed upon others as a more legitimate way of life, that non-Arab groups see the implied racism and counter it by various means; denied worth is implied domination.

State-making in the Sudan: An historical overview

As a political entity enjoying the status of a nation-state with internationally recognized boundaries and national flag, among other symbols of a national-state, the republic of the Sudan like many other African states is very much the outcome of colonial occupation and colonial definitions of territorial domains. However, there is a long history of state formation which has taken place within the present territories of the Sudan. A skeletal review of this history might be in order.

As early as the first millennium BC the kingdom of Kush[17] dominated the central Nile Valley and persisted up to about 330 AD when it was brought down by the kings of Ezana and Aksum: present day Ethiopia. However, Kush and the other kingdoms of antiquity, despite their indigenous nature, do not invoke emotions of affinity and political ancestry for the generality of the Sudanese groups for very many reasons. They were so remote and only accessible through historical studies which are only available through the formal educational system. As such they are accessible for the few educated

---

[16] Even the SPLA accepted *Uruba* (Arabic for Arabism) and Islam for that matter as part and parcel of Sudan's reality. "This aspect of our reality is immutable" (SPLA/SPLM: Department of Information, February 1989). (In Abdel Ghaffar M. Ahmed and Gunnar M. Sørbø (eds.), 1989:83–90). What many Sudanese object to is the chauvinistic claims made by the power elite about the content of Sudanese Arabism that transcends culture into race.

[17] The most recent archaelogical discovery in the Sudan was that made by a Swiss team led by Professor Charles Bonnet of Geneva University which puts this kingdom at 5,000 BP which makes it the oldest known black civilization, *The Independent,* 23 August 1992.

and even within these circles they are more or less perceived as Nubian affairs and not Sudanese. Thus they are reduced to being a one-group affair in the mosaic of ethnic groups that dominate the present day Sudan. The artifacts and archaeologically rescued material culture which is kept at the National Museum in Khartoum attracts mainly foreign visitors to the Sudan and the educated classes of the Sudanese. When Napata[18] was symbolically invoked as a metaphor for Sudanese nationalism in theatrical works and literary sources, it appealed to a special sector of the Sudanese educated class only, i.e. the secularly-oriented. For the generality of the Sudanese public in the west, south, the centre and the east, 'Napata' remains a witty play that was once enacted in the national theatre at Omdurman as a caricature of Nimeiri's regime by the forces of the Sudanese left. Historical metaphoric values and present day symbolism that the writer of the work wanted to embody in it were lost for the generality of the Sudanese.[19]

The kingdoms of Nubia, Maqarra and Alawa were treated in the same way but for reasons other than their remoteness. They were Christianized kingdoms to which none of the contemporary Sudanese groups wanted to claim affinity because of the fact that all the northern Sudanese groups are universally Muslim. Nor does the southern Christian elite claim any affinity because of the fact that those kingdoms happened to be in the geographical area defined today as Northern Sudan. However, the Funj kingdom which defeated both Alawa and Nubia is seen by most Sudanese elite and the public as a watershed which signalled the beginning of modern Sudan. Thus the fall of Alawa (the southern-most of the three Christianized kingdoms) and the rise of the Funj kingdom in 1504 as the first semi-centralized Islamized kingdom is heralded as the political precursor of modern Sudan. Though the Funj kingdom was indigenous and African, in the sense of internally arising and not externally propelled and showing in practice certain characteristics of the Sudanic kingdoms which arose across savannah and Sahelian Africa, it sought ideological inspiration in the great tradition of Islam. Not unlike the neighbouring, parallel kingdom of the Fur in the west (the Fur sultanate 1650–1916), cultural and racial supremacy was sought through attempts to belong to Arabism. Unlike many African Islamic traditions, for instance of west Africa where Islam is indigenized, the Fur sultanate and the Funj kingdom to which the beginning of modern Sudan is attributed, sought in the twin cultural process of Islam/Arabism the arbitration of an ideology of "greatness". These two kingdoms were parallel developments to each other

---

[18] During the last part of the seventies a theatrical work entitled *Napata Habibti* (Napata: my love) was shown in the national theatre in Omdurman. It was a satirical work criticizing the regime then in power (Nimeiri's regime). Though well attended, it was not censored by the regime which was not known for its tolerance or benevolence towards dissidents. The author, I was told, was harassed by the security.

[19] As the remote history of the Sudan is only available through the classroom, historical metaphor gets through only to the educated few.

and each maintained its independence from the other sometimes with active military invasion of the other. What was common between them was an ideology of an Islamicized state and a claim on the part of the ruling families in both polities of Arab ancestry. Abdalla Jamaa and his Funj descendants claimed Arab descent from the Ummayyad, and Sulayman, the founder of the Keira dynasty of the Fur, was simply known as Sulayman the Arab (Solong).[20] Thus Arabism in this sense became the arbiter of what was qualitatively good and the embodiment of what was sought after as an absolute value reinforced by Islam as a legitimizing principle. Arabism implied Islam and Islam implied Arabism in this context. This was why most of the "wise strangers"[21] who founded kingdoms and clans were Arabs. To reinforce this conception most of the tribal groups in the so-called Northern Sudan (including the west and the east) forged pedigrees that linked them to Arab ancestry either directly through descent or indirectly through marriage and affinity by virtue of the transformative ability of the patrilineal descent systems of the Arabs.

Indigenous state formation was interrupted by the Turco–Egyptian conquest of the Funj in 1821 and Dar Fur in 1873/74 (by proxy through Zubayer Pasha Rahma, a Jaali slave dealer). As a colonial power extending its domains through military conquest, the Turco–Egyptian rule obliterated the boundaries between indigenous kingdoms and imposed central rule from Khartoum. It was probably this period of colonial rule which created the bases for the strong centralization tendencies that were to be the hallmark of the Sudanese state for a century to come. The Mahdist state in Sudan (1885–1898) came as a result of an indigenous revolution led by a religious visionary in close alliance with Western Sudanese tribal groups. While the Mahdi's first encounter with the Turco–Egyptian regime took place on the Aba island in the White Nile in 1880, he had to migrate westward to the heartland of tribally-based political communities of Dar Fur and Kordofan to raise support for his cause which was no less than the liberation of the Sudan and the restoration of justice by purification of Islamic religion. He was overwhelmingly supported but not only because of his religious call.[22] The Turco–

---

[20] *Solonga* is Fur for Arab denoting light colour. For further elucidation of the Fur sultanate see R.S. O'Fahey (1980).

[21] The phenomenon of the "wise stranger" is quite common among the tribes of Dar Fur where almost all claim that their ancestor was a learned man of Arabic origin who was accepted by the original ruler of the groups and gave him his daughter in marriage. The running theme is that of Arab descent through the patrilineal descent system but African or indigenous affinity through marriage.

[22] The Turco–Egyptian rule is described as the most brutal and exacting period of colonial rule (1821–1885) that have dominated the Sudan. As early as the first years the *Jaaliyyin* tribes of the Matamma area, under the leadership of Mek Nimir, were to revolt, reacting to humiliation by Ismail Pasha the son of the viceroy of Egypt Muhammad Ali Pasha, and burn him with his troops. The brother-in-law of the deceased, the Difterdar, who was in Kordofan at the time, upon hearing the news went

Egyptian rule was one of the most brutal and exacting in terms of coercion and extraction. Hence more mundane political reasons have made the situation ripe for a revolution. The rallying call for all the discontent was provided by the Mahdist vision of Islamic religion. Across the multiplicity of ethnic groups, Islam provided the ideology of the revolution. Five years of mobilization and military encounters ended by the decisive defeat of the Turco–Egyptian rule when General Gordon was killed in the battle of Khartoum in 1885. Not long afterwards the Mahdi also died and his trusted follower and first disciple Khalifa Abdullahi took over the reins of the Mahdist state. As the Khalifa was from western Sudan, the riverain groups of whom the Mahdi was a member, though sublimated by his embrace of Islam as an ideology of universalism rather than the dominant kinship ideology, started conspiring against the Khalifa who was in this context non-kin. The Khalifa settled on a policy of confrontation where he asked the western ethnic groups to move *en masse* to the Mahdist capital of Omdurman. Inasmuch as the massive movement of ethnic groups from the peripheries because of political mobilization by the centre of Mahdist power was the modality, the Sudanese state at this stage was not only strongly centralized in terms of state ideology but it also showed clear tendencies of creating an ethnic core as a vehicle for state formation.

However, the Mahdist state was unique in the sense that rather than strengthening and building the internal structures of the new state, it sought active expansion propelled by an ideology of universalism[23] of Islam which brought it into confrontations with powerful empires to its detriment. Finally internal dissension[24] and external confrontation with the Egyptians and the British brought down the Mahdist state in 1898.

---

on the rampage scourging the White Nile area devastating the Hassaniyyia tribes among others. The levels of dissent were already high, upon mundane grounds, when the Mahdi started calling for a revolt in 1880 and, coincidentally, from the Aba Island in the White Nile.

[23] The Mahdist state pursued a policy of active expansion and with the idea of the *Jihad* so alive, after it has defeated the Turco–Egyptian colonial state in 1885, it was engaged in wars on several fronts. The Ethiopian empire to the east was one such front. However, Khalifa Abdullahi (the Mahdi's successor) called upon the Queen of England and the Khedive of Egypt to submit to the call of the Mahdi, through letters. But to follow rhetoric by actions, the Khalifa dispatched an army, led by the Mahdist Amir Abdel El Rahman El Nujumi, which was intercepted at Toshki in upper Egypt and was defeated. From then on the initiative was taken by the Egyptians and the British until, finally, the Karari Battle in 1898 sealed the fate of the Mahdist state of the Sudan.

[24] The Khalifa's policy of forced migration to Omdurman created a lot of dissension in various parts of the Mahdist domains leading to punitive action by the Mahdist troops which again furthered the internal dissension. But more than the dissension the forced migration led to serious shortfalls in the production of grains which culminated in the famine of 1890, with a great loss of human life. This is known as

The Anglo–Egyptian condominium rule was maintained in the Sudan as the colonial power up to 1st January 1956. It was the Anglo–Egyptian colonial rule, more than any of the intervening formative periods of state-making in Sudan, that made the present state of Sudan. Through a series of border agreements and demarcations of colonial domains, mainly with the French in addition to the initial act of conquest, the British created the territory which is presently covered by the political entity of the Sudan. The creation of the Sudan by the British was, to all effects, a juridical act rather than a natural process of a state formation which expanded gradually to cover a specific territory of a nation-state. It was primarily a result of British strategy to impose an upstream leverage on Egypt.[25] The unity that characterized the Sudan in this period was imposed by the British might rather than one that came on the basis of a political consensus of the body politic.

Power relations and political integration in the formative phases

While kingdoms of antiquity that dominated the central Nile valley and their successor—the Christian kingdoms of Nubia, Maqarra and Alawa—were important as a historical backdrop to the formation of the Sudan as a state, they are not so relevant to the understanding of the present day Sudanese politics for reasons alluded to above. Of particular moment for this endeavour are the three periods following from the rise of the Funj kingdom (1504) and the Fur sultanate (ca. 1650). These are the Turco–Egyptian colonial rule (1821–1885), the Mahdist state (1885–1898) and the imposition of the Anglo–Egyptian condominium rule (1898–1956). The importance of these formative stages lie in the fact they gave the Sudanese state its specific characteristics of the dominant position enjoyed by the twin cultural process of Islam and Arabism and the ascendency of the riverain central Sudanese elements in the power structures of the contemporary Sudan.

The Funj and the Fur Sultanates

The Funj and the Fur sultanates were indigenous Sudanese kingdoms of which the Funj and the Keira groups respectively provided the ethnic core around which these states evolved. However, today there are no tribes[26] by those two names, i.e. Funj and Keira. This can be explained by the fact that early in the history of those states their respective ethnic cores started claim-

---

Majaat Sana Sitta (Arabic), the famine of year six, Muslim calender year 1306 after the migration.

[25] I am specially grateful to Terje Tvedt, for drawing my attention to this point, while exercising detailed criticism of an earlier version of this paper.

[26] Apart from some people in Guli, Keili and Buk in the Southern Blue Nile region who claim Funj descent, there exists no identifiable tribal group which collectively claims this identity.

ing Arabic descent defining themselves outside and above the indigenous tribal and ethnic groups over whom they reigned. The Funj, as alluded to above, claimed an Ummayyad Arab ancestry and the Keira claimed Hilali Arab roots. The claim of Arab descent put these two groups, who formed the core around which these two states were built, a degree above the non-Arabic but Muslim indigenous groups, by putting the Funj and the Keira closer to the prophet of Islam to whom all other ethnic groups within their domains submitted. The close alliance between the Funj and the Keira royalties and the migrant Arab traders and religious preachers and teachers, to the extent that a diffuse kind of Islamic *Sharia* became the law of the court, reinforced the legitimacy of the ruling groups. This was not so much for the ability of Arabism and Islam in transforming the society, but because of the special status both Islam and closeness to the prophet, implied by Arabic descent, conferred upon the rulers.

The assumption of affinity to the prophet elevated the ruling elite above the multiplicity of ethnic groups that lived in their domains, leaving the latter as equals in so far as their relations to the sublimated rulers were concerned. Various ties of clientalism were established between the royal groups and the leaderships of individual ethnic groups, sometimes reinforced by intermarriages between the rulers and ruled, as evidence from both the Funj and Fur sultans might suggest. The political systems that emerged under both the Funj and the Fur were systems which were characteristically based upon loose coalitions with common interest in a certain territorial order. Smith puts it this way

> Some of the great empires were really no more than loose coalitions of super-ordinate and subordinate realms, each with its own ruler and local institutions, usually in some form of tributary relationship with an overall monarch. (Smith, 1986:235)

Under the Funj and the Fur Sultanates, the Sultans imposed territorial order within their respective domains as heads of state, but in close alliances with the heads of the constituent ethnic and regional groups who acted as their tributaries. Through the religious and tribal elites, whom they allocated land rights, gifts and sometimes brought into affinal relations through intermarriages, the Sultans regulated conflict by arbitration sometimes also by military containment. In essence what emerged as a system under both the Funj and the Fur sultanates was a consociational one. The nature of legitimacy which informed the position of the royal elite had a religious and divine character and as such, it was not far removed from what was the case under the Sudanic civilization.[27] The political systems that dominated these

---

[27] Abd Al-Rahim (1985:230–31) referring to the Sudanic belt writes, "Thus the medieval Arabs used the expression Bilád Al-Sudan to denote the lands of the Blacks in general and in particular the territories which today correspond to the Sudanic Group of African States". This, of course, is equivalent to the stretch of territory that

Sultanates, which were consociational, had also many features in common with the Sudanic belt of African states. Societies of contemporary West Africa, i.e. Liberia, Ghana, Siera Leone, Nigeria, Mauritania, Senegal, Mali, Guniea, Cote d'Ivore, Benin, Burkina Fasso and Niger, were also character-ized by consociational systems in pre-colonial times (Lewis, 1965).

In both Dar Fur and Sennar Sultanates the political society was character-ized by segmental cleavages of tribal, linguistic, cultural, economic and re-gional differences. However, a common society provided by the unity of reli-gious and temporal authority in the sublimated royalty which claimed both closeness to the prophet by the virtue of Arab descent and affinity to the lo-cal autonomous groups through recruitment of wives (to the royals as moth-ers to future monarchs), provided a common society whose maintenance was a kinship obligation as well as acceptance of Allah's will. The Fur and the Funj were not only black, they also had their own languages despite the fact that Arabic was the language of the court and all documents were drawn in that language. Physical appearance of the royal groups and their claims to Arabic descent in racial terms were not possible to reconcile with actual real-ity for they were distinctly Sudanese, i.e. black and negroid. Arabism as a culture and Islam as was lived then, therefore, made it possible for the royals to give a measure of credibility to their claims of affinity to the prophet. The ideological aspects inherent in this situation seem not to further Fur or Funj nationalism but rather underscored a strong drive to link the Sudan to a larger "something", i.e. the Islamic world. This drive was and is today very much an integral part of the elites' attitude. The Funj royals and the Fur sul-tans as well as today's riverain power elite in the Sudan, always looked at their country as a part of an Arab or an Islamic world. Thus Sudanese na-tionalism *per se* was born retarded from the very beginning: it was a "North-ern" affair that did not encompass the Southerners who wanted the British to stay a bit longer to guarantee, at least, a federal status for the South. Afterwards it was shelved and the past drive by the elite to make the Sudan an appendage of "something" Islamic or Arabic was recycled. The recycling of the past is at the very heart of the political decay of the Sudanese state. Citizenship was never an articulate part of the identity that was sought. But Islam and Arabism were always part of an ideal sought by the riverain elite.

The "original" Arab migrant who preached Islam in both the Funj and the Dar Fur sultanates was typically a layman missionary whose main occu-pation was trade. What they preached was not a sophisticated theology or high-powered Islamic jurisprudence but rather a folk-type of Islam. This type of Islam was accommodated into the cultural traditions that were encoun-tered and, inasmuch as that assertion approximated reality, the early type of Sudanese Islam exhibited by these formative kingdoms was of a limited transformative character. On the contrary it was transformed by the socio-

---

extends across the savanna Africa from the Horn in the east to the mouth of the River Senegal in the west.

cultural traditions it encountered. The evidence for this is found in the fact that both Funj royalty and the Fur sultans accommodated practices which were best characterized as non-Islamic. Moreover, the fact that individual ethnic and tribal groups within the boundaries of these early sultanates were internally autonomous in their political affairs implied that even Islamic *Sharia* practised at the Funj or the Fur court was not coterminous or co-extensive with the political boundaries of these sultanates in the sense of providing a unitary and mandatory juridical framework. The individual tribal groups practised their customs and traditions and only when they were in contact with the seat of the monarch, did they hear of *Sharia* as a legal arbiter. The record[28] from the Fur referred to the Sultan as "leader of the Muslim community" which implied again *Sharia* rules; but what was referred to as *Sharia* at the time was nothing more than an amalgam of traditions of cultural nature interspersed with quotations from the Quran.

The Arab trader/preacher and the various royal houses were to strike alliances cemented by movement of royal females in marriageable age to Arabs in exchange for Islamic teaching. Trade under these kingdoms was controlled by the royal houses; for caravan routes were under the direct authority and protection of the monarch. Trade items consisted of slaves and various raw materials which related to animal and forest products. Imports consisted of raw material and finished products. However, the most important item in trade was slaves which meant that each sultanate was to have a reserve which was by necessity populated by non-Muslims because a Muslim cannot be enslaved in that sense. Thus the antagonisms between the non-accessible southern and south-western parts of the present Sudan and areas effectively dominated by those early sultanates existed as the relation was one of slave raider/trader on the one hand and that of an evasive prey and "captivity avoider" on the other. It was then no great wonder if there was very little evidence of frontier Islamic missionary work, for extension of the territory of Islam meant conversely diminishing the territory for slave raiding. Thus the religious preachers remained within the court and in the proximity of the monarch's palace not only as a preacher but also as an in-law, a trade partner and a political ally that strengthened the legitimacy of the temporal authority of the monarch by religious justification through the manufacture of written pedigrees showing closeness to the prophet of Islam by descent.

As the state functions evolved over time and the state institutionalized the reproduction of itself, a specialized class of Islamic jurists developed. They were granted land rights by the monarch and through the resources they commanded they were able to support a specialized following and educational institutions which reproduced as well as refined the knowledge that became a basis for a special class of Islamic teachers named *Fugara*[29]

---

[28] See R.S. O'Fahey, 1980.

[29] *Fugara* is a plural for *Fagir* or *Faki* which denotes a person who has memorized the whole of the Quran (the Holy Book) and is able to put it into practical uses.

(Arabic) in both Dar Fur and Sennar. Later most of these institutions developed into Islamic brotherhoods, i.e. Sufi orders, which while refraining from seeking temporal authority sought to reinforce its legitimacy. Thus centralized political authority with quasi-religious character was decoupled from the specialized and professionalised religious institutions. Tribal groups, again, remained autonomous of both the centre of temporal authority represented by the monarch and his court and that of religious associations or brotherhoods, which were mostly formed by migrant religious men. The political system under these early sultanates was provided by four pillars

a. sublimated central authority represented in and occupied by the monarch and the royalty of each sultanate;
b. tribal and ethnic groups who remained autonomous of each other but in a consociational form;
c. religious associations and brotherhoods (established mostly by migrant religious men) which remained autonomous of but dependent on the central temporal authority for allocation of exclusive rights of access to land resources; and
d. the traditional cultural values of these three groups which though interacting remained fairly independent of each other.

Not only the cultural borders between these three groups which made the consociational state remained flexible, but also state borders on the peripheries remained flexible.[30] Thus the Funj sultanate as well as the Fur one extended and contracted their physical domains reflecting in the one hand the process of extension of frontiers of Islam and those of tribal groups opting out from one domain to another and the ability of the state in the centre to physically conquer new territory. The frontier land of Kordofan[31] which provided a kind of a buffer-zone between the Funj and the Fur sultanates changed hands between those sultanates many times. What is noteworthy is the fact that those early sultanates have been stable and provided the base for durable systems for about three centuries probably for no better reason than the fact that they were loose consociations despite the presence of a strong centre represented by the monarch of each kingdom.

Leading among these uses is the ability to teach it to pupils in the *Khalwa*, which is the Quranic school.
[30] The border area between the Fur Sultanate and the Sultanate of Waday remained open and whole tribes or part of the tribal group switched allegiance between the two kingdoms without leading to any major confrontations. O'Fahey (1985:87) refers to the presence of, "a series of petty states that owed allegiance, now to the one, now to the other", between Dar Fur and the Sultanate of Waday.
[31] Kordofan was, at this time, ruled by the *Mussabaat* who were neither Funj nor Fur though they shared some affinities with the Fur. A small group which carries that tribal name exists in Dar Fur today.

The Turco–Egyptian rule (1821–1885)

The nature of political integration under the sultanates treated above was provided by an amalgamation of the attributes of consociational existence where both religious and tribal elites cooperated, even if sometimes unwillingly, with the sublimated monarch whose legitimacy was rendered unproblematic by both pedigree and religion, i.e. closeness and affinity to the prophet of Islam. Under the Turco–Egyptian colonial rule the territorial unity of their political domain was imposed by conquest and maintained initially by a standing army. It was through the means of colonial domination that the territorial unity of the plural Sudanese society was maintained. Any revolt was decisively and brutally dealt with and taxes were ruthlessly collected.[32] In fact the motives behind the colonial expansion of the Egyptian domain to the South can be summarized into two main quests: men for the slave army and riches for the coffers of the viceroy of Turkish Egypt—Muhammad Ali Pasha.

One of the political consequences of the Turco–Egyptian rule was bringing the Sudan, including most of the Southern parts of the country, under one central authority whose seat was the riverain city of Khartoum. The movement of the power seat to Khartoum from Dar Fur and Sennar in the peripheries had major consequences for the political development of the Sudan as this meant the strengthening of the position of central riverain Sudan at the expense of the peripheries. Likewise, is the inclusion of the southern parts of the country which became a reserve for slave raids. Riverain Sudanese slave traders and raiders such as Zubeir Pasha Rahma later established themselves in those parts of the country and practised their trade under the blessings of the central power whose aims in invading the Sudan coincided, somehow, with the interests of such slave traders.[33] The basis for the ascendency of the riverain groups was also laid down by this regime when it employed Northern Sudanese groups (mainly JaaLiyyin, Shaiqiyya and Nubians) in the army, the police and minor administrative jobs.

---

[32] Reference has already been made to the revolt by *Mek Nimir* of the Jaaliyyin tribes and the massacres of the Hassaniyya of the White Nile by the Difterdar. In fact Mek Nimir and his group had to flee the carnage by the Difterdar to Ethiopia where a village by the name Matamma was created across the border. It survives even today.
[33] Before the relations between Zubeir Pasha and the Turco–Egyptian rulers went sour, it was Zubeir Pasha, the slave trader who brought Dar Fur under the Turco–Egyptian rule in 1874. The insensitivity of the dominant riverain elite towards how some groups feel about the historical memories of slave raids is reflected in the fact that one main street in Khartoum carries the name of Zubeir Pasha as a national hero.

The Mahdist period (1981–1898)

The significance of the Mahdi for the formative stages of the Sudanese state lies, perhaps, not in his call for an Islamic state but rather in the ability of the charismatic leader to exploit the conditions of discontent precipitated by the colonial Turco–Egyptian rule and unify the peripheral Sudanese to conquer the seat of central political power in Khartoum. Though his call was clearly based on messianic, anti-establishment Islam and propelled by the central concepts of *Jihad*, the followers of the Mahdi who confronted the Turco–Egyptian troops in the battle of liberation were singularly characterized by the variety of their motives. While some, like Khalifa Abdullahi and a core of Mahdist disciples who succeeded the Mahdi to the leadership of the state in 1885, were clearly motivated by the Mahdist vision of Islam, the Baggara tribesmen from western Sudan and the riverain slave traders were motivated by less sacred and more mundane motives.

The extreme oppression by the exploitative and exacting Turco–Egyptian rule and the charismatic personality of the Mahdi were the unifying magnets of the Sudanese tribesmen. As soon as the Mahdi died and Khalifa Abdullahi took over, conflicts based not on Islam but on ethnicity started profilerating. Khalifa Sharif, the cousin of the late Mahdi, led a rebellion against the Khalifa Abdullahi who succeeded the Mahdi not so much for differences of religious vision but because Khalifa Sharif's group was the *Awlad Al Balad*[34] (Arabic, the rightful sons of the land) as opposed to a Taaisha Baggara Arab who was at best a foreigner to the riverain Sudan. Khalifa Abdullahi dealt with this rebellion summarily and to further strengthen his position he called upon the Baggara tribes of western Sudan to migrate *en masse* to join him at the Mahdist capital of Omdurman. Those who did not do so voluntarily were forced to migrate. The Khalifa not only practised personal rule but also appointed his kinsmen to lead the Mahdist troops. Of the prominent Baggara princes that led the Mahdist troops under the Khalifa were Yonis Wad Al Dakim, Mahmoud Wad Ahmed, Osman Janu, Yagoub Jurab Al Rai and

---

[34] *Awlad al Balad* is an Arabic term which means the legitimate sons of the land. It has been used historically to refer to Sudanese of Arabic stock from the Nile valley. It prevails even today except for the fact that another term has been added to it so that it can assume more precision of connotation: *Wad Arab* or *Awlad Arab*, the sons of Arabs. In the Mahdist context, although the Khalifa was the leader of the Mahdist state as the legitimate successor to the Madhi, his *Taaisha* background put him beyond the connotative boundaries of *Awlad al Balad*. Khalifa Sharif who was the cousin of the late Mahdi was a riverain Mahdist, and by definition *Wad Balad*. Thus this term, in some senses, demarcates ethnic boundaries between the riverain Sudanese and the rest. Today people say, "He is *Wad Balad* and not *Gharbawi* or *Dinkawi*", meaning that he belongs to the rightful sons'—of the land—club and not from the Dinka or Western Sudan. The assumed superiority of the Awlad al Balad, i.e. riverain Sudanese, is taken as a matter of course (see also Mansour Khalid, 1990).

Sheikh Al Din. The last two were the Khalifa's brother and son respectively. The others were his cousins.

What was disputed between the Khalifa Abdullahi and Khalifa Sharif was, in fact, who would be the rightful son of the land *Wad Balad* and hence have rightful access to political power and authority in the country. This aspect of Sudanese politics is very far from being resolved even today. The riverain Sudanese consider and have always considered political power as their prerogative as *Awlad Balad* and *Awlad Arab* (sons of the land, sons of Arabs), and if any one from the peripheries was to be allowed to enter the club of the powerful and decide for the Sudan, that person or group must go through a sieve provided by a riverain-led organization[35] whether those were parties or military coups. This was very much confirmed by the post in-dependence period in the Sudan.

Weakened by tribal feuds, internal political conflict and famines as result of the mass migration of tribesmen to the capital as soldiers and the constant attempts to expand the Mahdist state into Egypt and Ethiopia, the Mahdist state was brought down by the forces of Anglo–Egyptian colonization in 1898. Though a major landmark in the political evolution of the Sudan, the Mahdist state was not only propelled by a spirit of Sudanese nationalism. The grand project of the Mahdi, using hindsight, was the resurrection of an Islamic empire and the vehicle of this resurrection was supposed to be by *Jihad* against the outside world. Its main drive was far from carving out a political territory that would become the Sudan to defend it against the out-side world. In fact it was an offensive movement which aimed at furthering a specific Islamic view point into Egypt, Ethiopia and the rest of the world.

The Anglo–Egyptian colonial period

While the death of Khalifa Abdullahi at the hands of the Anglo–Egyptian forces in September 1898 at Umm Dibaykarat effectively sealed the fate of the Mahdist state, sporadic resistance to the British rule continued in many parts of the Sudan until the nineteen thirties. The Fur sultanate which was revived by Ali Dinar after the battle of Karari (1899), was forcibly brought to an eclipse by the British troops in 1916 and was, thenceforth, formally annexed on 1 January 1917. However, one should note that it was only late in the thirties that certain stretches[36] of the western borders with the French

---

[35] Whether parties or military personnel that made the Sudanese regimes, the Awlad al Balad are always at the controls. Western, Eastern or Southern Sudanese are as a rule, coopted for reasons of giving some semblance of "national representation". Even those "co-opted" are hand picked by the riverain leaders so that their legiti-macy can come from the act of being picked up by the "Sadigs", the "Mirghanis", "Nimeiris", or the "Beshirs" of the riverain Sudan.
[36] For details see Theobald, 1965. However, this was a more general phenomenon where, e.g., the Nuer were not pacified before 1929, and borders with Ethiopia,

domain in Chad were agreed upon following the border protocol of 1924. What is significant here is the fact that the present day republic of the Sudan with its one million square miles of territory is a colonial creation and the mode of unity and integration maintained throughout the colonial period (1898–1956) was by imposition where military action to put down rebellious tendencies went hand in hand with international agreements with other colonial powers to ensure exclusion or inclusion of population groups in the juridically defined territory named the Sudan. Even within such defined territories, some of them were subjected to the Closed District Ordinance of 1922 to prevent the free interaction of population groups, e.g. the south and some parts of northern Dar Fur[37]. Such restrictive laws would have major detrimental consequences as to the development of attitudes of universally belonging to the same country. These restrictive laws were, of course, part of a wider British strategy, i.e. divide and rule.

The essence of the colonial policy of divide and rule was the manipulation of the segmental cleavages that were present in an extremely plural and ethnically diversified Sudan. Following from these politicies the southern parts of the Sudan became a *de facto* protectorate within the territorial domain of the Anglo–Egyptian Sudan. Access for elements from the other parts of the country was restricted by the Closed District Ordinance. A separate southern policy was followed where the initial aim was to allow separate development independent of influences from the so-called northern Sudan. Thus Christian missionaries of various Christian denominations were encouraged and given access to carry out not only activities of conversion but were also entrusted with education. In the north formal education was introduced and was carried out by the colonial government. Major agricultural schemes were also introduced there. By the time the southern policy[38] was reversed in favour of integration with the northern parts of the country in the late forties, major structural inequalities were already visible. Not least among them and with major political consequences for the independent Sudan was the development of two parallel elites in the country: a christianized missionary educated elite in the south and a formally educated riverain elite in the North. The latter was to inherit the colonial state at independence and the former was to be marginalized from access to the state and was to recourse to armed struggle.

Kenya and Uganda also remained soft just as is the case with Chad, Central African and Zaire.

[37] The reasons behind restricting access to Northern Dar Fur are not clear altogether though some people think that Major Guy Moore who was the District Commissioner for Northern Dar Fur until 1948 might have had "Christianization" on his agenda, an assumption which is not corroborated by any record.

[38] It was not before 1947 when the graduate movement, which became the backbone of the Sudanese Nationalist Movement, applied considerable pressure that the Southern policy was reversed by the condominium rule.

The war between the Khartoum regimes in the North and the Southern
guerilla movement continued for 17 years.[39]

The British indirectly reinforced their restrictive policies as far as free
movement of population between the two parts of the country was concerned by the introduction of "indirect rule". Native administration consisting of tribal elites, in direct contact with district commissioners, as a mode of
uncostly and minimum government whose concern was law and order, was
introduced. They also managed to integrate the religious leaders in their administrative framework at least in the North. This took the form of initially
promoting the anti-Mahdist Sayyid Ali al-Mirghani,[40] and the training of
ulama (Arabic), (Islamic jurists), to counter the Sufi orders, etc. Sayyid Abd
al Rahman al Mahdi was rehabilitated in 1915 and later he was awarded a
British knighthood. The integration of the religious leadership to the British
administration had also other aspects: to counter the influences of Egyptian
nationalism after 1919 on educated Sudanese. This could be seen in conjunction with the measure of popular support which these religious brotherhoods
have enjoyed among the masses of the rural population where Sayyid Abd al
Rahman al Mahdi commanded the religious allegiance of the Ansar of western Sudan while Sayyid Ali al-Mirghani commanded the religious allegiance
of northern and eastern Sudan through the Khatmiyya brotherhood's network. Thus religious sectarianism as represented in these two opposed religious brotherhoods as distinct from the officially trained and sponsored
Islamic jurists, i.e. *ulama*, which was to have major impact upon political developments in post-independence Sudan, owed its strong position in the
Sudanese political scene to the policies of the British colonial rule.

The colonial formal educational policy which was designed to generate
local clerical staff to support the colonial administrative system by providing
manpower to the lower reaches of the administrative hierarchy, was to generate a class of educated Sudanese who were to spear-head the anti-colonial
nationalist movement in due course. It was to form the basis of the graduate
congress[41] which led to the development of the two main traditional parties

---

[39] The Southern war started in August 1955, four months before the formal declaration of independence. It continued throughout two multiparty democratic regimes
(1956–1958 and 1964–1969) and one military regime (1958–1964). It was in June,
two weeks after Nimeiri took over in a military coup on 25 May 1969, that a declaration which came to be known as the "June declaration" was made by the new government with the intention of moving towards a peaceful solution. In 1972 Addis
Ababa provided the venue for the negotiations that led to the political solution of the
problem. Hence the agreement carried the name "Addis Accord".
[40] Sayyid Ali Al-Mirghani, the leader of the Khatmiyya religious brotherhood, took
refuge in Egypt during the Mahdist period and only came back with the Anglo–
Egyptian invading army to reconstitute his brotherhood: the Khatmiyya.
[41] The graduate congress, established under the leadership of late President Ismail al-
Azhari in 1938, was perceived to be a non-sectarian organization. As Ahmed Kheir
wrote, "enlightened opinion should become independent of disgraceful traditions, it
should free itself from personal cults" (quoted in Khalid, 1990:79). However, reli-

of the Umma, allying with the Ansar brotherhood, and the Nationalist Unionist Party (later Democratic Unionist Party) which allied with the Khatmiyya brotherhood. In addition to these forces, urban traders based upon the Jallaba riverain trade networks were also to develop as a distinct political force under the colonial period.

Thus under the colonial period, structural power relations were provided by a colonial central authority with its seat in Khartoum which provided the centre[42] and around which the Sudanese political forces of religious sects (sectarianism), the officially trained religious *ulama*, the urban traders, tribal groupings and the products of the colonial educational system (graduates) orbited. Each of these forces was somehow independent of the others, and sometimes antagonistic to the others, but all of them were dependent on the colonial central authority as a source of energy to stay in orbit. As such the sense of "Sudanese nationalism" was not developed except belatedly and when it finally came Sudanese nationalism was strictly political and riverain and the only programme it carried was to rid itself of the colonizer who was visibly a foreigner. This aspect of Sudanese nationalism is interesting for a number of reasons main among which is the fact that it evolved in close connection with Egyptian nationalism which was "Arabist" in nature. As such Sudan was always thought of as an Arab entity very much tied to the destiny of Arab nationalism. Thus most of the educated class in the Sudan during the nationalist movement believed in the unity of the Nile valley which meant unity with Egyptians and by extension Arab nationalism. This tendency was countered by some of the traditional forces based mainly, but not exclusively, on religious brotherhoods such as the Ansar or the followers of the Mahdi. Even then, these groups saw Sudan as an extension of the Islamic world and not a nationalist object of its own. All these views were expressed through sectoral interests be those religious sects, ethnic groups, geographical regions or an interest group, pre-empting in the process the creation of a national identity that is based on a loyalty to the nation as a whole rather than to a narrowly based sector of it. This fragmentary status of Sudanese nationalism remained to colour political developments in the country up to the present day.

---

gious sectarianism did not lose time in incorporating most of the graduates into its ranks. Thus most of the graduates become either members of the unionist movement, aligned to the Khatmiyya sect, or anti-unionist aligned to the Ansar sect.

[42] The central colonial authority provided a centre analogous to the solar system where all other political groupings were satellites to it (see Gaafar M.A. Bakheit, 1968).

The independence: instability and decay
Unequal worth: the dominance of the riverain

More interesting is the fact that whether fragmentary, sectoral or otherwise,
Sudanese nationalism, in a strict sense, expressed only the riverain viewpoint
because of the peculiar historical evolution which made both modern and
traditional elites of the Sudan to be dominated by the northern sedentarized
and riverain groups of, generally speaking, the northern provinces. The south
due to a different evolutionary process was left out or at best taken for
granted by this elite. Islam and Arabism entered this as ideologies enhancing
the dominant position of the riverain elite and not as cultural attributes of
the Sudanese people as a whole. What was called Sudanese nationalism expressed the riverain Sudanese point of view rather than the point of view of a
whole called Sudan for it did not exist at the time. The term "Sudanese"
somehow became tantamount to "riverain" reinforced in the popular political culture by dichotomies such as *Awlad Al Balad* (sons of the land) versus
Janubi (Southerner) and *Gharbawi* (Westerner), and *Awlad Arab* versus *Abd*
(slave) or *Nubawi* (Nuba). Such pejorative and value loaded terms are
prevalent even today in the popular political culture and they serve to enhance the worth of some groups as well as denying the human worth of other
groups. While slavery as a practice died a long time ago through abolition it
exists still in the minds of the people and still is used to degrade some groups
on the basis of ethnic or geographical region of origin. This is not a wild shot
for Khalid writes, "in the closed circles of Northern Sudan there is a series of
unprintable slurs for Sudanese of non-Arabic stock all reflective of semi-con-
cealed prejudice" (Khalid, 1990:135). The circles Khalid referred to in this
statement were no less than the circles of the ruling riverain elites of which
Khalid was once a member. The popular political culture which saw only the
northern part of the country as important and its culture as the only valid
one got its cues from such prejudices held by its leading elites. For example
Saddiq al Mahdi who was described by Khalid (1990:218) as "not just typical a member of the Northern elite, he is its archetype", as a prime minster
stood on a grave of a young northern officer killed in Bor district in the south
in 1966 and cried.[43] The army responded to the tears of the prime minister
and slaughtered 24 Dinka chiefs with impunity.[44] The army took the hint of

[43] See Mansour Khalid (1990:218) for the details of the incident. However, Saddig
al-Mahdi was of a completely different character when, in 1987 in response to public
pressure, he came to al Fasher to attend to a case of cold-blooded murder of six senior citizens by a police patrol in an act of indiscipline characterized by excessive police brutality and total disregard for human life. But then those were Westerners
(*Garaba*) and not real Sudanese (*Awlad Al Balad*) as this young officer who fell in
1966 was.
[44] Even today the army liquidates suspects with impunity in the South, the Nuba
mountains and in Dar Fur. And as those parts were declared "operation zones", the
military does not account for its methods of enforcing conformity.

who was more worthy than others from this emotional act by an incumbent prime minister of the country—the Sudan.

From the perspective of the dominant riverain culture which held political and economic power in the country, the culture of the developed triangle which assumed the representation of what is "Sudanese", the Sudanese ethnic multiplicity is reduced into five main identity groups. These are

a. the dominant group under the rubric of *Awlad Al Balad* or *Awlad Arab* (Northern riverain Sudanese including Nubians);[45]
b. Gharaba (or Fellata or Takarna) which included all the groups that stemmed from the West, the boundary of which started beyond the White Nile;
c. Hadendowa which is shorthand for all groups belonging to the Beja conglomerate;
d. Nuba; and
e. *Janubiyyin* which included all the Southern groups irrespective of whether they were Nilotic, Nilo–Hamitic or Sudanic.

This, of course, is a gross oversimplification, if not insulting, from the perspective of the groups so lumped together. But it served the purposes of the Riverain groups; for such a reduction, though *reductio ad absurdum*, served the purposes of hierarchization in terms of relative worth of such dichotomized identities. Needless to say that the category of *Awlad Al Balad* comes on the top of such a hierarchy and the category of *Janubiyyin* comes on the bottom of it. The remaining three categories, i.e. *Gharaba, Hadendowa* and *Nuba*, are intermediate categories which are pushed, sometimes, towards the lower reaches of the resultant ethnic hierarchy by the use of the criterion of Arabism and, some other times, towards the upper reaches by the use of the criterion of Islamism.

In terms of worth, such dichotomized identities are again reduced to two main ones. These are that of Arabs (embedded in *Awlad Arab*) and that of non-Arabs carried sometimes to the extremes of *Zurga* (black) and *Abid* (slaves). These prejudices have major political and economic consequences as they are, also, held by the power elite; for they, in many cases, define what is good for one or what one is supposed to be good at. As such they reflect, in a sense, the share each of these dichotomized identities could have in terms of power and economic well-being. Saying this should, in no way, minimize or explain away the historical developments that brought about the dominant position enjoyed by the developed triangle of the Gazira. However, in contemporary terms, one should not overlook the role played by these prejudices

---

[45] While the category of *Awlad Arab* should have been coterminous with Arabs, it, also, included Mahas, Danagla, Kunuz, etc., groups that belonged to the non-Arab Nubian conglomeration of tribes (see Sharif Harir, 1981 "Old-Timers" and "New-Comers", Bergen, Occassional Paper in Social Anthropology, No. 29).

in entrenching and enhancing this very dominant position. The continued marginalization of the peripheries, also, has something to do with this. All this was reflected in the post-colonial development.

Lopsided development: "Sudanese" or "riverain" mationalism?

The lopsided nature of Sudanese nationalism in which the viewpoint of one part of the country and one cultural trend were over-represented in terms of riverain elite domination, was underscored by its strictly political character which made it a tactical alliance between some elite segments just for the purpose of getting rid of an alien power.[46] It did not include, as parallel, major social transformation aspects, upon which a truly Sudanese nation-state would have been founded. By the time independence was formally achieved from within a Westminster style parliament, on January 1st, 1956, the major outstanding question of the relationship between the southern and the northern parts of the country had already deteriorated to armed confrontation which was sparked by the Torit rebellion of the southern corps of August 1955. Thenceforth, while governments changed in Khartoum and democratic and military regimes toppled each other in rapid succession, the civil war in the south continued to rage draining in the process the resources of the country, its infrastructure, and its institutions. After a short and precarious peace period, the war resumed again in 1983; this time with the Khartoum regime employing holy war *Jihad* metaphors, leading to an even more polarized situation; i.e. Islamic versus non-Islamic attitudes.

The central political authority which remained beyond the reach of the Sudanese elements under the colonial period except as junior collaborators and which kept each of the political forces in its orbit, disappeared through the departure of colonial powers. This in itself was not a cause of lament. On the contrary, it was an occasion for rejoicing as the Sudanese tricolour flag went into the Sudanese space ushering in an era of national sovereignty. However, the disappearance of the independent centre of political authority which held the country together, albeit by *fiat* and imposition, led to the appearance of distorted configurations of power centres. Religious sectarianism in alliance with the main two political parties (Umma and DUP) which subsisted on the blessing of the religious leaders of those sects, captured important portions of the central power and with it, central institutions of government. Other portions of it were captured by regional-tribal power configurations in alliance with some sections of those parties. Sudanization of the ad-

---

[46] Sudanese Nationalist movement shares a lot in common with the Nationalist movement in the third world whose final aim was to get rid of the alien power. Once that was achieved, no programmes for further social transformation were in place. For comparative purposes, see Basil Davidson, 1992 and S. Avineri, 1976. Avineri compares Arab nationalism which was, not unlike the African one, strictly political and the Israeli one which was transformative.

ministration reinforced the dominant position of the riverain development triangle; further marginalizing the South, the West and the East which were already marginalized by the colonial strategy of cotton production in the centre. In the process the newly emerging forces such as ideologically based groupings and trade unions, i.e. socialist forces of the left, were losers in this case of power capture. This was to be understood in the light of the fact that liberal Westminster style democracy with its emphasis on the supremacy of majorities was the adopted *modus operandi*, though the sectarian political parties were quite adept in avoiding the checks and balances that characterized such democracies in the countries of origin.[47] The electorate voted their "chosen sects"[48] to power. The choices were neither based on the merits of presented programmes of actions by the parties involved nor on any consensus of what the newly emergent nation was to be. They were based on blind loyalty to the leader of the religious sect who mentored the concerned party or candidate. But despite their antagonisms and differences the two dominant parties, e.g. Umma and the Nationalist Unionist Parties, which ushered in the independence represented the riverain political view. The southern viewpoint was put at the back burner for the time being. The western and eastern parts of the country were taken for granted as they were patronized by the leaders of the two parties. They voted, when they did, for the *Imam*, i.e. religious leader, and only by proxy to whatever parties or personalities the *Imam* or the *Sayyed* supported.

The lopsided political development led to a lopsided party constitution. The Umma party recruited the bulk of its followers from western Sudan based upon an adherence to the Mahdist teachings and was led by the Mahdi family. The Nationalist Unionist Party recruited its followers from urban central riverain Sudan and eastern Sudan which were dominated by the followers of the Khatmiyya religious sect. While the Khatmiyya was the religious sect led by the Mirghani, its political expression the NUP was led by

---

[47] In fact the sectarian parties proved time and again that the democracy they wanted had been the formal voting process where the electorate only delivered their votes. Accountability was not a part of that process, for they took it to be a mandatory rule once the initial choice was made. The voters in their turn made their choices between candidates not on party programmes but on the sectarian belonging of those candidates. Hence the choice has always been between the Mahdi family and the Mirghani family, which gave the Sudanese power politics its ever-present trait of personalities rather than issues.

[48] As Gabriel Warburg (1992:188) observed, "in the reality of the Sudan, one was born into a sect just as one is born into a family or a tribe". Thus *realpolitik* was not based on issues, as it was based on prior convictions. Dar Fur always voted Umma (*Ansar*) and the East and the North, invariably voted DUP (*Khatmyya*), in an ever present pattern of regional specialization of political following. The Umma party, for instance, used to send people like Ziyada Arbab and Abdalla Khalil to areas of Dar Fur which they had never seen before, armed with directives from the *Imam* to win elections. The local people voted for a person whom they did not know because of the *Imam's* backing.

Azhari—the man who hoisted the flag of the independent Sudan. But across their Islamic sectarian differences, the two parties were expressions of the dominant northern Sudanese political point of view and more precisely, even within the wider geographical territory designated the northern Sudan, these two parties were expressions of the political view of their respective riverain northern leaderships. Their sectarian religious nature ruled out the participation of non-Muslims; the overwhelming majority of the southern Sudanese were excluded by the Islamic criterion. Even among its diffusely defined northern constituency the hereditary nature of its leadership and their non-democratic constitution, ruled out the participation of non-riverain Sudanese in their leaderships as decision-makers. They were only followers whose votes were sought through religious directives issued by the religious leaders of such parties; and only occasionally. It was not surprising when regional parties emerged in the South as far back as 1953. But even then, the northern elite did not take this seriously. Rather they recoursed to MP buying to effect floor crossing among the members of the southern regional parties in the parliament. This has contributed to the creation of a stereotype of a southern politician not only on the level of popular political culture but even on the level of the northern elite as the 'slurs' referred to above might have indicated. The stereotype had it that a southern politician is a parliamentary member for sale to the highest northern bidder. Unfortunately, this led to a situation which dominated the riverain-led Sudanese politics of power: southern politicians cannot be taken seriously and there are no questions of principle to be discussed with them. Even the present regime of the National Islamic Front has an over-supply of Southern politicians who contradicted their Christian and other political principles and traded them for positions in the Government.

The first parliament which was elected in 1953 to deal with issues of self-determination was dominated by the two political forces of the North, i.e. the Umma and the NUP, and the regional political parties of the south. The NUP had 46 seats, the Umma 23 and the South 22 seats. In December 1955 the two religious leaders and the power behind the two parties agreed on the formation of a coalition government after independence but a national consensus, within the parliament, for independence was to be worked out. The most outstanding issue at this time was the question of federation for the South. It was somehow put under the carpet by the Northern politicians with great facilitation from the Southern politicians who accepted posts in the government in exchange for deferring the question of federation to after independence. No sooner than independence had been declared from within the parliament, than the term "federation" became a tabu, tantamount to subversion, in the political language of the Northern elite who on the eve of independence were assuring their southern "brothers" that they sympathized with the issue of federation. Khalid (1990) expressed this issue eloquently recalling some of the accompanying tactics of suppression—one of the three

Southern ministers appointed to the government was Stanislaus Payasama who was dismissed from the Government only a few months later accused of conjuring southern members of parliament to join him in subversion—'subversion' was the code name for Payasama's call for federation. In this way Southern politicians were only cultivated as long as their support was necessary to legitimize the independence motion and hand over power to the worthy sons of the land *Awlad Al Balad.* Southerners neither had the prowess nor the muscle, at the time to respond to this balderdash the way the Khalifa did with *Awlad Al Balad* of yesteryears. Not yet!" (Khalid, 1990:129).

But this was not the only factor that was conducive to political instability. Factional politics and political machinations were rife between the riverain elites of each party and across parties. Only six months after independence and in June 1956, Azhari, the prime minister of independence was forced to resign by shifting factional alliances.[49] Alliances came and went and without any one government being able to stabilize the political situation, it was no great surprise when the Sudanese army took over political power in a bloodless coup on 17 November 1958. The seeds of political instability were effectively sown, not unlike the rest of Africa where military and civilian regimes continuously battled each other for the seat of central political power in the capital city. The military regime which brought down the first democratic regime was in turn overthrown by a popular uprising on 21 October 1964. While general discontent with the state of civil liberties was very much at the heart of the causes of the October 1964 popular[50] revolution, the persistent civil war in the south was its last straw cause. However, the regime of the parties following on the heels of the overthrown military regime reverted to its traditional political inertia and recycled its infamous past of extreme factional politics, myopia, and the pursual of narrow sectarian interests to the detriment of the whole. But the major cause for the overthrow of the second democratic period by a military coup on 25 May 1969 was unmistakably the crisis of national unity. The May 1969 regime introduced a one party system which was a sharp departure from the direct military rule of General Abboud (1958–1964) as well as from the multi-party Westminister style democracy of the second democratic period (1964–1969).

Whatever the failings of the second military regime, it resolved the basic problem which bedeviled Sudanese national unity by negotiations in 1972.

---

[49] Factional infighting and political machinations were rife even before the formal declaration of independence on January 1, 1956. The emergence of the People's Democratic Party (PDP) led by a splinter group from Azhari's Nationalist Unionist Party (NUP) with the backing of the Sayyid Ali Al-Mirghani drew the majority-carpet from under Azhari's feet.

[50] It was a quarrel on the legality of a political gathering between the Khartoum University Students' Union (KUSU) and the police when the former was debating the Southern Sudan issue, that led to the precipitate events which culminated in the overthrow of the military regime of general Abboud in October 1964.

The longevity of Nimeiri's regime in power (16 years) despite concerted resistance, was largely attributable to the fact that it achieved the Addis Ababa Agreement. However, in 1983 the same regime was undermined by its abrogation of the Addis Agreement and the introduction of September laws. A popular upheaval brought down the May regime in 1985 and, after a short transitional period, ushered in a third multi-paraty democratic period as from April 1986. The traditional parties which dominated this period, i.e. the Umma and the Democratic Unionist Parties (DUP), recycled the past again. By 1988 the level of decay in the country was so staggering that it was clear to observers as well as to the main political actors that the days of the third period of democracy in the Sudan were numbered. The running theme among the public was that yesterday was better than today and tomorrow is definitely going to be worse than today. On June 30th, 1989 the present military regime took over supported by the National Islamic Front. External attempts of mediation towards a peaceful solution of the armed conflict, as exemplified by the Nigerian efforts which took place in the Nigerian capital, Abuja, have failed until now to produce the desired goal of peaceful agreement due mainly, but not exclusively, to the insistence of the present regime on carrying on with its Islamization programme as a mode of political integration in the country. The south was naturally off-board and its position was reflected by the Sudanese People Liberation Army (SPLA) which called for a secular democratic state.[51] The spectre of a war-divided country where the south remains largely under the control of SPLA and, "the national economy continues bogged down in debt and problems of production for which there is little prospect of respite while the conflict continues", (Woodward, 1990) continues as a disheartening, but realistic, scenario. The fact that the SPLA is now fighting for self-determination for the south, rather than a unitary solution does not change this scenario in any fundamental way as the central regime is not ready even to concede that. Rather, "such a scenario would probably presage continued decay of the state in all areas of its activity rather than some cataclysmic transformation" (Woodward, 1990:239). It echoes Nimeiri's unguarded relevation (1972) to the former colonial officer about how Sudan was "efficiently and competently run by the British", but so inefficiently and "incompetently" run by its own children!

"Germinative" or "irreversible decay"?

Looking at the context of decay of the African nation-state, Mazrui (1986) remarked prophetically that

---

[51] As recent as the Abuja talks in Nigeria June–July 1992, the SPLA was reaffirming its position that the Sudan should be a secular democratic state if it is going to accommodate the south.

Islam and westernism have been part of Africa's response to the imperative of looking outward to the wider world. But Africa's own ancestors are waiting to ensure that Africa also remembers to look inward to its own past. Before a seed germinated it must first decay. A mango tree grows out of a decaying mango seed. A new Africa may be germinating in the decay of the present one—and the ancestors are presiding over the process. (Ali Mazrui, 1986:21)

This was the time when "Afro-pessimism"[52] was imposingly dominant and optimistic remarks such as the one made by Mazrui were rare—even seemed baseless at the time and, as such, prophetic. The context was one which was dominated by the "killer" famines of the eighties, economic decline, social unrest, political decay and domination by barbarous, brutal and totalitarian regimes. Civil wars were not only recurrent, but spreading.[53] African performance in economic terms was decimal. The state was disintegrating and socially cohesive groups were disaggregating through a chaotic decade of social unrest. Politically, centralized repression and human rights abuse were very much in currency.

However, the 1990s saw a strong upsurge of social and political movements that were democratically oriented. Dictatorial regimes started crumbling. Mengistu of Ethiopia fell to be followed by Siad-Barré of Somalia—and before them all Nimeiri of Sudan. One party regimes started democratizing by adopting multi-party democracy; Zambia, Kenya and Tanzania were a few cases in East Africa. Ghana and Nigeria, in West Africa, were put on a course towards multi-party systems of democracy. In 1993 Ghana made the full transition to multi-paraty democracy and Chad conducted its first national constitutional conference for the first time in its post-colonial history. Zaire, Cameroun and Central African Republic were also under pressure from their own citizens and the international community to democratize. On the other hand, Somalia disintegrated calling for international military interference. Sudan might be on line. Is the mango seed germinating in its decay? On balance it seems so—yet a balance that reflects the international mood on the aftermath of the fall of the communist block and the formative stages of a new world order; free from the ramifications of the cold war and the binary oppositions between two super powers. As such it is difficult to assess in absolute terms whether the change in Africa is inherent in the system (ancestors awakening) or contingent on the disappearance of that binary opposition.

In the Sudan, while the levels of decay were very high by 1988, the developments that took place during the 1990s were opposite to and sharply contrastive to what was taking place in Africa. The Sudan moved in 1989 from a

---

[52] For an excellent exposé of "the Afropessimistic context" see Amundsen, Inge, 1992, "Afropessimism: A response from below?" Paper presented to NFU conference on Development Theory, Chr. Michelsen Institute (CMI), Bergen, 21–23 May 1992.
[53] Liberia, Chad, Ethiopia, Mozambique, Uganda, Sudan, Somalia and Angola were some of the worst cases.

multi-paraty democracy to a military dictatorship guised in an Islamic theocracy. Religious theocracy could not arrest the decay which, in the words of Woodward (1990), was

> Such decay has been going on for some years now, as most Sudanese admit, and intermittant disasters, such as drought in 1984–1985 and flood in 1988, make the wider world aware. Such is the nature of that decay—political, economic and social—that not only Sudan but the international community has a responsibility if it is to be reversed. (Woodward, 1990:239)

The new regime exasperated the pace and the levels of decay by polarizing the society into religious and secular forces and by pursuing the civil war. More than at any time during the meandering history of the Sudanese problem, the responsibility of the international community, at the present moment, towards the alleviation of the sufferings of the Sudanese becomes acutely needed.

While international factors and international responsibility remain a significant context of any state in today's world of interdependence where no state can escape influences emanating from outside its borders, there exist clear domains where each state must assume its internal responsibilities with a high degree of self-criticism in order to put its house in order. Colonialism, neo-colonialism and imperialism alone could not account for the internal decay of the African state in general or the Sudanese one in particular. Nor does unequal exchange or the unjust world economic order. In fact more than anything, the external-political-enemy conceptions magnified internal weaknesses and very little degree of self-criticism was practised, if ever. If our optimism of the mango seed that germinates in its decay is to be matched politically, internal issues of overhauling the existing social structures must be addressed with a high degree of self-criticism of the past experience. This field of political action is strictly a Sudanese responsibility which must be done with or without facilitation from the outside world.

FIELDS OF SUDANESE RESPONSIBILITY

Coming to terms with the reality of Sudanese pluralism

One of the basic factors that underlie the present Sudanese political decay is that the elites in power did not come to terms with the realities of the cultural pluralism and ethnic diversity in the Sudan. This happened despite a rich intellectual tradition that pinpointed[54] this very diversity recently. Governments always explained away tribal and ethnic affiliations as irrelevant in line with the dominant nation-building ideologies of the sixties. Owing to the peculiar historical developments that have put the riverain elite

---

[54] See Yusuf Fadl Hassan (ed.) (1985), Sayyid H. Hurreiz and El Fatih A. Abdel Salam (eds.) 1989) and Al Agab A. Al Tereifi (ed.) (1988) and (1989). See also F. Deng, F. and I.P Gifford (eds.) 1987 and D. Wai 1973 and 1981.

at the apex of central political power and the apparent, but deceptive, homogenizing tendencies of Arabism and Islam in the so called Northern part of the country, Arabism and Islam were made to be the central shaping ideological forces of nation-building process. The basic segmental cleavages that diversified the Sudanese societies such as language, region, culture, race and ethnic groups were somehow explained away or were totally set aside by the elite. But as shown above even in the northern part of the country which was thought to have been homogenized by Arabism and Islam, the assumed homogeneity was more apparent that real. The cultures of the Nubian groups in the North (Mahas, Kunuz, Danagla and Halfawiyyin) and the Beja groups (Hadendowa, Bishariyyin and Amarar) culturally, ethnically, linguistically and regionally, are clearly different from the so-called standard Sudanese culture with its strong emphasis on Arabism and Islam. Major ethnic groups in western Sudan, like the Fur, Masaleet, Zaghawa, Meidob and Tunjur, also show substantial and irreducible cultural differences from what is supposed to be represented by the central riverain cultures. Nonetheless all these groups are Sudanese. "Sudaneseness", rather than being Muslims, Africans or Arabs should have provided the common denominator for building a nation. But more than anything, the Sudanese elites' attempts at building a nation erred seriously in the area of dealing with tribalism and ethnic identity which is one of the main roots for political action in the Sudan. They dismissed it as a colonial making! Tribal and ethnic identities which are very real to the majority of the population in the rural areas were not only summarily dismissed as divisive, they, also, called for a considerable degree of enmity by the elite leading to strong handed actions by the successive governments. When, due to the inadequacy of the dominant sectarian political parties, regional groupings among the Beja, the Nuba and the Dar Furians started to appear, most of these were branded "racist", i.e. *unsuriya* (Arabic). Even though they later forced themselves to accept them as political movements, the elite in the centre still looked with suspicion at the leaders of these movements. Moreover, any political movement that came from the peripheries independent of the central elite, and irrespective of its declared "noble" political goals, was immediately branded as "tribalist" or "racist" and looked upon with extreme suspicion. Nationalism is practically equated to visions held by the riverain elites. The negative way the riverain elite looked at Philip Abbas Gabbush and his Nuba based movement and Ahmed Ibrahim Draige and the Dar Furi based movement illustrated the point.[55] Despite the fact that these leaders reached the central parliament through openly con-

---

[55] See Abdel Ghaffar M. Ahmed and Gunnar M. Sørbø (eds.) (1989) especially the contribution by Ahmed Ibrahim Draige (pp. 39–44). A university vice-chancellor of riverain origin told Draige, "We love the simple 'Westerner', but we cannot stomach the educated ones (*Muthaggafin*, Arabic)". (Draige, personal communication). I withhold the name because I belong to a culture which respects the dead and recalls only their "*good deeds*".

tested elections and on the basis of clear national political goal, major among which was the redressing of the unequal regional development, they were held in deep suspicion by the central elite if not with outright contempt.

The south is another case. While most of the central power elites admitted some special attributes to the south, e.g. being more African than the rest of the Sudan with mostly, but not exclusively Christian elite, etc., any calls by Southerners to a full recognition of that "specialness" were taken by the central elite as anathema to national unity. The case of the dismissal of Payasama from the first government of independence because of his attempts at reminding his riverain "brothers" of their promise to look into the "federation" issue bespeaks of this attitude. The civil wars which beset the Sudan were results of this attitude on the part of the central power elite, i.e. the *Awlad Al Balad*. This, of course, was the result of the most unfortunate myth that has endured for so long and has been sustained by both the riverain power elite and the world outside: that the Sudan is made of only two different parts; the North and the South. The implied homogeneity of each of the two parts unfortunately contributed to the inability of both Southern and Northern elites to come to terms with the extreme plurality and diversity of both parts. Such concepts of implied homogeneity have come as a result of a *reductio ad absurdum* where the common denominator for the northern identity was forced into Arabism and Islam and the southern identity into Africanity and Christianity. Both these situations are very far removed from social realities and as such untenable. The north as well as the south are homes for Islam, Christianity, and a host of other religions. Both are home for over one hundred languages and over a couple of hundred ethnic groups and cultures. On a more general level the inhabitants of the two parts of the country exhibit various degrees of Africanism and Arabism.

In the pursuit of this misplaced and unfortunate dichotomy the riverain power elite in the years following independence believed in a "melting pot" model of national integration. Moving from statistics which claimed that 70 per cent of the population of the country were Muslim and over 39 per cent were Arabs, the elite believed, even wished, that the minorities, despite their relative size, would eventually enter the pot of Arabism and Islam and melt into the image of the elite. The traditional political parties were supposed to be the vehicles of this political transformation. But as we have seen, the Islamic and the narrow geographical bases of the parties, ruled out the participation of the non-Muslim elements of the south and the Nuba. But even in the supposedly Muslim north, ethno-regional groups disillusioned with the narrow sectarian bases of these parties started developing their own political formations. Following the cue from the Beja congress which was formed by the Beja who were predominantly the followers of the Khatmiyya religious sect on 12 October 1958, the Dar Fur Development Front (DDF) and the General Union of Nuba Mountains (GUNM) were formed after October 1964 in the areas of western Sudan whose inhabitants were predominantly followers of the Mahdist Ansar sect. The rise of ethno-regionalism in the east, west and, before them all, in the south, would have been signal enough, had there been enough political will among the dominant riverain elite, that Sudanese diversity carried more than just Arabism and Islam.

Nimeiri's regime (1969–1983) tried very hard to reverse the political trends in which the Sudanese diversity was re-asserting itself. After banning the political parties, the regime outlawed all regional and tribal organizations as they were conceived to provide the antithesis of national unity. The only exception was the south where its special status was granted after the Addis Ababa Agreement. Nimeiri, in order to quicken the nation-building process and national unity, was to follow a strictly melting pot position. Only this time he did not leave the "pot" to be made of a diffusely defined Arabic/Islamic process. He provided the pot in the form of the Sudanese Socialist Union (SSU), as the only legitimate political party and the formula of the alliance of the people's working forces (regimental forces, professionals, labour movements, women and youth associations, pastoralists and farmers). Theoretically this formula might have worked but it was defeated by its one party overtones, among other things. However, what is important in this connection was the fact that political action within the SSU and the alliances that were formed, had strong regional and ethnic undercurrents. The Sudanese diversity refused to be suppressed.[56]

Towards the end of its years, the regime of Nimeiri worked against everything it earlier had worked for and introduced the Islamic *Sharia* laws while simultaneously abrogating the Addis Ababa Accord. The introduction of the Islamic *Sharia* laws by a presidential imposition was a trendsetter in Sudanese politics. It also brought to the surface a major political undercurrent which had always been there but which was not politicized by the parties under the previous democratic era. This was mainly the political elevation of the Islamic component of the twin cultural process of Arabism and Islam to the position of a core culture that was to become more legitimate than others. While the two main traditional parties, the Umma and the DUP, were based on Islam despite the fact of sectarianism, and were always talking about Islamic constitution[57] for the country, they never were able either to effect a permanent constitution for the country or push Islam to the political centre. It was the National Islamic Front who in collusion with Nimeiri introduced Islamic *Sharia* laws as the only legitimate corpus of law into the country. Since then the National Islamic Front has guarded its "imposition" with a religious zeal that ended up in appropriating the whole of government power in Sudan by effecting a military coup on 30 June 1989.

---

[56] See Sharif Harir, 1986.
[57] All constitutional drafts that came between 1956 and 1969 referred to Islam as a source of legislation.

The assumption of the existence of a cultural core in the Sudan that is based on Islam was statistically justified. The assumption goes: since the majority of the population are Muslims irrespective of the diversity expressed by their adherence to various schools and associations of Islam, it is a core which is stronger than any of the other segmental cleavages that characterized the cultural plurality of the Sudanese society. Some of the Nuba, some of the Southerners and some of the Ingessana are not Muslims, perhaps positively Christian. But by default, for had it not been for the colonial conspiracy against Islam which stopped its voluntary embracement by legislation (the Closed District Ordinance of 1922 and the introduction of Christian missionary activities in the South), Islam would have been prevalent in the whole of the country by now! As a legitimate core, while simultaneously representing the religion of the statistical majority, Islam should, then, constitute the law of the land. If some practical and haunting political questions arise, especially in today's world of human rights conceptions, a special status can be granted to the areas that are predominantly Christian by the application of a centrally controlled federal system. This was how the present National Islamic Front regime thought when it promulgated Islamic *Sharia* laws into the constitution of the country in 1991. However, the fact that opposition to the present regime came not only from Christians but also from Islamic-based groups in the North, i.e. the Ansar and the Khatmiyya, seemed not to bother the National Islamic Front. On the contrary, it argued that as long as what it tried to implement was Allah's *Sharia*, then it was not subject to validation or invalidation by political consensus or dissension. Being a "citizen" of Sudan does not give one an automatic right to object to the project pushed by the National Islamic Front. To have full rights as a citizen one must see things the way NIF sees them.[58]

As one may be able to discern, this point of view is slightly at variance with the "melting pot" model. While both presupposed the prior existence of a standard value towards which all other cultures should gravitate, the "melting pot" model does not rule out the rise of a uniquely Sudanese culture out of such interaction.[59] However, the Islamic "core culture" model presupposes assimilation into a carefully orchestrated Islamic culture which is

---

[58] In the document entitled "Sudan Charter: National Unity and Diversity" which was issued by the National Islamic Front in January 1987, NIF presented an ambiguous position for while accepting that the Sudanese were "diversified by the multiplicity of their religious and cultural affiliations", it went on to give the Muslims the right to dominate. It states "... the Muslims, therefore, have a legitimate right, by virtue of their religious choice, of their democratic weight and of natural justice, to practise the values and the rules of their religion to their full range—in personal, familial, social and political affairs". But for non-Muslims, in the Sudan, full range expression of their religion remains in, "private, family or social matter". See Abdel Ghaffar M. Ahmed and Gunnar M. Sørbø (eds.), op.cit. (pp. 133–144).
[59] See S.H. Hurriez and E.A. Abdel Salam (ed.s) 1989 (especially pp. 1–28 and pp. 29–68).

the absolute value and the only "correct" culture that, if necessary, should be guarded and furthered by the mobilization of the body politic of the faithful by Holy War, *Jihad*.[60] This seemed to be the case when state regimental forces and the popular defence forces were mobilized by the use of Islamic symbolism to fight the war in the South. What these forces were defending was not the Sudan—or a sovereign political entity—but the Islamic faith as viewed from the perspective of the National Islamic Front. Thus the recapture of Torit, the headquarters of the SPLA, was not portrayed in terms of a state dealing with a Sudanese rebel force, but in terms of Islamic Holy Warriors, *Mujahidin* (Arabic); dealing a final blow to *Satan*. Citizenship is not co-extensive with the political boundaries but with cultural boundaries.[61]

It goes without a say that the idea of "core culture" and its social relative "core ethnie"[62] have occupied central positions in the theoretical corpus of nation-building theory. It was the Arab philosopher and sociologist Ibn Khaldun who used the concept *Asabiya* (Arabic), i.e. core ethnic or ethnically based solidarity, as a necessary component of nation-state building. But more recently and reflecting European experiences of nation building, the presence of an ethnic core was made a prerequisite for understanding nation-building. This was based on the assumption that nation-states are more likely to reflect a co-extensiveness between geographical territory and homogenous ethnic community and hence a distinction was made between state-making, which may denote the carving out of territory into a state unit, and nation-building, which may denote the western concept of creating the "national participant society". Of course, very few nations in today's world, including those in the west, can conform to the criterion of co-extensiveness of territory and homogeneous ethnic community. Here one of the basic weaknesses of nation-building theory is revealed. The "core culture" approach seems not to be worried by these aspects. It proceeds a step further and imposes, *a priori*, a

---

[60] Colonel Yasin Abdel Gadir, the deputy commander of the People's Defence Force (PDF), a para-military militia created by the regime of General El Beshir after the 1989 coup, is quoted by Horn of Africa Bulletin (HAB, Vol. 4, No. 2 March–April 1992) as stating that "... the Sudanese Government's policy consisted of militarizing the entire Sudanese people to defend Islam's faith, the homeland and property". This policy was reinforced by the declaration of *Jihad* holy war against the SPLA.

[61] As *Jihad* is an Islamic concept to defend the Islamic faith, it, by necessity, must be directed against non-Muslims which only means the Southern and the non-Muslim Nuba area. If the campaign of militarization of the entire Sudanese people to defend the Islamic faith is meant to include only Muslims, then, it, by necessity, must exclude the non-Muslims from the designation 'entire Sudanese people'. By deduction, which is entirely congruent with the logic employed by the regime, non-Muslims are non-citizens.

[62] The idea of 'ethnic core' or 'core ethnie' is quite recurrent in the theoretical literature of nation-building where "the central difficulty of 'nation-building' in Africa is attributed the absence of 'core ethnie'". The basic weakness of such a view is the fact that it overlooks and slights over the consequences of the colonial intervention. See, for example, Anthony D. Smith (1986), in J. Hall (ed.), (1986:228–260).

selective "shared history" of its own making upon the communities that make the state and start building a nation—on its image. The reality on the ground does not bother it. The fact that a multiplicity of cultures exist in the same geopolitical territorial space, each no less legitimate than the other, escapes it somehow. This is precisely the case in today's Sudan as well as in many parts of Africa and for that very reason states recourse to centralized repression to suppress the multitude of cultures and multiplicity of ethnic groups for the benefit of an artificially and selectively created common culture. The response on the part of the multitude of suppressed ethnic groups is decentralized violence against each other and against the state. The recent ethnic wars between the Fur and the Arabs in the west and Arabs and the Southern groups along the lines of tribal overlap were but reflections of this process of decentralization of violence.

It is time to come to terms with the realities of the Sudanese ethnic diversity and cultural pluralism especially as the evidence showed a strong resurgence of ethnic politics. Despite the fact that rural-urban migration, rural-rural migration, the expansion of educational infrastructure and mass displacements of population resulting from droughts and wars, may have created opportunities for intensive interactions across ethnic and cultural lines, cultural distinctions remained salient and ethnic or tribal identity as a basis for corporate political actions remained strong. The persistent denial by the elite of the efficacy of such identities despite their saliency is also contradicted by the elite's manipulation of those same identities for their benefit.[63]

The first step towards coming to terms with the realities of Sudanese diversity is for the elite to admit that despite any pejorative connotations that they might have gained, tribalism and ethnic identity constitute a base for political action. As such they should not be summarily dismissed. Their expression in political life should be respected. This means, also, the legal disenfranchisement of ethnic identity as long as it seeks peaceful political goals. Statistical approaches to ethnic and cultural groups in terms of majorities and minorities are not only invalid in terms of conceptions of what ethnic identity is about, but also opens up the possibility for the domination by numerically superior ethnic groups over those which are numerically inferior. This leads to situations of internal colonization as conceived by dominated groups and hence to armed conflicts or instability. Once group identities are equalized in terms of validity of each as an identity of a specific group, the

---

[63] In actual practice, the elite maintain strong ethnic constituencies for themselves while they, at the level of rhetoric, deny and even attack ethnic attachments. This, in fact, is a widespread practice in Africa which extends across regimes and power elites, it has produced time and again, the so-called "Mobutist paradigm" (Basil Davidson, 1992) where the so-called 'nation-state' is 'privatized' (Ali Mazrui, 1986) for the benefit of extended family, tribe or an ethnic group. At the present moment one does see, in the Sudan, a clear power constellation based on a Jaali/Bedeiri ethnic base which is a part of the old riverain "old-boy" club. Only this time, Islam is used as an overarching ideology.

voluntary cooperation of the holders of those different identities in the interest of the common society could be sought. This will involve some consociational arrangements where political cooperation between the social and cultural segments of the polity will become the norm rather than the presupposition of segmental conflict which characterizes the current approaches. Other cleavages in society, such as religion, are also to be treated the same way. This is because relative numbers of followers of different religions should not have political implications in terms of access to structures of political influence in the state. This will leave the chance open for development of other types of interest groups whose constitution might cut across those fundamental segmental cleavages and give rise to political groupings based on wider national issues. Unfortunately in the Sudanese experience, segmental cleavages such as religion, region, race and ethnic identity, in most cases, coincided with the constitution of the political parties. Rather than leading towards the development of nationally based party politics, this coincidence reinforced and entrenched sectarian interests that led to the subordination of the national interests to segmental interests for the thirty-seven years of independence.

The constitutional debate and the format of the state in the Sudan

The constitutional debate that took place in the Sudan after independence suffered from the above mentioned misconception of the realities of the Sudanese cultural pluralism and found dubious ways of imposing an illusory identity based on Arabism and Islam upon the state. The debate was based, from the very start, on a foundation that was marred by racial and religious prejudices which extended a riverain elitist identity to cotermine with the state in the Sudan. This had an effect of limiting constitutional debate to remaining within the riverain elite circles because of the exclusivist character of its foundational basis. However, even within that limited circle of elites, consensus upon what an Islamic identity for the country would precisely entail, was difficult to come by. Up until Nimeiri took over power by a military *coup d'état* in 1969, the Sudan operated without a permanent constitution of its own, though there was no short supply of constitutional drafts based on committee work between 1950 and 1969.[64] Only in 1973 a permanent constitution was introduced by Nimeiri. But even then, the permanent constitution was not an outcome of a wide constitutional debate. It was authored

---

[64] The Sudan gained its independence by adopting the document drafted by Hight Court Judge Stanley-Baker in 1951 which came out of a failed effort by the so-called Constitutional Amendment Committee (CAC) which was formed by the then British Governor-General. Since that time three attempts at promulgating a permanent constitution failed on the two issues of Southern Federation and the role of Islam. Only in 1973 was Nimeiri able to impose a permanent constitution, only to be assaulted by him in 1983 and to be finally abrogated in 1985.

by the late Dr. Gaafar Mohamed Ali Bakhelt and was rubber stamped by
Nimeiri's hand-picked People's Assembly. In some respects this was a constitution by imposition because the main Sudanese political forces were excluded from debating it. Even then it did not resolve the issue related to the
role of religion in politics completely. The compromise it reached was to suffer from open interpretations later. But the whole of the permanent constitution was to suffer later from the imposition by the president of the so called
September Laws in 1983, when Islamic *Sharia* laws were imposed by presidential decree.

However, it is interesting to look briefly at what Article 16 of the constitution said on this question.[65] Item a) of Article 16 states, "In the Democratic Republic of the Sudan, Islam is *the religion* and society shall be guided
by Islam being the religion of the *majority of its people* and the state shall
endeavour to express its values". In contrast item b) states, "Christianity is
the religion in the Democratic Republic of the Sudan being professed by *a
large number of its citizens* who are guided by Christianity and the state shall
endeavour to express its values". As these two items stand it is difficult to
fathom the intention of the constitution makers for the issues here are
shrouded in semantic mysticism. In between the qualitative phrases of "the
majority of its people", and "a large number of its citizens", the intentions of
the law makers are not very clearly spelt out. If an equal role for both Islam
and Christianity was intended, this intention was compromised early on
when Islam was entrusted to provide guidance for the society. However, the
main compromising act was performed by president Nimeiri when he decisively went in favour of introducing Islamic *Sharia* laws in September 1983.
This act brought the constitutional debate to square one or where it always
began and ended concerning the Islamic identity of the Sudan. Throughout
the third democratic period following the overthrow of Nimeiri's regime
(1985–1989), the constitutional debate was conducted in terms of the Islamic
identity of the Sudan with the National Islamic Front guarding the gates of
the debate so that no unwanted viewpoints could enter. The Mahdists who
provided El Saddig Mahdi as a prime minister for most of this period, while
expressing viewpoints different to that of the NIF, were paralysed for most of
this period and were not able to change the track which the debate was taking. Until the overthrow of the third democracy by a military *coup d'état* in
30 June 1989, the National Islamic Front was able to blackmail the main
Northern political parties to acquiesce on the premises upon which the debate was based. When they sensed a change in the stand of the Mahdists towards this debate,[66] the NIF effected the *coup d'état*, using its elements in the

---

[65] See Mansour Khalid ibid.
[66] The NIF's abstainment from signing the "Charter for Defence of Democracy" was
enough signal, had there been serious politicians, as to the real intentions of the organization. This coupled with the fact that it was no great secret that it maintained
cells in the army would have been warning enough had it not been for the complete

national army.[67] Since then the debate was sealed by promulgating Islamic *Sharia* into the law of the land in 1991. A centrally controlled form of federation, as a format for the state, was imposed wherein state *wali* (Arabic for ruler) and state ministers were appointed by the central political authority after being carefully screened by the various NIF organs.[68]

The present situation is, of course, an outcome of long-standing processes of political evolution where all the various riverain Sudanese elites have contributed to it. It is not only a creation of the National Islamic Front. The self righteous assumption that Sudan is made in the image of the riverain culture based upon Islam and Arabism cuts across all urban-based riverain political forces. The differences in positions are only of the degree to which such positions are pursued. While the National Islamic Front pursued its position zealously and single-mindedly to the extent of imposing it by a military *coup d'état,* the Umma and the DUP were less consistent and more erratic but, nonetheless, embodying the main tenets of a northern, riverain position. What all these positions lacked was a broader, even a globalized vision, of the extreme plurality of the Sudanese society whose components should coexist on equal footing as its citizens despite their cultural and ethnic difference. Accepting such a broader vision of the plural reality of the cultures and groups that constituted the Sudan would have entailed ridding oneself of narrow-based ideologies, however, sacred they were held to be. Imposition by usurpation of central political power would not in any sense create a stable political system. It will only delay and in the process complicate the final disintegration—in the case of the Sudan the final decay of the Sudan not only into two states one in the South and the other in the North but unleash and spearhead regional instability in the whole of Sub-Saharan Africa. This will come from the fact that if one stretch of the boundary is undone, many stretches will come undone as those boundaries were not natural ones.

Bearing the facts of the Sudanese segmental cleavages in mind would imply a fundamentally different constitutional debate which would, in turn, call in a different format for the state in the place of the unitary form which,

---

incompetence of the party politicians of the third democratic era (1986–89). Anyway, what is important is the fact that the military coup by NIF came at a very critical moment when the parties, despite their utter incompetence, were moving towards resolving both the issues of the *Sharia* and the South. Some sources indicated that the very Friday, June 30, 1989, on which the NIF coup occurred was earmarked for making major concessions on the two issues of the *Sharia* and the war in the South. Instead, martial law was imposed and the Sudan continues to languish under it.

[67] The army was national but in name as its officer corps, with the exception of only a few, belonged to one party, ideological cell or similar.

[68] There are strong indications that all candidates, whether to carry political portfolios or to be appointed to the state bureaucracy, are now screened by the NIF information office. A handful of NIF leaders, then, vet the candidates who originated from their respective regions.

somehow, ensured the domination of the Sudanese politics by the riverain point of view. The constitutional debate will develop into the direction which Woodward attempts to point at in this collection, "perhaps the weakness of all forms of government hitherto will enhance the appreciation of the need to seek a consensus for a more effective constitutional structure than hitherto (whether in one country or two)" (Woodward, 1992). Seeking consensus as a political method to arrive at an effective constitution will transform the Sudanese reality of pluralism from being a liability (as is assumed today entailing necessarily the maintenance of political order by domination and force) into an asset which might make a major contribution to the creation of a stable democracy. This would also have implications for the format the state might take. As most of the segmental cleavages in the Sudan coincide with regional cleavages,[69] the federal format may be used. But federalism as a name-tag will not provide a panacea as the present form of federalism applied by the NIF regime has shown. It should be specified constitutionally and be used as a part of broader consociational approach (Lijphart, 1977). Islam, as it has been presented by NIF in the Sudan, is an extremely divisive force not only because it claims a dominant position which other religious creeds such as Christianity are denied access to, but because it is used to enhance riverain Sudanese "nationalism" as El Affendi observed (El Affendi, 1992:9). As Northern, or more specifically riverain, Sudanese identify is strongly associated with Arabism in racial terms, it goes without saying that Islam is used to enhance racial prejudices that are deeply harboured by northern Sudanese as far as assumptions of Arab superiority are concerned. What NIF successfully does is the galvanization of the riverain Arab/Islamic identity *vis-à-vis* the non-Arab but Muslim and the non-Muslim periphery. One has to undo the present situation of religious and racial prejudice and provide a balance between the extreme Arabism of the "riverain" and the extreme Africanism of the "South", if the country is to be kept together. Otherwise, the prospects are bleaker than most of us would like to think, not only for the Sudan but for the whole region.[70]

Nepotism, corruption and mismanagement

At the heart of the decay of the Sudanese state lie nepotism, corruption and mismanagement of public resources. Nepotism is a generally prevalent practice in the Sudan where holders of public office give relatives and tribesmen,

---

[69] Most of the Sudanese ethnic groups are territorial groups. Tribes, though intermixed today due to population mobility, have territorially defined homelands that carry their names.

[70] Sudan neighbours nine African countries (Egypt, Libya, Chad, Central African Republic, Zaire, Uganda, Kenya, Ethiopia and Eritrea) sharing restive ethnic groups across border overlap areas. Has the "Sudan" to become "two", there is no guarantee that it would not become "many".

undue and preferential access to public resources whether these are employment opportunities, public contracts or access to educational facilities. Known popularly as *mahsubiyya* (Arabic), it is effected through intermediaries *wasta* or *dhahar* (back, Arabic). It is a general belief that without a *wasta*, it is difficult for one to get access to, for instance, military or police academies; both prestigious institutions that confer considerable power in society upon its graduates not only in the daily life where the uniform opens many closed doors but as potential contenders to political power through future coups. Likewise is access to public contracts and state sponsored employment opportunities. Nepotism is, of course, the antithesis of merit and the public believe that if one is not from the riverain Sudan which is overrepresented in the state bureaucracy, one's opportunity situation is sharply curtailed irrespective of one's achieved merit or proven ability. Certain fields of employment, e.g. officers' corps in both the army and the police, hotel and tourism departments and diplomatic service, were believed, by Sudanese from Western, Eastern and Southern parts, to be exclusive fields of monopoly for the riverain Sudanese.[71] While the odd Southerner is seen, for instance, in the Ministry of Foreign Affairs as a diplomat, the entry of people from Western Sudan to that area is of a very recent date reflecting the gradual ascendency of Western Sudanese in the bureaucracy and politics.

Nepotism, though politically unacceptable, is practised in society as a moral fulfilment of kinship obligations which extend to include tribal and ethnic groups.[72] Thus rules are bent and regulations are overlooked to fulfil what public office holders consider a moral obligation. This is made all the easier in the Sudanese system which lacks both transparency and accountability and which is based on clientalism and patronage. As such it is practised by individual office holders as well as political organizations such as parties. Its main effect is not only the selective introduction of potential candidates to public-based opportunity situations using kinship and ethnic criteria, it also tends to protect corruption and mismanagement. In fact apart from very few cases of political[73] trials, at occasions of changes of regimes,

---

[71] The officer corps of both the army and the police was traditionally the monopoly of the *Jaali, Shaigi* and *Dongolawi* riverain ethnic groups though the picture is changing. Tourism and hotels were the exclusive domain of the Halfawi and Dongolawi groups. While the South has produced its odd ambassador in the diplomatic service, probably owing to the strong handed actions by various armed Southern movements (1955–72), the west, especially Dar Fur, had yet to provide its first third secretaries in the eighties.

[72] There exist very powerful social pressures in the Sudanese society, which very few High Office holders have successfully resisted up to now, to promote, unduly, relatives and friends in preference to other non-relatives, nonetheless qualified, co-citizens. While the pressure is generally felt, the overrepresentation of riverain elements in high office makes their nepotism stand out.

[73] Nimeiri (1969–1985), in his radical days, charged at least two ministers belonging to the outgoing regime with corruption which did not stick. In the post Nimeiri period (1985–1989), Nimeiri's accomplices were charged with the offence of "coup-

for the purposes of giving some credibility to slogans of fighting nepotism
and corruption, it is rare, if ever, anybody has been brought to account for
acts of nepotism, corruption or mismanagement. Even in those rare cases,
political considerations took precedence over considerations of legal accountability in the meandering paths of the ever shifting Sudanese political
alliances. This goes also for the *Jallaba* trade networks which enjoyed considerable protection from their kins in administration and politics. As a consequence, strong anti-*Jallaba* feelings were, and are, prevalent in Western,
Southern and Eastern Sudan.[74] These feelings led to regional movements in
Dar Fur, Kordofan and Eastern Sudan fuelled by a feeling on the part of the
inhabitants of those regions that they were excluded from access to state
power which is dominated by riverain Sudanese. Their dominant position
was protected and perpetuated through selective recruitment to the state organs by the use of nepotistic practices which are based on the *Jallaba* trade
and administrative networks.

Rather than taking these movements for what they really tried to express
beyond the manifest ethnic rhetoric which characterized them, the dominant
riverain elite strongly reacted to them and branded them "racist", thus dismissing the political questions which such movements raised with a characteristic riverain myopia. The second stage was the use of repressive measures
such as detentions, dismissals and, in extreme cases, physical liquidation,[75]
as ways of dealing with them. Understandably, most of the movements went
underground which pre-empted any chance of dialogue between them and
the dominant riverain elites. The Southern Sudanese movements were extreme cases of such reactions by excluded peripheries to have access to state

---

making". In the period after the latest coup (June 30, 1989) revolutionary courts No.
1 and 2, held centre stage. However, the only achievements (defeating the purpose of
justice) were the hanging of a currency dealer and the summary execution of some 28
army officers accused of a failed coup attempt.

[74] The term *Jallaba* denotes "long distance-trade" practitioner. However as this class
of people invariably came from the riverain Sudan and especially from the Jaaliyyin,
Shaiqiyya, the Musalamiyyia, the Mahas, the Danagla, etc. the term came to denote
a person from these groups even if he did not practise trade. At least, this is the case
in Dar Fur. In the South they were known as *Mandakoru* and in the East as
Balawayt. While the Beja Congress (BC), the Dar Fur Development Front (DDF) and
the General Union of the Nuba Mountains (GUNM) were politically articulate, re-
gionally-based groupings, the riverain power elite never made the small effort of dis-
sociating them from racism, thus dismissing them. More militant versions of these
groupings took place in Dar Fur in the early sixties when clandestine movements
such as *Soony*, and the Red Flame appeared. Later in the eighties the *Hadout* group
appeared among the Red Sea Hadendowa.

[75] Massive dismissals from the army which were directed against elements from Dar
Fur took place in 1965 in response to the appearance of *Soony*. Physical liquidation
was routinely practised by the army in the South during the First Civil War (1955–
1972) and now in both the South, Dar Fur and the Nuba Mountains
(1990/1991/1992).

power or structures of access. In Dar Fur, while movements like *Soony* and "Red Flame" which appeared in the sixties gradually disappeared, the ideas which were to be expressed by them have survived up to today. The fact is that regional inequalities in development and unequal access to the state power existed and whether what these movements tried to express in terms of *Jallaba* nepotism was right or not is far beside the point. The point is that mutual distrust has been built during the long process of interaction between populations of the Sudanese peripheries and the *Jallaba* (riverain Sudanese) where the former felt completely powerless to influence the state in their favour. As such while their reactions were a natural part of that process of powerlessness, they invited also reactions on the part of the dominant groups who were afraid of losing their dominant position. The dominant riverain Sudanese used Islam as an ideology to enhance its dominant position hoping not only to galvanize its own constituency of Arabized riverain Sudan but also the Muslim but non-Arabized Sudanese in Dar Fur and Eastern Sudan. The South, falling back into its relative Africanity, used Africanism as an ideology in the hope not only to galvanize its Southern constituency, but also in order to capture parts of the non-Arab but Muslim population in the West and Eastern Sudan. Christianity which is not a universal Southern religion but universally elite religion, is used only when it is advantageous. These two ideological positions are mutually exclusive and frightening to each other and imply the prevalence of one over the other. Perhaps in that lies the inability of the Sudanese to reach a solution in this context. Hence it would be natural that any solution that may not give a dominant position to one or the other and at the same time not exclude one or the other completely, may imply some proportional representation with a mutual veto to each. Otherwise separate existence may not be avoidable. That is because if the reproduction of the Sudanese state in its present form of riverain domination was based on nepotism, it becomes completely untenable now especially as some groups have taken to arms to redress this very situation.

FIELDS OF INTERNATIONAL RESPONSIBILITY

If the basic internal political questions which related to the realities of the Sudanese diversity were addressed with a degree of self-criticism and soul searching, there is a distinct likelihood that it might lead to a healthy constitutional debate. With constitutional debate I do not mean only the technicalities of a "constitution", but the more general processes of reconstituting a politically acceptable Sudan that may direct the loyalties of its citizens towards it as an object of national loyalty above all the segmental cleavages that are embodied in its status as a culturally plural entity. Only then would energies be directed towards the creation of a "Sudan" that transcends loyalties to segmental cleavages whether those are religious, ethnic or regional. Re-constitution will assume priority over attempts to put it in ideological straightjackets or create one for it. That being done, nepotism as a reproduction mechanism for the dominant elite will disappear and internal structural adjustments will be initiated. In no way do I claim that all these processes will take place peacefully, because achieving peace which may be conducive to most of these processes might require violence of some form to defeat the vanguard that perpetuates the present war situation in the country. That is because, as long as the National Islamic Front holds onto power, the war will be perpetuated as a holy war, *Jihad*. Furthermore, the ideological position of NIF will continue to be presented as the only correct and legitimate culture pre-empting in the process any movement towards acceptance of the Sudanese ethnic diversity and the concomitant cultural pluralism.

International pressure alone cannot achieve peace though it might bring belligerent parties to the conference table as the Abjua conference might suggest.[76] There must exist internal conditions, within the political environment, that are conducive to peace negotiations as was the case in 1972. However, reaching peace is also a degree easier than maintaining it as the 1983 turnabout may indicate. The international community has a vital and a central role to play in the maintenance of peace once achieved. This is because the whole issue of peace cannot be separated from the reality of the decay and the necessity of a total reconstruction of the whole country economically, socially and politically. An economic foundation that is able to deliver "public goods" will be supportive and conducive to an environment of sociopolitical stability. And conversely, however noble the ideals created during a peace process, a weak economy will undermine them. Following from the above, two clear fields of international responsibility stand out: reconstruction and development on the one hand and the debt question on the other.

Reconstruction and development

During the eleven years in which the Addis Ababa Peace Agreement functioned (1972–1983), considerable reconstruction and development effort was undertaken in the South by both the Sudan government and international agencies including expatriate non-governmental organizations. Though these efforts were not well coordinated due to the absence of coherent planning (as Johnson indicates in this collection) and suffered from the lack of adequately qualified personnel (as Tvedt indicates in this volume), they were nevertheless visible as achievements which have had developmental implications; even if they were characterized by uneven regional distribution (Johnson, 1992; Tvedt, 1992). But the onset of hostilities in 1983 and the continuation of the war up to the present, did not only pre-empt the promise which was carried by this period of reconstruction; it led to unprecedented levels of destruction.

---

[76] The attempts by President Jimmy Carter (1989) in Nairobi (Kenya) and President Babangida (1992) in Abuja (Nigeria), bear testimony to this assertion.

What happened during the first period of war in the South (1955–1972) cannot be compared to the destruction done during the present war for many reasons. During the first period (1955–1972) the war was a pretty straightforward and a simple matter that had had two parties: the Sudan government's troops vs Anyanya I rebel forces. The present war is a complex matter and has a multiplicity of parties. While the Sudan government's forces and the forces of the Sudanese People's Liberation Army are the main opposing parties, there exists a multiplicity of other contestants who might be smaller in size and scale but are no less destructive in this war especially as far as community life in the South is concerned. Early in the present war the government started supporting tribal militias from among the Southern tribes of Murle, Toposa and Mandari (Equatorian tribes) to attack the civilian populations of the Dinka tribes in the Jonglei and Lake provinces. Unlike the first war, civilian populations were specifically targeted and drawn into the spiralling war. The Anyanya II forces were also recruited by the government as "friendly forces" to fight the SPLA in and around the Nuer tribal districts in the Southern provinces of Upper Nile. In addition Baggara tribes (of Arabic stock) were recruited and supported by the government and organized in what came to be known as Murahalin forces (*Guwat al Marahil*, Arabic) with the manifest purpose of protecting the nomadic migratory routes of the Baggara Arabs to the South. But in actual fact, they raided the Dinka of Bahr El-Ghazal region for cattle—furthering the tradition of mutual cattle "rustling" and hostage taking; only this time with the support, connivance and complicity of the central government which is supposed to be the "peace keeper" and the "law upholder" among the diverse ethnic groups in the country.

The direct negative result of the presence of all these antagonistic fighting forces on the civilian, rural and agro-pastoralist communities was grave. Pastoralists were depossessed as a result of the massive cattle raiding and diseases started spreading among both human beings and livestock as a consequence of disruption of various services. The insecurity, famines and excesses of both the regular army and the irregular para-militaries led to massive population displacements and dislocations, first by draining the rural countryside into the garrison towns of the Southern region and then by sending a massive wave of migration towards the riverain towns; especially to the capital Khartoum. The disruption of services and amenities was followed by the disruption of the trade networks in the South.

Unlike the first war, the present one has also been one in which smaller towns and district centres have been subjected to extensive and repeated destruction leading to a complete stop of educational and health services among others. During this war many towns have changed hands several times between government forces and SPLA forces. Such towns and centres suffered destruction at least twice: once during the combat to take over from one another and second during the withdrawal of either of the forces from

them. It is reported by Johnson (1992) among others, that retreating government troops were in the regular habit of destroying "anything considered
of strategic value when they abandoned a town". Even medical equipment
and water pumps were blown up, if they could not be carried away which
was more often the case than not. The irony in this situation is the fact that
the bill for this wilful destruction will be borne at some future point by the
same treasury. It seems the fact that one day peace might come and that
equipment might be needed has never crossed the minds of the military
commanders.

These practices continued across three regimes which do not claim affinity
to each other. All this started under Nimeiri's regime which was ousted by a
popular upheaval in 1985 but continued through the transitional period of
1985–1986, only to be revived by the third democratic multi-paraty regime
of 1986–1989. The present National Islamic Front's regime, has elevated this
prevalent insensitivity to the future well-being of the country to a level of art
and religious duty by introducing yet another party to the war: an ideology
of Islamic militancy and a religiously motivated militia named the People's
Defence Forces (PDP) or *Mujahidin* (Arabic) holy warriors.

But the present war is different to the first one not only in the complexity
reflected in the multiplicity of its parties. Its geographical spread also, puts it
levels beyond the destructive ability of the first war. While the Anyanya I war
which continued for seventeen years was confined to the southern bush, this
war has moved out from the traditional "killing fields" of the South, to engulf the Nuba mountains in Southern Kordofan parts of Dar Fur in Western
Sudan and the Southern Blue Nile region affecting and displacing major
tribal groups who were not Southerners by the prevalent regional identification. Its destructive capacity has engulfed most of the Sudan. In the remaining part of the country where bullets and explosives were not destroying
buildings, medical equipment or communities the general economic decay
has brought it to parity with the destroyed South. Thus if peace is achieved
the formidable tasks of reconstruction and rehabilitation of, not only, the
South but the whole country will dwarf the first experience of reconstruction.

Given the nature of the decay which is total, (i.e. political, economic and
social), the responsibility of the international community must go beyond intermittent relief efforts to assist the country to stand on its feet. This is simply
because the way it is today the Sudan does not have the means to create
conditions that are conducive to the maintenance of peace even if it is
reached. Peace need economic qualifications.

The debt question

Throughout the years of economic mismanagement, corrupt governments
and privatization of the state the Sudanese people, for no good reason apart
from the fact that they did not have a say in what a government did, have ac-

cumulated an international debt that stands presently at USD 15.5 billion (*The Independent*, 23. March 1993). With a short fall on remittances which stood at USD 400 million in 1990, and the accumulation of interest from un-serviced debt, the figure of total debt must be considerably higher today, especially if one adds the continuous internal borrowing for the purpose of sustaining a USD 2 million per day war in the South. If the Sudan is to rise to its feet and be able to rebuild its economy and reconstruct its society, it becomes a responsibility incumbent on the international community that this debt must be written off. How this is going to be done is another matter.

THE NEW SUDAN

In between the three periods of democratic experimentation (1956–58, 1965–69, 1986–89) and those of military rule (1958–65, 1969–85, 1989 to the present), the formal state institutions have been steadily decaying. Feeding on the general atmosphere of political instability, war in the South (1955–1972, 1983 to the present), and natural disasters that were complicated by the myopic policies of its central power elite, the Sudan has been heading for an imminent disintegration. That it did not disintegrate could be explained by two factors that had strongly militated against that eventuality. On the one hand there was the external factor which related both to regional African and international world politics. The African state including the one that persisted in the post independent Sudan is a juridical expression of the international system that ruled out the formation of new states by the use of force. Hence, the legal fiction of the state was to be maintained by all means. On the other hand, many African states were suffering from the same types of conflicts that were taking place in the Sudan, e.g. Biafra in Nigeria, Eritrea as a part of the Ethiopian Empire etc. While the Africans were sympathetic to their "African brothers" in the South, it would not do any African state a service if Sudan was to be dismembered. Hence they brought pressure to bear on their African brothers to solve the problem within a united Sudan. Internally and despite the continuation of the war between Khartoum governments and the Southern movements, the Sudanese peripheries remained stable and the traditional socio-political systems and their institutions remained intact. In a sense there were two systems that existed side by side and while relating to each other in certain areas, the formal state remained a prerogative of the central elite and major national political events, such as shifts in regimes, were central events in which the periphery was not consulted. Under the various democratic periods, once the votes of the peripheries were elicited during elections for the sake of formality, the central elite ruled by mandate, and during military coups the peripheries were commanded to conform. In both cases they were taken for granted once Khartoum was under control.

On their part the peripheries depended on their traditional institutions, where native administration played a central role in conflict resolution, and ran their daily political life independent of the centre. But today it is not only the centre which is decaying. The presence of arms and militias combined with natural disasters and political instability led to a breakdown in those traditional institutions;[77] in brief, the periphery is also decaying. This is manifest in the fact that decentralized violence, as reflected in armed robbery and ethnic conflicts in which modern arms are used, are prevalent. The central state for its part is practising centralized repression as a means of survival. The question which poses itself here is whether a new Sudan will come out of the decay of the old?

Despite the pessimistic view expressed by many and contested by few, and irrespective of the immediate realities of the present situation (i.e. divisive religious bigotry, the devastating war, the demise of law and order in the peripheries, the economic bankruptcy of the state, the social turmoil and the decay of both state institutions and infrastructure), there seems to be a general consensus among the Sudanese public that Sudan should remain one country even if in a confederal or federal form. This is reflected in the fact that all dissension has been expressed in the form of rejecting domination by the central riverain elite but not in the form of questioning the rationality of being a part of a country named "The Sudan". Even the recent position taken by the SPLA of calling for self-determination[78] for the South should not be dramatized as a call for dismembering the Sudan. It should be understood as a tactical move in the face of the intransigence of the present Khartoum government and its adamant position towards proceeding with its Islamization programme. This assertion is supported by two categories of supplementary evidence while bearing in mind the original position of the

---

[77] Nimeiri's regime (1969–1985) liquidated native administration by decree in 1971 and tried in vain to fill the vacuum created by the Peoples Local Government Act (PLGA) of 1971. During all these years, the ex-native chiefs and leaders enjoyed a *de facto* power that was denied them *de jure* by a presidential decree. But the decay in this area was a reflection of the general social decay which became very apparent during the last part of the eighties when it was revived again. AK47 assault rifle-carrying bands attacked and liquidated at least two native chiefs—a situation which was unthinkable in the seventies. During the various tribal conflicts, especially in Dar Fur, the newly revived institution of native administration was not only unable to control their people, they were, over and above this, in constant fear of being attacked and liquidated by their own tribal youth.

[78] Self-determination for the South is an old idea and the thread runs through from the time when the Southern policy was reversed by the British colonial administration in 1947. Federation and self-determination have been on the agenda throughout the period following independence in 1956. However, the SPLA was not at all for self-determination until the Nassir split occurred in 1991. The complete insensitivity of the present regime towards the pluralistic nature of the Sudanese society which was confirmed during the Abuja peace talks (July 1992) led to the resurrection of the call for self-determination.

SPLA that a new Sudan should be born out of a thorough re-definition of the prevalent power relations which are neither holy nor just. This position is shared by most of the periphery and the moderate religious groups of the central riverain elite who are confirming their position by their daily opposition to the extremist Islamicist regime in Khartoum. To come to the supplementary evidence, the SPLA has been fighting, for nine years, a war which was guided by a "unitary solution" vision and in the process has recruited to its support groups that are definitionally "Northern" even if marginalised. Most of the Southern Blue Nile region, the Nuba mountains, groups from Dar Fur and the central riverain Sudan are among its fighting force. If self-determination for the South carried more than a tactical move, those groups might have deserted the SPLA and started their own groups which will also, logically, have to fight for their own self-determination. This did not happen and probably will never happen although there exists a theoretical possibility. But more weighty than this category of supplementary evidence is the fact that the massive population movements within the country that have been going on since independence in the form of labour migration and those caused by the last decade of multiple insecurity relating to the war in South, drought and famine in the rest of the country, have a precipitate effect of setting in motion a chain of diffuse but discernible integrative tendencies at the level of the identity "Sudanese", that it is very difficult to undo by the formal creation of new states in the one million square miles; the territorial space occupied by the Sudan. There is a whole generation from whom, (despite the fact that they can trace their regional, tribal and ethnic identities, for any practical purpose), to take away the third tier of their identity, i.e. "Sudanese" might be very difficult. Furthermore, both the South and the North will be faced by their very internal heterogenity in the event that the illusory homogenity is done away with by the eventuality of a "South" that is elevated to an independent "new" state. Fission will have a grave incendiary character upon the present Sudan to the extent that, although prediction is difficult if not completely obscene, only Dar Fur might survive as a politically viable entity. Even that is doubtful. But more than that we should remember a simple fact that the present regime came into being suddenly and out of the precipitate action of a fraction of the army to effect a *coup d'état*. It might disappear suddenly and become a non-issue, which is most likely, given the recent Sudanese political experience.

What is important in this picture is the fact that, historically viewed, the Sudanese "mango seed" is likely to give rise to a new Sudan in its decay. This is strongly supported by circumstantial evidence. However, the creation of two states one in the South and the other in the North, even if formally possible, as things stand today, will not provide a short-cut to improving the present state of decay. It will, on the contrary, exacerbate the decay of both even before they have had a decent chance to have a run. It is, in short, a non-starter. It is only by finding feasible political units among which a level

of political consensus can be found or achieved, which is a question of procedure, that it is possible to start negotiating a social contract that might
eventually perpetuate a new Sudan. Such units might be based on various
criteria which are provided and circumscribed by the multiple segmental
cleavages that are prevalent in the culturally plural and ethnically diverse society that the present Sudan provides. Only then will the ground be paved for
negotiation between the representatives of those salient segments within this
plurality. As a matter of procedure, and procedural matters are extremely
important in this situation (in fact necessary conditions for any success), this
must be done and the whole process must be informed by democracy.
Democracy here is not necessarily coterminous with the Westminster type
which was crippled by the intransigence of the central riverain elite three
times in as many decades of the political life of the independent Sudan. The
consociational alternative may be better suited to the Sudan in particular and
plural societies in general. Like Lijphart, I believe that

> ...there is—somewhat paradoxically an element of hope in the fact that the po
> litical development of many newly independent countries have actually been
> political decay and lapse into dictatorship. This means that there is now a per
> vasive disenchantment with Western democratic ideals and practices. Because
> the "Western" model is actually most often synonymous with the British
> model, the time may be ripe for consideration of the alternative consociational
> example. (Lijphart, 1977:175)

As the "consociational example" is defined (Lijphart, 1977) "in terms of
both the segmental cleavages typical of a plural society and the political cooperation of segmental elites", the question of the political unit that bears the
consensus of a salient segment whether that is a religious group, a tribe, an
ethnic group or a national party, becomes an important matter of procedure.
The questions that may arise as to the representativeness of elites will eventually be resolved by a democratic process that comes out of the multiple societal processes of definition of membership and political eligibility.
Federalism, confederalism or any autonomous arrangements will be a natural
part of such a democratic process. The whole process must, by necessity, lead
to the abandoning of the present untenable situation where the Sudanese
state is usurped forcibly by an "ideology" which was looking for a state
which could have been anywhere, though Sudan was the unfortunate casualty.

CONCLUSION

Despite the tragic state of affairs which characterized the Sudanese scene in
the last decade and the advanced state of decay which permeated all spheres
of life—social, political and economic—there is a glimpse of flickering hope
that is discernible: the "mango seed" is germinating in its decay. It clearly
indicates that dismembering the Sudan into two countries does not provide

any short-cut to ending the present decay. Such a dismembering will eventually be a precipitative act that will have incendiary effects far beyond the one million square miles.

An approach that bases itself on "one-country" but "many-states"[79] and is guided by a democratic practice that is able to accommodate the plural reality of the Sudanese society may provide the only feasible alternative to both the present state of decay and a safe-guard against a future probability of an incendiary instability. The important point to make is that if Sudan is to be divided into two countries, there are no guarantees whatsoever that it might not end up as more than a dozen countries.

REFERENCES

General

Avineri, S., 1976, "Political and Social Aspects of Israeli and Arab Nationalism", in E. Kamenka (ed.), 1976, *Nationalism: The Nature and Evolution of an Idea.* Edward Arnold, London.
Barth, F. (ed.), 1969, *Ethnic Groups and Boundaries: The Social Organization of Culture Difference.* Universitetsforlaget, Oslo.
Barth, F., 1984, "Problems in Conceptualizing Cultural Pluralism, with Illustrations from Sohar, Oman", in D. Maybury-Lewis (ed.), 1984, *The Prospects for Plural Societies.* The American Ethnological Society.
Connor, Walker, 1972, "Nation-Building or Nation-Destroying", in *World Politics* 24, No. 3.
Corne, Patricia, 1986, "The Tribe and the State", in J. Hall (ed.), 1986, *States in History.* Basil Blackwell Ltd.
Davidson, Basil, 1992, *The Black Man's Burden: Africa and the Curse of the Nation-State.* Time Books.
Hall, John A. (ed.), 1986, *States in History.* Basil Blackwell.
Issawi, C., 1969, *An Arab Philosophy of History.* London.
Kuper, Leo and M.G. Smith (eds.), 1969, *Pluralism in Africa.* University of California Press, Berkeley.
Lewis, W.A., 1965, *Politics in West Africa.* Allen and Unwin, London.
Lijphart, Arend, 1977, *Democracy in Plural Societies: A Comparative Exploration.* Yale University Press.
Maybury-Lewis, D. (ed.), 1984, *The Prospects for Plural Societies.* The American Ethnological Society.

[79] The contrary idea of "many countries" in the land mass presently occupied by the Republic of the Sudan will have grave consequences to both the regional and international order and there are very many strong regional and international interests that will militate against it. Regionally Egypt, among others, might not want to see several states springing up in the Nile valley: its life-line. But internally, also a strong "Sudanese spirit" which wants to see the preservation of a unified country but devoid of internal colonization realities, is there, despite all evidence to the contrary.

Mazrui, Ali A., 1975, "The De-Indianization of Uganda: Who is a Citizen?" in D.R. Smock and Bentsi-Enchill (eds.), 1975, *The Search for National Integration in Africa*. The Free Press.

Mazrui, Ali A., 1986, *The Africans: A Triple Heritage*. BBC Publications.

Smith, M.G., 1969, "Some Developments in the Analytical Framework of Pluralism", in Leo Kuper and M.G. Smith (eds.), 1969, *Pluralism in Africa*. Berkeley, University of California Press.

Smith, Anthony D., 1986, "State-Making and Nation-Building", in J. Hall (ed.), 1986, *States in History*. Basil Blackwell Ltd.

Smock, David R. and Bentsi-Enchill (eds.), 1975, *The Search for National Integration in Africa*. The Free Press.

The Sudan

Abd Al-Rahim, M., 1985, Arabism, Africanism and Self-Identification in the Sudan, in Y.F. Hassan (ed.), 1985, *Sudan in Africa*. Khartoum University Press.

Abdin, A., 1967, *History of Arabic Culture in the Sudan*. Beirut.

Ahmed, A.M. and G.M. Sørbø (eds.), 1989, *Management of the Crisis in the Sudan*. Centre for Development Studies, University of Bergen.

Alier, Abdel, 1990, *Southern Sudan: Too Many Agreements Dishonoured*. Ithaca Press, Exeter.

Al Tereifi, A.A. (ed.), 1988, *Studies in National Unity in the Sudan* (in Arabic). Khartoum University Press.

Al Tereifi, A.A. (ed.), 1989, *Decentralization in the Sudan: Present and Future* (in Arabic). Khartoum University Press.

Bakheit, G.M.A., 1968, "Political Authority and the Conflict of Loyalties in the Sudan", in *Khartoum Magazine*, No. 2, December 1968 (in Arabic).

Barth, F., 1967, "Economic Spheres in Dar Fur", in R. Firth (ed.), 1967, *Themes in Economic Anthropology*. ASA Monograph 6, London, Tavistock.

Barth, F., 1988, *Human Resources: Social and Cultural Features of Jebel Marra Project Area*. Bergen Studies in Social Anthropology, No. 42.

Bell, H., 1989, "Languages and Ethnic Identity in the Sudan and the Soviet Union: A Comparative Study", in S.H. Hurrei and E.A. Abdel Salam (eds.), 1989, *Ethnicity, Conflict and National Integration in the Sudan*. Khartoum University Press.

Beshir, M.O., 1968, *The Southern Sudan: Background to Conflict*. London.

Beshir, M.O., 1988, "Education and National Unity", in A. Al Tereifi (ed.), 1988, *Studies in National Unity in the Sudan*. Khartoum University Press (in Arabic)

Bob, Ali, 1990, "Islam, the State and Politics in the Sudan", in *Northeast African Studies*, Vol. 12, No. 2–3, 1990:201–219.

Bush, Ray and Kaballo, Sidgi, 1992, "The Sudan State: Continuity and Change", in *The Journal of Modern African Studies*, June 1992.

Deng, F.M. and I.P. Gifford (eds.), 1987, *The Search for Peace and Unity in the Sudan*. Washington, Wilson Centre Press.

El-Affendi, A., 1992, "Discovering Southern Sudan: Sudanese Dilemmas for Islam in Africa", in *The African Post Newsletter*, Vol. 1, No. 4, June 1992:9–10.

Evans-Pritchard, E.E., 1940, *The Nuer*. Clarendon Press, Oxford.

Gore, W.P., 1989, "Contemporary Issues in Ethnic Relations: Problems of National Integration in the Sudan", in S.H. Hurreiz and E.A. Abdel Salam (eds.), 1989, *Ethnicity, Conflict and National Integration in the Sudan*. Khartoum University Press.

Hassan, Y.F., 1967, *The Arabs and the Sudan from the Seventh to the Early Sixteenth Century*. Edinburgh.

Hassan, Y.F. (ed.), 1985, *Sudan in Africa*. Khartoum University Press.

Holt, P.M., 1970, *The Mahdist State in the Sudan 1881–1898*. Oxford University Press.

Hurreiz, S.H., and E.A. Abdel Salam (eds.), 1989, *Ethnicity, Conflict and National Integration in the Sudan*. Khartoum University Press.

Ibrahim, A.A., 1989, "Popular Islam: The Religion of the Barbarous Throng", in S.H. Hurreiz and E.A. Abdel Salam (eds.), *Ethnicity, Conflict and National Integration in the Sudan*. 1989:148–185.

Kameir, E.W., and Kursany, I., 1985, *Corruption as the "Fifth" Factor of Production in the Sudan*. The Scandinavian Institute of African Studies, Uppsala.

Khalid, Mansour, 1985, *Nimeiri and the Revolution of Dis-May*. KPI, London.

Khalid, Mansour, 1990, *The Government They Deserve: The Role of the Elite in Sudan's Political Evolution*. Kegan Paul International, London.

Malwal, Bona, 1981, *People and Power in Sudan*. London.

Manger, L.O. (ed.), *Trade and Traders in the Sudan*. Bergen Studies in Social Anthropology, No. 32.

Mazrui, A.A., 1985, "The Multiple Marginality of the Sudan", in Y.F. Hassan (ed.), *Sudan in Africa*. 1985:240–255.

O'Fahey, S.R., 1980, *State and Society in Dar Fur*. C. Hurst and Company, London.

O'Fahery, S.R., 1985, "Religion and Trade in the Kayra Sultanate of Dar Fur", in Y.F. Hassan (ed.), *Sudan in Africa*.

Sharif Harir, 1981, *Old-Timers and New-Comers: Politics and Ethnicity in a Sudanese Community*. Bergen Studies in Social Anthropology, No. 29.

Sharif Harir, 1986, *The Politics of "Numbers": Mediatory Leadership and the Political Process among the Beri "Zaghawa" of the Sudan*. Department of Anthropology, University of Bergen.

Sharif Harir, 1993, "Militarization of Conflict, Displacement and the Legitimacy of the State: A Case from Dar Fur—Western Sudan", in Terje Tvedt (ed.), 1993, *Conflicts in the Horn of Africa: Human and Ecological Consequences of Warfare*. EPOS, Uppsala.

Theobald, A., 1965, *Ali Dinar, the Last Sultan of Dar Fur*. London.

Thomas, Graham, 1990, *Sudan 1950–1985: Death of a Dream*. Darf Publishers Ltd., London.

Tvedt, T., 1986, *Water and Politics: A History of the Jonglei Project in the Southern Sudan*. Chr. Michelsens Institute, Bergen.

Wai, Dunstan, 1973, *The Southern Sudan: The Problem of National Integration*. London.

Wai, Dunstan, 1981, *The African-Arab Conflict in the Sudan*. New York, Africana Publishing Company.

Woodward, P., 1990, *Sudan, 1898–1989: The Unstable State*. Lynne Rienner Publishers, Boulder.

Warburg, G.R., 1992, *Historical Discord in the Nile Valley*. Hurst and Company, London.

Newspapers and Periodicals (1992–1993)

Africa Confidential (AC)
Al Guwat Al Musallaha
Al Hayat
Al Ingaz Al Watani

Al Sharq Al Awsat
Al Sudan Al Hadith
Horn of African Bulletin (HAB)
Indian Ocean Newsletter (ION)
SPLA/SPLM Update
Sudan Democratic Gazette
Sudan Information Bulletin
Sudan Monitor
Sudan Update (SU)
The African Post Newsletter
West Africa
The Independent

The Collapse of the State in Southern Sudan after the Addis Ababa Agreement

A Study of Internal Causes and the Role of the NGOs[1]

Terje Tvedt

The state administration in Southern Sudan and its post-1972 history provides a dramatic contrast to most other state administrations, not only when compared to the industrialized world but also when compared to other regions in Africa. Theoretical and universalistic concepts about "the state", the "Third World state", the "African state", "bureaucracy", "the African civil society" should not disregard the particular history of Southern Sudan.[2] Southern Sudan between 1972 and 1985 is also an interesting area for studying NGO-government relationship in a comparative perspective, because of the weakness of both the state and the "civil society" and the relative strength of the international aid agencies.[3]

This paper discusses the institutional and organizational characteristics of the state administration in Southern Sudan and its relationship with the foreign Non-Governmental Aid Organisations (NGOs) in the period between the Addis Ababa peace agreement in 1972 and the collapse of the administrative structure in the middle of the 1980s. It focuses on two different but interrelated phenomena. Firstly, an empirical description and analysis of the state and the structure of the public bureaucracy and its characteristics and strength in the Southern Sudan will be presented. Secondly, an analysis of the role of the NGO-sector will be presented. This effort at understanding the role and policies of the foreign NGOs in relation to the development of the state administration's is an implicit comment on a dominating conseptualization of the dynamics of NGO-government relations in Africa: that the NGO-sector plays an important role in the democratisation of African countries by strengthening and pluralising a civil society conceived as threatened by an overdeveloped, bureaucratic and parasitic state administration.

---

[1] I am grateful for valuable comments by Sharif Harir, Kjell Hødnebø, Gunnar Håland and Douglas Johnson.

[2] The type and quality of administrative structures is important also from a developmental point of view; it has been said that "administrative improvement is the *sina qua non* in the process of programmes of national development" in developing countries (Emmerich, 1969:1). A study of the theoretical problem of the relationsship between bureaucracy and modernisation or administration structure and socio-economic development is, however, outside the scope of this article.

[3] The empirical parts of this chapter is based on a fairly extensive collection of reports produced by government officials and regional government departments, NGOs, UN-organisations, the World Bank and a number of consultants working in the South during this period.

A study of the administrative structure of the state in Southern Sudan
should not reduce the state and its machinery to an arena for competing socio-economic interests; a locus of class struggle; an instrument of class rule or
an expression of core values in the surrounding society. More fruitfully the
state apparatus is approached as a separate socio-spatial organization, as an
actor which aimed at shaping social and political processes. The political and
administrative elite possessed an unusual degree of autonomy in relation to
the processes in the Southern agricultural and pastoral society. Financially
and politically the elite depended, however, upon support from Khartoum,
and the state therefore also became an object to be controlled for the purpose
of supporting clients. It should nevertheless not be conceived simply as a
typical clientilistic state administration, since the same elite saw this very
administrative system as a vehicle for reducing dependency on Khartoum in
the long run. The state administration is studied as an entity in itself and as
an actor by itself, but within the context of this particular political and socio-
economic setting. This first part will focus on the institutional means rather
than on the political aims. It will not focus on the performance of power or
on the relevance and receptiveness of the state administration's general policies and programmes. It will describe some aspects of the build up of an administrative structure and civil service, its role, potentials and limitations
within the state apparatus and its relation to the society; and focuses on its
strength, i.e. administrative stability and financial base.

As is well known, the Southern society, due to a number of historical,
geographical and economic reasons, was extremely structurally segmented
and culturally diverse. It was characterised by a lack of integration and
complementarity between various parts of the social system. It had a relative
absence of value consensus, the relatively broad support for the Addis Ababa
Agreement notwithstanding. The society was compartmentalized into relatively independent sub-systems, with only few points of contact with each
other. A great number of rural people and whole ethnic groups had only
marginal participation in a common money economy. In Durkheimian terms
such societies tend to be low on both "mechanical" and "organic" solidarity.
The state building efforts in the aftermath of the civil war could therefore
from this point of view, be seen as an effort at social integration. By subjugation of what was described as Southerners to a common body politic, a
specific point of contact on a supra-tribal and supra-ethnic level was established.

The state administration 1972–1981

To establish and build up regional and local state institutions was regarded
as the main task for the regional government after the Addis Ababa accord.
It was thought that the broader goal of reconstruction and development
would come to nothing without such structures. The aim was to turn these

instruments into motors of economic and social reconstruction and development and to secure a kind of semi-autonomy for the region, as embodied in
the spirit of the Accord. The old institutions had been partly destroyed by the
war, and a new bureaucracy was to be constructed:

a) the civil service (the district and provincial administration) was South-
   ernized completely; and
b) new political structures were created through the establishment of the
   Regional Government and the establishment of the Sudanese Socialist
   Union Party.

The Southern Provinces Regional Self-Government Act, 1972, which was
signed into law by Nimeiri on 3 March and officially ratified in Addis Ababa
on 27 March, meant that a new regional state apparatus should be established in the South; a legislature, an executive organ, a regional administration, three provincial administrations and district/rural administrations
should be formed so as to initiate and implement the reconstruction and development of the society. Khartoum should keep control over matters of defence, foreign policy and trade, national economic planning, transport and
communication, but the regional government was made responsible for the
preservation of public order, internal security, administration and development in cultural, economic and social fields. In April 1972, the Interim High
Executive Council was set up, headed by Abel Alier.

For the Council and the political elite in the South, the top priority was
the establishment of a new administrative structure manned by southern staff
and which should serve regional and southern interests. For the first time
Southerners were to govern Southerners, and in an institutionalised way. In
fact an entirely new type of authority was to be established in the South.
Compared to the region's colonial administrative and cultural history the aim
implied a far-reaching administrative, bureaucratic revolution. This revolutionary drive was also influenced by a dominant ideology in the early 1970s
in Africa in general, as well as in the Sudan after the 1969 revolution: the
state and its administration were seen as the "prime mover" in societal transformation and development.

These more overall aims and normative legitimation of the new state
structure, soon faced competition from more practical matters, often mixed
up with problems of a clientilist nature. Who were the Southerners to govern
and who should take command in the new state? There was the contradiction between Khartoum's strategy of appointing reliable and friendly staff
and Southern aspirations of regional autonomy bringing hardliners into the
government institutions, but also between the Southern exiles versus those
Southerners who had remained in the South or in Khartoum, between soldiers and intellectuals, between people from different provinces and between
people who could mobilize different ethnic constituencies. In addition, there
were reportedly about 20,000 Any Nya supporters returning from the bush

and many hundred thousands of refugees returning from neighbouring countries. The number of "soldiers" in Any Nya increased after the peace agreement. Some people joined the guerillas after the war in the hope of getting better job opportunities. When peace came, they all rushed to Juba and other regional centres competing for the new posts. It had important consequences that these posts were created in a period when free money and aid poured (relatively speaking) into the region as part of the relief and resettlement programme. From the very beginning this state administration had very weak economic links to the region it was supposed to serve.

The contradiction between the two dominating leaders, Joseph Lagu and Abel Alier, was both related to and reflected differences and conflicts within the Southern society. Lagu was part of a military bureaucratic hierarchy, being trained in the National Army before his defection, and had won his position as a soldier during the war. Alier had practised as a barrister and was an elected politician before being made a minister by Nimeiri in 1969. Lagu was from a small Equatorian tribe, the Madi. Alier was from Bor and a Dinka. Lagu was appointed Major General in April 1972. The same month Alier was appointed President of the High Executive Council. These two leaders represented different political and administrative networks, different types of leadership, different provinces and ethnic groups. The degree of conflict between these two men from 1972 to 1981, when Nimeiri dismissed Alier's administration, in important respects reflected the degree to which the Southern political elite and administration was unable to control centrifugal forces within itself, especially in a situation when these contradictions were fuelled by Khartoum's tactics.

The ethnic distribution of administrative posts had for decades been a central conflict in the South. The political struggle against Arab domination in the early 1950s had centred on Southernization of administrative posts. In the South the Sudanization of the British colonial administration was called Northernization. Since the elections to the Parliament in 1953 the political struggle had often centred on the manning-policy for the administration. The Liberal Party criticized the plans for the Sudanization programme, and the disappointment was great when the Sudanization Committee presented their recommendations; only six Southerners were found qualified for a total of 800 posts (four were found qualified for the post of Assistant District Commissioner and two for the post of Mamur). Later on the manifesto of the Federal Party called for a separate Southern Civil Service while the NUP president, Ismail al-Azhari, in the 1956 election campaign promised to appoint Southerners as District Commissioners and Governors (Arou, 1988:308). The emergence of a Southern political consciousness was closely related to the fight for a greater role of Southerners in the administration of the South. One might say, that the preoccupation with this question had, by 1972, become part of the educated and political elite's "common concern", of their political culture.

The competition among the returnees, the Anya Nya and the "insiders", was of course fierce, not only for jobs, but for the best jobs. After all, a high political or administrative position was a very important foundation of wealth and also a basis for conversion of value into political support and clientelism. The political economy of similar state structures in Africa has been called "the state as plunder capitalism" (Mamdani, 1986:46). In the Southern Sudan there was very little capitalism and not very much to plunder, the most important exception being money given by foreign donors or by Khartoum. High official posts were also important to gain regular business interests. In general, however, the jobs were less luxurious and the size of the administrative class smaller than in many other regions in Africa. In spite of this, the crux of the matter is, that the difficult economic and social and infra-structural situation in 1972 rendered, however, the state and its administration almost the only job alternative for many. Naturally, this reinforced the political interest in who was appointed where by whom and why. Within the relatively small circles which made up the political-administrative elite, the question of distribution of positions soon became an obsessive game. From the very beginning of the administrative build up, two sharply conflicting considerations influenced both the structure and the self-image of the employed administrators. Development and reconstruction of the society was on the one hand regarded as being dependent upon a strong, efficient and rule-governed state-machinery. At the same time there was a need to handle the manning problem with great care and with an eye to local, often particularistic and competing expectations.

When the Provisional Government was set up in Juba on 22nd April, it lacked almost everything a government usually takes for granted: administrative personnel, office-buildings and administrative experience.[4] One of the biggest problems in 1972 was thought to be the availability of adequate qualified manpower to run the various tasks of government. At the end of 1973 the Regional Government had an estimated 30 per cent of the manpower required to man and run the Regional Civil Service. The public services in the region had by December 1972, 284 administrative and professional personnel, 383 sub-professional and technical and 384 clerical personnel (International Bank for Reconstruction and Development, 1973:7), probably at that time the smallest administration and the most uneducated administration in the world when compared to an estimated population of 4,3 million (ibid., 8) and an area of 646,000 km². This implies that there were 11,227 persons and 2,278 km² per each professional administrator. The regional agricultural staff had 14 university graduates and 46 with lower level training (ibid.,22). The educated group was to a large extent returnees. In 1976, still only about half the required posts were filled (Alier, 1976:38). On the other hand 10,000 former, mostly uneducated, Anya Nya forces had

---

[4] See Alier 1976:7–8, for his description of the government-"infrastructure" in 1972.

been taken into civilian departments in 1972 to assist in reconstruction and development. The bulk of them were taken by forestry, wildlife, roads, agriculture, regional local government and education departments (*Peace and Progress*, 1972–1973, 1973: 4). As a comparison: the number of classified government personnel in the whole Sudan was 92,000 out of which 67,000 were in the central government (Al-Terafi, 1986:75).

But perhaps as important was the quality of the new administrative staff at hand. The bureaucratic culture and tradition was very weak among the Southern administrators in Southern Sudan. The legacy of British colonialism in the region had left few and weak bureaucratic structures and institutions. Although there were differences in the administrative set up between the heyday of the District Commissioner in the 1920s and 1930s and the evolution of more development oriented administration in the 1940s and early 1950s, the period of Condominium rule taken as a whole was basically a "law and order" administration, with weak infrastructural power and with limited functions. The overall strategy was "to interfere as little as possible" in the society and to work through tribal authorities. Where no such authorities existed, new tribal authorities should be created as the southern governors agreed in 1922. The British established a local government system based on local tribal and cultural units. There were regional dissimilarities, and different systems were developed at the state administrative level and on the level of rural and tribal administration. In the sedentary areas the chiefdoms were basically territorial units, while among the pastoralists they were basically lineage chiefdoms. On the higher, state-administrative level very few Southerners were recruited. The policy was in general restricted to implementing the policy of "care and maintenance", as it was called, and administrative expenses were cut to the bone.

Well into the 1940s at least, individual District Commissioners could represent in one man all the government functions in regions which might be of a size of an average European country. In 1937, for example, Mongalla and Bahr al-Ghazal were brought together to form the Equatoria Province. The aim was to reduce administrative costs. The new governor should administer this area from Juba. Sir James Robertson has underlined the problem with the enormous size of the administrative area and the limited administrative strength: "It was further from Nagichot, the most easterly of the district headquarters, to Raga, in the extreme west, than it is from London to Moscow" (Robertson, 1974:104). During most of the period it was anathema to create bureaucratic structures which would compete with native and tribal administration, as the historian G.N. Sanderson has put it. The result was an administrative apparatus which depended on the individual capabilities of British DCs and the potential rapid deployment of technologically superior armed forces. The development of a centrally organized bureaucracy with ordinary political, administrative and economic institutions was thus discouraged, very different from what was the case other places in the Nile valley, as in Egypt, the northern riverain Sudan, Kenya and Uganda. The British did not want to develop an educated elite of Southern administrators, since they feared a detribalized and discontented intelligentsia. The missionaries were allowed to start schools, but the mission schools had other aims than creating bureaucrats or administrators. The colonial policy on religion barred a possible development of region-wide religious organizations. As part of their Nile valley strategy and their Southern Policy, Islam was suppressed. The expansion of the Church did not lead to the establishment of an ecclesiastical hierarchy nor serve the interest of the build up of a strong, region wide state apparatus, partly because the South was partitioned between different Catholic and Protestant groups. No overarching religious hierarchies or bodies were established. The traditional religions were organized on a communal basis, often around a local cultic centre. These traditional religions were therefore incapable of providing an ideological and organizational foundation for administrative centralization or broad regional bureaucratic organizations. The British aims created state institutions which were designed neither to be instruments of economic development or economic exploitation (as in Egypt, Uganda, Kenya or the northern riverain Sudan) nor efficient channels of Westernisation or modernisation, but to maintain peace with low costs. The imperial army's technological superiority and the role of the alien DCs, which from a purely local perspective could be seen as neutral arbiters in local conflicts, made success in this respect possible. The more bureaucratic regulations of the Municipal, Township and Rural Area Ordinance of 1937 and the provision of Provincial Councils in 1947 did not have any important effect in the South and came too late to have any impact on institutional culture. Neither had the local government structure, suggested by Dr. Marshall (an expert on British government who in the late 1940s evaluated and recommended on local government in the Sudan) and incorporated into the Local Government Ordinance of 1951, any lasting consequences on Southern administration. The main reason was the less developed administrative structure in the South; the Local Councils in the South remained advisory and consulting agents to the District Commissioner. By 1972 the South had not experienced universally oriented and rule-governed bureaucracies and public administration.

Educationally, the Southern Region was probably the least developed in Africa. According to the 1973 census, 81 per cent of the population aged 7–24 had never attended school. 58 per cent of the workers employed in the modern sector in 1973 had received no education at all. There was moreover an imbalance in the distribution of educated people, not only between the North and South, but also within the South between regions and ethnic groups. When manpower requirements were first estimated in relation to the implementation of the government's Development Plan (1977/78–82/83), it was stated that there was a need for 2,400 graduates, 12,000 diploma and certificate holders and 16,000 school leavers by 1982/83. The estimated demand for university graduates in agriculture and related fields alone was 500 (Mills, 1977). The gap between estimated demand and potential supply can be indicated by the fact that there were in 1976 only about 250 Southern Region students in the whole of Sudan (International Bank for Reconstruction and Development 1981:54).[5] In 1978/79 less than 10 out of some 1,000 students following degree level agricultural courses at Khartoum University were from the Southern Region, a region where more than 90 per cent of the population were agriculturalists or pastoralists. The administrative language of the Southern bureaucracy was English, which only a few mastered better than they had mastered Arabic during the Khartoum-led administration in the 1950s and 1960s.

The character of the war prior to the peace and establishment of a state administration was not conducive to the training of administrators. Guerilla movements have in many other countries trained administrators during the struggle, through administering liberated areas for years. The Anya Nya did not build up such strong alternative administrative structures in the areas they controlled. Some chiefs and trained administrators defected to them and the Sudan Penal Code was used, but this did not create anything that resembled a unified, bureaucratic system. Those who represented the Southern movement at Addis Ababa and those who after the Agreement took up high posts in the regional government had therefore little administrative experience. The "insiders" had more experience, but they were on the other hand generally less trusted by the people.

The Southern movement was very disunited. Legal instruments of conflict resolution or bureaucratic institutions for policy implementation had not been established within and between the different factions. This fluid situation came to the fore time and again. A period of three years from 1967 saw for example, a number of different southern "governments", the Southern Sudan Provisional Government, the Nile Provisional Government, the Sue River Republic and the Anyidi Government. This lack of organization was also noted by contemporary observers; "in places other than the Sudan (this) might have proved fatal" (Eprile, 1974:97). It was only when Joseph Lagu, in 1970, managed to establish a military leadership over both the Anya Nya and a new political wing, the Southern Sudan Liberation Movement, that one can say that the movement became united. Unity was imposed by a "bush coup". This organizational weakness could work during the war, due to its character, but the shortcomings were exposed in ordinary institution building

---

[5] The Bank compares this with Somalia, which is "generally reckoned to have one of the least developed educational systems" and having about the same population as the Southern Sudan. Somalia had nearly 2,700 students at university undertaking undergraduate courses in 1977, against the Southern Region' s 250. In 1980, the Bank anticipated, there were likely to be a mere 500–700 students passing the secondary school certificate—compared to 3,500 in Somalia (International Bank of Reconstruction and Development 1981:54).

efforts. Lagu's authority was to a large extent derived from his ability to de-liver goods, i.e. military hardware and training (through the Israelis). This was a kind of authority which proved to be unstable and difficult to transfer to peace conditions.

In addition, two legal factors were important for the manner and form the administrative build-up took. The Self Government Act came into existence before the promulgation of the new national Constitution in 1973. Some of the articles of the former differed from and contradicted articles later written into the Constitution. When such fundamental legal instruments talked with two tongues, it was of course not conducive to the establishment of a rule-oriented administrative system; on the contrary it added to the uncertainty and confusion. The region, in line with Section 22 of the Act, was directly under the jurisdiction of the President, although the amending law was not enacted until July 1977 (Wieu, 1988:48.) From the very beginning and dur-ing its formative years the build up of a Southern public administration was *formally* guided by legal provisions and rule-oriented, i.e. a bureaucratic au-thority was to replace the traditional authority of Native Administration. In reality, however, the administrative implementation of the Act was funda-mentally personalized, since it depended to a very large extent on Nimeiri's opinions and attitudes. What took place represented a "centralized" decen-tralization, by which Nimeiri delegated some of his Khartoum based author-ity to Juba.

Personalist polities are the very opposite of universalistic, rule oriented administration. The difference has been defined by the fact that in the former, rulers themselves are the source of state norms (see Heper, 1987:15). In the case of Nimeiri, the central "norm" became unpredictability (for ex-amples and discussions, see Khalid, 1985 and Woodward, 1991). In the South especially, due to the Constitutional arrangements and Nimeiri's very strong position among the regional politicians and in the popular opinion, the fundamental arrangements were personalistic. Seen from the South, Nimeiri was the man who had given the Southerners peace and regional au-tonomy, or more precisely, he was seen as the only leader in Khartoum who could safeguard that peace, and was given southern support on that under-standing. For the Southern elite in this context, with their multiplicity of local loyalties and the conflicting loyalties between supporting Nimeiri and pleasing the centre on the one hand,[6] and promoting the Southern cause

---

[6] It is important to remember the strong support Nimeiri had in the South through the 1970s because of the May Revolution, the Peace Accord and the fact that Nimeiri, due to the role of the region as his "Southern constituency" for some years responded positively to Southern aspirations. Malwal wrote in 1981: "Second, the South has come to trust President Nimeiri personally very much, so much so that they do not question the basis of his decisions, even if those decisions could adversely affect the South" (Malwal, 1981:217).

more directly on the other, it was difficult to formulate and implement a consistent long-term policy on which the administration could work.

Additionally, this initial build-up of an entirely new administration was guided by the regulations and instruments of the People's Local Government Act, 1971. The aim of the act was to create a politicised administrative system, in support of the May Revolution of 1969. This had important consequences in the South, because the new regional, provincial and local administration, both its core administrative system and administrative personnel, were given shape and identity by guidelines directly contradicting the idea of a "neutral, bureaucratic" administrative system. The highly politicized atmosphere in the South turned the staff-appointments into a tense struggle among competing interests, authorities and statuses. The core administrative personnel from the very beginning conceived their role as a political role, and were so regarded by the ruled. Many had got their bureaucratic posts in order to represent "particular" interests within the state administration rather than to promote "universal", regional, state administrative interests. Promotions were often too rapid, and many were given jobs which they had no competence for.

The Act moreover, gave the People's Province Executive Councils responsibilities and functions that were virtually impossible and self-contradictory. Their membership were to be locally elected and appointed. Legally it was a body which should represent the local will and interests. The councils should promote all kinds of development initiatives: primary and intermediate education, public health, agricultural development, village and town planning, recreational activities etc. On the other hand they were to mobilize public support behind government policies and maintain public security. Generally, it failed in both respects. In reality it was the Commissioner who was the strong man, also according to the 1971 Act. He was appointed by the President in Khartoum and answerable to him only. He was chairman, treasurer and convener of the council sessions. He had supervisory and disciplinary powers over the staff. He was to report on the seconded staff to their respective ministers. He was at the same time SSU-secretary of his province. Due to his almost autocratic position *vis-à-vis* the rest of the civil service and the elected politicians locally (Badal, 1983:90), the Commissioner's role eroded the possibilities for establishing a bureaucratized, rule-oriented system of government. If anything went wrong he was to blame. If no sugar, grain or petrol was available in the market, it was the fault of the Commissioner. More often the Commissioner became a symbol of anti-institutionalism and anti-routinization; and he often used or misused the local councils haphazardly to boost personal political backing as he deemed fit (see Malik, 1983:95).

The state administration was from the beginning an administration of a very special type since it did not depend on extraction of local resources or taxes for its existence. In this it resembled the British colonial state in the

South. But contrary to what was the attitude and practice after 1972, the British had as a main administrative interest the extraction of taxes, not primarily as a source of state income but as a symbol of administrative state power and as a symbol of local submission to an externally imposed state administration. Administrative expenditure in Equatoria Province for instance was about double the receipts during the early 1930s (see different memoranda by the Governor-General on the Finance and Administration and Condition of the Sudan). The government's taxation policy was therefore implemented in a rudimentary way and with the "ears to the ground". The chiefs were responsible for tax collection and were usually given a certain percentage of the taxes collected. The often personalized relationship between the District Commissioner and the local chiefs, created a system of government based more on clientilism than on bureaucratic rules. Although taxation on a certain scale by a central authority in the South was started by the British, a "coercion-extraction" cycle never seemed to have taken off. General political mechanisms behind state formation have been described as the "extraction-coercion cycle" (Finer, 1975:95). Extracting economic surpluses from the population makes it possible to maintain a state machinery, a permanent army etc. which in turn serves to extract further surpluses and so on. It also makes the state rulers accountable to the ruled. No such cycle ever existed in the southern Sudan.

The financial regulations of the new regional administration were chaotic. The basic rules were governed by Presidential Decree No. 39 of 1972 and the Self-Government Act, 1972. Appendix B of the 1972 Act, "Draft ordinance of items of revenue and grants-in-aid for the Southern Region", was an instrument which fostered internal quarrels within the regional and provincial administration. Administrators and politicians fought for their own interests or those of their own constituencies while trying to enlarge their slice of the "grant-in-aid" cake sent from Khartoum. It could exploit both as a carrot and stick *vis-à-vis* the South. Paragraph 15 reads

> New Social Service Projects to be established by the Region or any of its Local Government units, and for which funds are allocated, shall receive grants from the National Treasury in the following manners:
>
> - Education Institutions, 20 per cent of expenses
> - Trunk and through Roads and Bridges, 25 per cent of expenses
> - Relief and Social Amenities, 15 per cent of expenses
> - Tourist Attraction Projects, 15 per cent of expenses
> - Security, 15 per cent of expenses
> - Grants for Post Secondary and University Education within the Sudan, 20 per cent of grants, outside the Sudan 30 per cent of grants.
> - Contribution for Research, Scientific Advancement, and Cultural Activities, 25 per cent of expenses."

The PECs were paid a "deficiency grant" by Khartoum through the Regional government, based on approved deficiency in the submitted budgets. This grant should cover provincial/local budgeted costs of personnel only. This led the provinces to prepare their budgets more or less as a "bid" for the central grant. The gap between budget figures and actual disbursement widened every year.[7] The executive councils were moreover unable to collect more than about 50 per cent of their modest, budgeted local revenues (Malik, 1981:6). According to some estimates, the tax revenue as percentage of total government revenue was about 15 per cent in 1975–76, as compared to 74.9 per cent in Kenya, 81.7 per cent in Zaire, 87.2 per cent in Ethiopia and 89.1 per cent in Uganda (Sodhi, 1981:35). This affected the administrative system in two important ways. Firstly; the administrative system became very vulnerable and the staff continuously frustrated since their salaries depended upon an uncertain and varying central grant. Planning problems in Khartoum were immediately felt in the South. In rural councils in remote areas, at the bottom of the disbursement chain, money never arrived in time, if it arrived at all. This helped create a work-environment which diverted the civil service's attention away from administrative routine matters to personal matters. Secondly, since the personnel generally was paid by the north they did not have to cultivate relationships with local communities or to justify their work or lack of work to the local people. It became more important to be in the right offices in Juba when money arrived from Khartoum, than to be in the villages to improve relationships and strengthen administrative infrastructure. From the very beginning there was not established an extraction-coercion cycle, or an extraction-accountability cycle. If no services were established locally the administrators could simply blame the "centre", it was a system for writing off responsibility. At the same time these administrators depended upon this very "centre". For the "centre" itself this system also functioned as a dumping ground for Southern grievances and criticism. When money was disbursed the payment of salaries was a first priority. These regulations therefore further alienated the administrator from the local societies, since it regularly diminished the money left for investment in development locally. With the size and character of this financial base, the local administrations' penetrative power in the Southern rural societies had to be very weak, indeed. Not only that! As most of the Southern provinces established so-called Liaison Offices in Khartoum for follow up of business with the bodies which allocated resources, the South was soon governed directly from

---

[7] A table given in Malik 1981: 5, shows this (figures in £S 000)

Years	Total Grant Received	Distribution Reg.Min.	PECs	Budgeted Reg. Min.	Expenditure PECs
1977/78	20,800	12,721	8,079	19,742	15,671
1978/79	23,500	14,200	9,300	22,039	17,241
1979/80	36,000	16,200	19,800	22,148	29,990
1980/81	40,000	19,293	20,707	24,714	37,853
1981/82	48,000	21,962	26,038	34,377	55,443

Khartoum. Even the High Executive Council was running the South from Khartoum. In the end, the "minimalist" administration had to a large extent been transferred *de facto* to the centre. The South was gradually evacuated administratively.

Concerning development initiatives the Province Council was to combine former Provincial Council Revenue with sources of income of the local councils and central government grants. The Province Council kept the purse and decided what to give to which Town/Rural Council and what to keep. The Province could form subordinate councils and perform their development functions at district and sub-district levels through the People's Town/Rural Councils and Village, Residential, Trade, Market and Neighbourhood Councils. In 1973 there were no sub-province Local Councils in any of the provinces but 35 rural councils (*Peace and Progress*, 1973:11). In 1976 there were 24 Rural/Town Councils in the South. In 1980 it was necessary to budget for 53 Rural/Town councils. A number of the local councils which reportedly were established, existed only on paper. The Development Committees at the various sub-levels did not function as a general rule. Legally the base councils—the village and residential area councils—were to be elected first. These should send delegates to the higher councils. Thus the People's Province Executive Council should, according to the regulations, be composed of delegates from the Town/Rural Councils in the provinces plus the appointed members and the civil servants. Local Council budgets were being prepared as appendices to Provincial Budgets (Bior, 1982:61) and the commissioners continued to draw money from Local Councils' treasuries during the whole period. The policy of decentralisation became therefore already at this early stage an activity which more resembled a symbolic ritual than effective devolution of power.

States and state administrative systems have generally tried to maintain their legitimacy and authority *vis-à-vis* those who are governed by a claim to "universalism". When the state is seen to favour particularistic, special ties to kin, locality, ethnicity etc., it has tended to loose authority and legitimacy. The strength of tribalism in the South and the elite's political culture, obsessed with job-distribution, caused the Dinka domination issue which was raised with growing strength at the end of the 1970s. It became fatal to later state building. "External" factors like the high floods in the 1960s caused conflicts over grazing land/agricultural land between the Nilotic and the Equatorians, such as the Bari, and among the Nilotes themselves, and thus contributed to the growth of ethnic animosity in the 1970s and 1980s. Whatever universalistic ideology about a "Southern cause" existed among state administrators in the first years after regional autonomy was attained, evaporated quickly in this inter-tribal conflict about control and jobs. The Jonglei Canal crisis in 1974 was the first open attack on the terms of the 1972 agreement. The Akobo uprising in 1975 and the arrest of Benjamin Bol and Joseph Oduho on Alier's order, because they called for a return to the bush (Alier, 1990), had already demonstrated a political split among the Southerners and sharpened the conflict between "insiders" and "outsiders". In 1978 Lagu retired from the People's Armed Forces and joined the ranks of the politicians. He was elected President of the High Executive Council. Alier was ousted. Two years later Lagu raised the issue of re-division in a petition to Nimeiri.

In his publication, *Decentralisation* (1980), Lagu warned against what he saw as Dinka domination and Dinka expansion. Taking the title of his pamphlet as a starting point, he could have focused on the deterioration of the regional and local economy and government structures, but such matters were made peripheral in his assessment of the Southern problem. Lagu gave figures and tables of the ethnic background of the politicians and administrators, but did not discuss economic or administrative indicators. He focused on the same job-distribution issue which had dominated election campaigns in the South since 1953, but in a different form and with different contenders. Re-division was now, for many, another word for "anti-Dinka" sentiments. The tribal factor and the "insider–outsider" dichotomy were also reflected in different viewpoints and attitudes towards the state, the state administration and the bureaucracy between the two main political rivals, Alier and Lagu. Alier was more concerned about building up bureacratic structures and regulations than was Lagu. From his first days in office he concentrated on building up public administration and, being a lawyer by education, he tried to put emphasis on regulations and rules. The Peace and Progress Reports published during Alier's first period in office underlined the importance of regulations and rules. A number of bills were enacted to strengthen public administration; the Southern Region Service Act, 1975, the Southern Region Public Service Pensions Act, 1976 and the Southern Region Employees Discipline Act, 1976. Lagu's policy statements, in comparison, put little weight upon administration and administrative regulations and rules. Lagu voiced more populistic opinions. Their different emphases regarding this question can be exemplified by Lagu's inauguration speech in 1978. He said that the Southern citizen had been a "victim of officialdom"; he should therefore be liberated "from institutional oppression". The government should work to cut "the web of bureaucratic red-tape" (Lagu, 1978:7).[8]

Alier and his High Executive Council planned to establish a state administrative structure based on western models and replicate what was in the North (see for example Peace and Progress and Alier's speeches from the 1970s). Seen from the perspective of the existing traditions, culture and or-

---

[8] The expression "red-tape" derives from the twine which the state administration in England used to tie around their big piles of old documents. In the South, most ministries never established a proper archival system, and the red-tape of the administration was not rule-oriented or based on organised institutional memory, but more influenced by particularism and clientilism.

ganizational experience, this represented a bureaucratic revolution. Alier was trying to guarantee southern access to these bureaucratic arms of the state, at the same time as Nimeiri was trying to subordinate the state to himself, partly through the SSU and partly through the 1973 constitution.

The state administration 1981–1983

During 1981 the regional administration received a mortal blow. In March 1981, twelve Southern MPs in the National Assembly asked Nimeiri to dissolve the Southern government and decree division of the South. On 5 October 1981 both the Regional Assembly and the High Executive Council were dissolved and Alier's administration was dismissed. Nimeiri appointed in its place an interim administration headed by Major General Gismalla Abdalla Rasas. His main task was said to be the supervision of the referendum on division/re-division. The reactions in the South were mixed. The divisionists generally supported the dissolution. Others saw it as part of a large strategy by Northerners to fragment the South. The struggle between the divisionists and the anti-divisionists, created a situation where again the manning of the administration became a question of paramount importance.

The People's Local Government Act of 1981 was therefore soon overshadowed by the consequences of re-division (see below). The central government's Regional Government Act in 1980 left largely intact the administrative framework in Southern Sudan. The main importance of this Act in the South was that it was one act in a row of legal instruments that contributed to the instability and deepened the difficulties of creating a viable state administration.

One central purpose of the 1981 Act was said to be the correction of what was described as disadvantages stemming from the concentration of powers at the provincial level in the previous Act; i.e. to devolve administrative power from the provincial to the district level. It abolished the Provincial Executive Councils. The aim in the South was to increase and place the responsibility for local affairs in 25 Area Councils. The Area Councils should be the central instrument of the government's decentralization policy and their role was to serve as the link between the people in rural/town areas and the Regional Government, and at the same time to be the centre's main instrument to rally support around government policies. In addition they were to initiate and support social and economic developments of their areas and be directly responsible for providing the essential services to the people.[9]

---

[9] In the Annex to the Act the functions of the Area Council were specified. Concerning economic development it is mentioned:
  1. Preparation of socio-economic plans in accordance with the delegated powers and presentation of necessary recommendations thereon to the Regional Executive Authority.
  2. Organization of statistics in all fields and supply of necessary data which are capable of being depended upon.

In the 1981 Act, the Area Councils were given wider discretion in respect of budgeting and disbursement of expenditure than the Executive Councils had previously had. They were now to exercise a financial, supervisory and co-ordinatory role in respect to the sub-councils. But none of the fundamental problems had been solved. Rather they were magnified by the new Act. Local governments at different levels continued to inflate their budget estimates, hoping that the central government would fulfil its declared promise of meeting any budget deficits. This situation was described in the following way in 1981 by a discussant at a UN seminar; "Everybody tries to lower their expected revenue and to raise their expected expenditure so as to increase the gap". This became especially important for the Area Councils taking into consideration the new responsibilities they were given, but which, based on realistic local revenue, they were totally unable to fulfil. But since Khartoum was virtually bankrupt, it could not possibly meet all the demands, no matter its actual Southern strategy. The 1981 Act empowered the Area Councils to decide on and approve their own budgets, and in Section 23 the sources of revenue available to the Area Councils were spelled out. But no arrangements were made for the Council to receive further, additional revenues to those already assigned to local government under the Appropriation of Taxes Ordinance, 1954, increasing further the cash shortages. Grant-in-aid from the central government was by far the major source of income. But even more important; it became a prerequisite for their very existence. Total local revenues, if fully collected, were not capable of financing more than 20 per cent at most of the budgeted recurrent expenditure.

Local tax in 1980 should have met, according to the regulations, the demand for local investments in development projects, recurrent costs of maintaining and running schools, road building and maintenance etc. The regional government could and did levy a special development tax. Two years after the agreement they promulgated the Finance Act 1974, which was intended to yield a revenue of 2,7 million Sudanese pounds already in 1974/75 (Sodhi,1981:30–31). As during the British period the social service tax or the poll tax was the most important local tax, often forming more than half of the local revenues of the Local Councils. The actual amount collected was, however, far from meeting the targets, due to the lack of cooperation from the people, the seasonal movements of pastoralists, the immigration of youth to the towns but, first and foremost, lack of administrative strength, capability and will to levy and collect taxes. There had been a certain improvement; while tax revenues in the region constituted 15 per cent of total revenue in 1975–76, the percentage had reached 34 per cent in 1980/81, which was still extremely modest compared to its African neighbours (Sodhi, 1981:35). The machinery for the collection of taxes levied by the central government but collected by the regional government (personal income tax, land rental tax

---

3. To work for carrying out studies and preparation of research which are aimed at promotion of the Area in socio-economic fields.

and business profit tax) was, however, strengthened over the years. It started as a one man office but gradually the staff was increased to 33 officers and 119 tax collectors and base level staff. But this system also faced great difficulties, especially in collecting the personal income tax.

In 1982 the Area Councils and the Town/Rural Councils in the three regions combined employed about 250 professional administrators (Malik, 1983:97). Before the re-division there were, for example, eight Area Councils in Equatoria Region (four were temporarily dissolved in December 1983). Financially the Area Councils in 1982/83 were not viable units and needed a subsidy of 60 per cent of their total budget expenditure (Inter-Regional Training Project, 1983:1), a deficit which unavoidably increased, as it was expected that more and more social services should be rendered to the population at the same time as the transfer from the North decreased.

The Area Councils' administrative, professional, technical and support staff was on secondment from the Regional Ministries. This made them a dumping ground on which to off load inefficient and incompetent staff from more central administrative organs, since the Councils became responsible for their salaries. In spite of this, UNDP reported for 1981 that, for example, over 50 per cent of the provincial and local book-keeping and accountancy posts were vacant. At one stage, only one out of six posts of the Controllers of Accounts in the Province was filled (Malik, 1981:5–6). The Commissioner post continued, but his powers were reduced as spelled out in Section 10 of the Act. He was now only to supervise and check the activities of the Local Councils and not directly to participate in them. But the Act did not address the power vacuum the reduced role of the Commissioner created. Hence an additional unclear administrative structure was established.

The training problem which was highlighted already in 1972, remained a crucial issue. For example: not before 1982 was the *National Training Regulation 1976* translated into English and made available in the South; a Regional Civil Service Training Institute was never established; the Regional Institute of Public Administration was conceived, created by decree, but never materialized. A training centre offering courses in book keeping and accounting, budgeting, auditing and tax administration was conceived in 1975. Official approval of the project was secured first in 1978. In July 1981 the Regional Accountancy Training Centre was officially started. The Training Advisory Board and the Steering Committee, established to provide policy and administrative guidance, never did manage to function! Contributions from three regional governments were unpaid by November 1984 (See UNDP 1984).

The state administration after re-division in 1983

In this rather chaotic and unsettled administrative situation, marked by very unclear management structures, serious shortages of trained staff, a weak *esprit de corps* among the administrators, and first and foremost—with no adequate finances to pay either for the administrative staff or for development initiatives—came the re-division of 1983. Without waiting for the planned and promised referendum, Nimeiri, on June 6th 1983, decreed the establishment of three new regions in the South. The Presidential Order No 1/1983 created three new regional governments and a number of new departments, Area Councils etc. The Regional Ministry of Finance and Economic Planning of the Southern Region Government (RMFEP) was, for example, split into three regional Ministries of Finance and Economic Affairs. The three regional governments divided the assets and resources of the former ministry, with the Equatoria Regional Government inheriting the building of the former RMFEP. The distribution of personnel depended on which region the officers and employees belonged to (UN 1987:1). The Nilotic and other people from Upper Nile and Bahr al-Ghazal provinces were forced to leave Equatoria and *vice versa* (Badal, 1988:21–23). An untenable administrative situation which was wrought with fundamental uncertainties about basic regulations was created.

In a situation where educated people were few,[10] and where money was in short supply, the establishment of more administrative units added to the already unsolved staffing problems. In the regional assembly, it was said that the only surplus manpower was politicians, and they were the only ones who would benefit from the creation of new posts in the new regions (the Speaker of the Regional Assembly, Angelo Beda, quoted in Arou, 1988:171). The councils came to depend entirely on grant-in-aid from the central government. This was released to the Regional governments which in turn allocated parts of it to the different area councils. A regular formula for how this money should be allocated was never established. Furthermore, most of the book-keeping, accounting and clerical personnel staffing the Area Councils were not trained at all. Since the budgets were seriously under-financed—as were the budgets of the provinces before the 1981 Act, disbursement of approved expenditures in the recurrent budget could not be done owing to lack of authorization for the release of funds. In this transitional atmosphere regional and local politicians often tried to influence the posting of the officers in such a manner that the "right officer was not posted in the right place" (see Khamis, 1984:172).

The re-division made it impossible to generate both a rule oriented and an efficient public administration. Before the re-division quite a few Area Councils used to have their separate development budget. Between June 1983 and October 1984 the situation had deteriorated so fast that no money had come to the Area Councils in Equatoria for development purposes. The sit-

---

[10] The trained pupils at intermediate schools in the whole region, were, according to the official statistics, 189 in 1980/81. The number enrolled in primary six the same year was 14,812.

uation was regarded as so difficult, that the area councils did not even bother to prepare any development budgets for the years 1983/84 and 1984/85.

The ambiguity of the regulations continued. The relationship between the Chief Executive and the elected members of the Area Councils had not been settled. The legislature in every region should have been partly elected and partly appointed. The executive power in the region rested, however, with the Governor, appointed by Nimeiri. He was to be assisted by a deputy and five ministers all responsible to the Governor. The Governor was to be solely responsible to the President in Khartoum. The administration did not have enough money to pay for recurrent expenditure, and such categories as teachers were rarely paid. In 1984, for example, all the primary schools under government control were closed down for more than three quarters of the year. Neither did they have instruments by which administration could become possible. Almost all the Area Councils, even in Equatoria, did not have vehicles for their operation; at best they had some few bicycles.

The decree by Nimeiri led to absurd situations. When, for example, the new Regional Executive Authority of Bahr el Ghazal came into being no facilities had been provided to cater for the new regional government. The administrative headquarters had to be established in the previous premises of the Headquarters of the former Bahr al Ghazal Province. None of the five new regional ministries in Bahr al Ghazal had offices, inventory or personnel. The new ministries were waiting for months for the arrival of furniture distributed from Juba. During this initial phase no work was done (Bahr el Ghazal Region Group 1984:154). In its turn the Province headquarters of eastern Bahr el Ghazal Province at Aweil had to move into the premises of the previous Aweil People's Town Council. The same happened in Western Bahr al Ghazal province. The problem of staffing these new ministries and councils was solved by "applying speedy promotion" (ibid., 155). It offered job opportunities for the lesser qualified among the educated elite. In Bahr al Ghazal the Regional Ministry of Services, Department of Education upgraded the primary school teachers to intermediate school level "overnight", and a great number of teachers were shifted to the Regional Ministry of Administration. Education suffered, and little administration was done. In Equatoria it led to further delays in the payment of salaries, to transfer of office furniture from Juba to Wau and Malakal while "personnel took extra long leave" (Gillo et al., 1984:37). Some departments became overstaffed, due to the "influx of Equatoria Region personnel returning from the other Regions" (ibid.), while other departments experienced serious manpower shortages.

The administration of the Western Area Council as of October 1984 can be used as an example to indicate the staffing situation in Equatoria, the most administratively developed region. In the Area Council 895 were on the pay-roll. These included General Administration Department (49), Agricultural Department (26), Education Department including teachers etc.

(694).[11] Agriculture and Veterinary Department (26), Forestry Department (39), Health Department (86) and Social Welfare Department (1) (sic!) Staff shortfall was estimated at more than 50 per cent (Pickering and Davies, undated:33–39). This description of the Western Area Council would also hold for the Central Area Council and for the Eastern Area Council.

By 1985 development efforts undertaken by the government had almost been brought to a complete stop. The staff had gone on strike and in the schools there were neither schooling material nor teachers. Many councils had stopped working during 1984 and 1985. Added to this came the staff-transfer policy. The senior administrators in the Western Area Council were changed three times during the three years between 1981 to 1984 (Pickering and Davies, :54). Efforts at improving, for instance, budget procedures and structures became almost impossible due to instabilities. In 1982 the government had appointed a number of technical committees to advise on rules and regulations for the effective implementation of the systems as laid down in the 1981 Act. The first budget procedures of the Area Councils these influenced were for the fiscal year 1982/83. "Unfortunately", as it is stated in a UN report, these procedures were not followed by the councils the next year due to further decentralisation (Inter-Regional Training Project 1983:2). The re-division required new procedures and regulations. Everything had to be done again, but now in three regions, by even less trained staff and with less money to undertake the work than ever. The 1983 decision led to the fragmentation of an already weak administrative system, and supplanted it with new administrative structures whose fragility and limited administrative capacity were only matched by the paucity of financial and other resources at their disposal.

In the Southern Sudan, where ethnic groups as social categories have been more important than social class, one of the paramount problems in building up the administration has been one of "ethnic arithmetic". The difficulties in implementing universalistic bureaucratic principle in a context of ethnic rivalry and conflict were demonstrated again and again. Here we have analyzed the failure of the Southern Regional Government in a primarily southern context. This focus does not relate the whole story, of course. It was a semi-autonomous state, to a large extent dependent upon the political will and decisions in Khartoum and Nimeiri.

---

[11] The Education Department had no vehicles, but three bicycles were available for visits by the Inspectors of Education. Books and educational materials—including chalk, were practically non-existant).

NON-GOVERNMENTAL AID ORGANIZATIONS, SOCIETY AND THE STATE ADMINISTRATION[12]

The 1980s, in Africa, has been called the "NGO decade"; then the NGOs "entered the limelight..." (Bratton, 1989:569). In Southern Sudan the NGOs came to play a very important role already in the 1970s.[13] The enormous task of socio-economic reconstruction of the whole region after the first war, the emergency assistance to more than half a million Sudanese returnees and later to about 200,000 Ugandan refugees fleeing to Southern Sudan between 1979 and 1983, and a weak and new state administration without enough money, people or experience to carry out these tasks alone, made the region an early and natural place for extensive NGO involvement.[14] In Juba alone in 1985 there were 38 foreign aid organisations.

There can be no doubt that many of the NGOs were rather efficient development agents. The Norwegian Church Aid/Sudan Programme, which will be especially focused on in this chapter, definitely helped to improve the living standards in their programme area on the East Bank of the Nile in Equatoria Province. The area covered 86,000 km² and had an estimated population of around 500,000. Approximately 90 per cent were small farmers. About 20 different ethnic groups lived in the area; the most important

---

[12] The term non-governmental organization (NGO) has no clear meaning, and denotes different type of organisations in different countries and different settings. The very term is a residual expression which describes what the agency is not; i.e. it is not part of a government administration. Here it will mean foreign non-profit-making development agencies which are not initiated or controlled by the beneficiaries and which raise funds from the general public and receive support from the development budget in the home countries for development purposes or which provide development services as sub-contractors in the aid system. (In the Southern Sudan many NGOs were sub-contractors of UNHCR.)

[13] At the Relief & Resettlement Conference on Southern Region in 1972, 38 representatives of different foreign NGOs participated (Proceedings of Relief & Resettlement Conference on Southern Region, 1972, 51–52).

[14] Some of the western NGOs operating in Southern Sudan during the period of study were Action Committee for Relief of Southern Sudan (ACROSS), African Interior Mission, African Medical and Research Foundation (AMREF), Catholic Relief Service, Euro-Accord, German Volunteer Service (GTZ), German Leprosy Relief Association, International Volunteer Service, International Summer School of Linguistics, Lutheran World Federation, Missionary Aviation Fellowship, Norwegian Council for the Prevention of Blindness, Norwegian Association for Disabled, Norwegian Church Aid/Sudan Programme, Oxford Committee for Famine Relief (OXFAM), Save the Children Fund, Seventh-Day Adventist, Sudan Interior Mission, Swedish Free Mission, Voluntary Service Group, Swiss Interchurch Aid, , Voluntary Service Overseas and World Vision. This list of NGOs is compiled from Madison, 1984, 174–191, and personal notes of implementing agencies for UNHCR, Juba. (The author worked in 1985/1986 as a Programme Officer for United Nations High Commissioner for Refugees in Juba, being responsible for social services for all the Ugandan refugees in the South and for the rural settlement programme for about 40,000 refugees on the East Bank.)

being Tophosa, Boya and Didinga in the eastern part of the programme area, Latuka, Lapit and Lokoro in the centre and Madi, Acholi, Lokoya, Luluba and Bari in the western parts of the area. After 1983 it covered Kapoeta, Chukudum, Ikotos, Torit and Magwe Area Councils in addition to the east bank of the Nile in Juba Area Council. Norwegian Church Aid built a number of new roads in the area and organized repair and maintenance on others. They helped establish 15 dispensaries and 40 primary health care stations. They constructed 30 primary schools and six secondary schools and 16 schools which they helped to initiate on a self help basis. They drilled hundreds of wells and installed Indian Pump II. Through their active support Torit District Cooperative Union was able to organise 139 co-operatives at village level. Broadly speaking, NCA was an efficient aid organization, primarily concerned with doing a good humanitarian job while trying to stay out of local and regional politics. The NGOs will, however, in this chapter not be evaluated as to their ability to reach the target groups and deliver the goods. Their impact will be analysed in relation to the dissolution of state administrative functions and institutions in the South, and to the whole underlying question of social integration and particularism versus universalism.

The state–civil society dichotomy

In recent years much research on NGO-government relationship has focused on the differences and contrasts between the political role and characteristics of states versus those of voluntary organisations. This theory gives the NGOs a crucial role in the democratisation of African countries: they are to strengthen and pluralize what commonly is called the civil society. The NGOs are conceived as representing instruments for organising local initiatives and for promoting local participation and diversity as opposed to the state, whose approach is seen as dirigiste and top-down, and which expresses the interests of a bureaucratized, alienated elite in search of control. The emergence of NGOs on the African scene has been analyzed as an organisational expression of particular interests or objectives within the body politic which are not adequately represented within the political governance system.

The 1980s were an NGO decade, but it was also a decade of NGO mythology. Influenced by strong anti-state ideologies and criticism of "big government", which dominated the political debate in the United States and Great Britain, especially under President Reagan and Prime Minister Thatcher, the private or non-governmental organisations were as a group given common positive characteristics and roles, as contrasted to the state, which was generally painted in dark colours. The term "civil society" with its present meaning emerged in Europe in the beginning of the nineteenth century. It expressed a reaction to the strong, all-pervasive state which developed during and in the wake of the industrial revolution. It was important to curb the role of the state in order to safeguard private initiative, individual freedom etc. The sudden dominance of the term "civil society" in the vocabulary of social sciences and in the jargon of the development aid community in the 1980s (it is extremely rare to find the term in development aid documents of the 1950s, 1960s and 1970s, even in dictionaries of social sciences and political thought the term was often not mentioned at that time), can be seen as an expression of the strength of this ideological trend. This dichotomy has obvious ideological connotations. But more importantly; the power of this concept and its inherent perspective has given birth to a mythology which has tended to disregard the differences in relationships between the state and the society under industrial and post-industrial capitalism and in societies where 90 per cent are subsistence farmers. The term has also, when dogmatically applied in prescriptions about NGOs' contribution to development, failed to distinguish between African societies with a long and internally rooted state tradition (as in Egypt, Ethiopia and to a lesser extent Dar Fur, which is studied in this volume), and African societies in which the state is a very recent phenomenon, introduced from above and maintained by external sources. Moreover, the actual and potential role of the third sector in African countries varies according to its homogenity, its organisational history, its exchange relations with the state sector etc. Analytical perspectives which study NGO-government relations in Africa within frameworks based on general assumptions about a bureaucraticised and parasitic state on the one hand, and the existence of a civil society with supra-ethnic or supra-tribal organisations fighting to curb the role of the state supported by NGOs as agents of micro-developments on the other, can, of course, be fruitful. I will show that in the case of the Southern Sudan it is not very illuminating. The impact of the NGOs must be analysed concretely. It depends on the specific character of the state system and the "civil society" in which they operate.

The relationship between governments and non-governmental organisations is fundamentally a question of the legitimacy of the various types of institutions which exercise power and authority. I will argue that, in the Southern Sudan, the NGOs contributed unintentionally to the erosion of the authority of the very weak state. The NGOs did not organise the civil society against the state, or consciously promote and strengthen the civil society, as the present rhetorics suppose. Basically they themselves became local substitutes for state administration. The NGOs assumed in a very efficient manner the welfare functions of an ordinary state (which, as shown above, the state in the South was unable to fulfil). As the state was "withering away", (though not in the way Karl Marx described)—in the first instance it was ephemeral and in the second its role as service provider was abdicated—whole districts or sections of ordinary government ministries' responsibilities were handed over to the NGOs to run. The NGOs put up their own administration and authority systems thereby undermining the state institutions without establishing viable alternative structures, partly because there simply was no familiar "civil society" to root them in. The project proliferation, therefore, imposed potential and long-term burdens on state administration and state finances. The NGOs represented different types of organisational behaviour, different types of bureaucratic systems and development philosophies. Their practices therefore came to express institutional and ideological opposition to region-wide, rule-oriented and universalistic state administration and bureaucracy.

These points will be substantiated mainly by a closer description of the programme of the biggest NGO in the region, the Norwegian Church Aid. NCA was in important respects more concerned about developing good relations with the state and its administrative structures than many other NGOs. They continuously emphasised the need for mutual discussions and formal agreements with the state authorities. NCA warned against the danger of establishing institutions the government could not take over and stressed the necessity of local participation as a way to root the projects locally.[15] Other agencies were apparently less concerned about the long term sustainability of their projects. This situation makes NCA especially interesting, and the extensive documentation of their project activities combined with their relative openness, makes their history accessible to outsiders.

Formal relations

Both in Juba and locally there were now and then open tensions between the state administration trying to execute administrative command and control of all the different NGOs and the NGOs' defence of their autonomy. In the first years after the Addis Ababa Agreement regular monthly meetings with the NGOs were coordinated by the Regional Ministry of Finance and Planning (NCR/SP 1975:31). But these meetings gradually developed into empty rituals; the government representatives were formally in charge, but their words carried less and less authority. They had little administrative power to back their proposals and objections. Some of the government representatives also irritated the action-oriented agencies; they demonstrated a combination of "officialdom" and lack of knowledge about what was going on in the rural communities. There were NGOs which did not bother about whether they were registered by the host-government. Some of them did not want to discuss their projects with the regional or local authorities, although they would inform them about their plans. Many organisations had formal agreements approved by the central or regional government (some donor countries like Norway made this a requirement for financial support), while

---

[15] In 1986/87, when their long-lasting integrated rural development programme had been brought to a halt due to the civil war, the NCA also reassessed their past policies and decided that in future development assistance programmes in the Southern Sudan more emphasis should be given to institution building including support to local state institutions.

others looked upon this as unnecessary "red tape". What is more interesting than these formal questions, however, and what will have far-reaching consequences in a longer historical perspective, is the imprint of the existence of different forms of authorities and different types of organisations and bureaucracies on the local society.

Infrastructural power

The NGOs had in certain areas very strong infrastructural power as compared to the state. In total NCA's activities on the East Bank for the years up to 1986, including the refugee aid, amounted to about USD 75 million. This was almost 20 million more than the regional government invested in the whole region.[16] In a land-locked economy, Juba being about 5000 kilometres from the nearest port, and in a society where there were no regular newspapers, one local radio-station which was on the air some few hours a day, no inter-regional mail- or telegraph-system which functioned, the NGOs and their employees in important areas monopolised distribution of both information and things due to their well-developed logistic systems, communication networks and superior means of transport. The British NGO, ACROSS, had more than 100 vehicles. When petrol became very scarce in the mid-1980s, this power relationship tipped even further to the side of the NGOs, since the few government cars had often to be supplied with fuel begged or bought from the NGOs or the UN.

---

[16] For comparative purposes, Malik's (Malik, 1981:11) data on expenditures, revenue and grant-in-aid to different government hierarchies can be given.

Budgeted expenditure/revenue recurrent £S(000)

Items	1978/79	1979/80	1980/81	1981/82
Expenditures				
Regional	28,138	34,236	38,203	47,122
Executive Councils	13,192	29,990	32,383	46,381
Local Councils	4,050		5,470	9,063
Total Exp.	45,380	64,226	76,056	102,566
Revenue				
Tax & Non-Tax Rev.				
Regional	11,412	14,371	15,054	18,114
Provincial	2,896	7,143	2,680	8,333*
Local	4,523		4,682	9,062*
Total Rev.	18,831	21,514	22,416	35,509
Grants-in-aid				
Regional	14,200	16,200	19,293	21,962
Provincial/Local	9,300	19,800	20,707	26,038
Total	23,500	36,000	40,000	48,000

* Includes Savings

Hilieu, just outside Torit, was the administrative centre of NCA. It had excellent secretarial services, radio communication with Khartoum, Nairobi and most of the East Bank, a functioning mail service and flight services. (For comparison: the regional government in Juba did not at times have a functioning photo-copying machine.) Hilieu had three office blocks and the whole programme had approximately USD 600,000 for stationery and office equipment (Norwegian Church Aid/Sudan Programme 1986b, Annex 11:5). Hilieu had a fleet of about 200 vehicles and with no felt fuel shortages. Most of the vehicles on the roads on the East Bank in the mid-1980s were NCA vehicles. NCA built up 6 administrative centres, with administrators, logistic officers, researchers and secretarial staff and stationery and radio communication. NCA had, until the evacuation in January 1985, about 50–60 expatriate personnel. The expatriate colony in Hilieu was comprised of about 200 people, including family members.

In Arapi Rural Development Centre (RDC), in Loa district, there were between five and ten expatriate experts who had lived and worked there for years until 1985. The centre had two administrative buildings, much better than any house owned by the government or any other person in the area, well equipped with stationery and clerks. The RDC had radio-links to both Juba and Hilieu, had plenty of vehicles, fuel, a mechanical workshop etc. The local government in Loa, being responsible for the same area as Arapi RDC, was housed in an old building which was badly in need of repair. In addition to the Head Chief there were only one cashier and a typist/secretary, with one typewriter. The Head Chief had a bicycle, and when he had business with the government in Juba he often came cycling to NCAs Development Centre to ask if he could borrow NCA's radio. This infrastuctural weakness of the Sudanese state would have been a fact whether or not the NCA had been there, but the existence of this efficient and successful programme demonstrated the state's weakness to the people and thus eroded its legitimacy. NCA had become not only a state within a state, but the "state". The NCA not only delivered services, they could also respond to local requests, they could bring sick people to hospitals etc. The government's ordinary administrative authority was more or less confined to the radius of the old chief's bicycle. (The police, the military or the coercive power of the state was of course another matter. This we do not include in the analysis.)

This led to what can be described as a process of local brain-drain. The NGOs had relatively minor staffing problems as compared to the state. They did not necessarily pay higher wages, but the salaries were regularly paid and there were certain fringe benefits, such as access to cars, motor-bikes etc. In addition, to work for an agency generally brought higher work satisfaction because the organization functioned properly. The number of local Sudanese staff varied, but for years it amounted to more than 2,000 people, which made NCA the biggest employer on the East Bank. It had a management staff as per 1 October 1985 of about 90 persons (Norwegian Church

Aid/Sudan Programme 1985:36–37), of whom 70 were Sudanese. NCR/SP's report for 1974 reported in line with the Regional Government that also their "greatest problem in the period has been lack of staff in all projects (Norwegian Church Relief/Sudan Programme 1974:11). The agricultural staff of the NCA project in 1974 numbered already 174 people. In 1983 the number of permanent Sudanese staff had increased to 317 (NCA/SP 1984:28), with 69 working at both Arapi Rural Development Centre (RDC) and Palotaka RDC, while the whole Department of Agriculture employed 80 (Norwegian Church Aid/Sudan Programme 1986:13). None of the later reports mentioned lack of staff as a serious problem, contrary to the situation within the government where staff-shortage was a permanent problem.

Local monopoly in the social service sector

The NGOs' strong position reflected the fact that they could supply something which was very much needed and something which nobody else, and especially not the state, could deliver; social services. As shown, the state administration had very little money for development projects and social services projects.[17] It did not even manage to pay some of the recurrent expenditures for teacher salaries causing government schools to close down temporarily, while agency supported schools functioned.

One might say that the big NGOs and the Khartoum government shared one thing in common: because of their purse they held the Southern government machinery hostage. Most government financed projects in the South were not implemented. Many of them were big and well-known projects, but as the government admitted in 1977 "though the list of projects is impressive, in fact the majority of them were not implemented" (Peace and Progress, 1977:38).

The local government on the East Bank naturally did not pay much heed to collecting unpopular social service taxes, since these services were provided anyway. By easing this burden of governing, the NGO at the same time further alienated the state from the society and *vice versa* and reduced its potential role as meeting point between the compartmentalized unities in the society. By establishing what can be described as competing tax systems (in order to mobilise what was commonly called the "sense of responsibility" among the local people and the level of "popular participation", the agencies demanded that the local people should pay for pump-repairs, stationery etc. to the agency or some local committee established by the agency), the "extraction/accountability cycle" was affected. Most normal functions of a

---

[17] According to Madison (1984), the Regional Government expenditure on Regional Ministry of Agricultural and Natural Resources up to 1981/82 totalled around 7 million Sudanese pounds (Madison, 1984:148). The Regional Ministry of Communication, Transport and Roads had spent about 2.5 million pounds on undertaken projects.

government became the domain of the NCA as in other areas it had become the domain of other NGOs.

Both compared to the government administration and the institutional and organizational features of the local societies in which they worked, the NGOs did represent and, in many areas, did introduce different organizational modes and cultural values. The NGOs were goal-oriented organizations, organized in principle on a temporary basis. They were in the context of the surrounding society more ad hoc "problem solvers" than "rule-oriented" bureaucracies. They furthermore operated within geographically limited areas with limited objectives, and therefore did not have to develop more general, universalistic types of organisations which were adapted to different types of activities and different types of cultures.

A local government bureaucracy was anathema to the NGO sector, as it had been to the British, although for different reasons. The NGOs' relationship to the state administration was often based on individual and personal contacts. These contacts were important when it came to speeding up the removal of official stumbling blocks which hindered efficient project implementation. The NGO-government relationship was therefore also personalized, and not rule-based, in many ways identical to the clientilistic system which had been developed within the state administration itself. Their relations to the recipient society contrasted with cultural attitudes within the beneficiary groups, and they also played by different rules than these which are presupposed by western bureaucratic culture. From their expatriate compounds the aid workers made development excursions into the surrounding society.[18] A relationship was established which had no traits of that reciprocity which has been said to be typical for the local socio-cultural relations.

The NGOs as a rule did not try to establish anti-state structures or organisations. There was no deliberate policy of strengthening such organisations to counterbalance the state. The "civil" organisations which were established, like women groups, cooperative societies etc., were in line with government policies and priorities and were no stronghold for anti-government policies. Their fundamental basis was, however, money supplied from foreign sources. The kind of development institutions which were established through popular participation had therefore difficulties in growing roots in the local soil or in breaking down ethnically divided polities. Little consideration was given to the problem of organisational sustainability in this context, independent of aid injections. The NGOs created bases for alternative entities, but entities that did not possess the universalistic outlook of a regional or provincial administration and which ultimately depended on external money to survive.

---

[18] In Juba there were eight separate compounds for the aid workers. NCA/SP also had their own compound at Hilieu, where, for example, the Sudanese employees had no admission to the dining room before 1985/86.

The way in which the services were provided was perhaps as important. For some of the NGOs money was not the deciding constraint on their scope of activities. What affected the project size and the project components was in general not the purse, but arguments about what was morally right and most conducive to local development. Generally, the NGOs acted within a culture of absolute affluence, where services and goods were not priced. When the NCA now and then tried to counter this unsustainable economic culture, as when they were informing the UNHCR that if they needed NCA lorries for transport purposes, they would have to pay, this was met by strong objections from the aid community. It was by central actors in the aid community characterised as greediness, although the sum did not cover the cost involved. It was difficult to question the principle that aid was free and in some mysterious way outside the realm of economic realities.

The NGOs could moreover decide what kind of exchange relations should be subject to negotiations among the people, the state and the NGO. When a specialized agency worked in an area (education or health for example), they delivered their specialities. An organization geared towards aid for education or the disabled could not, or was not, willing to respond to proposals which, seen from a local or government perspective, were more important to the society as a whole. On the East Bank, it was in the NCA development centres and ultimately in Hilieu that decisions in reality were taken where to drill bore-holes, where to assist self-help schools, which agricultural produce should be supported in what areas, which primary societies should receive most support. Through their control of the Co-operative Union they also fixed the prices of crucial agricultural components such as seeds and ox-ploughs. The local people influenced the decisions as did the government, but at the end of the day NCA decided.

A particularistic, target oriented development strategy

The dominant development strategy of the NGOs, that of realizing the people's basic needs, had consequences for both how the agencies conceptualized the NGO-government relationship and for the social, economic and political integration process. The NGOs had a particularistic strategy for development and a particularistic approach to the administrative system they tried to establish.

Most of the NGOs had a target oriented strategy, aiming at reaching the poor people living in their villages. The NGOs had different approaches, and implemented different aspects of the basic needs strategy. Some only worked in the health sector and with small pockets within it, like combating blindness and helping the disabled. Others concentrated on educational services, while some NGOs, like NCA, implemented comprehensive integrated rural development projects. What was common for almost all these projects was that, in order to meet the goals and also the need to report success stories, to maintain the support from the home country or the UN family, the NGOs sought to circumvent the inefficient state institutions and work directly with the beneficiaries. The better they did it, the more the authority and legitimacy of the local government structures were eroded. There was a contradiction between establishing programmes for costly social services and the state's potential for becoming a vehicle of economic transformation. The NGOs established social services which, although differing in the level of ambition, had running and maintenance costs which could not be financed by local surpluses or local revenue, not even in the foreseeable future.

The realization of people's basic needs was considered as a right by both the NGOs, by the local people and by the government's declarations and rhetoric. But the recurrent costs of these had to become, also in the long run, a serious drain on the already strained budgets of the local councils. The legitimacy of the state institutions was undermined and, therefore, also the chances for building institutions which could penetrate competing and localised institutions. The possibilities for the local administrations and state institutions to take upon themselves a more active role regarding new investments etc., were simply not there, no matter what the personal attitudes or the wishes of the local administrators or government representatives. The NGOs were instrumental in relieving the government from would-be pressures by carrying out projects within the service sector. On the other hand, by fulfilling this role, the state, as a potential supra-ethnic and universalitic entity, could not point to its record as service provider to strengthen its position.

There was, therefore, also a contradiction between projects aiming at realizing certain target groups' basic needs at a local level and projects aiming at strengthening the regional or national economy, or between a successful local project and a beneficial regional project. Since the aid input was so heavy and the local development councils and committees so weak, this uneven relationship also created uneven development between people and areas defined as target areas and areas outside the spheres of development aid organisations. The ambitious programmes and projects and the lack of reflections on the administrative and financial situation in the Southern Region created a situation in which there was little correlation between development activities and implementation capacities in the would-be implementing institutions.

The NGOs were apportioned different parts of the region, in many ways similar to the British government, decades before, divided the region between different missionary societies. The NGOs tried to establish local institutions and local accountability by the policy of "popular participation". They established formal administrative structures and informal authority networks independent of the state institutions and partly in competition with them. The by-passing of the local state institutions took different forms, unintended in some cases and deliberate in others. The general impact of their activities, aiming at reaching the target groups with basic needs projects, further marginalized the state in many areas and made the local and provincial councils more or less redundant.

A giving, care-taker "state"

A type of development administration was created with very unusual traits. The aid handed out was mainly grants and the improvement of the lot of the people did not reflect an improvement in state finances. In at least important parts of the South there were no "tremendous setbacks" in the meeting of basic needs of the rural people in the early 1980s, as the World Bank reported to be the general rule in Africa. On the contrary, there was an increase in living standards and without doubt there was an increase in collective services at least in Equatoria. This development was mainly caused by foreign donors and NGOs as implementing agencies. The aid helped the local people. But the aid mechanism and the asymmetric relationship between the weakness of the infrastructural power of the state and the strong infrastructural power of the NGOs caused the state institutions to play an even more peripheral role in large parts of the region. There had been established a system whereby the people expected initiatives and development projects to come from individual foreign organizations rather than from a bankrupt, inefficient government. What had happened was an improvement of social and economic conditions but, due to the particular conditions of the region, it is questionable whether it represented a strengthening of the "civil society". It weakened the possibility for building state institutions and a potentially universalistic, rule-oriented bureaucracy. A practice was established, however, whereby predominantly subsistence farmers started to talk to their government about their rights regarding education, clean water, health facilities etc. There had taken place a revolution in expectations, more profoundly than at any time in the region's history, without a parallel improvement or the state's ability to fulfil them or to guarantee these rights.

The success of the NCA programme and the consequential growth of their budgets and activities, created a "state", an administrative machinery, which represented a "revolution from outside" on the East Bank as far as development administration was concerned. In the perspective of a local state building process, however, this machinery represented a perpetuation of some of those processes which had helped to block a locally rooted state building process in the past. Its actual and immediate role was, however, very different; it built and did not destroy, it gave, but it did not take anything. Both in a historical and contemporary perspective this "state administration" was a novelty. It was a state as a service institution, without functions either of suppression or extraction. The relative autonomy of *this* state in relation to the economic and social basis of the society was complete, since its activities depended on money from abroad and the moral-political judgements of the aid workers. These "state officials" were social workers rather than rulers and parasites. New institutional structures and new normative models of state behaviour had been created, but structures and models which can hardly be implemented by any future Southern state. What had taken place was what can be termed a *privatization* and an externalization of the state, at the same time as the Government continued their rhetoric about the state building socialism.

The accountability problem

The NGOs also had conflicting and multiple loyalties and created an organizational system marked by lack of accountability. Important ordinary state functions had been taken over by a Norwegian private organization which legally was answerable first and foremost to Oslo, the capital of Norway, although morally to the local people. The lack of clear lines of administrative authority in the region in general was further blurred. From one point of view the NGO-sector deepened the general problem of accountability. It was an in-built problem of the whole structure, since the personnel and the organization were rewarded for implementing the project target within an alternative and fundamentally external reward system. It was "downwards" accountability to the people and upward accountability to the NGO's HQs, while the local state institutions were often regarded as inefficient, time-losing institutions that preferably were to be circumvented.

NCA had established formal institutions and informal networks which not only were a counterweight to the state, but an alternative. In the same way as the British "indirect rule" policy created traditions and practices which influenced the framework for the administrative build up of the Southern Region after 1972, the NCA programme and its operation will have a legacy for future state building. NCA and the other NGOs were not important enough to bar the development of a universalistic bureaucratic rule over the whole region, but by establishing its own localised bureaucracy with stronger infrastructural powers than the regular state in important sectors of the society, they represented one of many centrifugal forces. While the programme area locally was called "Little Norway", the Sudanese administrative staff were called "Black Norwegians".

NGO mythology versus southern realities

The character of and relationship between state and society vary considerably between countries, reflecting historical developments, economic situation, the degree of social integration/compartmentalization etc. A productive relationship between NGOs and the host government's administrative system will therefore have to adapt to different roles and potentials of the third sector. In the case of the Southern Sudan a kind of conceptual dogmatism played an important role; the dominant perspective underestimated the weakness of the state institutions and overestimated the degree of social integration and value consensus in the social system. One example, in 1974 NCR/SP stated typically, and in line with government aims, that their reconstruction programme should be incorporated in "the existing government structures at the end of the 3-year programme" (Norwegian Church Relief/Sudan Programme 1974a:4), i.e. in 1977. In 1977 the programme was further from being handed over to the government than it had been when started. The Southern politicians and the NGOs both underrated the region's very special "state-history" and its financial difficulties. One example: the agency meetings (which were few, partly because of competition and mutual suspicion) mostly reported on the development within the different organisations' areas, and never did consider more macro-oriented issues like regional integration or regional universalism. The NGOs made important contributions to the improvement of local living standards and they mobilised people locally for development and social change. But the impact of NGOs, insofar as they are involved on such a relatively massive scale as they were in the Southern Sudan, cannot be properly understood within the micro-perspective and grasroot-perspective which have been part and parcel of current NGO-mythology. They also had important and overlooked impacts on the state administrative system; impacts which were not intended but which must have influenced, although on a limited scale, both the dissolution of the Southern state and the breakdown of the administrative system.

REFERENCES

Al-Terafi, Al-Agub Ahmed, 1986, "The Civil Service: Principles and Practice", in Muddathir Abd Al-Rahim, Raphael Badal, Adlan Hardallo and Peter Woodward (eds.), 1986, *Sudan since Independence*. London, Gower.
Alier, A., 1976, *Peace and Development in the Southern Region. A Statement*. The Democratic Republic of the Sudan, Ministry of Culture and Information, 1976.
Alier, A., 1990, *Southern Sudan; Too Many Agreements Dishonoured*. London, Ithaca Press.
Arou, M.K.N., 1988, "Devolution: Decentralisation and the Division of the Southern Region into Three Regions in 1983", in M.K.N. Arou and B. Yongo-Bure, 1988, *North-South Relations in the Sudan since the Addis Ababa Agreement*. Khartoum, Khartoum University Press.
Arou, M.K.N. and B. Yongo-Bure, 1988, *North-South Relations in the Sudan since the Addis Ababa Agreement*. Khartoum, Khartoum University Press.
Badal, R.K., 1983, "The Role of the Commissioner under the People's Local Government Act, 1981", in Inter-Regional Training Project, 1984, *Selected Papers from Seminars Organized during the Years 1981 to 1984*. Edited and compiled by Project SUD/83/002, Juba.

Badal, R.K., 1988, "The Addis Ababa Agreement Ten Years After", in M.K.N. Arou and B. Yongo-Bure, 1988, *North-South Relations in the Sudan since the Addis Ababa Agreement*. Khartoum, Khartoum University Press.

Bahr el Ghazal Region Group, 1984, "Decentralization Issues in Bahr el Ghazal", Seminar Paper, Seminar, 21–23 November 1984, in Inter-Regional Training Project, 1984, *Selected Papers from Seminars Organized during the Years 1981 to 1984*. Edited and compiled by Project SUD/83/002, Juba.

Bior, Ajang, 1982, "Evolution of Local Government in the Sudan", Seminar Paper, Seminar 4–8 October, 1982, in Inter-Regional Training Project, 1984, *Selected Papers from Seminars Organized during the Years 1981 to 1984*. Edited and compiled by Project SUD/83/002, Juba.

Bratton, M., 1989, "The Politics of NGO—Government Relations in Africa". *World Development*, 17, 4, 569–87.

Emmerich, H., 1969, *A Handbook of Public Administration: Current Concepts and Practices with Special References to Developing Countries*. New York, United Nations.

Eprile, C., 1974, *War and Peace in the Sudan, 1955–1972*. London, Newton Abbot.

Finer, S., 1975, "State and Nation-Building in Europe", in C. Tilly (ed.), 1975, *The Formation of Nation States in Western Europe*. Princeton.

Gillo, A.L., R.V. Rajan and M. Lauya (eds.), 1984, *Proceedings of the First Regional Conference on Health and Social Welfare in Equatoria Region, Southern Sudan*. Juba, Directorate of Health and Social Welfare.

Heper, M., 1987, *The State and Public Bureaucracies. A Comparative Perspective*. London, Greenwood Press.

Inter-Regional Training Project, 1983, *Guidelines for Annual Budget and Monthly Financial Statements of the Area Councils. Compiled under the supervision of the UNDP/DTCD/PROJECT SUD/83/002*. Juba, The Democratic Republic of the Sudan, Bahr el Ghazal Region, Equatoria Region, Upper Nile Region.

Inter-Regional Training Project, 1984, *Decentralisation. Tasks Ahead. Report on the Colloquium Held on 27 and 28 October 1983, the Council Room, University of Juba*. Juba, UNDP/DTCD Project SUD/83/002, ODA project AMTP.

Inter-Regional Training Project, 1984, *Selected Papers from Seminars Organized during the Years 1981 to 1984*. Edited and compiled by Project SUD/83/002, Juba.

International Bank for Reconstruction and Development, International Development Association, 1973, *Report of a Special Mission on the Economic Development of Southern Sudan*. Country Programme Department, Eastern Africa, No 119a–SU, Washington.

International Bank for Reconstruction and Development, 1981, *Project Performance Audit Report. Sudan—Southern Region Agricultural Rehabilitation Project*. (Credit 476-SU), Washington.

Khalid, M., 1985, *Nimeiri and the Revolution of Dis-May*, London, KPI.

Khamis, C., 1985, "Decentralisation Issues in Equatoria Region", Inter-Regional Training Project, 1985, *Selected Papers from Seminars Organized during the Years 1981 to 1984*, 170–174. Edited and compiled by Project SUD/83/002, Juba.

Lagu, J., 1978, Policy Statement Given by the President of the High Executive Council, H.E. Joseph Lagu, to the 2nd end (sic!) People's Regional Assembly, in Democratic Republic of the Sudan—Southern Region. *Regional Government. Policy Statement March 1978*, Juba, The Regional Ministry of Information & Culture.

Lagu, J., 1980, *Decentralization. A Necessity for the Southern Provinces of the Sudan*. Juba University.

Madison, B.B., 1984, *The Addis Ababa Agreement on the Problem of Southern Sudan: A Study to Evaluate the Distribution of Benefits and Social Groups in the Southern Sudan and to Determine the Impact of this Distribution on the Region's Political Stability.* Ph.D., University of Denver.

Malik, J.R., 1981, "Issues of Local Finance in the Southern Region", Seminar Paper, Seminar 1–3 December, 1981, in Inter-Regional Training Project, 1984, *Selected Papers from Seminars Organized during the Years 1981 to 1984.* Edited and compiled by Project SUD/83/002, Juba.

Malik, J.R., 1983, "Decentralization of Powers to the Councils", Seminar Paper presented 27 and 28 October, 1983, in Inter-Regional Training Project, 1984, *Selected Papers from Seminars organized during the Years 1981 to 1984.* Edited and compiled by Project SUD/83/002, Juba.

Malwal, B., 1981, *People & Power in the Sudan—The Struggle for National Stability.* London, Ithaca Press.

Mamdani, M., 1986, "Peasants and Democracy in Africa", *New Left Review*, 156, March-April:37–51.

Mills, R.L., 1977, *Population and Manpower in Southern Sudan.* Geneva, International Labour Organization.

NCR/CP 1975, Norwegian Church Relief/Sudan Programme, *Progress Report 2,* 1975. Juba, NCR.

Norwegian Church Relief, 1974a, *Continuation and Expansion of Relief and Rehabilitation in the Southern Sudan. Preliminary report Prepared by the Norwegian Church Relief Survey Team. Part 2. Basic Rrinciples and Detailed Outlines of Programme.* Oslo, Norwegian Church Relief.

Norwegian Church Relief/Sudan Programme, 1974, *Progress Report.* Torrit/ISP.

Norwegian Church Aid/Sudan Programme, 1984, *Agricultural Extension. Processing and Marketing Study. East Bank Equatoria. Final Report.* Herst (England), Hunting Technical Services Limited.

Norwegian Church Aid/Sudan Programme, 1985, *Annual Report.*, 1985.

Norwegian Church Aid/Sudan Programme, 1986, *Economic Development. Potential Study, East Bank, Eastern Equatoria, Sudan.* Herst (England), Hunting Technical Services Limited.

Norwegian Church Aid/Sudan Programme, 1986b, *Proposal for Norwegian Church Aid Sudan Programme 1987–90.* February 1986, Torit.

Peace and Progress 1972–1973, 1973, A report of the provisional High Executive Council of the Southern Region of the southern Sudan marking the first anniversary of the Addis Ababa Agreement and the establishment of regional self-government in southern Sudan, Regional Ministry of Information and Culture, Southern Region, Juba.

Peace and Progress 1972–1976–77, 1977, Regional Ministry of Information and Culture, Juba.

Peace and Progress, 1974, Regional Ministry of Information and Culture, Southern Region, Juba.

Pickering, A.K. and C.J. Davies, (undated), *Decentralisation Policy and Practice in the Southern Sudan. The Case of the Western Area Council.* The Inter-Regional Training Project, Development Administration Group, University of Birmingham and UNDP project SUD/83/002.

Robertson, J., 1974, *Transition in Africa. From Direct Rule to Independence.* London, C. Hurst.

Sodhi, P.S., 1981, Financial Issues—A Perspective, in Inter-Regional Training Project, 1984, *Selected Papers from Seminars Organized during the Years 1981 to 1984.* Edited and compiled by Project SUD/83/002, Juba.

Sudanow and Ministry of Guidance and National Information, 1983, *Perspectives on the South. An Analysis of Trends and Events Leading to the Final Decree of Regionalisation of the Former Southern Region of the Sudan*. Khartoum.

Democratic Republic of the Sudan, 1972, *Proceedings of Relief & Resettlement Conference on Southern Region 21–23 February 1972 (Khartoum)*. Khartoum, Ministry of State for Southern Affairs.

UNDP (United Nations Development Programme), 1984, *Sudan. Accountancy and Financial Management Training in the Southern Region of Sudan. Report of the Evaluation Mission*, SUD/80/015, Washington DC.

United Nations. Department of Technical Cooperation for Development, 1987, *Accountancy and Financial Management Training in the Southern Sudan. Project Findings and Recommendations*. New York, UNDP DP/UN/SUD-80-051/1.

Wieu, A.W.R., 1989, "Southern Sudan Institutional Structure, Power and Inter-Governmental Relations Yesterday and Today", in M.K.N. Arou and B. Yongo-Bure (eds.), 1989, *North-South Relations in the Sudan since the Addis Ababa Agreement*. Khartoum, Institute of African and Asian Studies, Sudan Library Series, 14.

Woodward, P., 1991, *Sudan, 1898–1989. The Unstable State*. London, Lester Crook Academic Publishing.

Political Cleavages within the Southern Sudan
An Empirical Analysis of the Re-Division Debate
Raphael K. Badal

POLITICAL CLEAVAGES AND THE DEMISE OF AUTONOMY

This paper focuses attention upon political cleavages within the Southern Sudan with special emphasis on the debate provoked by a controversial proposal to split the former Southern Region of Sudan into its constituent parts, provinces or sub-regions. The debate itself is used in illustration and to highlight political divisions within the Southern Sudan. Cleavages within Southern society are not a subject that has often attracted the attention of scholars interested in Sudanese, more specifically, Southern Sudanese, affairs. Yet, time and again it has been splits or divisions within the ranks of Southern Sudanese political leadership or freedom fighters at crucial and decisive moments that have had radical impacts upon subsequent events.

For instance, at the Juba Conference in 1947 there was unanimity of views amongst the Southern delegates on the first day to the effect that the South should, for a trial period, have a separate administrative conference of its own as well as a legislative assembly for political education. Strong sentiments were expressed against any hasty union with the North. On the second day all that had changed as a result of splits and behind the scenes wheeling and dealing that occurred in the course of the night.

The first Southern Liberal Party formed in 1952 succeeded in uniting and consolidating Southern Sudanese political opinion. It was so popular in the South, on account of its federation platform, that in the 1953 elections it won all the 40 seats allocated to the South to become the third largest Party in Parliament. None of the major religious sectarian parties in the North, the Umma and National Unionist Party (NUP), dared form the Government without inclusion of the Southern Liberal Party. So strong was the position of the South and the Party that, according to its chairman Mr. Stanislaus Paysama, it almost held the trump card. Had the Southern MPs stood as a bloc, they could have demanded and got any of the powerful portfolios or even have delayed the self-government process if they had so wished. But, when it came to the election of the Prime Minister, the Party experienced lots of floor crossing so that, at the end of the day, its size dwindled to about 20–25 MPs. Paysama was shocked and heart broken and resolved to leave politics altogether when the military took over power in November 1958. Later on, many years afterwards, he recorded the incident in his memoirs thus:"The money was there, a great amount of money, from the Government and the Umma Party, and every time elections [voting] came, they [the Southerners] are destroyed like this" (Dellagiacoma, 1990:69).

Diagram 1. *The nexus of political changes in the South*

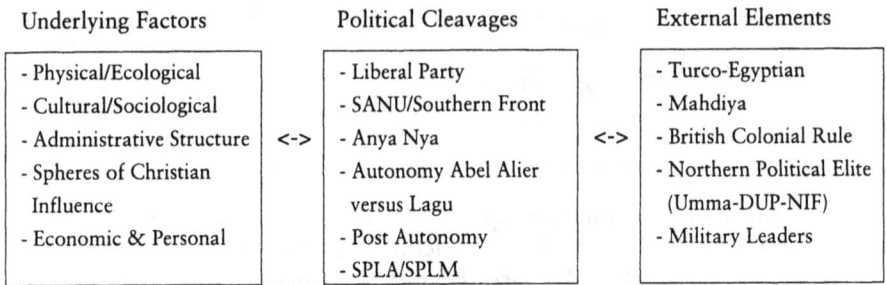

Underlying Factors		Political Cleavages		External Elements

- Physical/Ecological
- Cultural/Sociological
- Administrative Structure
- Spheres of Christian
  Influence
- Economic & Personal
	<->	- Liberal Party
		- SANU/Southern Front
		- Anya Nya
		- Autonomy Abel Alier
		  versus Lagu
		- Post Autonomy
		- SPLA/SPLM
			<->	- Turco-Egyptian
				- Mahdiya
				- British Colonial Rule
				- Northern Political Elite
				  (Umma-DUP-NIF)
				- Military Leaders

According to other disclosures by S. Paysama in his autobiography, published in 1990, the South, but for disunity, could have been granted local self rule as long ago as 1965 instead of seven years afterwards, in 1972. He gives a narrative account of a tea party held by Sir Abder Rahman al Mahdi at which both Azhari and Abdallah Khalil, two veteran independence nationalists, were in attendance. Asked point blank by Sir Abder Rahman what the Southerners wanted, separation or federation, Paysama replied that Southern Sudanese aspirations centred on autonomy, self government for themselves and the right to manage their own affairs. Sir Abder Rahman then drew the attention of Azhari and Abdallah Khalil thus

> Do you hear? Why then don't you do like that? Please, go and discuss these matters [with the Southerners] and let these things go on. Give them what they like. Look here: when the Turkish government came here, they were unable to conquer the South; again my father, the Mahdi, could not subject the South to his rule, and the British did it with great difficulty: you might hear now and then there were murderings of the British officials or fight against the Government ... you see? Let us sit down, please, and look into this Southern question, so that we get satisfied with it. (pp. 69–70)

Political divisions, disunity and personal rivalries within the Southern leadership contributed to a large extent to the failure of the Round Table Conference (RTC) of March 1965, convened ostensibly to find a solution to the Southern question. Theoccasion this time was the termination of the military regime of General Ibrahim Abboud in a popular uprising in October 1964. While Northern Sudanese political parties were quickly revived and new ones sprang up, the Southerners in Khartoum organized themselves into a political bloc named the Southern Front (SF). Its chairman was Mr. Clement Mboro, a veteran Southern Sudanese administrator and a controversial participant in the 1947 Juba conference. For some time the SF claimed to be the representative and spokesman of Sudan African National Union (SANU), at that time the only Southern political Party formed by politicians in a self-imposed exile. In February 1965 Mr. William Deng, then Secretary General of SANU, broke ranks with his colleagues and returned to the country to organise his own wing of SANU. One outcome of the split was the emergence of two wings of SANU: SANU-inside under the chairmanship of William Deng and SANU-outside under leadership of Mr. Aggrey Jadein.

Almost immediately, William Deng called for self-dissolution of the Southern Front now that SANU had come to operate inside the country. The SF responded by registering itself as a political party. Political battle lines and rivalries had been drawn. The late Paysama recounted how he had advised Clement Mboro and the late William Deng not to create or start another party but to revive the Liberal Party, which had had strong grassroots support and the sympathy of peoples from both Western Sudan and the Nuba mountains. At a later stage he urged them to dissolve the two political parties, SANU and the Southern Front, resurrect the Liberal Party, with one of them taking the chairmanship and the other becoming its Secretary General, for a trial period of two years for the sake of unity of the South. He soon discovered in agony that the two could not and would not compromise. Diagram 1 shows the political cleavages in the South.

Southern political leaders in 1965 carried their differences, disunity and rivalries into the conference room as evidenced by lack of consultations, coordination and, above all, a unified political platform. After delivering an emotional speech in which he did not envisage any grounds for unity between South and North, Mr. Aggrey Jadein, the leader of the SANU-outside delegation called for secession of the South and left the conference immediately. The SANU wing of William Deng put forward a proposal for federation while the SF demanded a plebiscite to be carried out in the South to decide on one of the four options: autonomous rule, federation, unity of the country or separation of the South. The Round Table Conference was an international conference with seven African states including Egypt, Nigeria and Ghana participating as observers. All efforts at persuading the Southern delegations, whether by observer states or Northern Sudanese politicians of goodwill, to close ranks and present a unified proposal were in vain. Meanwhile, influential Northern politicians such as Azhari, Abdallah Khalil and Mohamed Ahmed Mahgoub kept pressing or pestering Paysama, who was not himself a conference participant, to tell the Southerners to unite. However, disunity carried the day.

The conference ended in deadlock. A 12-man committee was set up to study and follow up the recommendations of the conference. As for the South, Northern goodwill and the general euphoria created by the demise of the military regime quickly wore off. The newly elected Umma Government headed by Mohamed Ahmed Mahgoub was militant and resolved to punish the Southerners for intransigence and lack of political foresight or seriousness or both. The July 1965 massacres of the educated Southern elite in both Wau and Juba towns bore testimony to the changed attitude and policy of the central government towards the South. The subsequent savage persecution of the Southerners both in Khartoum and in the South had all the hallmarks of the

policies of the military regime which had been overthrown seven months earlier.

As has already been seen, exiled political movements of the Southerners
enjoyed no special immunity from this established pattern of leadership split
and internal power struggles. This was reflected by the formation of a myr-
iad of governments in exile: the Anyidi Revolutionary Government; the Nile
provisional Government, first under Aggrey Jadein and then Gordon Mayen
Mourtat; the Sue River Republic; the Sudan Azania led by Ezboni Mondiri,
and, finally, the Anya Nya guerilla organization and its political wing, the
Southern Sudan Liberation Movement (SSLM) under the overall leadership
of Colonel Joseph Lagu. Of the proliferations of governments a former
Southern Sudanese student leader and activist, who had closely monitored
the activities of exiled politicians, explained:"Tribalism has plagued all
Southern politicians outside the Sudan ... The formation of Anyidi
Revolution Government (for example) was basically tribally motivated, and
aimed at countering the Dinka dominance in the Nile Government" (Wai,
1973:165). Expressed differently, ethnicity coupled with sheer personal ambitions encouraged internal power struggle and internal divisions, which led
to the creation of meaningless governments abroad which followed more or
less tribal lines.

Political cleavages in Southern Sudan were neither a function of class
struggle, ideological polarization nor religious differences. Social stratifica-
tion, class conflict and class analyses are, for the time being at least, quite irrelevant in the context and of the recent history. Ideological under-pinnings
and Christian religious denominations, Catholicism or Protestantism, have so
far played only a relatively minor role in Southern Sudanese politics.

In physical, geographical terms a rough distinction may be drawn between
swamp ecology versus the ironstone plateau, corresponding respectively to
the Nilotics on the one hand and Bantus or non-Nilotic groups on the other.
Sociologically the divisions reflect the existence of pastoralists or semi-
nomadic pastoralists occupying the swampy areas while sedentary agriculturalists live on the high or table plateau. This is, of course, a rather gross
over-simplification as there are real internal differences within the two broad
categories. For instance, the Bari and Latuka of central and eastern Equatoria
differ considerably from the Azande of Western Equatoria in many important respects. Equally, even amongst the Nilotics the Shilluk and their Anuak
kindred differ greatly from the Dinka and Nuer in terms of social structure
and organization.

Administratively, the South had been governed for most of its recent history as three provinces. Under British colonial rule the three provinces comprised Upper Nile, Bahr El Ghazal and Mongalla down to 1906; then Upper
Nile, Bahr El Ghazal and Equatoria to 1936, after which time an administrative reform amalgamated Bahr El Ghazal and Equatoria into one huge
territory under the name of the latter, so that the South had only two

provinces: Upper Nile and Equatoria, with their capitals at Malakal and Juba. In a sense, Bahr El Ghazal and its capital Wau were reduced to the statuses of a sub-province and a sub-provincial headquarters. In 1948 Bahr El Ghazal was detached from greater Equatoria and the South reverted to the pattern of three provinces with corresponding capital towns at Malakal, Wau and Juba respectively. The picture remained the same until independence day on January 1, 1956. At the Round Table Conference and during the deliberations of the 12-man Committee the one point upon which the Southern Sudanese delegations were in agreement was that the South, whether as autonomous region or a federal state, should be reconstituted into one administrative unit and the its capital be at Juba.[1] The Northern delegation was adamantly opposed to this proposal and this difference was not resolved until the Addis Ababa agreement of 1972, which stipulated that the three provinces of the South should constitute an autonomous region with its capital at Juba. For one decade at least, save for financial constraints, the South enjoyed a large degree of autonomy. The first regional premier of the South, known as the President of the High Executive Council, was Mr. Abel Alier a lawyer and formerly Secretary General of the Southern Front. He came to power in April 1972 and was succeeded seven years later on July 1st, 1978 by Joseph Lagu whose term of office lasted till July 7, 1980 when he was replaced by Abel Alier. Abel's return to power was short-lived because of the re-division issue which terminated his term of office on 5th October 1981. Gismalla Abdallah Rasas headed an interim administration for six months, but the man who actually supervised the regional administration was Mr. Joseph James Tambura, who was elected to office in April 1982. The presidential decree No.1. of June 1st, 1983 proclaimed the demise of the Addis Ababa agreement and annulment of the autonomous status of the South.

The following pages will focus on the re-division debate prior to the dissolution of Southern autonomy. The emotionally charged and acrimonious debate aptly captures the political atmosphere in the South at the time and exposes the divisions within the Southern community. It is argued that, in an important respect, the current political predicament of Sudan stems, in a large measure, from the division of the South and the subsequent imposition of Islamic *sharia* laws upon the whole country. The Sudan People's Liberation Army/Movement (SPLA/SPLM) are a direct result of these misguided and misconceived policies. The participants in the debate, more specifically the cons, had foreseen these developments and had sounded a warning which was never heeded. Let us now turn to the debate itself.

---

[1] In this respect it is important to note that the late Joseph Garang, a leading Southern Sudanese intellectual and a prominent member of the Sudan Communist Party, had proposed Wau, rather than Juba, as the future capital of the South.

THE DEBATE

The debate and controversy over the "re-division" proposal lasted for well over two and a half years. Launched in February 1981 the debate continued unabated until the former Southern Region was dismantled by a Presidential Decree in June 1983. The opposing camps each attempted to give their particular viewpoint intellectual credence and respectability. The debate had only one primary objective: to persuade the general public and to win the support of President Nimeiri in Khartoum. The actual task of disputation consisted in either pointing out the beneficial effects of re-division or its obnoxious fall-outs. In the latter case there was constant appeal to emotions and nationalist sentiments. Thus while the opponents assumed a nationalist posture and barely made allusions to ethnic domination, for the propounders ethnic hegemony was the crux of the matter. To the divisionists the unity of the South was anathema; to the antis, the unity and solidarity of the South was more or less sacrosanct and the call for re-division of the South was tantamount to high treason.

The venues of the debate were mostly public and academic fora such as National and Regional assemblies, the University campuses of Juba and Khartoum and the media. However, the most telling part of the whole exercise was contained in secret and confidential petitions and correspondences to President Nimeiri himself.

It has not always been easy to disentangle the rather confused, contradictory and sometimes facile arguments advanced by the pro-division lobby. This picture contrasts sharply with that of their adversaries who presented a rather well-argued and coherent position. In the pages that follow the reader is served summaries of argued positions rather than a dialectical discourse or point-by-point refutations of opposing views. The re-division debate has been such a bitter, acrimonious and divisive matter that Southern opinions are easily polarised into pros and cons.

Arguments against re-division

The arguments advanced against the re-division may be broken down into five broad categories:

(i)   Economic viability
(ii)   Instigation and fanning of "tribalism"
(iii) Balkanization of the South
(iv)   Destruction of the special autonomous status of the South
(v)   Constitutionality

The first point is so obvious that it does not require much elaboration. It simply states Sudan's economy was an ailing and shrinking economy so that reasons of economy and financial constraints militated against a regional proliferation scheme in the South. As Sudan's foreign debts were in excess of 8 billion USD, it was a financial and economic folly to propose a scheme of administrative re-organization when the coffers were empty. Put rhetorically, if there were barely sufficient funds to run the existing Southern Regional Government based in Juba, how were the proponents going to finance three Regions? In brief, further regionalization of the South would only put an unwarranted burden upon the Sudan's meagre financial and other resources.[2]

The anti-division group possessed foresight and some of their warnings were prophetic indeed! The battle-cry of the divisionists had been tribal domination, more precisely, Dinka domination: re-division was to put an end to this alleged domination of the South by one tribe. The anti-divisionist movement charged that the call for splitting the South on account of ethnic domination amounted to tribal instigation; that this was a deliberate fanning of ethnic and tribal animosities. The fears and warnings of the antis have been vindicated by the current internecine tribal warfare in the Wau area in the Bahr El Ghazal, the organization and arming of tribal Militia, first in Equatoria then in Bahr El Ghazal and Upper Nile and in the two Western Provinces of Dar Fur and Kordofan. In retrospect, it is quite impossible to escape the force of argument for the charge of tribal instigation and fanning of tribal animosities.

At least one debater accused the chief proponent of re-division of either presenting self-contradictory arguments or being insincere. The so-called Dinka domination could not have been the product of a self-conscious and calculated policy. Otherwise, how could one account for the election of Lt. General (Rtd) Joseph Lagu to be the President of the High Executive Council (HEC) by the second Regional Assembly in February 1978 despite the fact that he was not a Dinka? In his hour of euphoria and jubilation Lagu is reported to have stated that "the *unity of the Southern people* which had enabled him to acquire the leadership in the Region reflected political maturity of the Southern people and that that unity should be promoted, *safeguarded and preserved*".[3] That statesman-like speech had earned him applause then because he, Lagu, (who comes from the Madi, a numerically small tribe), could not have come to power without the support of the other ethnic groups (i.e. Dinka and kindred) who commanded the majority of the seats in the Regional Assembly. The same critic concluded that the re-division proposal was being pursued by what he called "a knot of disgruntled politicians who cannot wait for another round of the recognized political tournament (i.e. general election)".

---

[2] Phrased from the records of a debate organized by the Southern students in the University of Khartoum, March 1988. The students were organized in the African National Front (ANF).

[3] Isaiah Majok, *Sudanow*, April 1982. The "political maturity of the Southern people" refers to the fact that the regional assembly, which has a sizeable Dinka component, has opted to elect a non-Dinka for the highest regional post.

The perception of the Southern Sudanese student body in general, and of the University of Khartoum in particular, has always constituted something of a touchstone of Southern Regional sentiment. Traditionally, the students echoed the genuine fears and aspirations of the Southern masses. It is no wonder that they raised some of the most pertinent points in the anti-division camp. For this and other reasons I have quoted them at length. For instance, the very ground upon which the re-division proposal had rested was thought of as most unhealthy. Re-division, if effected as a device for checking ethnic domination,"will keep our (i.e. Southern) people away from one another almost for ever" (Document B). Furthermore, re-combination or re-constituting the South will be an impossible task. The students cited the example of the partition of Korea in substantiation.

Arguments Nos. 3 and 4 are best taken together as they are closely intertwined. Balkanization of the South and the consequent destruction of its special autonomous status were probably the most potent weapons in the armoury of the anti-division movement. The gist of it all was that the proposal to divide the South into two or more smaller Regions was none other than the familiar colonialist strategy of divide and rule, long entertained and cherished by its enemies. If that were to happen (as it did afterwards), then the South would lose its special African identity and be reduced to a mere geographical expression (Document A). Balkanization would grievously weaken the South in anticipation of Nimeiri's and the Muslim Brotherhood's grand design to Islamize the entire country, including the South. It was patently clear at that time that President Nimeiri was bent on implementing the policies engineered by the Muslim Brotherhood and their allies. Southern students in the United Kingdom and Ireland got the clue when, in October 1981, the Minister of Cooperatives addressed a group of Sudanese students in the City of Manchester in the following manner

> Nimeiri is a sick man and spent force. He will hand over the Government to us (meaning the Muslim Brothers and their allies). But we told him that he should hand over the South to us as he found it before 1972. We know how we will deal with them (i.e. the Southerners). Whether the Southerners like it or not, Nimeiri is going to divide the South. (Document C)

Having detected the machinations of President Nimeiri, the students hastened to warn him. In a terse and intimidatory tone, indicative of the shape of things to come, their letter to President Nimeiri continued thus

> If your intention is to take back the South to the pre-1972 period ... then the people of the South will not stand aloof to see their legitimate and constitutional rights being tampered with. We deem it our duty to defend the existence and *identity of the South by all means and at any cost*. The South will seek political, moral and material support (they did not indicate from where) and call upon the people of the other Regions of the Sudan to terminate the so-called Central Government of minority interests.

The students' letter actually proceeded to call upon "our people in the South, the West, the East and other peace-loving peoples of Sudan to rise and to resist these concerted conspiracies" with a view to installing a democratically-based Government of the majority in the Sudan. In an outburst of anger verging on disrespect the Executive Committee of the Student's Union of Southern Sudanese (SUSS) stated categorically that "the Southern People do vehemently reject and ostensibly condemn and will resist treacherous moves by you, Mr. President, to divide and fragment the historical entity of the Southern Sudan".

In a separate memo of the same date addressed to Southern Sudanese compatriots, the Executive Committee of SUSS made a passionate plea for Southern unity. Having stated that President Nimeiri was about to deal a final blow to African identity in the Southern Region the memo emphatically reminded fellow Southerners that, historically, they were one and the same people no matter what: a united community with a common destiny and a common struggle. Re-division should not be permitted to drive a wedge into their ranks. Because Nimeiri had succeeded in dismantling the military wing of the Southern Sudan, the Anya Nya, he expected no meaningful military opposition against re-division. But "we tell the man (i.e. Nimeiri) that the people of South have never lost the will to defend their interests and their existence and identity" (Document C). On an ominous note the students warned that unless the Southern Sudanese remained united, peace and prosperity would be impossible in the future. Needless to say, the current civil war is but a vindication of this statement. Finally, they called upon the "oppressed and exploited" peoples of the Sudan as a whole to join the Southern people in condemning the minority clique Government in Khartoum and in asking it to refrain from the politics of re-division.

The Southern students at the University of Khartoum organised ostensibly under the banner of the African Nationalists Front (ANF) attempted to hammer the last nail into the coffin. The ANF was at pains, and went to great lengths, in an attempt to demonstrate the gravity of the impending evils of re-division. Their point of departure was that the year 1972 (of the Addis Ababa Agreement) marked a sharp turn in the history of the Southern people. It was a landmark in that the South accepted something far less than their original demand. This compromise solution was dictated as much by practical politics as the Nimeiri regime's overt and sincere recognition of the Southern problem. The Southerners accepted that compromise in good faith and thenceforth the concept of a Southern Region within the context of one united Sudan was developed. However, events leading to the demand to split the South had demonstrated quite convincingly that President Nimeiri had ceased to be the godfather of Southern Regional autonomy.

The students were unshakeable in their belief that balkanization was not to be seen or taken in isolation. On the contrary, it came at the end of a succession of events each of which entailed Northern ill-intention toward the

South. For instance, there was a proposal in 1977 for the creation of a Unity Province to encompass the oil zone based at Bentieu and to be administered directly from the republican palace. Southern Sudanese MPs in the National Assembly successfully fought and warded off the idea. The plan was instantly dropped. The next move was the North-South border dispute of 1980 (Badal, 1983), the effect of which would have been to annex the oil fields and other resource-rich areas of the South to the adjacent provinces of the North. Because the Southerners were united in their opposition to the attempt to alter the borders, the scheme was foiled. Realising that the unity and solidarity of the Southerners were stumbling blocks to their secret oil designs, so argued the students, Nimeiri and his political allies conceived of a device to weaken the South by preoccupying the Southerners with a divisive issue thereby distracting them from the real issues.

The educated Southerners, as distinct from their illiterate compatriots, were supposed to play a leading role in the fight against these divisive policies from the North. Time was opportune for them to play their historic role of leadership guidance, enlightment and to speak for the Southern masses. Previously, Southerners had the excuse that they were not sufficiently equipped either politically, culturally or educationally. All that had changed the memorandum continued:"Today, and for the first time in our history, we have all types of professional men and soldiers. If we fail to anticipate the obvious dangers involved in the issue (of re-division) neither the coming generations nor the international community will forgive us. Our responsibility is to think clearly and critically before we support or reject disintegration of the South".

The students, in this respect, exhibited an extraordinary display of foresight and political maturity. It was as if someone much older and wiser was putting words into their mouths. Undeniably, short-term benefits would acrue from the regionalization of the South to a restricted sector of the educated Southerners. Nevertheless, anybody with a clear mind and conscience could not fail to foresee the permanent damage it would cause to the South's social and political standing. It was incomprehensible, said the students, that some Southerners were calling for fragmentation at a time when the South was in dire need of unity, solidarity and social cohesion. Then, almost solemnly, the students' memorandum came to the very core of the matter. They advised fellow Southerners against drawing a false analogy between regionalization of the Northern Sudan and division of the South; these were two entirely different things: *"We had to lose lives and property to get the little that we talk of today"* (my emphasis). Rather than calling for re-division the Southerners should have been demanding something greater, nay, a strong federal system.

The constitutionality argument is derived from the Addis Ababa Agreement and the Self-Government Act of 1972. The Act was entrenched into the permanent Constitution of 1973 as an organic Law. The argument was based on the fact that splitting the Southern Region would amount to violation of the organic Law and the constitution itself. The Addis Ababa Agreement was an internationally recognized peace treaty and its unilateral abrogation by the Sudan Government would signal a dangerous precedent, not to mention the severe damage it would cause to Sudan's image abroad. Besides, there were technical hurdles ahead to be overcome.

The purely technical point of how in fact to go about dividing the South (if partition there must be) generated just as much controversy as did the original proposal. It became a hotly contested issue because the adoption of the correct, legal and constitutional methods might not lead, contrary to expectations, to the splitting up of the South after all. Some of the divisionists were fully aware of this fact hence their insistence that the President of the Republic should effect division of the Southern Region by decree.

The dilemma of the legal pundits may be expressed briefly thus: which is prior in time and importance, amending the Constitution first and then the Act or the other way round? If, by first amending Article VIII of the Constitution to allow for the existence of more than one Region in the South, but subsequent referendum upheld the *status quo*, then what will happen to the Constitutional amendment? Article 8 of the national Constitution prescribes the following:"Within the unitary Sudan there shall be established in the Southern Region a Regional Self-Government in accordance with the Southern Provinces Regional Self-Government Act, 1972, which shall be an organic Law and shall not be amended except in accordance with provisions thereof". That provision may be found in Article 34 of the Act, which is even more difficult to amend than amending the National Constitution.[4] The Act could only be amended with the approval of "a majority of two thirds of the citizens of the Southern Region in a referendum to be carried out in the Region".[5] The Constitution was much easier to amend because it required only a vote by a three quarters majority of the members of the people's assembly.

A referendum was not a simple matter either as it had never been carried out in the Sudan before. It had never been a common practice in Sudan, leave alone the South, except for the periodical mock plebiscitary democratic method by which the President of the Republic was elected. Given the dearth of accurate census figures, the poor skeletal transportation and communication system, the extensive borders with neighbouring countries and many Southern tribes astride them, especially in Equatoria, the referendum must be a daunting task, indeed! Electoral fraud, faked figures, counterfeit results, and further disputations leading ominously to violence could be the order of the day. When the issue of re-division was introduced to the floor of the Regional Assembly in Juba on 22nd. March 1981 in an extraordinary ses-

---

[4] For further details see Deng Awur Wenying in *Sudanow*, 7 (1), January 1982.
[5] The Southern Provinces Regional Self-Government Act, 1972, was a derivative of the Addis Ababa Agreement of 1972, which terminated Sudan's first civil war.

sion, it was roundly defeated. After a week of discussion the resolution finally adopted on 28 March rejected the proposal on the ground that the Self-Government Act and the relevant provisions of the permanent Constitution of the Sudan would be adversely affected.[6] So what sense was there in a referendum?

Arguments for re-division

Broadly speaking, the position of the divisionist movement may be summed up in the following terms:

1. Administrative failures and malpractices
2. Advantages of partition
3. Popular participation
4. Reply to critics
5. Dinka hegemony

The principal indictment of the former Regional Government system had been its failure to deliver the goods i.e. the basic needs of the Southern People. Viewed retrospectively, the aims and objectives for which the Southern masses shed blood for 17 years, had been totally ignored by the Regional Government (Rephrased from Document D). Further allegations had it that the system had nurtured incompetent people who only allowed malpractices to flourish. There then followed a litany of abuses

> A few people have benefited at the expense of the Southern public. Corruption has been rampant and accepted as a mode of administration. Individuals have acquired properties, built huge houses, opened farms, loaded (sic) their houses with public vehicles, spent thousands of public funds on buying unprofitable (sic) cattle, acquired many residential plots on premium land in Juba and even commissioners (of Provinces) have turned to black market practices with Government blessings, resulting in soaring prices of essential commodities throughout the Region. (Document D)

Furthermore, it was alleged that victims of flood, epidemic diseases, hunger and other natural disasters were often left to fend for themselves and, where donations were made, these went to private pockets. Having realized the inadequacy of this system, some Southerners were prompted to demand an alternative system, namely, the splitting up of the Southern Region into three governments and three assemblies instead of one corrupt, inefficient, and centralized Government based in Juba. This position was then backed by invocation of the decentralization policy in the rest of the country.

Taking stock of the same Regional Government performance one critic[7] with considerable experience in the operation of the system had this to say

---

[6] Proceedings of the Third Regional Assembly, Juba, March 1981.
[7] Philip Obang, a former Ambassador of Sudan to Uganda, former Commissioner of Upper Nile and several times Regional Minister of Education.

The Anya Nya forces in the Army, Police and Prisons as a fighting force to protect Southern gains have been destroyed; the 1974 Jonglei Canal Scheme riots in Juba resulting in deaths and brutalities could have been avoided by the provision of adequate information system in advance; the South's total absence from representation in the Central Government institutions and parastatal bodies was due to the Regional Government's desire to avoid risking damage to its reputation of the "good guys"; the disappearance of accountability from the administrative and political vocabulary of the South and its substitution with the right to mismanage and dispose of public funds by officials for selfish interest; salaries not paid for months on end for the same reasons; and, above all, the despicable practice of false witch-hunts by state security agents for alleged enemies of the Addis Accord, the SSU and national unity.[8]

The thrust of this argument was that the policies pursued by the Regional Government during the one decade of its existence had undermined, distorted and counteracted the development of Southern nationalist consciousness. Selfish, sectional or factional interests had certainly caused untold damage to the common good of the South.

When it came to the benefits of a re-divided South, the divisionists put forth the argument that dividing the South would make for faster socio-economic development of that Region; that it would foster the competitive spirit and bring the elite closer to the masses. In the words of Lt. General Joseph Lagu, the former leader of Anya Nya until the Addis Agreement was signed in 1972

> Further regionalization makes for easy administration, quick and faster development of the South; it will instill the spirit of competition in the Southern people. Some form of competition is healthy for the progress of the South and the South should be able to compete even with some Northern Regions. It will bring the elite closer to the masses. Spreading out the elite to Wau and Malakal will bring them nearer to their people and avoid their concentration in Juba. (Document E)

In view of the almost "primitive" economic conditions of the South and the case for economy of scale, the very tiny size of the Southern Sudanese elite whether political, administrative or otherwise, the hollowness of this form of argument is self-evident. It is not clear whether the elite in question is a political, administrative or commercial and business elite. The great majority of the commercial and business elite in the South came from the Northern Regions anyway. Furthermore, neither habitational contiguity nor physical proximity can bridge the elite-mass gap.

Similarly, one may dismiss as naive the suggestion that dividing the South into smaller Regions would "dilute some of the tribal aspects of our politics, remove tensions that are developing as a result of grievances caused by tribalism and pave the way for greater harmony among our people" (Document

---

[8] Quoted from a letter by Philip Obang addressed to Southern Sudanese compatriots and dated 19th March 1981, Khartoum.

D). Nor can it be taken seriously, when the divisionists in their election manifesto of 1981 claimed that a vote for their candidate was "a vote for the permanent removal of corruption, nepotism, bribery and other (unspecified) malpractices" (Document D). The aftermath of the re-division has not substantiated any of these arguments.

As a matter of fact the list of the alleged advantages of the re-division was almost endless, with each item sounding more promising than the preceding one. Consider the following benefits

> It (re-division) will arrest the drift of rural population to urban centres, in this case Juba, and thereby avoid the social dangers of such migrations; it will bring the decision-makers closer to the masses where Regional problems can be more effectively resolved. This is so because the authorities will be better acquainted with the local conditions, problems and mood of the people than the present Regional Government in Juba. Internal trade will be stimulated and each Region will specialize in the exploitation of its own resources and thereby encourage exchange and economic activity between Regions. For instance, Equatorial Region will specialize in production of tea, coffee, fruits, timber products and building materials which it can trade for cattle and fish that are so abundant in the Upper Nile or rice and animal products in Bahr El Ghazal on the basis of comparative advantage. It will enable each Region to identify its own priorities and to allocate the scarce resources accordingly... (Document D)

As for the popular participation argument there was first, the terminological muddle between the two terms "decentralization" or *la markazia* (Arabic) and "regionalism". Regionalism as political devolution was confused with the broad category of decentralization, for regionalization could mean either the strengthening of an existing Region by increasing its powers and functions or simply splitting it up into two or more sub-Regions. The divisionists taking their cue from the fact that Regional units in the Northern Sudan were conveniently patterned on the basis of the old provinces, jumped to the conclusion that the South should be treated in a similar fashion. One argument which held its ground was that Juba was increasingly behaving like another central authority *vis-à-vis* the Provinces and the Local Councils. Crudely put, "Juba took power from Khartoum and kept it to itself" (Document E). This practice is said to have limited the scope of popular participation, a fact which ran counter to the official policy of the SSU and the May Regime. "The pattern of having small, manageable Regions had been set by the North and the emulation of this experience by the South would satisfy the aspirations of the greatest number of people possible" (Document F).

The *antis* re-division movement had laid a number of charges and accusations at the doorstep of the proponents of re-divisionism, by charging them with greed, cupidity and playing into the hands of Northern politicians. The net result of all this would be a weakened South *vis-à-vis* a determined North. One exponent of re-division dismissed the fears of Northern domination as baseless and self-motivated, arguing that the North could not have dismembered itself in order to dominate the South. The *manifesto* of the divisionist candidates also played on the same tone:"Our opponents charge that by having three Regions the Arabs will come back to dominate and rule us. This is a baseless and naked lie. The three Regions, three Parliaments and three Governments will be run by Southerners from these three Regions. Each Region will elect its own Members of Parliament, appoint its own administrations, police, prison warders and supervise its own hospitals, schools, development institutes and schemes" (Document D).

One serious accusation was that the call for re-division was an unpatriotic and treasonable act. The anti re-division movement issued a stern warning that should re-division of the South be pushed through, there would be bloodshed all over the South. Once again the reply of some proponents exhibited naivety:"How is bloodshed going to come about? Who is going to fight who? Is it because some tribes have been armed by the previous Regional Government against Equatorians?" (Document D). Lt. General Lagu, the chief architect of the re-division proposal, argued bitterly and emphatically that nobody could give him lessons in patriotism:"I cannot be accused of selling out Southern interests; I fought for them for ten years."[9]

Equally serious was the accusation that dividing the South into smaller Regions would sound the death knell of the Addis Ababa Agreement. Some of the leading Equatorian politicians were unimpressed. They argued that splitting the Southern Region would be done in accordance with the Articles of the Self-Government Act of 1972 and that the boundaries of the Southern Sudan would remain as they were on 1.January.1956. They stated that,"the people of the Southern Sudan will continue to remain within the same boundaries" (Document B). To substantiate this conviction Lt. General Lagu addressed the politbureau of the SSU, of which he was member, in the following manner:"Allow me Mr. President, (reference here is to President Nimeiri), to solemnly declare before you and my colleagues that upon my honour, as a former officer in the Sudanese Armed Forces, I not only cherish this document, but I am prepared to lay down my life for its defence just as I (would have) laid down the same life to bring it about." (Document F). On another occasion, Lt. General Lagu stated quite categorically that the Addis Agreement was neither the Bible nor the Koran as to be so secret and unalterable as the laws of nature.[10] In the heat of argument the obvious contradiction between the two statements went unnoticed by the general.

The actual or deeper motives of the advocates of re-division centred upon the desire to break an alleged Dinka hegemony. Lt. General Lagu, for instance, made no secret of his desire to eliminate what he considered as Dinka domination. With rare vehemence he declared that Dinka participation in the 17 year civil war had been nominal and yet they were the primary beneficiaries of the local autonomy:"The civil war was fought mainly by people from

---

[9] Lt. General Lagu in an interview with the *Middle East*, No. 90, May 1982:23–24.
[10] Phrased from a televised interview with Lt. General Lagu conducted by Sudan Television in January 1982.

Equatoria, but since the Dinkas are the biggest single tribe they have tried to monopolize the political posts."[11] Venting a tribalist sentiment he continued:"It is time we cut the Dinkas down to their original size. They must go home; they have nothing to do in Equatoria".

However, conclusive evidence of a Dinka secret plan to dominate the South was never produced. Crude statistical evidence hastily compiled by Lagu to demonstrate the extent of Dinka hold over the Regional Government was less than convincing (Document G). The figures produced pertained to the Government of Abel Alier (1981). He did not have statistical data covering the period right from the inception of the Regional Government down to 1981 or statistical data of Dinka high office - holders compared to their percentage of the population as a whole. At the same time, Lagu could not account for the existence of a disgruntled section of Dinka political leadership which he himself skilfully manipulated to the advantage of his own faction. Lagu also maintained a circle of confidants which included certain key figures of the then defunct SANU Party. I wish to venture the hypothesis that the re-division campaign itself may have in fact galvanized Dinka unity and solidarity which, previously, was non-existent. The key to the success of that campaign by Lagu had little or nothing to do with persuasive arguments. Rather, it had to do with the artful playing on the fears and tribal sentiments of the Equatorians coupled with the steady support and encouragement of President Nimeiri.

Some Equatorians have argued that re-division of the South was a foregone conclusion; that it was foreseen and, indeed, predictable in view of the policies pursued by the Regional Government for the first eight years of its life. They singled out educational policies which envisaged lower intake marks for the provinces of Upper Nile and Bahr El Ghazal while it raised the hurdle for Equatoria. Much cynicism also surrounds the waves of student unrest throughout Southern schools which forced the departure of Equatoria students from the old and established secondary schools such as Rumbek and Bussere, both located in Bahr El Ghazal. It was alleged that the students' violence against each other was politically motivated.[12] A rational response to the suspected Dinka hegemony (or to a tendency thereto) would have been for the non-Dinka to have checked it through their combined electoral strength in the regional assembly. The Dinka, who constitute the single largest ethnic group in the South, cannot be completely isolated or excluded from the Government of the South. As MPs in the central Parliament put it: "If any Dinka leader has become a tribal chief and is turning regional institutions of the South into [a] Dinka platform, the majority of the non-Dinkas have the power to bring such a leader down and destroy the structures he has

---

[11] Interview, *Middle East*, op.cit.
[12] Personal communication with Jimmy Wango, John Oller, Gajuk Wurbang and Deputy Governor, Francis Wanjo, (intellectuals from Equatoria), December 1984.

built" (Document H). Diagram 2 on page 24 shows the realignment of forces along the North-South fault line during 1985–1989.

Diagram 2. *Realignment of forces along the North-South fault line*

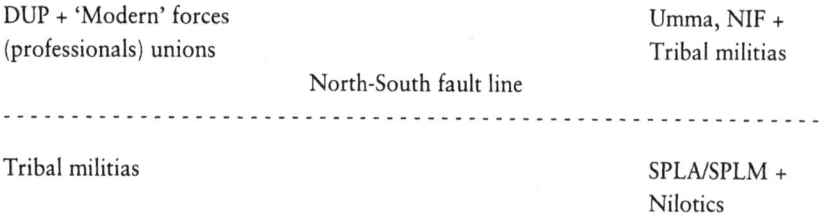

DUP + 'Modern' forces	Umma, NIF +
(professionals) unions	Tribal militias

North-South fault line

- -

Tribal militias	SPLA/SPLM +
	Nilotics

CONCLUSION

The re-division debate exposed the extent of Southern Sudanese cleavages and their exploitation or manipulation by the political elite at the centre. The fear of ethnic domination, real or apparent, electrified counter group opposition deeply committed to breaking the alleged "Dinka domination" through the device of splitting up the Southern region. However, the proponents of re-division would not have succeeded in their scheme had it not been for the machinations of President Nimeiri and the Muslim Brotherhood. Dr. Turabi, the present General Secretary of the National Islamic Front (NIF) was, in the early seventies, head of the Muslim Brotherhood organization and a political/religious adviser to President Jaafar Nimeiri. Some argue that Nimeiri and the Brotherhood had conjured up, in collaboration with Lagu, the re-division of the South as part of their grand design to weaken the South in anticipation of, or preparation for, imposition of Islamic Sharia on the whole country. Once decreed, it would then become impossible for any Sudanese Muslim leader to undo it. The presumption was that Southern disunity would militate against any serious opposition coming from that quarter.

The re-division of the South took place in circumstances of a gradual erosion of Southern Sudanese nationalism. Tribalism was surely a scapegoat and a camouflage for the political failures of Southern Sudanese leadership. In this regard the whole spectrum of Southern Sudanese leadership and intellectuals is to blame, in the post-Addis era it seemed to possess no vision nor sense of direction for the South. It was as if acceptance by the South of peace, unity and security precluded either articulation of a special Southern interest or protection of its identity. The Southerners had accepted a political system whose operation compromised their national identity and was ultimately antithetical to it. Hence over-display of Southern Sudanese nationalism became a political taboo. Elite and authorities alike shied away from glorifica-

tion of Southern heroes and martyrs. For instance, there was no special re-
membrance day for the martyrs of the Torit uprising; no statue erected in
commemoration of the victims of the July massacres in Juba and Wau; not a
single road, street or school or hospital named or erected in memory of some
of the greatest Southern Sudanese national heroes such as William Deng
Nhial, Rev. Fr. Saturino, or Aggrey Jadein, to name but a few. Equally, the
multiplicity of conflicting loyalties between supporting Nimeiri and pleasing
the centre, while treading delicately on the path of promoting the Southern
interests, were other restraining considerations that made it difficult if not
impossible for Southern leadership to formulate and implement a coherent,
consistent and long-term policy for the South.

The greatest weakness and cardinal sin of the autonomy arrangement
must be the lack of definite, predictable and assured sources of finance for
the regional government. Availability of funds would have given support to
ongoing development projects, facilitated local planning and fulfilled recruitment needs, thereby easing incessant client/patron pressures that partly
triggered the re-division demand. Starving the region of necessary funds
meant the centre could, and naturally did, use purse strings to control and
influence political behaviour of regional politicians, in a way that was quite
inimical to the interest of the South, by playing off one faction against the
other.

The lure of politics and the privileges of power added another dimension
to an already complex situation. The attraction of the profession of politics
to the Southerners stemmed from the fact that the state and its bureaucracy
were the chief employers. Politics was seen as providing a short-cut to riches,
power and prestige and to the exercise of patronage; it thus attracted the
highly limited number of Southern professional and technical staff as well as
the sub-professional and peasants. It was not uncommon to find the South's
best trained teachers (especially), doctors, lawyers and engineers lured away
from their professions. Furthermore, politics was not viewed as requiring any
special skills or training. It was a profession which attracted both the doctor
and the farmer; the mechanic as well as medical assistants, none of whom
had ever read any textbook on politics or a political biography. In circumstances of this kind, all the service sectors suffered greatly while intense pressure was exerted upon the political system, which itself lacked independent
sources of cash or sufficient funds to go all round.

As for the political cleavages that developed and led ultimately to the destruction of Southern autonomy, conflict of personalities of the two dominant leaders, Lt. General Lagu and Abel Alier, partly reflected some basic
socio-political divisions within the South as well as other differences and
anomalies. As discussed by Tvedt in his paper, Lagu was a military man
while Abel Alier was a lawyer and administrator; the former came from a
small Equatorian tribe, the Madi, Alier was a Dinka and from Bor. Lagu
who led the Anya Nya and the SSLM did not form the first regional

Government as might have been expected of a victorious or semi-victorious liberation movement. Instead, he was appointed Major General in the Sudanese army in April 1972, the same month Abel was appointed regional premier. Obviously, the two represented different traditions, different provinces, ethnic groups, and different networks. I would agree with Tvedt that the degree of conflict between these two leaders, until the splitting up of the South in 1983, reflected the extent to which the South was unable to control or counter centrifugal forces within itself.

Thus for the South history repeats itself; indeed is always repeating itself: at the Juba Conference in 1947, the Round Table Conference of 1965, in the Anya Nya movement, during the autonomy experiment and, most recently, within the SPLM-SPLA. The August 28 split in the SPLM-SPLA represents a water-shed, a turning point, and a decisive moment. The point is, where do we go from here? What is the next line of action for the South?

The preceding discussion has uncovered three key variables, namely, external element or factor; financial independence or lack of it; and internal cleavages. The third and last point is very important since the management and resolution of the first two depend upon it. Political divisions exist in any society; they are part and parcel of the natural order of things. The question is not so much how to do away with them as how to transcend them, turn them into a manageable device for reconstruction. The realization that the enemy is liable to exploit any crack that develops within the Southern community should serve as incentive for a unified stand. As it is, Southerners have two options or courses of action open to them. They can persist in the present trend of regional, ethnic and personality rivalries supported by an uncompromising attitude. A corollary trend is the formation of alliances dictated by the political expediency with political forces in the North, e.g. tribal militia in alliance with the religious sectarian parties and Islamic fundamentalists, viz., Umma, DUP and the National Islamic Front (NIF); while the SPLM/SPLA has the sympathy of the so-called progressive forces in the country. The end result of such development will be the eventual Arabicization and Islamization of the South and complete eradication or obliteration of an African identity and Christian in the South. After one hundred years the Southerners, as Professor Ali Mazrui once said, will not only be Muslims but will also claim that they are Arabs (1986:Ch. 7). This course of action naturally aids the process of national integration, save that it would mean permanent subjugation, not partnership, of the South and the other peripheries by the clique in the developed triangle.

Alternatively, the Southerners may realize that there are greater stakes involved in the unity and solidarity of the South: the need for preservation of Southern identity, the protection of its natural wealth: land and waters from the Jonglei canal, oil from the oil wells in Bentieu, forestry products and minerals; gold, uranium, copper, manganese, etc. Survival in a united Sudan also imposes the necessity for unity of the Southerners, regardless of ethnic origin and despite regional and personal rivalries. The imperatives of confronting the central government elite as a bloc are there. The strategy is to revive the old Southern Front ideology, solicit the alliance and cooperation of other peripheral groups in the North such as the Nuba, Fur, Zaghawa, Beja etc., to force adoption of a genuine federal structure for the country as a whole, with adequate financial provisions for the federating states.

Since cleavages in the South are about the question, "Who governs?", this point must be addressed. Governance by some persons or groups in any place and at any time is unavoidable. After re-division, the Dinka became the dominant group in Bahr el Ghazal. Given their numerical superiority there, that is unavoidable. In upper Nile the Nuer are in a controlling position. That fact, too, cannot be avoided. In Equatoria, the swing of the pendulum or tug of war is between the Azande in western Equatoria and the Bari-speaking groups in the centre. It seems that the fact of who governs does not matter much. There will always be someone or some group in power at any one time. The essential point relevant to the South is the creation of a supra-ethnic and supra-regional organization, whereby the elite will have a special role, a special task and duty. Ethnic partnership demands that the political elite must stand up and resist, not succumb, to pressures for preferential treatment from their respective communities. They will have to play an educative role by reminding their fellow tribesmen that there are others like them with equal needs, entitled to a just and equitable treatment, that each and every group in the South has its inherent worth, for there is good in every society.

REFERENCES

Books and articles

Badal, R.K., 1983, *Oil and Regional Sentiment in Southern Sudan*. Discussion paper No. 80. Syracuse University, Dept. of Geography.
Fr. Dellagiacoma (ed.), 1990, Stanislaw Payasama, Autobiography: *How a Slave became a Minister*. Khartoum.
Mazrui, A.A., 1986, *The Africans: A Triple Heritage*. BBC Publications.
Wai, Dunstan, M. (ed.), 1973, *The Problem of National Integration*. Frank Cass and Co. Ltd, London.

Magazines and popular press

Deng Awur Wenying, 1982,"As I see it". *Sudanow*, 7(1), January 1982.
Isaiah Majok, 1982,"As I see it". *Sudanow*, April 1982.
Lt. General Lagu, 1982,"An interview", *Middle East Magazine*, No. 91, May 1982.
Lt. General Lagu, 1982,"An interview", *Sudan Television*, January 1982.

Unpublished documents

A. Record of live debate on re-division organized by African Nationalist Front (ANF), in the University of Khartoum, March 1981.
B. Memorandum on re-division addressed to concerned citizens of Southern Sudan by ANF, 13th December 1981.
C. Letter of the Executive Committee of the Southern Students' Union (SUSS) in the United Kingdom and Ireland to President Nimeiri. London, 22nd. December 1981.
D. Manifesto of the candidates for Re-division in the National Elections of 1981. Equatoria Central Committee, 1981.
E. Seminar presentation by Lt. General Lagu to the Department of Political Science, University of Khartoum, September 1981.
F. Address speech by Lt. Lagu to the Politbureau of the Sudanese Socialist Union (SSU). Khartoum, September 1981.
G. Lt. General Lagu, 1982, Decentralization: A necessity to the Southern Provinces of the Sudan.
H. The Re-division of Southern Sudan: Why it must be rejected? The Solidarity Committee of the Southern Members of the 4th People's National Assembly. Omdurman, no date.

Destruction and Reconstruction in the Economy of the Southern Sudan

Douglas H. Johnson

This paper draws primarily on two assessment missions to the rural areas of the Southern Sudan on which I was employed by the World Food Programme in 1990 and 1991.[1] It attempts to answer the question: how far is the reconstruction of the Southern Sudan possible before peace is secured? I will first give a very brief summary of the scale of destruction in the rural areas and some of the towns most directly affected by the civil war since 1983. This will be followed by a general assessment of the relief activities undertaken during the three years of Operation Lifeline Sudan (1989–91), and some of the constraints upon those activities. I conclude with a discussion of the prospects for rehabilitation.[2]

PRE-1983 DEVELOPMENT AND POST-1983 DESTRUCTION

The Southern Sudan's historic underdevelopment is the cause of a continuing bitter political grievance among Southern Sudanese; yet despite the disappointment at the failure of development to meet expectations during the brief period of the Addis Ababa peace (1972–83), considerable sums of money were spent on development in the South, and a number of development projects were undertaken by governmental, non-governmental and international agencies. While recognizing that the overall concentration of economic wealth and power remained in the northern Sudan during that time, it nevertheless has to be recognized that by 1983 numerous places in the north were lagging far behind some of the more developed areas of the Southern Region.

Development projects were both small and large scale, focusing on the improvement of infrastructure and services, as well as experimenting with improving the overall economic productivity of the South. There was, however, very little coherent planning of development needs and priorities by the Southern Regional Government, nor was there much practical co-ordination of development projects undertaken by different agencies. For the purposes of this paper it is not important to calculate the total amount of money spent

---

[1] United Nations, Life Line Sudan, an investigation into production capability in the rural Southern Sudan. A report on food sources and needs (Nairobi, June 1990), and report of the WF/FAO/UNICEF crop, food and emergency needs assessment Mission, Southern Sudan, 29 October–14 December 1991 (Rome, December 1991).
[2] Both the analysis and opinions expressed are my own, and in no way represent the opinions or policies held by the World Food Programme, or any other agency working within the relief umbrella of operation Lifeline Sudan.

on development in the South during the eleven years of peace; nor even to judge whether the money was efficiently spent. What is important is to note the unevenness of development. Most projects were concentrated in Western and Eastern Equatoria provinces (especially Torit, Yei River and Yambio districts), including road projects (both trunk and feeder roads), agricultural and forestry projects (both small scale and commercial), and a host of health and education sector improvements. Development proposed for Upper Nile and Bahr El Ghazal tended to be either large-scale and long-term, such as the Jonglei Canal, or experimental, like the Aweil Rice Growing Scheme; neither of which provided any real development for the regions in which they were located before war forced their abandonment. There was, however, some improvement of basic services and infrastructure, especially in the provision of rural water supplies (through deep bore wells, hand-pumps and *hafirs*) in Jonglei Province. The Jonglei Executive Organ managed to get school and health dispensary buildings built as a spin-off from the construction of the Jonglei Canal, but such buildings were not well staffed or equipped. The veterinary service, which was supported by a number of development agencies, did function well in preventative cattle vaccination campaigns, but less well in overseeing the general health of rural livestock.

In addition to this there was some expansion of indigenous commercial activity which began to rival (in however small a way) the northern Sudanese based *jallaba* network. This was especially so in the dried-fish trade, which was largely in the hands of Dinka and Nuer fishermen and traders, and which contributed significantly to the Southern Region's export earnings. It was also true of the cattle trade, whereby the pastoral economies of Bahr El Ghazal and Upper Nile not only supplied the meat markets of the towns of Equatoria, but also met some of the demand in the northern Sudan.

The civil war began in earnest after the Bor Mutiny in May 1983. The disruption of the rural areas was far more immediate and far more severe than anything experienced during the fighting in the first civil war in the 1960s and early 1970s. This was because the rural population in many of the Nilotic districts became a specific target as part of the government's military strategy to deny the SPLA active civilian support in those areas where the guerrillas were most strongly represented. Thus at a very early stage in the war the governments in Khartoum and Juba supported tribal militias among the Murle, Toposa and Mundari in attacks on the civilian Dinka population of Jonglei and Lakes Provinces. With the internecine fighting between the Anyanya II and the SPLA most of the Nuer districts of Upper Nile Region, as well as some of the border districts of Bahr El Ghazal Region, too, were sucked into a spiral of civil violence in which armed bands preyed on unarmed communities more than they fought each other.[3] The Murahalin raids

---

[3] The SPLA/Anyanya II war has usually been described as a Nuer/Dinka war. In fact, it was far more a Nuer civil war than a tribal conflict, with the Anyanya II at-

deep into Bahr El Ghazal in 1984–88 are well known, and their devastation of the civilian population well documented.

Among the first casualties of the war were the rural services and commercial networks in the areas immediately identified as providing support for the SPLA. Cattle vaccination campaigns ceased throughout most of Jonglei Province after 1983. In the northern Bahr El Ghazal area around Akon, where Baggara raids spread insecurity even before the civil war had begun, cattle vaccinations ceased even earlier, the last being 1982. There were no further government vaccination programmes after 1984 in Yirol District of Lakes Province, Nasir of Sobat Province, and Ler of Unity Province. Veterinary staff continued to try to carry out their duties in many of the rural areas, but as rural violence increased, contact between the districts and province capitals where medicines could be obtained was extremely tenuous. In areas under direct government control, or where an alliance with the government had been established, some veterinary services were maintained for a few more years. Oxfam-UK supported Mundari para-vets out of Tali until about 1988, by which time the SPLA were well established there.

Commerce also suffered. In Kongor district, where there was very little actual fighting, the bush shops closed down as early as 1981. In Ler shops stopped selling grain in 1981, but continued to sell other items until 1986, when they, too, closed. Quite apart from the effect this had on the food supply, rural people were no longer able to replace their fishing nets and agricultural implements once they wore out; nor were they able to get replacements for clothes, mosquito nets and blankets, all of which had an effect on general health. Currency came to be in short supply in the non-government held areas, especially as the SPLA initially banned the use of government currency in its territory for many years.

The cattle trade, too, suffered. Very quickly cattle auctions held at court and administrative centres ceased. The lack of currency inhibited private transactions, and the barter of livestock for grain became the standard means of exchange. Large-scale cattle raiding also interfered with the rural cattle market: the raiders (usually supported by the government) took the cattle they stole for sale to government centres, and the rural pastoralists herded their cattle further and further away from government areas for their own protection. Despite this, some cattle trade between government and non-government areas did continue, especially from Yirol (where there was little fighting after 1984) to Tali, and from there to Yambio and even Juba (see Diagram 1).

The war directly affected other services. As guerrilla sieges of government towns became common in the late 1980s any building could be pressed into service as a barracks or fortification. This included hospitals as well as

tacking Nuer, as well as Dinka communities, and Nuer soldiers in the SPLA fighting Nuer (and Shilluk) in the Anyanya II.

schools. Both the Bor and Nasir hospitals, for instance, were badly damaged by shell fire in the fighting which preceded the SPLA capture of those towns; in 1990 most buildings of the Bor hospital were still covered in graffiti left over from the occupation by Sudan government paratroopers. Government troops destroyed anything considered of strategic value when they abandoned a town. All medical equipment which could not be carried away from the Maridi hospital was burned by retreating government soldiers.[4] In Ayod and Waat donkey pumps were removed and wells blown up. In many of the rural districts hand pumps were similarly destroyed. The most serious problem for rural water supplies was not deliberate destruction, however, but deterioration through lack of maintenance: *hafirs* silted up, hand pumps broke down and could not be repaired.

The disruption of commerce and services, insecurity which led to large-scale migrations outside of the Southern Sudan, the contraction of subsistence activities and exchange networks, were all war-related factors which contributed to the decline of the rural economy. Most pastoralists had suffered livestock losses through raiding and disease, and very few families had been able to accumulate sufficient food reserves to see them through any period of natural calamity. The floods of 1988, which affected large parts of Upper Nile and Bahr El Ghazal regions thus had an exaggerated effect, and resulted in serious food shortages and local famines. The well publicised famine of northern Bahr El Ghazal in 1988, however, was entirely a result of the war in that area, not natural catastrophes. This was the state the Southern Sudan had reached when Operation Lifeline Sudan began in 1989.

OPERATION LIFELINE SUDAN: CONSTRAINTS UPON RELIEF

In the public criticisms which have often been made of the performance of UN agencies in Operation Lifeline Sudan (OLS) since 1989, there has been little recognition of the constraints which accompany any relief effort in the Southern Sudan. These affect not only the UN, but to some degree all agencies involved in relief, whether or not under the umbrella of OLS.

Organizational constraints

Through the agency of the UN an agreement was reached by both the Government of Sudan and the SPLA to allow relief (mainly in the form of food) to be supplied to civilians on both sides of the battle line in 1989. The agreement was helped by the momentum which was then building in the Sudan in favour of a negotiated constitutional settlement to the civil war.

---

[4] Action Africa in Need, Needs Assessment and Proposed Interventions, West Bank, Southern Sudan (Yambio, Maridi, Mundri, Yei and Kajo-Keji Areas) (Nairobi, June 1991).

The government of Sadiq al-Mahdi was under considerable pressure from public opinion in the north to reach an agreement with John Garang. Garang, on his part, appeared conscious of the need to conciliate Southern opponents to the SPLA who had formed political parties and were represented in the National Assembly. It is probably fair to say that when agreeing to the terms of OLS both leaders assumed that the level of fighting in the rural areas would diminish throughout 1989 and probably beyond. The continuation of the relief effort would thus coincide at least with a period of truce, and possibly with the beginning of a new period of peace.

The military coup of June 30th 1989, only a couple of months after OLS began, altered the circumstances in which the relief effort would take place. The new military rulers ended the process of negotiation and ultimately declared their intention of continuing the war. This meant that when the World Food Programme (WFP) announced that it had reached its relief targets towards the end of 1989, the Government of Sudan (GOS) declared OLS at an end and withdrew flight permission to locations under SPLA control. No permission was given (to UN agencies at least) to transport relief items (especially food) into SPLA territory. Fighting was renewed throughout the dry season of 1990, with the government achieving very little, and actually losing territory in the Kajo-Keji and Kaya areas of Western Equatoria. Only in April 1990 were flights resumed, and a UN assessment mission was allowed into the South. It was agreed that the UN would send two teams, one to the GOS held towns and one to the SPLA-controlled territories, and that the needs of both areas should be assessed and reports submitted. These reports would be considered by a Joint Technical Committee (JTC) sitting in Nairobi, consisting of representatives from the GOS, SPLM/A, the UN and the donors. In the end the JTC never met because the GOS representative failed to show up. Only one report, that for the SPLA areas, was published. The UN, on its side, then proceeded with its relief effort without the formal agreement of either side as to the priority of needs, the quantities of relief, or the methods of supply.[5]

This was to be the pattern for the next two years of OLS. The government proposed new restrictions to the allocation and movement of food into the SPLA-held areas at the end of 1990, and by objecting to convoys moving in the dry season. The WFP office in Khartoum (which had authority over the WFP relief operation running out of Nairobi and Kampala) acquiesced. Agreement to move UN convoys came only at the beginning of the 1991 rainy season. UN flights resumed then, but did not include all those locations which the UN assessment mission had earlier identified as needing relief (such as Bor, Kongor, Akon). Nor did it include those towns in

---

[5] A three month plan was agreed with the Sudanese Relief and Rehabilitation Association (SRRA) of the SPLM to cover the implementation of relief from August to November 1990.

Western Equatoria which the GOS itself claimed had needed relief prior to their capture by the SPLA. The UN was unable to bring both the GOS and the SPLA together to negotiate the conditions for continuing the relief effort; though the SPLA agreed to such face-to-face meetings chaired by the UN, the GOS did not.

Thus in 1991 there were no agreed modalities between the UN and the two combatants. This affected mainly the operations of the WFP in the SPLA-held areas: supplies of food from WFP and other agencies continued to be flown into the government-held towns without serious obstruction from the SPLA. UNICEF-supported programmes (in health, education, agriculture and veterinary vaccinations) continued to operate uninterrupted in areas accessible by road from East Africa. A number of other NGOs operating in Equatoria continued to carry out their programmes despite the government's obstruction, and the occasional lack of co-operation from the SRRA. The ease with which the GOS obstructed OLS operations in the rural areas, while maintaining the flow of relief supplies to some of its own areas, demonstrated the vulnerability of OLS to political constraints. It is to those constraints we now turn.

Political constraints

The difficulties the UN faces in intervening effectively in a civil war without the backing of the major powers are perhaps more clearly appreciated now, in the aftermath of the Gulf war, the Kurdistan and Somali operations, than they were at the beginning of 1989. The undertaking of humanitarian relief is a political decision, which must be backed by political will if it is to succeed. The political will is often lacking if that intervention must be made within a civil war in a member state; for to provide any sort of assistance to a segment of the population no longer under the control of the member government will almost inevitably be interpreted as a hostile act by that government. In the absence of any international consensus for sanctions against a given regime, the UN, as a body, cannot independently take action against one of its member states. No such formal consensus existed regarding the current government of the Sudan. The restoration of human and political rights in the Sudan was not high on the international agenda.

Quite apart from the constraints of international politics, the very structure of country representation of UN relief and development agencies inhibited a truly impartial distribution of relief in a civil war. UNICEF and WFP, the two main participating UN agencies in OLS, have country offices in Khartoum. These offices are overseeing existing relief and development programmes unrelated to the OLS' sphere of operations, which are confined entirely to the war zone. Thus, obstruction of OLS by the GOS did not affect the agreements concerning other UN projects in the northern Sudan. As the area under government control shrank, so did the GOS commitment to OLS;

increasingly, it had little to lose, even if OLS ceased altogether. What this meant in practical terms was that UNICEF-funded EPI and anti-rinderpest vaccination campaigns continued in the northern Sudan, even when the cancellation of UNICEF/OLS flights severely curtailed similar programmes throughout the Southern Sudan. The ban on WFP convoys into SPLA held territory did not bring with it the risk of a similar halt to WFP convoys to Kassala, Kordofan or Dar Fur. A GOS prohibition on school-feeding programmes in schools under the SPLM's Sudan Relief and Rehabilitation Association (SRRA) control did not lead WFP to cancel its long-standing school-feeding programmes elsewhere in the Sudan (including Wau and Juba). Since the new relief operations in the war zone were being implemented through the same agencies already committed to long-standing development programmes, OLS was subordinated to existing development concerns. The UN, therefore, showed no inclination to use its leverage against a government disinclined to honour its own undertakings.

This does not mean that it had no leverage. The WFP office in Khartoum in 1990-91 appeared to have very little interest in OLS, Southern Sector (the operations run from Nairobi into the SPLA-held territories), but showed considerable interest in securing for itself a leading role in organising famine relief in the northern Sudan. There appeared to be a convergence of interests between the GOS and the Khartoum office of WFP, in that both set greater store in programmes in the north than in the south (which were largely beyond their control), and neither wished to jeopardise those programmes. Many independent observers felt that WFP in Khartoum could have combatted GOS interference in OLS, Southern Sector far more than it did. For reasons which are still obscure to me, this biased behaviour on the part of the WFP Khartoum office was tacitly endorsed by the UN, since neither the WFP headquarters in Rome, nor the UN general secretariat, were willing to press their commitment to an impartial supply of relief to the point of antagonizing Khartoum.

The GOS was thus in a position to impose restrictions on the relief effort in the SPLA areas without fear of SPLA retaliation. Not only did the GOS interfere in the movement of food, it prohibited support to projects it considered of strategic value to the SPLA. It objected to any programmes of road improvement, whether with heavy machinery or by food-for-work road gangs: it objected to the use of river transport for the movement of relief items within SPLA-held territory (and in 1990 bombed Bor several times in an unsuccessful attempt to destroy an ICRC barge moored there); it objected to the repair of wells in the rural areas destroyed by government soldiers (but has repeatedly requested the complete overhaul of the Malakal water filtration system, which broke down due to lack of investment and care before 1983); it objected to the rehabilitation of hospitals and health centres; and it objected to school feeding programmes.

Much of what the GOS objected to in the SPLA territories would be classed as *development*, rather than *relief*. In the opinion of most relief workers attached to OLS they are absolutely essential as part of the rehabilitation of the Southern Sudan which is needed if relief operations are to be effectively carried out. And it is important to note that much rehabilitation work was being undertaken, despite government objections, either by NGOs on their own, or supported by the UN. It is also true to say that by the end of 1991 it was mainly NGOs who began to define their task in terms of rehabilitation and development. The UN agencies were still inhibited by the fear that they would not get Khartoum's approval for the renewal of OLS if they began to emphasise development in their proposals. This certainly influenced the way the assessment of the South's needs were finally presented.

The inhibitions do not stem entirely from Khartoum's war plans. Many donor governments were reluctant to sanction development for budgetary as well as political reasons. As a matter of fact, practical financing relief and development come under different budgets, often under different agencies. To switch money from one to another often requires a shift in political priorities within the donor government or agency. Politically, very few governments were willing to support the SPLA (even before the current split); and money for development implied such support.

In many ways the SPLA acted as if it did not fully understand that relief does not imply political support, and its response to the relief effort did little to encourage the development of the political support it both wanted and sometimes assumed it enjoyed. The SRRA was ill-organised in 1989 when OLS began, with no clear overall policy.

Most of its field representatives had been selected not only from the military wing of the movement, but from the security wing as well. Throughout OLS the SRRA often gave the impression that it was the procurement department for the SPLA, at least as far as food and medicines are concerned. Frustrated by Khartoum's obstructiveness, it often responded by being uncooperative itself. This never really impeded the flow of relief supplies into the government held areas, but it ultimately impeded the relief effort in the rural south. Many of the SRRA's criticisms of the UN operations have been justified (particularly in the perceived lack of impartiality), but with no detailed and realistic development plan of its own, and no proven overall competence in implementing complex programmes, it did not establish its own credibility in the eyes of a sceptical international relief community. Its representation of itself as the humanitarian wing of the SPLM was undermined by its subordination to the SPLA. At present most donors appear more sensitive to the SPLA diverting relief supplies to its military effort than they are to the Sudan government's more efficient diversion of similar supplies to its own troops. This may be inherently unfair, but it is a fact of political life which the SPLA has yet to recognize.

Resulting inequalities

Because of the weakness of OLS structures, the UN agencies failed to implement their relief programmes with the full degree of balance, impartiality,
and transparency they pledged. This has caused understandable resentment
within the SRRA, and a certain amount of justifiable criticism from other
NGOs. All of this further hampered the UN in the one field in which it is
better placed to do good than any NGO; over-all planning and the setting of
regional and sector priorities. No other agency involved in the relief effort
has been able to provide a comprehensive survey of the whole of the
Southern Sudan. The only reports produced in the last two years which have
attempted a comprehensive assessment of the relief needs of the South were
produced by the UN (though certainly with the co-operation of other agencies). With no overall priorities established, there has been no systematic approach to the relief problems of the entire region. Virtually the whole of Bahr
El Ghazal (the most populous of the three Southern regions) has been excluded from the relief effort, though its need was considerably greater than
either Torit or Yei River Districts, where so many NGOs have been active.

NGOs are often more efficient in implementing smaller scale projects
than the UN, but their limited resources have tended to restrict their range of
operations. Most NGO activity has been concentrated on those areas
accessible from Kenya or Uganda; areas which received the greater share of
the Southern Region's development before 1983 and suffered less damage
and dislocation than Jonglei, northern Bahr El Ghazal or eastern Upper Nile.
Thus some of the inequalities which led to the outbreak of the civil war have
been perpetuated in the relief operation.[6] Unfortunately, the imbalance of the
relief effort, with very little in the way of food, medicines, cattle vaccinations, well repairs, or school materials getting north of Kongor (and by far
the majority of all efforts being concentrated in the area *south* of Bor) has
contributed to the internecine fighting that broke out between the two SPLA
factions in 1991. The raiders who devastated Kongor and Bor in November

---

[6] It is little wonder that smaller organizations who feel greater pressure to demonstrate the success of their projects would be attracted to Equatoria, where there has
been a higher degree of education and development than most other parts of the
Southern Sudan. With the availability of resources and trained or semi-trained personnel, the prospects of early results are increased. At a meeting at Kopera market
in Yei River District in September 1990, out of a group of about 75 men I met some
23 had training or experience which would have been immediately useful in any
relief/development project. There were 7 students, 1 teacher, 5 market gardeners
from Yei town, 4 clerical personnel (including a former UNHCR administrator of a
Ugandan refugee camp), 4 men with mechanical skills, 1 medical trainee, and 1
trader. One would be hard pressed to find the same concentration of relevant experience anywhere in the Upper Nile Region, where even rinderpest vaccination
campaigns have often come to a halt due to the lack of suitable local veterinary
staff.

and December 1991 were able to recruit extra fighters from the civilian population of Ayod because it was popularly believed that "Bor" was hoarding relief supplies. In this case both the SRRA and the high command of the main SPLA faction must be absolved from most of the blame for the inequality of the distribution of relief supplies. It stems mainly from the weaknesses within OLS itself.

A further inequality has been the obscuring of relief priorities themselves. Because OLS began as an emergency relief operation the dominant relief item was food. Food remained the main relief item brought in, and most relief plans revolved around the delivery of food. In reality the need for food was not as great as the need for other items throughout 1990, the first half of 1991, and probably throughout most of 1989 as well. The return of the refugees from Ethiopia, the displacement of the civilian population around Bor and Kongor, and further displacement by fighting in 1992 has now increased the need for emergency food supplies, but before June 1991 agencies would have been better employed putting their efforts into means of increasing local food production and stabilizing the population. The provision of fishing equipment and tools, and the redistribution of local (as opposed to exotic) seeds was of far greater importance than the provision of emergency rations. Such supplies were distributed far more widely than relief food, but not as widely as the known need. Widespread rinderpest vaccinations were carried out, but this was because it could be funded under the Pan-African Rinderpest Campaign (PARC). Other veterinary needs remained undeveloped, with most devastating consequences in the recent trypanosomiasis epidemic in Bor. To encourage dislocated populations to settle down in order to increase food production other sectors, too, had to be supported. This meant the repair of flood protection embankments, the improvement of rural water supplies, the resurrection of some primary health care system, and the reopening of local schools (as opposed to the contentious boarding schools, long suspected of being SPLA training camps).

Some work was done by many agencies in all of these sectors, but again, the work was not comprehensive. The repair of the flood embankment from Jalle to Kongor could not be attempted with the heavy machinery it needed, because it was a "strategic" facility. Rural water supplies were not improved to any significant degree outside Eastern Equatoria. Training programmes for health and medical staff were frequently interrupted. Local schools often could not stay open for lack of adequate school feeding programmes. Bombing of towns by the Sudanese air force often led to local authorities closing schools and even some health facilities after evacuating civilians to outlying villages.

PROSPECTS FOR RECONSTRUCTION

Given the political constraints outlined above, what were the prospects for any sort of reconstruction in the rural Southern Sudan during the brief period of OLS, and were there any realistic alternatives to relief operations? Both questions are part of a larger one, relating to the potential for an indigenous reconstruction of the rural economy, and must be answered together.

Local markets and reconstruction

Emergency relief usually did not contain many of the items rural people felt they needed to improve their welfare or their subsistence activities. Basic necessities such as clothing, mosquito nets, blankets, tools, fishing line, water containers, cooking pots, etc., which had formerly been obtained through the commercial network, were generally considered too expensive, too bulky to transport, or too marginal to the emergency to be included in any substantial quantities in relief programmes.[7] People living in areas secured from fighting, which also had access to currency and goods from outside the war zone, attempted to make good these deficiencies on their own. The pattern described below began in some areas as early as 1986, but the main developments took place in 1989–91, after the Sudanese army had been cleared from most of the rural areas and the threat of government militias had been contained or removed.

The collapse of the rural commercial networks (described above) led to a considerable contraction of the economy, and fighting made any commercial or economic activity highly precarious. Yet the battle line was never impermeable, and there was small scale, individual trading going on between some areas controlled by the government and some controlled by the SPLA. Thus, prior to 1989, Dinka and Atuot herdsmen could drive their cattle from the SPLA-held Yirol area to government-held Yambio, the provincial capital of Western Equatoria, and a centre of strong anti-Dinka sentiment. Yambio is inside the tse tse belt, has limited access to meat in its immediate vicinity, and prior to re-division in 1983 had been supplied with meat largely from Lakes province. This trade was interrupted first by the division of the Southern Region, and then by the war. The inhabitants of Yambio were willing to set aside their public hostility towards the Dinka and the SPLA in order to obtain supplies of fresh meat. In the early years of the war the SPLA banned the use of Sudanese government currency in the areas it controlled. This inhib-

---

[7] Most agencies, including UNICEF, did provide some or all of these items in projects, usually, involving specific groups of a displaced population. The ICRC always had a more comprehensive approach to its relief project than did the UN and provided far more of such items (along with a full food basket which included pulses, salt and oil, along with grains). Yet all agencies had problems of targeting, allocation, distribution and monitoring.

ited the further development of commerce across the battle line. and it is not yet known whether the herders from Yirol risked taking currency home with them, or used the cash from the sale of their livestock to purchase items in Yambio which were scarce back home. Nor is it yet known how many of these herders were similarly involved in cattle sales to Juba, via the government outpost at Tali, or were even going as far afield as Kaya on the Sudan-Zaire-Uganda border, then a flourishing smuggling and trading centre.

Farther north, along the border between Southern Kordofan and Upper Nile, trade between Northerners and Southerners was being conducted on a large scale as early as 1986, even when militia raids were devastating the economy of northern Bahr al-Ghazal. The SPLA Area Commander of Western Upper Nile actively encouraged northern Sudanese merchants, including many from the Missiriya Baggara, to come into the border area of his command, there to deal with southern Sudanese traders licensed by the SPLA. A cattle auction and trade centre was established at Rupnyagai, not far from the government garrison of Bentieu. Here local Nuer herders brought their cattle and sold them for cash, often using that cash to buy items also brought in by the northern merchants. Southern traders also accumulated both Sudanese currency and trade goods (mainly items of clothing), and with these supplied their own bush shops and markets further south in SPLA controlled territory. In this way the use of Sudanese currency was promoted in Western Upper Nile, even though it was banned in other SPLA territories.[8] But an important aspect of this trade was that the SPLA administration was able to limit the activities of northern merchants, requiring them to work with licensed southern traders. Thus the network of southern-owned bush shops in the district was protected from better financed northern competitors.

The market in Rupnyagai was connected with another one in Ler, the SPLA district headquarters. Here the market was much reduced from its pre-war days, but cattle auctions were regularly held at least up until 1991, where cattle were bought and sold in Sudanese currency, and trade goods from the north could also be bought for Sudanese currency. The Ler cattle market was similarly linked to the cattle market in Yirol. Yirol, which had been a centre for cattle auctions since before Sudanese independence, grew in importance not only as SPLA security in the immediately surrounding rural areas increased, but also as the SPLA secured their border with both Southern Kordofan and Uganda.

The SPLA contained the Missiriya and Rizaigat raids into Bahr al-Ghazal only in 1988/ 89, by occupying large stretches of the Bahr al-Arab (or Kir). The Murahalin continued to ambush parties of Southern Sudanese who at-

---

[8] The use of Sudanese currency was so well organized that Western Upper Nile was able to exchange all of its Nimeiri pounds within a period of ten days, prior to their being withdrawn as legal tender. Nimeiri pounds were still in use as far south as Torit and Kapoeta in 1991.

tempted to make their way overland from the government town of Abyei in Southern Kordofan, but despite this active commerce grew up between Abyei and Milo, the market attached to Akon, an SPLA-held centre between Aweil and Gogrial. Sudanese currency circulated freely in Milo, and trade goods from Abyei were available in an abundance unheard of for most other parts of SPLA-controlled Southern Sudan (at least as of May 1990). Though the Sudanese government and army attempted to stem the flow of goods and currency out of Abyei, particularly through the practice of confiscation from Southern civilians leaving Abyei, the commercial incentives were strong enough for individual merchants and soldiers in Abyei to collude in the contraband traffic.

Cattle were in short supply in northern Bahr al-Ghazal, not only because of Murahalin cattle rustling, but because the surviving herds had been taken to safer pastures far to the south. Thus while there was no cattle trade between Milo/Akon and Abyei to match the trade between Rupnyagai and Abyei, the market at Milo/Akon was used by local Dinka to replenish their herds from Yirol. The scarcity of goods in the interior was such that any person bringing commercial goods from Akon to Yirol was likely to realize over 100 per cent profit on each item, so that the overland journey of some seventeen days by foot with a highly portable bundle of cloth or clothing would result in a tidy profit, as the following table of comparative prices in May 1990 indicates.[9]

Table 1. *Commercial goods, May 1990*

Commercial Goods	Milo/Akon (£S)	Yirol (£S)
Jallabyia/men's wear	100–120	250–300
Women's cloth	100	250
Women's dress	120	250
Sirwal/Trousers	70	200
Rubber "ship-ships", i.e. flip-flops *)	60	130

* Sandals made of rubber and which have just one grip by the big toe, a single cross strap and no uppers.

The cost of cattle, on the other hand, was high. The seemingly lower prices in northern Bahr El Ghazal represented an equal scarcity in grain and cattle for exchange, rather than altogether cheaper animals available. The figures were obtained in May 1990 and were said then to apply to rates of exchange the previous February, when some grain was still available. The prices in Yirol, also for May 1990, showed a slight decline in livestock prices from the previous year. Most livestock sales in Yirol were for cash, rather than grain, but for ease of comparison a conversion rate is given below.

---

[9] For both tables, see United Nations, Lifeline Sudan, *An Investigation into Production Capability in the Rural Southern Sudan. A Report on Food Sources and Needs*, pp. 56, 65–6.(Nairobi, June 1990).

Table 2. *Cattle exchange rates, early 1990*

Animal	N. Bahr al-Ghazal	Yirol
Heifer calf	1 x 90 kg sack dura	2 x 90 kg sack dura*
Pregnant heifer	2 x 90 kg sack dura	2-4 x 90 kg sack dura

* 2 x 90 kg sack dura = £S 1000

By mid-1991 the Yirol market was also linked to the border market at Kaya (taken by the SPLA from the government in February 1990). In Kaya merchants operated on both sides of the Sudan-Uganda border, and a far wider range of commercial items and locally produced food was on sale for either Sudanese pounds or Ugandan Shillings (at the rate of between 12 and 20 U Sh. per £S). Herdsmen from Yirol (mainly Atuot cattle traders), drove their cattle to Kaya for sale, and spent the proceeds on manufactured goods. Some of the cattle were also taken to Uganda.

Another commercial network, active in 1989–91, was centred on the main Sudanese refugee camp at Itang, Ethiopia. Some small goods (such as torch batteries) and relief food were on sale in and around Itang, and pastoralists along the Sobat and the border brought their cattle there during the dry season to obtain Ethiopian currency with which to buy food. Subsidiary markets, where goods coming from Ethiopia were sold for either Sudanese or Ethiopian currency, grew up at Nasir, Jokau (on the border), and perhaps other sites along the border. The amount of goods and currency which entered the Southern Sudan along this route appeared to be much smaller than that which came in from Southern Kordofan or Uganda. It also ended abruptly with the evacuation of all Sudanese refugee camps in Ethiopia in May–June, 1991.

The main trading networks operating in the areas under SPLA control by early 1991 are outlined in Diagram 1.

The extraordinary extended network which encompassed Abyei, Akon, Ler, Yirol, Kaya and Uganda is indicative of just how much security had returned to that area under SPLA control. It could not carry a heavy volume of goods, as almost all travel was by foot (the only part of the network which saw regular lorry traffic was that part between Southern Kordofan and Rupnyagai). With the failure of the UN to secure a rail corridor between Kordofan and Wau, it was also the only network by which any supplies could be got to the civilian population. Despite this, neither the UN nor the other relief agencies made effective use of it before the fighting in 1992 brought all relief in this area to a halt.

The Eastern Equatorian towns of Kapoeta and Torit also received a supply of foreign currency and commercial items from Kenya and Uganda, mainly through the 'official' channels of the New Sudan Council of Churches, the SRRA, and the National Economic Council of the SPLM. Despite the fact that relief convoys could travel from Kenya and Uganda through these towns up to Mongalla, Bor, Kongor, and on occasion to Ayod

Douglas H. Johnson

Diagram 1. *Flow of goods, currency and cattle*

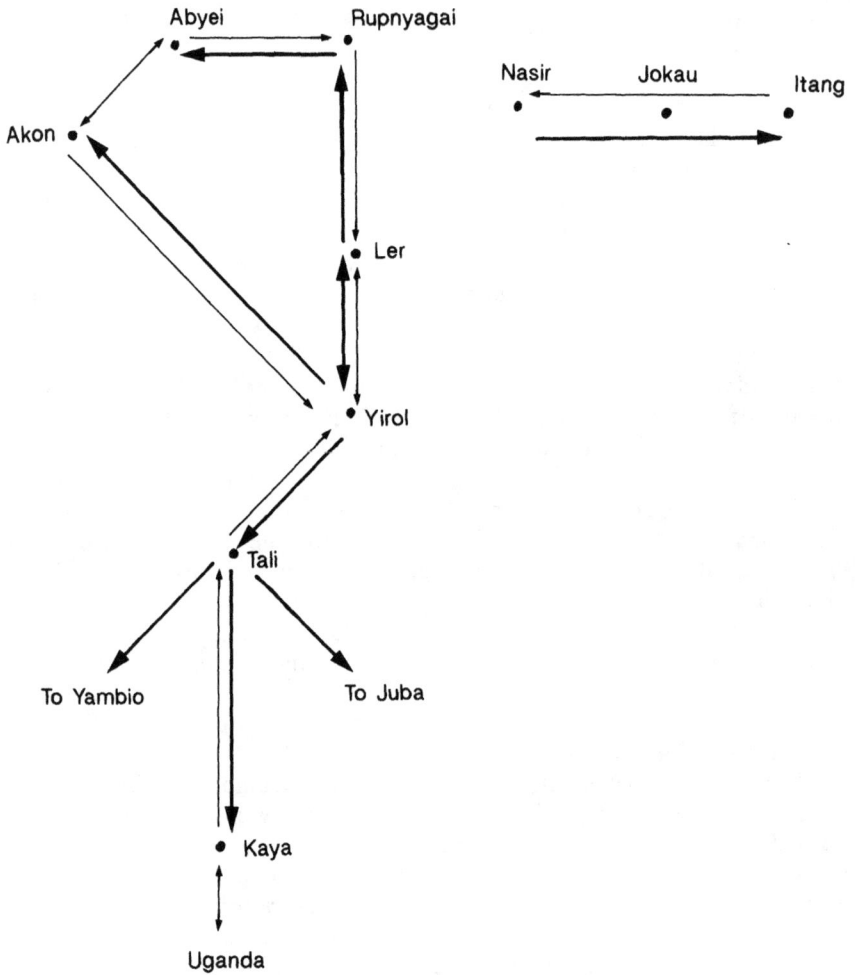

Key:

—————— Currency &/or goods
—————— Cattle

and Waat, this tenuous commercial link with East Africa had very little impact on the local economies of areas outside Eastern Equatoria.Very few commercial goods appeared in the small markets between Mongalla and Kongor (and those that did seem to have been brought out of Juba by Mundari traders). The currency which was exchanged (officially or unofficially) in Kapoeta and Torit did not stimulate markets and cattle auctions further north.

If the UN and other NGOs failed to make the best use of routes and networks established by local peoples inside the Sudan, the SPLM/SPLA command and the SRRA do not seem to have considered that there would have been advantages in strengthening local infrastructures (as in undertaking their own repairs of the major roads, rather than insisting on relief agencies taking on that task), or encouraging markets and commercial networks. On the contrary, many SRRA representatives seemed to wish to keep relief workers ignorant of local markets, fearing that their very existence would undermine demands for large amounts of relief supplies.

In short, there was potential for the limited rehabilitation of the subsistence economy in many parts of the rural Southern Sudan, and that potential was demonstrated by the efforts of local people who did have access to resources from outside the region. The agencies operating within the umbrella of OLS were slow to recognize that potential, and the SRRA never encouraged them to do so. In the end the break down of internal security, following the split in the SPLA, made it impossible for agencies to act on even their belated recognition.

The renewal of fighting in the rural areas

The split between the "Nasir" and "Torit" factions of the SPLA increased the obstacles already inhibiting relief and rehabilitation projects inside the Southern Sudan. It gave Khartoum new opportunities for interference and undid much of what was accomplished between 1989 and 1991. Agreements, which were difficult enough to obtain between Khartoum and the SPLA, had to be made between Khartoum and two SPLAs, something which, in the end, proved impossible. Khartoum's desire to widen that split was evident in its response to the new relief needs. Flight permission to areas still loyal to Garang's faction of the SPLA were denied, while flights to the territory held by the Nasir faction were renewed. Relief supplies were sent to Nasir from Khartoum by both air and barge, whereas objections were still raised about sending relief to any area controlled by Garang. Security deteriorated even in some areas not directly involved in the factional fighting. The work of relief personnel and even agencies came under renewed political suspicion: Garang's SPLA accused the UN of abetting the Nasir coup, and the Nasir faction accused the Norwegian People's Aid of supplying Garang with military and propaganda support.

Areas which were free of serious fighting since at least 1989 were once again engulfed in war, beginning as early as October 1991, when the two factions of the SPLA began fighting each other in the area between Kongor and Ayod. The serious damage done to expatriate relief headquarters in both Kongor and Bor (which were systematically looted by *both* factions of the SPLA) meant that they could no longer be used as centres co-ordinating agricultural, veterinary, and health programmes, as had been done in 1990-91. Attention had to be focused in any case on the simpler, but urgent, emergency food and medical needs of some two hundred thousand persons displaced by the fighting who had fled south of Bor. Since then the government's drive into Jonglei and Eastern Equatoria has led to further displacements, and the creation of new refugee populations along the Sudan's borders. By July 1992 the Southern Sector of OLS had been wound up. Relief efforts were being focused on refugees fleeing out of the Sudan.

CONCLUSION

At the end of 1990 it was possible to look forward to a gradual transition from relief to rehabilitation. Many relief workers advocated this as a logical development of existing projects. The restrictions placed on the relief effort in the dry season of 1991 effectively stifled such a development, and clearly demonstrated that the international community lacked the political will to implement any meaningful rehabilitation policies. Political developments since then have increased the need for emergency relief but have also increased the difficulties in meeting that need. The expansion of fighting into the rural areas of the Southern Sudan inevitably destroyed much of what little the various agencies have accomplished on the ground since 1989. In fact, the pattern of fighting in those rural areas where OLS was formerly most active has provided a strong argument against investment into non-emergency reconstruction projects, or even an extended relief/development network. Agency attention is once again being focused on the emergency needs of refugees fleeing into neighbouring Uganda, Kenya, and even Ethiopia. The prospects for rehabilitation and development before rural peace has been secured are very small indeed.

REFERENCES

Action Africa in Need, 1991, *Needs Assessment and Proposed Interventions, West Bank, Southern Sudan*. Nairobi, June 1991.
Galaty, J.G. and Bonte, P. (eds.), 1991, *Herders, Warriors and Traders: Pastoralism in Africa*. Westview Press, Boulder Co.

Johnson, D.H., 1986, "The Historical Approach to the Study of Societies and Their Environment in Eastern Upper Nile Plains", *Cahiers d'Etudes Africaines* 101–102, 26/1-2, (1986):131:44.

Johnson, D.H., 1988, "Adaptation to Floods in Jonglei Area; an Historical Analysis", in D.H. Johnson and D.M. Anderson (eds.), 1988, *The Ecology of Survival: Case Studies from Northeast African History*, 173–92. London: Lester Crook Academic Publ./Westview Press, Boulder Co.

Johnson, D.H., 1988, "Environment and History in the Jonglei Area", in P. Howell, M. Lock and S. Cobb, (eds.), 1988, *The Jonglei Canal: Impact and Opportunity*, 211–24. Cambridge, C.U.P.

Johnson, D.H., 1989, "Political Ecology in the Upper Nile: The Twentieth Century Expansion of the Pastoral 'Common Economy'". *Journal of African History*, 30/3, 1989:463–86.

United Nations, Lifeline Sudan 1990, *An Investigation into the Production Capacity in the Rural Southern Sudan*. Nairobi, June 1990.

WFP/FAO/UNICEF, 1991, *Crop, Food and Emergency Needs Assessment Mission, Southern Sudan*. Rome, December 1991.

"Arab Belt" versus "African Belt"

Ethno-Political Conflict in Dar Fur and the Regional Cultural Factors[1]

Sharif Harir

The purpose of this paper is to demonstrate, by the use of case material from the prolonged Fur-Arab war, how limited conflicts over natural productive resources can develop into a regional ethnic war of a quasi-international character. A quick transformation of the nature and scale of the conflicts was made possible when the concerned governments abdicated their role as peace-keepers, either due to weakness or partiality. This situation was and is made more complex by the presence of alien forces which maintained some interest and supported one of the parties to the conflict. This paper also focuses on how peace may be restored by reconciliation.

Though drawing on other conflicts for comparison and contrast, the main body of my empirical material comes from the Fur-Arab conflict which dominated Dar Fur between 1987 and 1989 and which keeps on erupting like an active volcano, albeit on a limited scale. The sedentary farming communities of the Fur took the brunt of the destruction caused by this war. Over 2,500 Fur tribesmen lost their lives and hundreds of them have been disabled. The Fur also lost 40,000 head of livestock and 400 villages, containing 10,000 residences, were burned out of existence.[2] The numbers of displaced Fur people who became refugees in urban areas in this region ran into the tens of thousands. The small but vigorous and modernized horticultural sector in the Fur economy experienced a serious setback. Fruit trees were either uprooted or completely burned down by Arab groups. Considerable investments in motor vehicles, diesel-driven water pumps, ploughs and flour-mills (or what one can term the small but expanding modern sector of the Fur economy) were lost. The Arab groups, the other party to the conflict, suffered about five hundred deaths, a couple of hundred were disabled, 3,000 head of livestock were lost and approximately seven hundred tents and residences were burned.[3] As the Fur area represented the strategic

[1] I am deeply indebted to Richard Holton Pierce, Gabriel Jal, Sean O'Fahey and Terje Tvedt for valuable comments.
[2] This statistical information is compiled from the proceedings of the tribal reconciliation conference held in Al Fasher, the capital of Dar Fur region, Western Sudan, between 29th May and 8 July 1989. These figures include only those which entered the police records prior to the commencement of the conference.
[3] This information is also compiled from the proceedings of the reconciliation conference held in Al Fasher in 1989. However, as many people did not report their losses during the height of the war, I have a feeling that the damage was far greater

safety valve for food supplies in Dar Fur, it was not surprising that most groups in Dar Fur experienced a severe shortage of food materials during and after the war. Food prices soared sky high.

This war, did not spare even public property or government property. Public utilities, such as mosques, schools and dispensaries, were burned down. Unlike many other ethnic conflicts which took place in Dar Fur, the destruction that came with this war was total. The government forces failed to stop the war even when they tried half-heartedly. The parties to this conflict neither believed in the efficacy of the government forces as a deterrent nor trusted them as neutral. The central government, until July 1989, favoured the Arabs, while the regional government, until Dr. Sese took over in early 1988, as a rule favoured the Fur. The conflicting parties knew this, therefore the war became all the more destructive and vengeful. Its brutality was sustained by both sides. The Arabs using mounted *razzias* called "knights" (*fursan*, Arabic), cut the throats of their Fur victims and burned them alive when they survived their machine guns and rocket-propelled grenades. The Fur did likewise whenever they had a chance, using their combatants called "militias" (*malishiat*, Arabic). The Arabs violated Fur farms and burned their produce and uprooted orchards. The Fur counter-attacked by burning pasture and by denying their enemies access to water sources. The Arabs looked to Libya for the supply of armaments and as a source of ideological inspiration; the extension of the "Arab belt" (*al hizam al Arabi*, Arabic) in Africa and the liberation of the Arab world. The Fur looked at the model presented by the Sudan People's Liberation Army (SPLA) for inspiration, but towards Hissein Habré and, via him, to the anti-Libyan mosaic (United States of America and Egypt) as possible sources of armament. In between, their respective educated elites mobilized resources to guarantee supplies of arms and ammunition from the local market. The two parties also sought alliances with the political parties at the centre in order to further their case within the government apparatus to their own advantage or the disadvantage of their opponents in the conflict; the Arabs were closely allied to the Umma party and the Fur were allied to the Democratic Unionist Party (DUP) who were coalition partners at the time.[4]

The appointment of Dr. Sese in 1988 as the ruler of Dar Fur led to a serious search for a peace formula. Dr. Sese, a Fur himself, broke with the tradition of partiality and opted for finding a formula for peaceful coexistence

---

than what was reported. In fact, many areas engulfed by this war did not have police posts to report to.
[4] This was clearly shown during a protest demonstration organized by the National Council for the Salvation of Dar Fur in Khartoum on 12 March 1988. The dominant coalition partner, i.e. the Umma party did not only instruct its 34 parliamentary deputies not to join the demonstration, it tried to get an injunction from the judiciary to outlaw the demonstration. Deputies from the DUP, i.e. the junior coalition partner, marched in the demonstration.

between the Arabs and Fur in the area of conflict. He had a deep conviction
that the existing war was the making of alien powers. The efforts he began in
February 1989 were to bear fruit in July 1989. But when the final peace
agreement was signed Dr. Sese was out of office and under political detention
due to the *coup d'état* of 30 June 1989 which brought the National Islamic
Front to power.

To understand the conflict it is necessary to reproduce the positions taken
by the parties to this conflict in the opening session of the tribal reconciliation conference in Al Fasher, the capital of Dar Fur, on May 29th 1989.
(These are translated from the original Arabic text by me.) These positions
were shrouded in a great deal of diplomatic language compared to the glaring brutality of the killings and burnings which had been going on outside in
the areas engulfed by the conflict. The rhetoric reflects, in a sense, the desire
of the "leaderships" of the parties to the conflict for a peaceful resolution,
and, also, a conscious attempt by each party to put the blame on the other
party by pleading "reaction" rather than initiating action. However, most
importantly, the diplomatic language notwithstanding, each party presented
its ideological justification for its position and its understanding of the immediate causes of the conflict unmasked.

POSITIONS OF PARTIES TO THE CONFLICT

The Fur position

The Fur delegation was led by Dimingawi Fadl Sese of Dar Dima (brother of
Dr. Sese, the ruler of Dar Fur), the territory in which most of the clashes had
taken place. In his 110 man strong delegation, the Dimingawi had representatives of other Fur territories that are scattered all over Dar Fur. As the
meeting was preceded by months of painstaking negotiations by a neutral
committee (Ajawid, Arabic) representing neutral mediators who were agreed
upon by both the Fur, the Arabs and the government, the unified position of
the Fur was delivered by the secretary of the Fur delegation, a young primary
school teacher

> The dirty war that has been imposed upon us [i.e. the Fur], began as an eco-
> nomic war but soon it assumed a genocidal course aiming at driving us out
> of our ancestral land in order to achieve certain political goals. We have
> followed, with dismay, all the different phases of this war from the time its
> took the innocent appearance of unrelated incidents of theft until it devel-
> oped into armed robbery that targeted Fur individuals only. At a later stage
> it aimed at the destruction of our economic base and the lifeline of our sur-
> vival by making it impossible to practise agricultural activities by the con-
> stant and brutal attacks on farmers and farming communities. We watched
> with the greatest degree of alarm the sinister development which aimed at
> full economic siege of our communities by making the movement of com-
> modities impossible through robbing markets and isolating urban areas from
> the rural hinterland. At the present time we are witnessing yet another and
> yet more sinister phase of this dirty war: the aim is a total holocaust and no

less than the complete annihilation of the Fur people and all things Fur. How are we to understand the brutal mutilation of Fur victims and the burning alive of residents of Fur villages? The message is quite clear: empty the land and do not allow any Fur survivors to come back and re-establish their villages. All this, of course, is a step in the chain of effects that aims at the complete displacement of the Fur and their replacement by the invading [Arab] elements that are [a] party to this conflict. How are we supposed to understand the mobilization of 27 Arab tribes, including some from across regional boundaries and others from across international boundaries, against only one tribe? The basic fuel of this war is racism. This conflict is about their attempt at dividing people of Dar Fur region into "Arabs" against "Blacks" (*Zurga*, Arabic), with superiority attributed to the former. The racial nature of the conflict is clearly revealed by the organizational vessel adopted by them, "The Arab Congregation" (My translation. From the opening address by the Fur delegation on 29 May 1989.)

The Arab position

The delegation of the Arab tribes was led by Al Hadi Eisa Dabaka, the Nazir of the Beni Helba Arabs, whose territory borders on the neighbouring Dar Dima of the Fur. In his 110 man strong delegation 27 Arab tribes were represented: the informed consensus of the Arabs. Their position speech was also delivered by a young school teacher who acted as a secretary to the Arab delegation

> Our Arab tribe [note the singular form] and the Fur coexisted peacefully throughout the known history of Dar Fur. However, the situation was destabilized towards the end of the seventies when the Fur raised a slogan which claimed that Dar Fur is for the Fur "Dar Fur for Fur". This coincided with the fact that the first regional government of Dar was led by a Fur individual who did not lift a finger to quell this dangerous trend. To further exacerbate the situation some Fur intellectuals in the Dar Fur Development Front and the Independent Alliance have embraced the "Dar Fur for Fur" slogan. The Arabs were depicted as foreigners who should be evicted from this area of Dar Fur. To give substance to this slogan, Fur "militia" forces were trained under the supervision of the Fur governor of Dar Fur in the period between May 1986 and September 1986 replacing, thus, the traditional throwing sticks, clubs and spears with AK47 and G3 assault rifles and rocket-propelled grenades. Ours is a legitimate self defence and we shall continue defending our right of access to water and pasture. However, let us not be in doubt about who began this war: it is the Fur who in their quest to extend the so-called "African belt" (*al hizam al Zunji*, Arabic) wanted to remove all the Arabs from this soil. (My translation)

The Government's position

As mentioned above, it was Dr. Tigani Sese who, as the ruler of Dar Fur and, appointed by the Umma party, initiated the search for peace. However, what is significant is the fact that for the first time during the conflict the ruler made a firm and an official commitment for peace

In this meeting let us remind ourselves of the fact that our people in Dar Fur have lived together in peace throughout history. As the result of our peaceful ways, Dar Fur has became a standard quotation for many parts of our world as far as stability and peaceful coexistence are concerned. The ability of the people of Dar Fur in solving tribal conflicts is exemplary. I need not labour much for examples of tribal conflicts which were solved in the "Dar Fur way" of amicability: Rezaiqat vs Maalia, Gimir vs Fellata, Northern Rezaiqat vs Beni Helba etc. ... But despite our rich experience in containing tribal problems, we witness today a conflict that has been conducted in ways completely out of character with our spirit.

The conflict we are trying to resolve today began as an ordinary conflict between nomadic pastoralists and sedentary farmers over natural resources. The extraordinary aspect of the Fur/Arabs conflict is not in the manner in which it began but in the speed with which it spread out from the Jebel Marra areas to engulf communities in Wadi Salih, Zalingei, Kas, Kabkabiya and Nyala rural council areas. The reckless use of firearms to ruthlessly massacre our peaceful citizens and the macabre mutilations are completely out of character with the people of Dar Fur. Never before, were whole village communities annihilated and women, children and the elderly so mercilessly mowed down by machine guns.

It is my conviction that this brutal war has been imposed upon us by external forces that did not like our democratic way of government. The war in the south is but a manifestation of such malignant external forces. Today we are united in the search for a strong and durable peace. The Government at both levels would spare no effort in supporting the armed forces to impose the authority of the state and its supremacy in order to maintain peace once it is achieved.

The position of the mediators

Sultan Abdel Rahman Baher El Din of the Dar Masaleet led the mediators *ajawid*. In his long tenure in the office as Sultan, the Masaleet leader had acted as a mediator in many tribal conflicts in Dar Fur. Within the Dar Fur maze of ethnic conflict the Masaleet have managed to maintain a reputation for neutrality which is, in fact, interesting but irrelevant to the purposes of the present topic. The mediating group was composed of a 26 man strong contingent. Its membership was drawn from the ranks of tribal leaders from Dar Fur, Northern and Southern Sudan, high ranking civil servants and officers from the Sudanese regimental forces. The parties to the conflict formally had the right to veto any member of the mediating body. The legitimacy of mediators was therefore, largely, due to the fact that both parties had accepted them. In fact most of them were tested in the period between February 1989 and May 1989 when they were moving physically in the field, trying to disengage groups of combatants and to reduce tensions in preparation for the meetings which started on 29 May 1989. At least one member of this body was killed in the cross-fire when he was trying to disengage combatants in the field. Sultan A. Baher el Din delivered the position speech of the mediators

We would like to thank everybody who has contributed to the preparation of this conference which might pull out our beloved region from imminent doom. It is hoped that at the end of the day we shall come out of this more unified so that our efforts may be directed towards the development of our region for the benefit of future generations: our children. We would also like to thank the regional government and the tribes concerned for bestowing their valuable confidence upon us. We want to reaffirm our complete neutrality. We shall favour nothing but justice. (My translation. From the opening address by the mediators, 29 May 1989.)

WHAT WAS THE PROBLEM?

Both the Arabs and the Fur, while each disclaiming responsibility for starting the conflict by blaming it on the other, unanimously attributed the conflict and the way it was conducted on the ideology of racism harboured by the other. The Fur, in fact, made quite explicitly clear that the war was about the Arabs' attempt to conquer the Fur's territory, propelled by a racist ideology which aimed at the extension of the "Arab cultural belt" into black Africa, through the destruction of the "Black Africans" who owned the territory. For that purpose, the Fur argument went, the Arabs had mobilized 27 Arab groups which were not even related under normal circumstances, but which were, for all other purposes, antagonistic to one another. Those 27 Arab groups, according to the Fur, included a number of non-Sudanese groups from the area of Salamat in Chad which were in opposition to the Chadian regime. As they received logistical support from Libya, the weapons they brought to bear in this conflict situation were far superior to and relatively more lethal than any weapons the Sudanese Arab groups which were parties to this conflict could possess. This fact notwithstanding, some of the Sudanese Arab groups received arms from the central government in Khartoum on the pretext of defending themselves against raids from the southern elements of the Sudan People's Liberation Army (SPLA). Those guns were used against the Sudanese Fur. This strengthened the theory of an "Arab conspiracy" against the black Africans. It was, according to the Fur, an Arab conspiracy which extended from the central government in Khartoum to the local Arab tribes in Dar Fur and on the basis of the ideology of Arab nationalism as espoused by Libya, included non-Sudanese Arabs.

The Arab tribes involved in this conflict, and the subsequent war, dissolved their tribal boundaries, and buried their differences. They behaved as if they were a single tribe by calling themselves "our Arab tribe". They blamed the whole problem on the Fur intellectuals and the regional government of Dar Fur which had been led by people of Fur ethnic background since 1981. According to them this war was a legitimate self-defence as access to pasture and water in the Fur territory was of the utmost importance for their very existence. Furthermore, the Arabs claimed that it was the Fur who started the whole thing by their attempt to extend what they termed the "Black African" (*ifirigia al souca*) or "Negro belt" (*al hizam al Zunji*), aimed at excluding the Arabs who should have enjoyed equal rights of access to natural productive resources as citizens of the Sudan. They quoted the Sudanese constitution to reinforce their assertion.

The regional government of Dar Fur, and especially Dr. Sese in his quest for a peaceful solution, did not blame any party to the conflict. He appealed to a joint history of peaceful coexistence, a rich heritage of finding "civilized" ways of resolving problems and an exemplary "Dar Fur spirit" which had never allowed conflicts to reach the appalling level of disregard for human life that had become typical of this conflict. He was able to point out a basic element in this conflict without blaming any of the parties for it: it is natural to have conflicts between pastoralists and agriculturalists. This truism enabled the leader of the Dar Fur government to skirt the sensitive question of responsibility and blame which would, at this crucial moment, not only be undesirable but destructive. Without closer specification Dr. Sese blamed external powers for this situation. Now that Dr. Sese was able to re-gain for the regional government some semblance of credibility as being neu-tral and committed only to peace, the mediators, (*ajawid*), were to do the job of mediating peace and to help the process of social reconstitution. These mediators affirmed their neutrality and their commitment to peace and jus-tice in the area of the conflict. That their position was the most difficult one was evidenced by the death of Al Tahir Misaid Gaidom, a member of the mediating body, while trying to disengage combatants in the field.

All the above stated positions show some manifestations of the conflict but by no means its complexity. And as these positions were arguments in a negotiation process, they have a tendency to oversimplify and, sometimes, mystify things. In the following sections we shall pursue the conflict in some of its various contexts. To start with this conflict in essence, was based on the ecology of the area. Later, political developments began to reflect some of what is termed as the general "Sudan problem": the inability of its elitist governments to see beyond Khartoum and problems of daily supplies there. This helplessness is reinforced by tendencies towards explaining away "real problems".

Dar Fur and the Sudan

Dar Fur is the western-most province of the Republic of Sudan and lies be-tween latitudes 10°N-16°N and longitudes 22°E-27°30'E with an area of 160,000 square miles. It was the last province to become part of the Anglo-Egyptian Sudan in January 1917, after its last Fur Sultan, Ali Dinar, was killed by British-led forces on 6 November 1916. The boundaries between it and French Equatorial Africa (presently Chad and Central Africa) were not agreed upon before the signing of the border protocol between the French and the British on 10 January 1924. Some of the border stretches were not delimited until as late as 1938. However, when this operation was finally completed at the formal level, a considerable number of the groups in the border area were divided into two by international borders.[5] MacMichael summarized this situation as follows to Wingate on 29 May 1919, "the main point is that we have let the French keep *Tama* and they are letting us keep *Masalit* and *Gimir*. Further North, we are giving them their protege *Haggar Toke* (the Western end of *Dar KoBe*, North of *Tama*), though they are *Zaghawa*, and all the *Bedayat* and the *Quraan*, and we are accepting the line of Wadi Howa [Howar] as a Northern boundary of Dar Fur". (Quoted in Theobald 1956:9.)

People and society in Dar Fur

The recorded history of Dar Fur tells that as from about the mid-seventeenth century, ca. 1650, a centralized polity which came later to be known as the Fur Sultanate started to emerge in the tableland area of the Jebel Marra massive which is the dead-centre of the present day Dar Fur region. Parallel to this emergent Sultanate was the Funj Sultanate which dominated the river-basin of the Sudan as from the beginning of the sixteenth century (1504). From a purely nationalistic perspective, it would seem quite tempting to trace the origins of the Republic of the Sudan to those relatively distant dates. Both kingdoms espoused Islamic ideologies, but remained strongly independent and even hostile toward one another as is witnessed by offensive military activities and attempts at invasion by one against the other, which vitiates the usefulness of extending the nationalist interpretation to those antecedents of the Republic of the Sudan. The buffer region between the two Sultanates, i.e. Kordofan, changed hands many times until the fall of the Funj Sultanate at the hands of the Turco-Egyptian colonial forces in 1821. In fact the Fur Sultan Tayrab (1752–1787) carried active invasion to the very heart of the Funj sultanate when, after overrunning the rebellious Musabaat in Kordofan towards the end of his rule, the Dar Fur army advanced as far as Omdurman on the Nile. After its emergence in 1650, the Dar Fur sultanate maintained its independence well into the twentieth century, though sometimes very precariously and extremely tenuously. It was finally brought to a definite eclipse by the Anglo-Egyptian forces on 6 November 1916, and formally became a part of the Anglo-Egyptian Sudan in January 1917. There have been two periods during which this independence was negatively influenced by external forces. The first period was the brief brush with Turco-Egyptian overlordship from November 1874 to 1883 and the second period was the Mahdist period from 1885 to 1898. However, those two decades were ones of confusion in which the centre of power on the Nile at Khartoum never exercised effective gov-

---

[5] The border agreement between the French and the British was signed on 10 January 1924. It was described by Theobald thus: "the settlement was one of exhaustion, rather than of common-sense—but at least it was a settlement after twenty-five years of dispute". (Theobald 1956:225.)

ernment, let alone did away with the various contender Sultans in Dar Fur who claimed the throne independent of these forces. These contender Sultans, in no small way, maintained the continuity of the Dar Fur tradition of leadership.

As the Sultanate gradually extended itself from the Jebel Marra massif, the vehicle for which had been a combination of affinal[6] ties in which women crossed ethnic borders in marriages and thus cemented relations with the rulers and predatory expansion by military force, the Fur sultans brought into their orbit, as tributaries as well as incorporated territories, other ethnic groups. The first Fur sultan was, in fact, a descendant of such an affinal alliance between an Arab father and a Fur princess and was referred to as Sulyman Solong which means Sulayman the Arab. In effect the Sultanate of Dar Fur was made to appear like a scale in which the balancing centre in the middle was provided by the sedentary Fur who provided the Sultans with nomadic cattle-raising Arab tribes to the south and semi-nomadic, non-Arab groups in the north. The balancing act was provided by military incursions, either to the south or the north depending upon who deserved chastisement in the eyes of the rulers who recruited fighters from the one group, but never simultaneously from both. Only in expeditions against neighbouring independent Sultanates did recruitment to the Fur army approximate anything that can resemble a national army, with both "Northerners" and "southerners" taking part. Of course, this operational wisdom was less adhered to towards the end of the Sultanate. But the most important thing to note is that the power centre of Dar Fur remained stable most of the time during which the Sultanate lasted while the northern and southern extremes of the scale were most of the time unstable and less quiet and peaceful.

This stable atmosphere which was created by the Sultanate was favourable for the incorporation of smaller and sedentary tribal groups into the inner circles of the Sultanate. These groups consisted mainly of the present Berti, Marareet, Mima, Daju, Birgid, Tunjur and Dadinga as well as migrant *fugara* (religious men) from West Africa. The state, i.e. the Sultanate, provided for the public security of these groups. On the other hand the nomadic and semi-nomadic peoples, were less controlled by the state and hence were occasionally coerced by military power but more often than not were also coaxed to act as tributaries by forging affinal ties with their respective leaders. The same applied to the numerous nomadic Arab groups, though military confrontation between them and the Fur was more often the case than was the forging of affinal ties.

The present spatial distribution of ethnic groups in Dar Fur is not drastically different from what it was at the time of the Sultanate. This is because most of the ethnic groups of Dar Fur, are also still territorial groups; each group has a defined territory as its home-land. Broadly speaking the Fur still

---

[6] A number of Fur Sultans were born of Zaghawa mothers (see O'Fahey 1980:14–28) and a number of Fur princesses were married out of the royal clan.

continue to claim the centre of Dar Fur and are surrounded by a number of smaller ethnic groups which, like the Fur, engage in agricultural production. The Zaghawa and the Meidob continue to claim the northern semi-arid belt of Dar Fur interspersed with some nomadic camel breeding Arabs such as Northern Rezaiqat and the Zayadiya. The area to the south of this region is still occupied by nomadic and semi-nomadic Baggara Arabs who breed cattle (Rizaigat, Habbaniya Taisha and Beni Helba) and are interspersed with recent in-migrant communities from various parts of Dar Fur. Thus the region can be divided into three main zones according to the predominant production systems. The central parts are dominated by farming communities which produce the staple crop *dukhun*, i.e. bulrush millet, the southern parts by nomadic and semi-nomadic Baggara cattle herders, and the northern parts by camel herders. However, these systems are not mutually exclusive and, in fact, most of the production systems can be characterized as agro-pastoral. Despite the existence of tribal *dars*, wherein each tribe depicts itself as a territorial unit exclusive of others, the seasonal disposition of pastures and water sources leads to considerable movement across tribal territories, a practice which leads to conflicts caused by competition over natural productive resources. Most of the tribal groups whose economies and societies depend on animal husbandry have every year to negotiate rights of access and passage through the territories belonging to a number of other tribal groups. Intermittent conflict occurred among these groups over access to resources often leading to armed feuds, involving the government authorities as potential arbiters. In most cases tribal reconciliation conferences, supported by the state, are conducted to resolve these conflicts.

Ethnic inter-relationships in contemporary Dar Fur

Despite the apparent "separateness of ethnic groups", expressed and misleadingly reified by separate ethnic territories, separate languages, autonomous internal political systems and considerable variations in cultural and societal forms, they are interdependent as groups sharing the same region which has been subjected to centralization of the state over a long span of time. These interdependencies were reinforced by regional webs of exchange and trading links, the growth of markets and urban centres and by the considerable ease with which population groups moved from one place to the other in search of both natural resources and employment opportunities. This was especially the case as the state, after the incorporation of Dar Fur into the Sudan, had progressively assumed the role of the arbiter of public peace and security, through a series of legislative and administrative organizations and reorganizations. In addition the state, through the introduction of forensic institutions, such as courts and police, assumed the monopoly of legitimate coercion and violence. With these it undertook the extension of educational, health and other services on a universal basis. The weekly rural and urban markets and the fora presented by the state bureaucracy and service agencies were especially supposed to be ethnic-free fora. They all became subject to the overlordship of the British colonial rule and not to the overlordship of any particular local ethnic group as had been the case during the Fur Sultanate. This situation helped to remove the basic contradiction between the dominant position of the Fur and the cliental position of the Baggara to the south and the Zaghawa and the Meidob to the north; a contradiction which had marked the Fur Sultanate. The colonial state was also successful in curbing the rampant mutual raiding across ethnic borders and a considerable reduction in livestock thefts was achieved as police, courts and prisons started functioning in the region.[7] While the occasional flaring up of conflict between pastoralists and pastoralists and between pastoralists and sedentary farmers was to continue intermittently, on the whole the situation was stable and peace was felt.

The formalization of native administration by the extension of the Powers of the Shaikhs Ordinance of 1928 and the reorganization of native administration reinforced the peace among the ethnic groups of the region. The native administration constituted the corner-stone of British colonial policy which was based on 'indirect rule, security and good government'. The British were successful in establishing internal peace. On the other hand, they also created structural conditions that subsequently led to the marginalization of Dar Fur and the Dar Furians *vis-à-vis* the Sudan. The whole region was regarded as a security hazard and was kept in an iron grip to the extent that the Closed District Ordinance of 1922, which was mainly applied to the southern part of the country, was extended to cover certain parts of Dar Fur. This imposed isolation was to prove disadvantageous to Dar Fur under independent Sudan when external colonialism was replaced by what might aptly be termed "internal colonization". The domination of Dar Fur, both administratively and economically, by riverain Sudan was to generate strong antipathies later.

Riverain domination and the emergence of regional identity

When the Sudanese flag went up at independence on 1 January 1956 replacing the two flags[8] of the condominium powers, Britain and Egypt, the pro-

---

[7] This aspect of the colonial rule is nostalgically remembered by the elderly generation in Dar Fur when talking about the present predominant insecurity. The unfortunate comparison between the colonial ability to maintain peace and security and the inability of the national governments to do so, ends up by the elderly enquiring mischievously "whether the *Turuk*, (a local reference to the British,) are coming back or not".

[8] It is worthwhile to mention, in this connection, that in 1952 the Union Jack was burned by nationalist demonstrators in Al Fasher, the capital of Dar Fur. It is also worthwhile to allude to the fact that the motion for independence from within the Parliament in 1955, was tabled by a deputy from Dar Fur.

cess of Sudanization of the national civil and military services was accelerated. This effectively sealed the dominant position of the riverain Sudanese. This was due to the implications of the structural conditions created by colonization in which education, which gave basic qualification for government employment, was by and large concentrated in the riverain Sudan. The Dar Furians found themselves and their affairs being run by an elite that, though Sudanese, was alien to them. In addition trade was also dominated by the riverain Jellaba traders who were the ethnic kin of the local administrators and the decision-makers.

On a more fundamental level of economy, the central riverain Sudan was comparatively much more developed than Dar Fur, whose economy was fundamentally traditional and subsistence-oriented despite the presence of "market forces". The presence of big agricultural schemes, like the Gezira in the centre, and the concentration of manufacturing industry in the capital, Khartoum, made those areas targets for labour movement from Dar Fur. The west/east axis of labour movement has continued as the disparities in development and hence in opportunities increasingly persist. On the national political level, Dar Fur has continued to be a domain of the Umma party whose leadership was mostly riverain but whose connection with the Mahdist movement evokes considerable religious emotions among the Dar Furians. The Dar Furians, submissive to the manipulated religious context of this party, were included as voters and followers but excluded as politicians and leaders. The Sudanese army, during the first Civil War was predominantly Dar Furian in its rank and file but exclusively riverain in the officer ranks. The young educated Dar Furians and those who served in the army felt totally excluded. The reaction of the young educated Dar Furians to this situation was intensified by the revival of the image of a Dar Fur which has remained independent long after the rest of the country, of which it later became a part, was colonized.

Clandestinity was the major characteristic of a number of Dar Furi movements that aimed at getting rid of the domination of the Jellaba traders and the riverain administrators in the region. The anti-Jellaba sentiments were not expressed in terms of development disparities but in terms of cultural differences, between the Jellaba and the Dar Furians. They were expressed in terms of a dichotomy between Westerners and Northerners wherein the situation was depicted in such terms as that the "honest" and "brave" Westerners were dominated by the "dishonest" and "cunning" Northerners. The "northern" Jellaba used the state and its institutions as a means of oppression hiding, as it were, behind courts and police. These institutions, it was said, have favoured the Jellaba because state administration was manned by their ethnic kin. Dar Furians applying to enter military or police academies as well as those who generally applied for jobs were defeated by the riverain nepotism which used the Jellaba networks to promote the Jellaba machine of domination—exclusive access to state authority.[9]

Between independence and the October revolution in 1964, two clandestine groups dominated the scene of Dar Furi disaffection. A group that named itself *al-Lahib al-ahmar*, literally the "Red Flame", threatened actions against the Jellaba by distributing leaflets in the main urban centres of Dar Fur. We do not, to date, know the extent of proliferation of this group on the Dar Fur scene. However, apart from the initial panicky reactions the leaflets created among the Jellaba communities, the Red Flame did not endure long. A second group, which was taken more seriously by the government because its members were recruited from the army rank and file, came into being in 1963. Though underground and clandestine Soony, the name of a place just below the peak of Jebel Marra, was much more felt. Its membership was largely drawn from the regimental forces but also included a few civilians. Its ethnic basis was quite diverse since it presented itself as a fighter against the Jellaba for the benefit of Dar Furians. Though wide arrests occurred as the result of launching Soony, the security agencies of the central state could not uncover the extent of its membership and the perimeters of its organization. They contented themselves with adopting a pre-emptive strategy whereby mass dismissals from the regimental forces of Dar Furi elements were undertaken, as well as tightening the chances of entry of Dar Furians into the military and police academies. To pre-empt such tendencies ideologically, the government also had recourse to a propaganda campaign in which regional movements were branded racist.

In the wake of the Soony and Red Flame movements, an internal debate which had started among the now growing body of educated Dar Furians on the merits of having an open, above-the-ground organization that fought the politically legitimate battle of Dar Fur bore fruit and Dar Fur Development Front (DDF), was launched in Khartoum in 1964. Unlike other regional organizations that were launched around the same time, the Beja Congress (BC) and the General Union of the Nuba Mountains (GUNM), and which were characterized by a distinctly narrow ethnic base, the Dar Fur Development Front was founded on a wider ethnic base that made the whole region its base of recruitment. The founding members of the DDF were highly educated Dar Furians, belonging to diverse ethnic groups. Though a regional organization designed to serve regional interests, the founding members decided not to play themselves out of the national political game. To put this decision into effect the first chairman of the Dar Fur

---

[9] A.A. Ibrahim in an unpublished Ph.D. Thesis, Sussex, 1985, shows this very clearly. In a sample survey he carried out in 1981 about occupants of senior positions in civil service, the findings were as follows: 5 per cent Khartoum, 20 per cent central region, 14 per cent Northern region, 8 per cent Kordofan and Dar Fur's share was zero. Of 90 senior positions at ambassorial level in the Department of Foreign Affairs, not a single one is from Dar Fur.

Development Front, Ahmed Ibrahim Draige, decided to align the group with the Umma national party as a tactical move in order to be able to further Dar Furi interests by exploiting the national political base provided by that party. However, this move eventually compromised the DDF when its chairman, Ahmed Ibrahim Diraige, ended up as a leader of the Umma parliamentary opposition in 1968. Rather than maintaining a separate identity as a regional movement, the DDF was swallowed by the Umma party. Later when some groups from Dar Fur attempted to revive it in 1986, after the overthrow of Nimeiri and the restoration of multi-party democracy, the DDF came to be viewed by the majority of the Dar Furians as representing not a regional base but as the Fur.

Regional autonomy, the Dar Fur upheaval and the involution of ethnic conflict

Under the May regime (1969–85) President Nimeiri banned all political parties as well as regional movements, and instituted the now defunct Sudanese Socialist Union (SSU) as the only legitimate political party. The political parties, before they were banned in 1969, and irrespective of whatever shortcomings they might have had, cut across ethnic boundaries and most of them possessed a diverse ethnic base. When these were banned and all other political groups were made illegal, political struggle within the SSU tended to be carried out through revitalization of tribalism. This does not imply, of course, that political ethnicity was accepted by the regime. Rhetorically the regime was very harsh on ethnic identity and tribalism. However, there was no way that it could control ethnic processes. Ironically the regime's crusades against what were termed "racism" and "tribalism" only made them more entrenched in the political process. Most of the leaders of the political parties went into exile and organized an opposition movement against the regime in power in Khartoum. However, most of their followers inside reverted to their ethnic identities as vehicles for political activity. This was most clear as one moved from the centre into the regions. Dar Fur can provide such a test case in a much broader sense.

The political thinking behind the introduction of the SSU as the only party was to create unity in the Sudan through a model which was informed by a "melting pot" philosophy. The SSU aimed at dissolving all political barriers between the population groups in the country by banning their political parties as well as regional and tribal groupings and by the introduction of new labels based on profession and occupation, such as farmers, nomads, professionals, regimental forces or what was called the alliance of peoples working forces. The appeal of this rhetoric was limited only to a very small sector of the society, i.e. the urban and educated people. For the rural people, the reduction of their multitude of identities to labels, such as farmers and nomads, did not make sense. For the rural people, everybody, whether nomads or farmers or office workers, belonged to tribes. It was only logical that in pursuing political goals the members of the only party, SSU, used tribal or other criteria that were explicitly rejected by the regime then in power, albeit in ways shrouded in subtlety.

The May regime decided to extend the Regional Autonomy Act of 1972, to cover all the other regions of the Sudan in 1980. This would have satisfied the regional sentiments of the Dar Fur people had it not been for the fact that the governor of Dar Fur, who had been appointed by the centre, was not a Dar Furi himself. It is to be remembered, in this connection, that the establishment of the Dar Fur Development Front and other more clandestine movements in Dar Fur throughout the sixties was largely based upon this sentiment. Hence it was not a great surprise when Dar Fur erupted in 1981, in what came to known as *intifadha* (or upheaval), demanding equality with the other regions of the Sudan by having a Dar Furi appointed as the ruler (governor) of the region. The central government in Khartoum attempted to crush this upheaval, *intifadha* by using the riot police. However, as the demonstrations grew in force and clashes with the police resulted in casualties, the central government gave in, and Draige, the first chairman of Dar Fur Development Front, was appointed as the first Dar Furi to govern Dar Fur since the death of Sultan Ali Dinar at the hands of the British troops in 1916. This, ended the situation aptly referred to by intellectuals as "internal colonization period".

The euphoria of the people of Dar Fur, surrounding what they consider to be a glorious achievement was boundless. But the remarkable regional unity vis-á-vis the centre did not last long. It was short-circuited by the involution of conflict in Dar Fur manifested in confrontations between ethnic groups. While there were many factors underlying the various ethnic conflicts that took place in Dar Fur, the ecological deterioration that pushed population groups into southern Dar Fur was one of the most important, their continuation and later politicization was the work of a narrow-minded elite who took sides in these conflicts. This aspect of the conflict situation cannot be understood without examining the role played by the autonomous regional government which inadvertently increased tensions.

Draige's government, 1981–83

Not long after the formation of the regional cabinet, conflicts within the cabinet started to leak out to the public. The cabinet was split into two camps—one camp was led by Draige, and the other was led by Mahmoud Beshir Jamma, his deputy. This divide did not at that time represent any clear political-ideological dichotomy; for under other circumstances Draige and Mahmoud were, in reality, members of the Umma party and hence subscribed to the same political ideological stance. Furthermore at the time the split started to appear, both were leading members of the only legitimate political party, the SSU. They were, in fact, the chairman and the deputy chairman of the Sudanese Socialist Union *ex officio*. So what was the problem?

The SSU was a party by default inasmuch as no other political parties were allowed to exist legitimately by the regime in power. Rhetorically the regime portrayed the SSU as the ruling organization and not an organization which was subordinate to any specific government at any specific time. Hence, for a person to be in the government the prior membership of the SSU and a public subscription to its ideology were prerequisites at the normative level. However, many of the actors who were manning key posts in the SSU, kept their previous party loyalties, albeit secretly, though the manifestations of this "residual resistance" were weaker among the members of the traditional sectarian parties—the Umma and the Democratic Unionist Party, DUP. The Muslim Brotherhood (MB) which was more ideological and better organized were an exception. As some of its leading members were associated with the leadership of the Dar Fur upheaval of 1981, residual resistance by the Muslim Brothers was much more discernible than that offered by the others, especially as they had opted, after the 1978 national reconciliation with Nimeiri, to build their organization from within the regime's institutions. All the above named political parties, in fact, had opposed the regime in Khartoum prior to the national reconciliation as constituent parties of the exiled National Front in Libya. It followed that most of the members of the regional government in Dar Fur were reluctant servants of a regime which they openly opposed up to 1978 and which they still passively opposed at heart. The apparent contradiction involved in this stance was never fully resolved until the fall of the Nimeiri regime in 1985.

Given that all the members of the Dar Fur regional government were at one time opponents of the central regime by party and ideological affiliations and were then co-members—even leading members—of the SSU, what was the "difference" which made differences between them? In other words, what was it that caused disagreements between the members of the regional cabinet and to what constituencies did the emergent factions appeal for support? To answer this question a broad description of the Dar Fur scene might be fruitful. In pre-1980 Dar Fur, most of the leaders of both the civil service and regimental forces were from riverain Sudan. The rulers, decision-makers, judges and, not least, the jailers were riverain Sudanese whom the Dar Furians generally regarded as alien to the region. With total and absolute power over the people they ruled, disdain, arrogance and exploitation were part and parcel of the behaviour of the riverain overlords. The feeling of being excluded from power, was so strong as to give birth to movements like the Red Flame and Soony. However, as these strong feelings waned, more balanced and constructive movements arose, e.g. the Dar Fur Development Front, supported by most of the educated Dar Furians who, by the very virtue of education, expected it to be their rightful destiny to replace the relatively alien riverain Sudanese in the administration of the region. The Dar Fur upheaval of 1981 made such a prospect a reality whose tangible manifestations were Draige and his all Dar Furi government. This political fusion of ethnic identities nurtured by the strong feelings against the dominant centre was soon to be undermined by processes of fission in which each ethnic groups claimed rewards from the Dar Fur government. The ruling elite under such pressures allowed itself to fall into the "ethnic trap": appease the ethnic group to which one belonged at the expense of others or indulge in wholesale nepotism.

The Dar Fur public, especially in urban areas, was divided into two opposing groups in the immediate aftermath of the 1981 upheaval—those who participated in the upheaval through demonstrations and those who tried whenever possible to sabotage the upheaval. The former category came to be known as upheavalists *muntafidh*, and the latter category came to be known as *kilab el Leil* (dogs of the night).[10] This connotation came from an incident in which a smaller group of inhabitants of Al-Fasher demonstrated against the Commissioner of Northern Dar Fur province at night. The incident took place while the upheaval was in the making and the expression, "dogs of the night", came to mean any person who went against the popular call that Dar Fur must be governed by a Dar Furi—a person who belonged to Dar Fur ethnically. The upheavalists, at least in urban Dar Fur, expected that the all-Dar Fur government should keep obstructive individuals and groups who played the role of saboteurs at an arm's length, at any rate, from the power centre in the region. But to isolate those individuals and groups was not what was in the minds of the regional government.

For those who took active part in forcing the central government to transfer power to Dar Furians through successive demonstrations, the elements of the old riverain dominated regime and their local collaborators which they politically associated with exploitation and arrogance were to be excluded from participation. Hence they wanted no part of them. Against this background of devolution of political power, frustrated public expectations and rational, but locally implausible positions taken by the newly instituted government, an involution of conflict eventually occurred. However, its disruptive ramifications and societal consequences cannot be fully fathomed unless we give a description of some aspects of the ecological situation in Dar Fur and of some of the international factors which made Dar Fur either a staging area, logistical back-up area or a war theatre for international groups.

---

[10] These labels were so dominant in popular political discourse at Al Fasher in 1982, that people were "pigeon-holed" into those categories as a matter of course, just like any other social identity such as tribe or family.

Involution of conflict

Prior to the devolution of power and the institution of a Dar Fur government manned by ethnic Dar Furians, ethnic conflict occurred, either because groups were competing for natural productive resources, pasture and water, or because of mutual raiding for livestock. Most of these conflicts remained under the control of government agencies and were, in most cases, settled by tribal reconciliation conferences supported by the district or province authorities with *ajawid*, bringing the two hostile parties to the conflict into agreement. The government authorities usually played the role of neutral go-betweens and later the guarantors for the fulfilment of the terms of such agreements. One reason for this enduring practice was that most of the government personnel was either totally alien to the parties in conflict, as was the case of the British colonial officers or that of the riverain Sudanese groups who did not have any affinities with the local tribal groups. Hence they were primarily interested in the maintenance of the *status quo* and the restoration of a stability that guaranteed their dominant position.

After 1981 the conflict situation changed dramatically. People who shared tribal and ethnic affinities with parties to conflicts held the reigns of power. While taking sides does not necessarily follow from this fact, unfortunately, as time went on many, though not all, government employees started taking sides in local ethnic conflicts. Very early in 1981, the leaders of the Dar Fur government started identifying their opponents in such categorical terms. This was done in private conversations the contents of which soon started leaking out to the public. It was at this stage that the two opposing political alliances crystallized; the *Zaghawa*, the nomadic Arab groups and the doctrinaire Muslim Brotherhood on one side and the Fur, Tunjur and elements of urban Dar Fur elites on the other side. The former group was to be led by Mahmoud Jamaa, (the then deputy ruler an ethnic Zaghawa) and the latter by Draige, (the then ruler an ethnic Fur). The elections for the post of the ruler were held in early 1982 and were won by Draige.

Ecological deterioration and increased competition

By the time the Dar Fur revolution was successfully concluded and an all-Dar Furi government was instituted, environmental conditions had already deteriorated to an unprecedented degree in the northern half of the region. This caused a massive movement of population groups and livestock into the farming belts of central Dar Fur, the heart-land of the Fur, and of other Dar Fur ethnic groups, which has a long tradition of settled rain-fed cultivation, based upon land tenure systems which excluded non-members: the *hakura* system.[11] The *hakura* system is based upon lands allocated by the Fur sultans to leaders of specified ethnic or family groups for the common use of the members of those groups. In each locality, as the practice was among the Fur, a headman allocated usufruct rights in land to the members of a diffusely constituted ambilineal descent group. While strangers and individual non-members, can be allocated land on usufructuary terms in return for remitting one tenth of the produce at harvest, massive influx of non-members created a number of problems. While an individual or a few migrant families were always granted temporary rights of utilization of lands and were in due time incorporated into the local system, an influx of whole tribal groups created problems, not only confined to the availability of arable land resources, but raised political questions about future alienation of land and, as a consequence, questioned the system of political authority. Animal thefts across ethnic borders were also rife and, though localized, nonetheless gave rise to serious and frequent inter-ethnic conflicts. Such was exactly the situation when Draige assumed the leadership of Dar Fur.

The areas of the Fur, Birgid, Berti and Daju were flooded by displaced groups from northern Dar Fur. The Zaghawa and various camel nomads of Arabic origin whose traditional pasture lands suffered even more under the ecological crisis were to be accommodated. In this already chaotic situation, the famine of 1983-1984 struck the area with devastating effect. As the very survival of particular groups was at stake, due to the combined effects of the ecological situation and the famine that ensued, localized ethnic conflicts began to get out of hand and encompassed whole ethnic groups and a wide geographical area. The settled farming ethnic groups—the Fur and Birgid—tried very hard to exclude the migrant groups from their lands; they feared that their sheer numbers should change ethnic balances and hence affect the customary rights of the host groups. Under relatively ordinary conditions in which the number of migrants into settled communities used to be low, the Fur traditionally received their guests with hospitality and shared their resources with them. If any migrants chose not to go back to their homes of origin, they became a part of the local political and social systems.[12] Even if not fully assimilated in cultural terms they were integrated into the local political system. It was not an advantage for the migrants to insist on their difference in terms of ethnic background hence they played down those differences. Moreover, relations between these in-migrants and the Fur were cemented through intermarriages and border maintainance operations were

---

[11] These were lands granted by the Fur Sultans for which the title holder got a sultanic deed written and stamped. Though the Sultanate was finally conquered by the British in 1916, these deeds continue to be legal documents accepted in courts.
[12] Håland (1969) shows these mechanisms as operating when destitute Baggara Arabs cross ethnic boundaries and become sedentary farmers and when Fur sendentary farmers who have accumulated livestock become Baggara by joining Baggara nomads.

minimized. Even language differences were, in a matter of few years, sur-
mounted in favour of the language of the host community. Thus Zaghawa
became Fur and similarly Arabs became Fur. These were voluntary societal
processes not so very different from those reported by Håland in 1969–1972.
Ethnic coexistence was peaceful in so far as the migrants absolutely recognized the Fur ownership of land.

The influx of ethnic groups into the Fur area which took place in the early
seventies and eighties was, however, of a completely different character.
Fleeing from drought-stricken areas and hunger the displaced groups were
there to stay on a more permanent basis. To forward their interests they
opted for a different concept relating to access to natural productive resources. They were to be seen as Sudanese nationals who had inalienable and
equal rights to all productive resources available. The gap between this new
concept and the customary *hakura* system of land tenure prevalent among
the Fur was bridged by various ethnic wars. Each position was backed by a
different ideological rationalization which was racist in content. Each group
overplayed its cultural differences from the other and hence justified culturally the call for a separate administration, not on a geographical but on an
ethnic ground.

The Regional Cabinet overwhelmed by these ethnic problems, was also
divided along ethnic lines—each group or groups supporting discretely the
claims of one or the other of the parties to the conflict. As the ruler was from
the Fur the other groups played precisely on that, convincing themselves that
they were unjustly treated because it was a Fur led government. They acted
towards the Fur accordingly and incidents of armed robbery were occurring
in the farming belt of central Dar Fur. Then suddenly Draige left the region
in protest against the reluctance shown by the Central Government in
Khartoum in acknowledging publicly the extent of the famine in 1983.

International factors in the ethnic conflict
The influence of the Chadian factional conflict

It is to be remembered that the Sudan and Chad have a long border in common and hence they share a number of ethnic groups. The instability and the
long-standing wars in Chad affected the Sudan because the warring factions
always sought refuge among their ethnic relatives across the borders. The
border areas which provided pasture for both Sudanese and Chadian livestock were in periods inaccessible, partly or wholly due to the prevailing insecurity. Pastoralists on both sides of the border were pushed into ever-de-
creasing and badly deteriorating pastures in the interior of the Sudan where
cultivation was also practised. This concentration of both livestock and cultivation in extremely narrow corridors in the interior had the effect of exac-
erbating the already deteriorating ecological conditions caused by continuously failing rains and overutilization of the productive land. Localized eth-

nic conflicts were already quite prevalent when the 1983-1984 famine struck
the area, pushing the local populations further southwards towards the central farming belt of Dar Fur. The concentration of pastoral and semi-pastoral
groups with their livestock in an area already occupied by sedentary cultiva-
tors, whose land use patterns included orchard growing and year-round
farming of vegetable fields, was bound to lead to many forms of confrontations, especially when the parties belonged to diverse ethnic groups. The government which sat at that time in the regional capital of Dar Fur was led by
the Fur as stated in the study.

In 1982 Hissene Habré forced Goukoni, the then Libyan-supported president of Chad, out of office. The staging ground was Dar Fur, with military
aid provided by the US and Egyptian governments and with the Sudan government of Nimeiri playing a leading role in the military operations. The alliance between the Sudan, Egypt, USA and Habré's rebels was sustained by
the desire of those powers to frustrate Libyan ambitions to expand to the
South. In an effort to regain a place of influence in Chad, the Libyans attempted to fight by proxy through the use of the so-called Islamic Legions (*al
failag al Islami*)—a multinational force made up of migrant workers and the
remnants of Chadian opposition groups. In Chad the ethnic composition of
the ruling alliance under Habré's post-1982 government was composed of
the representatives of the following tribal groups: Sara (Christian southerners), Goraan (Habré's group), Zaghawa and Hadjerai. As all these ethnic
groups were non-Arabs, the Libyans started recruiting Arab tribes whose exclusion from power in Ndjamena was already apparent. This drive was
backed up by an ideology which advocated the extension of the Arab belt in
Africa. Recruitment among the nomadic Arab groups that straddled the border area between the Sudan and Chad was not difficult. Libyan arms, ammunition and money travelled easily across the Sudanese borders and easily
found their recipients among the nomadic Arab groups, both Sudanese and
Chadians, in and around the southern and western slopes of the Jebel Marra
in the Fur heartland.

The hindrance which the Libyan military operations met was the government of Nimeiri, acting in alliance with the USA and Egypt. This obstacle
was removed when Nimeiri fell in 1985. The political chaos that followed in
the Sudan during 1985–1986 was effectively exploited by the Libyans to
strengthen their lines of supply to the Chadian opposition and the nomadic
Arab groups in Dar Fur. Chief among these groups was the Conseil
Démocratique Révolutionaire (CDR) of al Sheikh Ibn Omer which consisted
of nomadic Arab tribes whose tribal areas straddled the Chad-Sudan borders.
While the main recipients of the Libyan weapons were the Chadian Arab
groups which intended to destabilize Chad, Sudanese Arab groups, such as
the Missriya Zoroug and the Beni Helba, were also armed by the same
source. Of course, the massive supply of weapons found its way indirectly to
other tribal groups in Dar Fur, although the shipments were not intended for

them in the first place. The need to secure food supplies and to gain support led each Chadian faction to arm local allies in Dar Fur. Weapons were cheap and readily available. A kalashnikov assault rifle (AK 47) with accessories, for instance, was sold for less than USD 40 in 1986. The same held true for rocket-propelled grenades and other more destructive weapons.

However, what was more pertinent in the Fur-Arab conflict was the fact that most of the Arab-based Chadian opposition groups moved with their livestock into the Fur areas because the Jebel Marra range provided some natural protection, the terrain being difficult for Chadian government expeditionary forces to adventure into. The Fur, being settled farmers and peaceful people, encountered many problems in the wake of the influx of the nomadic Arab groups and their livestock into a predominantly agricultural area. These problems arose from animal trespass onto farms, destruction of crops and general competition for productive resources; for most of the watering areas in the Fur area were situated within heavily cultivated areas. Conflicts caused by the destruction of crops by Arab herds led quickly to mutual retaliatory acts of banditry—stealing from each other's herds, burning unharvested farms, burning pasture grass by the Fur and the Arabs, irrespective of whether these Arabs were Chadians or Sudanese. Chadian forces pursued the Arab opposition from Chad into the Sudan and Chadian para-military forces rustled camel herds belonging to the Chadian nomads who were fleeing from persecution. This made the Fur area problematic even for the Fur as well. Major battles frequently took place there with the Fur individuals falling as a "collateral damage".[13]

Being under these pressures, the Fur decided to take action. They resorted to the mass burning of pasture fields with a view to forcing the Arabs to move to other pasture areas, and attempted to withhold access to sources of water and retaliated in kind when their livestock were stolen by Arabs. The Arabs started retaliating by burning Fur villages and farms, by uprooting trees from the orchards and destroying Fur farm equipment, such as water pumps, ploughs and trucks. Sudanese Arab tribes, neighbouring the Fur, came to assist their "brother Arabs" of Chad. The war soon took ideological and racist leanings which were heavily laden with tribal bigotry. Arab bands called *janjawid* (hordes) and *fursan* (knights) roamed the Fur areas, burning villages, killing indiscriminately and appropriating Fur property at will. The Arab *janjawid* slaughtered anyone whose tribal identity was Fur or looked like a Fur in complexion or facial appearance, whether on a highway or in a village. The Fur also started developing their own groups, the *malishiyat* (militias) and responded in a similar manner.

---

[13] This situation was repeated in 1990 when Chadian army units pursuing "rebels" burned fourteen Fur villages in the areas of Ein Siro and Jebel Si in Northern Dar Fur. The Chadians also mined and booby-traped water sources in this area and many individuals lost limbs as a result.

The Libyan-backed elements, not only distributed arms and funds, but they also passed the message that the Arabs were the power in the local area. On the other hand, the Fur elements in the leadership of the Regional Government of Dar Fur, at the time, did not handle the situation in such a manner as to dispel the fears held by the Arabs. The Fur were behaving towards them as if the Fur Sultanate of the seventeenth century was back in place. The Arabs thought they were fighting with their backs to a wall: they were chased across the border by Chadian militant and paramilitary forces and opposed by the Fur. The Arabs sought the support of other nomadic Arab groups in the Sudan, especially from the neighbouring Kordofan province and in the end formed an organization called "the Arab Congregation". It included 27 Arab groups, not bound by kinship ties, although they all claimed Arab origins in racial terms. This congregation's declared hostilities were directed against any Zurga (blacks). A central feature of this conflict was the fact that each side developed a racial ideology against the other. This helped to create cultural and political justifications for the mass killings and burnings across Fur-Arab ethnic lines. The *janjawid* were the vehicle of the Arab racial position against the Fur and by extension the blacks of Dar Fur. *Milishiyat*, the militias, were the Fur's vehicle for self-defence and were later used to forge links with the SPLA.

The influence of the Libyan-Chadian wars

After the successful installation of Habre in Ndjamena in 1982 Libya continued her efforts to exert influence through direct military actions, with a view to destabilizing the US, Egyptian, Sudanese (and sometimes Iraqi) backed regime in Ndjamena. The only deterrent against the invasion of Chad was the clear commitment of France to safeguard the national integrity and sovereignty of the former colony by maintaining an active military presence there. The area below latitude 16°N was a no-go area for any form of Libyan presence. However, from 1986 a military initiative was taken by the Habré government in Ndjamena on the pretext of liberating the Aouzou strip which was previously a *de facto* Libyan enclave in Chad. Enjoying the backing of a number of major international and regional powers aiming to destabilize Gaddafi's Libya, Habre's forces went on the offensive and war broke out in 1986–1987. But before a cease-fire agreement was reached between the two countries in the last quarter of 1987, the Chadian troops were in control of the northern part of their country and were pushing deep into Libya proper.

Two points of this international conflict are relevant to the discussion of the Fur-Arab conflict. In the first place, the humiliation of the better equipped Libyan troops by the Chadian rag-tag army of various guerilla forces, although discretely and sometimes openly supported by French Air Force, only sharpened the Libyan clandestine attempts to bring down the

Habré regime. But as a direct consequence of this action Dar Fur became more and more enmeshed in these complex international conflicts. In the second place, however, as they were defeated on the battle field and prevented by the French Air Force from having a second military go against Habré, Libyans did not have much choice, but to recourse to a war by proxy and use the nomadic Arabs, the only group which was not included in the ethnic balance in the Chadian power distribution arrangements. As a consequence of this, more armaments, ammunition, and funds poured into Dar Fur. Their influence was strengthened by the culturally saleable ideological propaganda that the Arabs were the dominant power in the area. Up until the fall of Nimeiri in 1985, Libyans could not use the Sudan as a conduit to Chad. Relations between the two governments had become extremely sour after an attempt by the then exiled Sudanese opposition group, the National Front, to bring down Nimeiri with massive Libyan backing in a short-lived invasion in 1976. Once Nimeiri was out of power in Khartoum, the Libyans could resume using western Sudan, i.e. Dar Fur, as a conduit to Chad. By backing the Umma party of Saddiq el-Mahdi financially in the 1986 elections, the Libyans had somehow ensured their cooperation with Saddiq's regime which lasted for three years (1986–1989).

The premiership of Saddiq el-Mahdi, who owed so much to Tripoli as a result of the 1986 parliamentary elections, made it easier for the Libyans to become more and more open about their presence in Dar Fur in spite of the fact that the Dar Furians were highly critical of it. This was at the time when the Chadian-Libyan war broke out wherein a sizeable Libyan force was taken as prisoners of war by the Chadian army from Ouadi Doum. The anti-Libyan alliance worked to transform the Libyan prisoners of war into a contra-force to bring down the Libyan regime. Libyan activities in the Dar Fur became even more intensive as they moved troops and armaments to this front, since the northern front was barred by the French.

In this military situation the Chadians also needed allies among the Sudanese ethnic groups in order to weaken the Chadian nomadic Arabs who provided recruitment ground for the Libyan backed opposition groups. But as the Libyans had found a local ally, the militia force of the Beni Helba Arabs, the Chadians started running a para-military force recruited mainly from the Bedayat Zaghawa to harass the Arabs and rustle their camels, the backbone of their economic survival. This action was regarded by the Chadian government as a legitimate operation to recover Chadian national wealth which had been illegally smuggled out from Chad into the Sudan. Though the Chadian government never admitted responsibility for these paramilitary forces, its military forces later disregarded international laws and crossed into the Sudan, mounting military operations with some degree of impunity. The Chadian violations of the Sudanese territory were regarded as a counterbalance to the complicity of the Sudanese government in the Libyan operations.

In addition there appeared small independent groups, which had splintered off from different Chadian and Libyan backed factions. They started to operate outside the control of any of the governments or major ethnic groups involved in the conflict. Armed with Gronovs, kalashnikovs (AK47) and G3 assault rifles, RPGS, explosives and heavy machine guns—showing that they once were either sponsored by Libya or Chad—these groups operated from bases on the fringes of the semi-Saharan areas of the northern Dar Fur mainly as armed bandits. Influenced by these factors, the Fur-Arab conflict erupted into a full-scale ethnic war. Given the fact that the Arabs were already sponsored by external powers and that shortly afterward some of their groups were provided with arms by the Sudan government in order to ward off the SPLA in the southern fringes of Dar Fur, these developments in the region imperatively forced the Fur to look for internal and external allies for similar support. Although they were able to open an office in Ndjamena during Habre's reign, (up to December 1990), during most of the period of the conflict, the Fur were on their own.

Consequences of devolution of power and the involution of conflict

The following table shows some of the major ethnic reconciliation conferences which took place in Dar Fur after independence.

This table was compiled from the administrative files of the office for tribal affairs in Al Fasher by the author in June 1990.

As the table shows, the major causes of these conflicts were access to natural productive resources—pasture and water and animal thefts. These conflicts also occurred between pastoralists as well as across the pastoralist/agriculturalist divide. Moreover the likelihood of ethnic conflicts occurring between pastoral Arab groups was as high as the likelihood of its occurrence between nomadic Arab groups and nomadic or agricultural non-Arab groups. Six out of the thirteen cases in the table were conflicts between Arab pastoral groups. However, nine out of the thirteen occasions on which reconciliation conferences were conducted, involved pastoral Arab groups as parties to those conflicts. Four cases involved conflict parties who were both non-Arabs. It is also to be noted that only four cases involved parties to the conflict in which one party was of Arab identity and the other party was of non-Arab identity. Of the two provinces of Dar Fur region, southern Dar Fur seems to have the highest numbers of reconciliation conferences, convened to resolve ethnic conflicts. Nine of the thirteen reconciliation conferences were convened in southern Dar Fur and only four were held in northern Dar Fur. This is explained practically by the fact that southern Dar Fur is by far the richest in terms of pasture and agricultural production and that the receiving areas for pastoralists migrating from the north lay in those territories.

Reconciliation Conferences

Date	Parties to the conflict	Main issues
1957	Meidob vs Kababish [Northern Dar Fur].	Mutual raiding for camels [territorial access].
1968	Rezaiqat vs Maalia [Southern Dar Fur].	Grazing lands, animal thefts [territorial access].
1969	Zaghawa vs Northern Rezaiqat [Northern Dar Fur].	Access to pasture and water, animal thefts [territorial access].
1974	Zaghawa vs Birgid [Southern Dar Fur].	Access to agricultural land, animal thefts [territorial access].
1976	Beni Helba vs Northern Rezaiqat [Southern Dar Fur].	Access to pasture and water and animal thefts [territorial access].
1980	Northern Rezaiqat (Umjallul, Mahriya, Eraiqat and Etaifat) vs Beni Helba. Birgid, Daju and Fur [Southern Dar Fur].	Access to pasture and water and animal thefts [territorial access].
1980	Taisha vs Salamat [Southern Dar Fur].	Access to pasture and water and animal thefts [territorial access].
1982	Kababish and Kawahla vs Meidob, Berti and Ziyadia [Northern Dar Fur].	Access to pasture and water and animal thefts [territorial access].
1984	Missairiya vs Rezaiqat [Southern Dar Fur]	Access to pasture and water and animal thefts [territorial access].
1987	Gimir and Marareet vs Fellata [Southern Dar Fur].	Access to pasture and water, animal thefts [territorial access].
1989	The Fur of Kabkabiya vs Zaghawa [Northern Dar Fur].	Territorial access and animal thefts.
1989	The Fur vs 27 Arab tribes [Southern Dar Fur].	Territorial conquest, racial prejudice and political subjugation.
1990	Gimir vs Zaghawa [Southern Dar Fur].	Territorial access and animal thefts.

Apart from the case involving Fur and 27 Arab tribes, ethnic conflicts are usually attributed to livestock thefts, mutual raiding and denial of access to productive territories, either during "lean years", suspicion of animal diseases or even fear of over-grazing. As a rule, all the conflicts involve losses of human life and animal property which are settled by *diyya* (blood money) and material compensation between the parties to the conflict. The district and provincial government authorities act as guarantors for the fulfilment of the terms of such agreements reached in the conferences. The continued observation of the implementation of terms and the responsibility of the local chiefs who were signatories ensured the durability of the settlements reached.

The Fur/Arab case presents an ethnic conflict of a different character in this particular spectrum: while territorial access might have been the initial cause, the conflict was quickly transformed into a racial war, fuelled by ethnic bigotry and racial prejudice that entailed territorial conquest and political subjugation. The battle-cry was absolutely based on the manipulation of racial symbols on both sides. The Arab *janjawid* strove, to expand the "Arab Belt" by attempting to annihilate the Fur by burning their villages, slaying their people and appropriating their property. Public utilities, such as schools, mosques and dispensaries were never spared, let alone Fur women, children and the elderly. The Fur militia responded in similar ways and justified their actions with slogans about the "African Belt" in Dar Fur. This war was beyond the control of the traditional local chiefs; young educated people on both sides strove to mobilize their urban based constituencies for the war. Moreover in order to starve the Arab groups and their herds in the Fur lands, the militia forces burned pasture and denied them access to watering areas. Into this bloody and scourged field entered a body of profiteers that rustled both Fur and Arab livestock. The blame, of course, fell on the warring parties and this only increased the frequency of violent conflict between them.

While this conflict was the only one which took on the character of a racial war, by 1988 ethnic conflicts had proliferated in Dar Fur; a situation of all-against-all generally prevailed in the region. The central and regional governments were equally paralysed and the relationship between ethnic groups was so bitter that prospects for any reconciliation were worse than gloomy. In addition the security forces were adding fuel to the fire by committing atrocities against the civilian population whenever they were called out to disengage combatants or to pursue bands of robbers. Neither the regional government nor the central government had, at this time, much credibility in rural Dar Fur. In fact, the central government tried to explain away the problem by attributing it in some cases to what it called armed robbery and at other times to the educated class in Dar Fur. At the end of the day the situation looked as if a drastic change was needed in order to come to grips with the ethnic problems of Dar Fur.

The National Council for the salvation of Dar Fur

Within this grim situation a non-official body, the National Council for the Salvation of Dar Fur (NCSD) was created in Khartoum in March 1988. The initiative was taken by some Dar Fur intellectuals based in Khartoum. It was a result of continuous informal discussions carried out by educated Dar Furians who were fed up with the accusations that it was the educated Dar Furians who were fuelling tribalism and manipulating ethnic conflicts in Dar Fur. An executive of the National Council for the Salvation of Dar Fur was formed in a meeting held at the University of Khartoum in February 1988 as an attempt to surmount narrow ethnic affinities—hence the affix "national". The motto which the NCSD adopted was: "the salvation of Dar Fur is a national duty". Members included University professors, members of the parliament, (representing different constituencies in Dar Fur), businessmen, office workers and workers of Dar Furi origin in the capital. For various reasons relating to party politics, 34 members of the parliament, who belonged to the Umma party, walked out from the first meeting of the council, while members belonging to the Democratic Unionist Party (DUP) and to the National Islamic Front (NIF) remained active in the council and led practical work.[14]

After issuing a number of press releases which made clear the objectives of the council, the NCSD called for a "silent" demonstration in protest against what it regarded as the passive stance of the Umma dominated government over the issue of the presence of Libyan troops and Chadian opposition factions in Dar Fur. The Umma party, attempted to prevent the demonstration from taking place in Khartoum. Of course, its Dar Furi contingent of 34 parliamentary representatives were directed not to take part in that demonstration, a directive with which they complied.

The informal NCSD managed to mobilize 40,000 (Salih, K.M. 1990) demonstrators, representing a cross-section of the Dar Fur population. A silent march went to the Council of Ministers on 12 March 1988 with a petition protesting about and criticizing the presence of Chadian and Libyan forces in western Sudan. This brought what was happening in Dar Fur to the centre of political debate. The Umma party, aiming to preserve its followings in Dar Fur, took the situation even more seriously. It was in this context that Dr. Sese took the initiative, mentioned in the beginning of this article, for a reconciliation of the Fur and the Arabs. Dr. Sese's initiative bore fruit in the Fur-Arab peace agreement which was signed on 8 July 1989. However, the signing took place under a different government, for the multi-party coalition government of the Umma party of which Dr. Sese was a member, was overthrown on 30 June 1989 by a military coup; what was later known as the Revolution of National Salvation. The new government banned all political and non-political organizations, including the NCSD.

The Reconciliation Agreement between the Fur and the Arabs

From February 1989 until May 1989 a committee of mediators, comprising most of the tribal leaders of Dar Fur, toured the conflict area and talked to the parties, attempting to make them accept the principle of peaceful negotiations as the only means of settling disputes in the region. It was not until the beginning of May 1989 that the leaders of the Fur and Arabs agreed to meet in Al-Fasher. The date for this first meeting was agreed to be 15 May 1989. However, on 13 May the uneasy truce which was reached through the painstaking work of the mediators broke down, and violence continued until 17 May 1989. The violence was all encompassing and spared no one.

---

[14] The parliamentary deputies belonging to the Umma party understood the whole exercise as a conspiracy by the other two parties against the Umma, especially as the coalition government was not working. It is also worth mentioning that two parliamentary deputies belonging to the National Islamic Front (NIF) crossed the floor to join the DUP not long after the formation of this council.

When, finally, the meeting of the two main parties to the conflict took place on 29 May 1989, peace was nowhere nearer than before; each of the parties blamed the racist attitude of the other. The negotiations continued until June 1989 when they reached a deadlock. However, the military coup on 30 June 1989, had a positive effect on the negotiations. One week after the coup, the agreement was ready and on 8 July 1989 the reconciliation agreement was signed by the parties and the mediators and was soon ratified by the government in power in Khartoum.

The following are some of the basic stipulations of the Fur-Arab Reconciliation Agreement (as I translate them from the proceedings)

1. The liquidation of Fur militias and those of the Arabs or of any other tribal groups that are armed. The presence of the government in the form of armed forces should be guaranteed and a dateline should be fixed for handing in any illegal arms held by the tribes in return for a generous reward.
2. The government shall deport any aliens entering Dar Fur illegally.
3. The government undertakes to open routes of migration for the nomads according to standing agreements. It shall also maintain a heavy presence to safeguard the rights of both pastoralists and farmers.
4. The government shall evict any groups that have occupied villages or farms during the dispute and shall reinstate their original population.
5. The government shall dissolve any organizations that do not work according to the law and shall put its members under surveillance.
6. The government shall scrutinize carefully the activities of all foreign organizations working in the region.
7. The government shall issue laws which mete out severe penalties on those who burn pastures, close migration routes, erect unnecessary air exclosures, (*Zaraib al-Hawa*, Arabic), cut trees or destroy farms.[15]
8. Any party which breaks these agreements shall receive the maximum penalties stipulated in the Sudan Penal Code.
9. A committee for migration routes, pasture and water shall decide all issues related to these aspects.

The conference asked the Arabs to pay a total of £S 43,218 773 as a compensation to the Fur, accounting for deaths and destruction of property. The Fur were asked to pay £S 10,883 459 as a compensation. The central government was asked to contribute £S 10,433 350 to both parties to the conflict. These protocols were signed by 110 Arab representatives, 110 Fur representatives and 21 mediators in the presence of the military Governor of

---

[15] *Zaraib al-Hawa* (Arabic) or air exclosures as the nearest translation, denotes a thorn fence around a piece of territory with the intention of putting it beyond access to livestock. In this sense it stands for that part of range taken out of public access.

Dar Fur. But would the terms of this agreement be implemented and re-spected by the parties?

Unfulfilled reconstruction

The reconstruction period that was supposed to follow the formal signing of the peace protocol was aborted, even before it was given a chance to start. Only a few months after the agreement, killing started all over again. The Fur accused the Arabs of armed banditry, cattle rustling, highway robbery and burning of Fur villages. The Arabs accused the Fur of denying them ac-cess to the watering points, burning pastures, continued terrorization and bombardment of their camps. The Arabs claimed that the Fur militia forces were intact while the Fur claimed that the Arab militia forces were intact. Both parties claimed that the government was conspicuously absent from the most vulnerable conflict areas.

An "atraditional" tribal conflict

Most of the tribal conflicts which took place in Dar Fur were straightfor-ward cases of competition over productive resources in which two parties were involved. The Fur-Arab divide was an atypical case in the sense that it involved a multiplicity of partners and had a clear ideological drive. The lo-cal Arab tribes such as the Beni Helba and the Beni Hussein had lived with the Fur in what can be described as symbiotic peace for quite a time. With the amicability of relationships and their complementarity it was even possi-ble for the Fur to become a part of the Baggara nomadic groups and for the Baggara to settle down as farmers (Håland 1969).

However, the external support the Arabs enjoyed in terms of the supply of arms and the self-confidence that arose among the Fur after the devolution of power in 1981 and the assumption of the office of the governor by persons of Fur background fed on each other to create feelings of superiority in both camps. The Arabs wanted to conquer the Fur territory by force of arms with racial ideologies providing a cultural justification for massacring Fur. The Fur, on the other hand, tried to revive the mythical greatness of the Fur sul-tanate, and assumed the role of the bearer of the "Black African" heritage in the area.

In all this the Fur found support among certain sections of the regional government, especially under the leadership of Yousif Bakheit in the period between May 1986 and September 1986. The Arabs, on the other hand, re-ceived some support from the central government when parts of their con-stituency were armed by the government to ward off the SPLA operations in southern Dar Fur. The central government turned a blind eye to the arms supplies coming into Dar Fur from Libya. When they finally petitioned the central government about how they were excluded from power in Dar Fur in late 1987, the Arabs did not even mask the so called Arabic congregation—the vehicle for the racist ideology of Arab superiority in Dar Fur. In their firm belief that they had the support of the central government, they played on what they supposed were feelings of "Arabism" shared by the prime minister: Saddiq el Mahdi. They even quoted a verse of an old Arabic poem which claims that: "Injustice from relatives inflicts more pain than an Indian sword," the "unjust relative" here being the prime minister.

The failure of the Prime Minister and the government to react to this petition was shocking for the rest of Dar Fur, including even Arabic groups which did not want to be a party to this racist congregation. It was the strong abhorrence of these racist tendencies by the majority of Dar Furians that led to the formation of the informal body of the National Council for the Salvation of Dar Fur.

Militias vs knights?

Unlike the Fur, the Arabs, because of their segmentary organization and its potential for mobilization by the process of fusion of lineages and clans, were able to engage in corporate action. Their systems were readily able to mobilize groups for corporate action when faced by external threats. Their mobility, either on horse or camel-back, made it easier for them to move out of danger zones and thus avoid retaliatory action by the sedentary Fur. Therefore, it was no great surprise that the Fur suffered heavy losses at the beginning of this conflict. But, however, shortly afterwards the Fur began to address the balance of "naked" power by training their own militia forces.

The devolution of power that brought persons of Fur background to the leadership of the regional government of Dar Fur also precipitated conflicts between the Fur and other ethnic groups of Dar Fur. This was because other ethnic groups interpreted the behaviour of the Fur, at least that of their leaders, as if the Fur Sultanate had been revived. The Zaghawa and the nomadic Arabs felt that the Fur and their leadership were intent on denying all of them access to natural productive resources, especially when the northern Dar Fur was devastated by the Sahelian drought, which caused their mass movement into the Fur area. In 1982 there was a strong movement among the Fur communities, spreading from Kutum in the northern Dar Fur to Kabkabiya and Zalingei in the southern and southwestern Dar Fur, to get rid of the immigrant groups. In response the nomadic Arabs and the Zaghawa were forced into an alliance of convenience. These differences were played out in the elections to the SSU during 1982–1983 when the Fur of Kutum expressed open enmity towards the Zaghawa and the nomadic Arabs whom they referred to as the *nazihin ajanib* (displaced aliens). In addition the Fur accused the Zaghawa of perpetrating acts of armed robbery against them.[16] The regional government, for its part, dealt with the problem of law and order through heavy handed action against those tribal groups which were collectively accused of armed robbery. Whole tribes came under fire from the government forces which adopted a mode of operations code-named "combing"—essentially consisting of ransacking whole villages, beating up men severely to force them to confess that they were armed robbers and sometimes shooting people at random.[17] As a direct result of these operations a deep hostility began to develop between the persecuted groups and the Fur-led government. 1986–1987 saw a different turn of events. Small bands of armed men started ambushing government forces in the field in addition to undertaking retaliatory strikes against Fur local chiefs in northern Dar Fur. Simultaneously, the threats of execution of certain police officers who were accused of brutality against the civilian population started coming to the northern Dar Fur district headquarters in Kutum. As most of these actions were taking place in northern Dar Fur where the Zaghawa presence was heavy, the accusation that the Zaghawa were the perpetrators of the actions against the Fur was strengthened. The heavy-handed actions of the government continued and spread out to include all areas of Zaghawa concentration in the central farming belt of Dar Fur.

The outbreak of war between the Fur and the Arabs in 1987 provided a respite for the Zaghawa. The accusation of armed banditry was now turned against the nomadic Arab group and forces of Chadian opposition in Dar Fur. Certain leading elements in the Fur dominated regional government went so far as to align the forces under their command directly with the cause of their kin, the Fur. Under cover of recruiting more police to cope with the security problem in Dar Fur, some of those leaders mobilized the Fur to join the police to use the cover of legitimacy that was provided by the uniform to help their kin.[18] The Arab elements in the armed forces in Dar Fur began to behave in a similar way. By the time Dr. Sese came with his peace initiative in February 1989, the government forces which were supposed to bring this ethnic war under control were themselves divided, each group favouring its ethnic kin. This was reflected in the many recorded incidents of "non-response" by government forces to reports of violence which demanded swift action from those forces, the failure depending upon the ethnic background of the reporter and the ethnic background of the com-

---

[16] In a meeting in Kutum, the headquarters of Northern Dar Fur district on 25 November 1987, it was revealed that the Fur of this area had started arming themselves with AK47 assault rifles and were harassing Zaghawa travellers (Source: The security committee of the district, Wednesday 25 November 1987).
[17] Six elderly people belonging to the Bedayat Zaghawa, were extra-judicially executed by the police in an area named Alawona (about 25 km from Al Fasher) in 1987. In the same year the army in Kabkabiya, extra-judicialy executed 3 Bedayat Zaghawa including the *Imam* (religious leader) of their village.
[18] The names are withheld for obvious reasons.

mander of the force at that time. If the two—reporter and commander—
happened to be from the same ethnic background, the government forces responded in record time, albeit, biased in their interference.

It was partly due to this situation that the Fur were unable to mobilize
other groups which fell on the African side of the dichotomy between Arabs
and Zurga. Although there were a number of meetings between the Zaghawa
and Fur representatives with a conscious attempt to merge their forces in the
Zurga camp, the Zaghawa refused to be drawn into those blocks, mainly due
to their bitterness because of the many years of persecution by the Fur-domi-
nated regional governments and partly because they saw the latent danger of
dragging the whole of Dar Fur into a civil war by forming alliances based
largely on race. The Zaghawa always saw themselves in an intermediate position between the two extremes of the racial continuum.

Between the formation of NCSD in 1988 and the military *coup de d'état*
of 30 June 1989 a different thinking began to dominate the Dar Furians in
Khartoum and urban Dar Fur proper. This was due to the revival of a regional identity that was threatened by so many years of ethnic conflicts, biased and heavy handed central and regional governments and a foreign presence which threatened the very fabric of a peaceful and civilized life in Dar
Fur. Here it is important to remember that Dar Fur experienced centralized
states from around 1640. How to get an equal share of national power and
wealth became the issues for discussion after the coup in 1989. As the coup-
makers' first statement made the Dar Fur issue one of the justifications for
overthrowing an inept regime which was to be blamed for the situation there,
the Fur and the Arabs quickly reconciled their differences and within a week
after the coup a peace protocol was signed by the conflicting parties. In the
political fanfare which followed this event (8 July 1989) the Arabs claimed
that the reconciliation was a present from the Arabs to the Revolution of
National Salvation. The Arabs' representative in his closing address to the
session in which the peace protocol was signed by the parties stated that

> On this blessed day, 8th July 1989 we [the Arabs] present the most valuable
> gift to the Revolution of National Salvation because we feel that the revolu-
> tion is sincere about its national orientation. Dar Fur for all, the Sudan for
> all and Dar Fur for the Arabs and the Fur. We would like to see the revival
> of tribal administration with full force and authority. We would also like to
> see the Sudanese state regaining its respect, might and awe and that its
> armed forces should be spread all over to maintain law and order. Equally
> we would like to see this region "taken" out from its state of backwardness.
> Finally we say to our Fur brothers, "stop your militia forces from harming
> us [Arabs], we will stop our "knights" from harming you [Fur].

The representative of the Fur made it explicitly clear in a reply that

> At this moment we would like to draw the attention of this respectable con-
> gregation, once again, to the causes of this tragic conflict: a) external influ-
> ence with its imported ideologies premised on racism such as Arab Belt,
> Zenji Negro Belt and liberation of Arab lands, b) internal influences relating

to political expediency and the opportunism of the now-banned political parties coupled with individual and collective ambitions which worked to manipulate tribal feelings to serve their political ends. This was assisted by the weakness of the state and its diminishing authority owing to its partiality in these matters and the ineffectiveness of the judicial apparatus. It is our view that reconstruction could begin by the quick relief of the displaced persons of this war and the urgent task of rehabilitation of villages and public utilities that were destroyed. The safeguarding of our international borders in the face of unwanted migration and the termination of foreign influences (Chadian and Libyan) are integral to the survival of our reconciliation. History does not repeat itself, but events similar in nature occur in different times. We should remember that exactly one century ago Osman Janu of the Taaisha Arabs wreaked havoc in the Fur area as an army commander of Khalifa Abdullahi in Omdurman!

The military ruler of Dar Fur who ratified this protocol representing the central government of the Revolution of National Salvation conveyed the following message to the parties to the reconciliation conference

After we have achieved this great reconciliation, I would like to warn everybody that I will not tolerate any of those words and terminologies that led to the collapse of law and order in Dar Fur. From this moment onwards I will not want to hear such phrases as "the Arab Congregation", "Dar Fur for Fur" or "militia forces" and "knights". Neither do I tolerate such empty phrases as "Arab Belt" or "Zenj Belt".

The Command Council of the Revolution of National Salvation which had sent two of its members to attend this session had the following to say

This conflict has its roots, first and foremost, in the scramble for political power which followed the regional government Acts of [1982]. As a result of it development effort in this part of the country came to a standstill. Later, the leaders of political parties and politicians were to contribute to this bloody conflict by their very lack of vision. This callous attitude from politicians of different levels had led to the deaths of a great many "children", ... the personnel of the armed forces and other security forces. The integrity of these forces was questioned and accusations against them were forwarded by one or the other party to the conflict, irrespective of the self-denial practised by these forces. I would like to assure you all that these forces will not abdicate their responsibilities and they will be the eye that watches and the hand that firmly strikes at any individual or party that attempts to breach this agreement.

However, only a few months after the peace agreement was signed violent breaches of the terms of this agreement were reported. The Fur complained of increased activities by Arab elements in rustling their cattle, committing highway robbery and burning trucks and villages. Indiscriminate killing of Fur, appropriation of their property, uprooting of trees in the orchards and destruction of irrigation pumps were on the rise. Moreover most of the terms of the agreement, especially those that related to the evacuation of armed non-Sudanese groups, were not fulfilled. The Arabs, for their part, complained of Fur intransigence, especially of that relating to denial of access to watering points and the burning of pasture in order to starve their animals. Markets were closed to the Arabs and daily shelling of the Arab camps by the Fur heavy guns was on the rise. In short, eight months after the peace agreement was signed, the Fur "militia forces" and the Arab "knights" were engulfed in a full-scale war in which Fur villages were burned and Arab camps were shelled daily. The ideological phrases "Arab Belt" and "Zinji Belt" were current again. What was it that went wrong?

Basic but unresolved issues
Land ownership and access to productive resources

This conflict, although manifesting a multiplicity of causes, basically revolves around the question of ownership of natural productive resources, especially of land resources. In central Dar Fur

> ultimate title to land derives, in the Fur view, from two disparate sources: sovereignty, and first use. According to Sudanese law, the State is the ultimate title-holder to all land, and fields revert to the State if cultivation is discontinued for more than two years. This more or less perpetuates the practice of the Fur Sultanate, whereby the Sultan exercised the authority to seize land from occupants, and to give land as fiefs to his followers. On the other hand, the Fur also claim title to land from ancestors who were the first to take the land in use. Such traditional rights are held collectively by a whole groups of descendants, and are maintained to varying degree in the face of the rights as defined by the state. (Barth 1988:9)

In the Fur tradition, which was upheld through the operation of the Fur Sultanate 1640–1917, the sovereign allocated *hakura* rights to a collectivity through a title-holder who represented the sovereign. This title holder could have been a village *sheikh*, or an *omda* of a number of villages, or a *shertai* of a specific district of the Fur administrative hierarchy. Individuals, within a *hakura* system, have access to land, either through the allocation of usufruct rights by the title holder or through traditional claims derived from ancestors. In both cases land is inalienable through sale. When use is discontinued for any reason, land reverted to the sovereign or the collectivity of traditional claimants. Authority, both political and administrative, in the local Fur context went with the hakura system. He who has land can claim both administrative and political authority over those on it. Access is conditional only on Fur ethnic identity (see Barth 1982:26). These aspects of land ownership never used to be problematic, although one may expect some internal conflicts as increasing portions of *hakura* lands started coming under permanent agriculture through orchard growing and vegetable production in intensive form, as from the fifties. The problem here stems from the fact that orchard growing takes out land from the redistribution system, especially as the economic value of orchards is becoming increasingly evident.

The nomadic Baggara Arabs and Fulani tribesmen who used to frequent Fur areas were temporary sojourners who stayed in the *wadis* in the dry season and spent the rainy season elsewhere. Only a few stayed in the Fur area and cultivated the staple *dukhun*, and they were mostly destitute Baggara who cultivated in the hope of accumulating enough cattle to go back to the nomadic sector. However, this process was not unilinear. Some Fur who accumulated enough cattle became a part of the Baggara nomadic mode of life (see Håland 1972). The small minority of Baggara Arabs who farmed in the Fur territory were allocated usufruct rights to land in the same traditional way as was done to Fur individuals, except for the small difference that they had to remit what is normally called *usher*, (one tenth of the produce) to the title-holder as regular traditional dues. The economic value of such a remittance is negligible as it was not fulfilled in many cases and was, in all probability, replaced by a symbolic presentation of a bowl of porridge or *marisa* (local beer). However, its political significance cannot be over-emphasized, for its remittance by the user meant the recognition of the right of the owner of the land and his sovereignty. In terms of the political-administrative framework, the users of land thus allocated followed the authority of the "allocator". As clients to Fur patrons they were not expected to have independent administrative or political authorities that might correspond to their separate ethnic identities. The same held true for the nomadic camel Arabs of the northern Rezaigat, particularly the Jallul, who frequented this area for grazing in the dry season. Equally, this situation obtained for the Zaghawa non-Arab camel nomads when they migrated into the Fur areas.

In fact relations across ethnic lines were characterized by symbiosis and complementarity; and the Fur made use of these ethnic groups as farm labourers, paid them in kind and trusted them with their livestock. Groups like the Zaghawa and Jullul also provided load camels for the transport of Fur farm produce, either from the fields to the store houses or to the nearest markets for sale.

But the size of the migrant population in the Fur territories was increasing; and their sojourns had been gradually taking on a relatively more permanent character during the last twenty years. This was partly due to adverse developments in the natural and political environment of the northern and western areas of Dar Fur. Within the Fur territory another kind of development which would have serious implications for the traditional form of land ownership was taking place with serious consequences for the pastoral groups which used to frequent the *wadis* of the Fur area during most of the dry seasons. This was reflected by the extensive practice of making "exclosures" where access to pasture by the public within their perimeters was restricted. These are referred to locally as *Zaraib al-Hawa,* literally "air exclosures".

Except for the Beni Helba Arabs whose home-territory overlapped that of the Fur, the majority of the nomadic Arab groups which had been a party to this conflict did not even possess tribal territories as was traditional in Dar Fur. However, as drought persisted over the last two decades and after they had entered into many conflicts with the farming communities of Arab and non-Arab stock, this group of Arabs started to demand specific home-territories from the government authorities in the region. But as there were no empty lands to allocate to whole tribal groups, all government efforts were directed toward seeking the consensus of groups to any conflict through conciliation councils (see the table above), toward delineating migration routes and keeping them free of obstacles, such as farms and protective exclosures in addition to preventing farmers from cultivating around watering points and agreeing on the dates of entry of the nomads into the farming belt. In fact, owing to the practice of the Beni Helba of the southern Dar Fur of building extensive protective exclosures, a tribal war of tragic consequence took place between them and the northern Rezaigat camel nomads. It was reconciled in 1980. Håland (1991) reports on exclosures in the following manner

> ... in this situation, members of some local communities, particularly the Beni Helba of southern Dar Fur, have taken active steps to protect their communal wealth. By extending the perimeter fence around farm land to include several kilometres of pasture they have, on a local community basis, tried to protect the land from grazing during the rainy season. (Håland 1991:23–24)

Although exclosures are illegal in the strictest sense of the law, they do *de facto* lead to claims for exclusive rights in pasture on a local basis which contradicts communal access to pasture on the level of a wider society. As the Fur also possessed considerable herds, they also started adopting exclosures as a means of protecting pasture. The mutual exclusion from each others' near pastures practised by these two neighbouring groups, the Fur and Beni Helba, was bound to lead to conflicts in the future. It was, in fact, no great surprise when in the context of the present conflict the neighbouring Beni Helba came out as leaders of the confederate Arab tribes (27 in all) who waged the war of local destruction against the Fur.

While the demands of the nomadic Arabs for ethnic home-territories were almost impossible to meet, the regional government in Dar Fur made administrative arrangements elsewhere which made it possible for the northern Rezaiqat to have a local nomadic council. Such arrangements were not extended to the Arabs in the Fur area because the lack of an ethnic territory of their own weighed heavily against them. Authority went with territory, and without territory one remained a client to the ethnic groups that traditionally owned the territory or so argued established tradition. This was obviously one of the mistakes committed by the regional government which was dominated at the time by Fur elements. If it was possible for the Northern Rezaigat to have their own nomadic council even though they did not possess a traditional ethnic territory in northern Dar Fur, why was it not possible to create similar nomadic councils in the Fur area, where the number of nomadic Arab tribes people exceeded by far the three tribes which constituted the northern Rezaiqat? It was through such rhetorical questions that most of the nomadic Arab groups in the southern Dar Fur were mobilized by their educated elites against the Fur ruling elite, long before the birth of the Arab Congregation which eventually waged a destructive war against the Fur and, by intent, against all Zurja of Dar Fur.

The majority of the nomadic Arab groups which, under the leadership of the Beni Helba, waged that war against the Fur were groups originating from Chad or were formally Chadian nationals but *de facto* Sudanese since they have kin in the Sudan and hence did not ask for refugee status. This group was running away from an unstable Chad, where wars of some kind or other have been going on since 1965, and was trying to settle in the relative safety of the Jebel Marra area. With these people came the armed opposition groups and Libyan supplied arms. Pursued by Chadian military and paramilitary forces and faced by a hostile local group, the Fur, the nomadic Arabs preferred to face the Fur; for they, in this context, were the weakest of all the adversaries they had to face. As for the Sudanese nomadic Arabs some of which received arms from the central government whose policy of arming tribal groups to fight wars by proxy could be traced back to colonial times (see Theobald 1956:103), this was a chance to solve a basic problem of their existence: how to conquer territory to become their *de facto* ethnic homeland. In fact similar situations, although of less dramatic nature, obtained elsewhere in the Sudan where the Rashaida nomadic Arabs of eastern Sudan were attempting through political manoeuvring to gain access to Hadendowa land. The situation between the migrant Zaghawa and a host of farming groups in central Dar Fur had the same explosive potential which the Fur situation possessed.

In fact, internal developments within Fur agriculture made less land available for allocation to migrant tribes. In the last two decades cultivation of orchards and vegetable gardens, whose products found ready markets in the expanding urban sector in Dar Fur and beyond, led to heavy investment in ventures related to these activities. Diesel driven water pumps as well as other technological innovations, such as ox drawn ploughs and tractors, brought increased areas of prime pasture land into the orbit of agriculture. The *wadis* which constituted the watering points for the livestock of the pastoralists became heavily cultivated. As farms proliferated animal trespass and the problems generally associated with it became more and more frequent in the area as a whole, in many case sparking off ethnic conflicts.

The *modus operandi* of the Arab *janjawid* and knights was not only characterized by brutality towards fellow human beings as long as they were Fur, it also opted for a complete destruction of orchards, farms, vegetable fields and villages. It was deliberately designed to end up in the migration of most of the Fur from their home territory which could have become a *de facto* Arab home-territory as a result. In fact, the extension of the Arab Belt as an ideology was reinforced by the naming of the territories temporarily occupied during this war as "liberated territories". Whole Fur *omodiyas* (districts) were occupied after their populations were forced to migrate under the threat of extinction by horse-mounted and gun-blazing Arab *janjawid*.

As these questions of territorial ownership and the vacation of occupied territories were given only cursory treatment, leaning heavily on the side of blood money and compensation for material damage, the conditions were created wherein the Fur would try at a point in the future to recapture their lost territory. This was due to happen when the Fur forces felt that they had the necessary training and armament to conduct a war. It did not take too long.

External forces

While every conference which dealt with security in Dar Fur that had been convened during the previous five years, has mentioned the external influences which were behind ethnic conflicts, none of them developed this thesis to the point of being able to deal with the problem. Since most of the Chadian groups were military groups with relatively advanced training and destructive fire power, they opted, more often than not, to settle their problems with the unwelcoming Fur by the use of military force. Even if the Fur did not lift a finger in their faces, they came to the aid of their ethnic kin, the nomadic Arabs, as soon as there was an armed confrontation.

The very ideology which they worked to further and their claim of home-territories in Dar Fur made it possible for these Arab groups to have powerful external backers which supplied them with advanced weapons. As the ideological unity between the regional suppliers and the political goal of destabilizing and eventually bringing down a common enemy, Habré, coincided with the territorial needs of the Arabs, arms supplies were increased to the extent that the opposition forces were even able to arm their local allies. The tacit, if not overt, complicity of the Khartoum regime was secured through the threat of calling in debts in addition to the promise of extension of military aid to them.

The Fur, in their turn, looked for internal allies. Habré allowed the Fur to open an office in Ndjamena, but that was closed when Habré fell from power in December 1990. The Fur continued to fight, though weakened by the fact that they did not have reliable access to external support.

The neutrality of the government forces

Despite the continuous complaints against the partiality exhibited by governments and government forces, the discussions around this issue were muted. In some cases the parties to the conflict named names which were linked with brutality and excesses against the civilian population of one group or the other. But this is a topic which has to be broached very carefully. The fact that the Sudanese state forces, whether security or military, have conducted conflicts with excessive brutality against civilian populations has never been exposed in internally acceptable debates. The conduct of the war in the southern Sudan and the conduct of various purportedly law enforcement operations leave much to be desired from legal and human perspectives.

Whenever such issues were raised, the army command brushed them aside by pointing out how many army and other security personnel were killed by the recalcitrant tribal bandits. This was evident in the closing remark made by the representative of the Revolutionary Command Council (cited above). Suspicions about the army's conduct have not been allowed to be raised, either in courts or in internal debate, because the argument goes the army is fighting a war in the southern Sudan. Moreover the army is a dangerous "power constituency" that needs to be appeased by overlooking minor irregularities. The only solace for the victims of army excesses is that the Sudanese army is not unique in this respect! Thus many tribal groups were forced to suppress their grievances against the excesses of the Sudanese army lest they be construed as committing a treasonable act.

The educated Dar Furians

The operationalization of the Regional Autonomy Act of 1980 which brought Dar Furians to govern Dar Fur in 1981 was repeatedly cited as an anchor for security problems and ethnic conflicts in the area. In disregard of the fact that Dar Furians were excluded from running their own affairs for the better part of this century, from 1916–1981, the educated Dar Furians have been condemned as "trouble-makers" because of the performance of a few individuals for a combined period of less than eight years. Even during that short period effective power remained centralized in Khartoum! The government found it reasonable to exclude Dar Fur intellectuals from taking part in the resolution of the conflicts in Dar Fur and from 1989 the governorship reverted once again to being a prerogative of riverain Sudanese. It should be remembered that in the context of the reconciliation conference about 220 local chiefs, who were largely powerless, and thirty five tribal groups and dozens of so-called "national figures", meaning figures from the centre, took part. The exclusion of the Dar Fur intellectuals was glaringly clear.

The National Council for the Salvation of Dar Fur was formed, in this light, to cater for the participation of the educated Dar Furians, even if informally, in the process of finding solutions to these problems. The role it played in bringing the issues concerning Dar Fur and the callousness of the political parties then running the Sudan to the centre of political discussion cannot be minimized. Their thesis was that the problems in Dar Fur were mostly structural, relating to the relationship between a dominant centre and the marginalized periphery. In short the Dar Fur question, like the Southern Sudan question, is essentially a Sudan question. In this context NCSD was a much needed moral victory for the educated Dar Furians and the region.

CONCLUSION

It is my thesis that ethnic conflicts in Dar Fur in particular and in Sudan in general cannot be understood without taking into account the general political environment at local, regional, national, and international levels; for the geopolitics of the area is volatile and rife with armed conflicts. This is not a novel thesis, but it is often overlooked in the Sudan and conflicts are usually reduced, either to the bellicosity of ethnic groups and their bigotry, or to the actions of self-seeking local elites.

Environmental conditions, such as those which were dominant in Dar Fur and the Sudan, in general, created suitable preconditions for ethnic conflicts. However, were it not for the prevalent local, regional, and national political situations, in addition to the geopolitics of the area which made the continuous supply of "cheap" arms possible, this conflict might have not been so brutal a war as it became in Dar Fur.

Major structural issues were not discussed and resolved in the reconciliation efforts which officially ended the war. As a result the war is still raging today, pre-empting any serious reconstruction work, which requires nothing less than an overall development of the region under structural conditions that could ensure real sharing of both power and national wealth. As it stands today, Dar Fur may become yet another "South" Sudan albeit in the West.

REFERENCES

Aguda, Oluwadare, 1973,"Arabism and Pan-Arabism in Sudanese Politics", *The Journal of Modern African Studies*, 11, 2, (pp. 177-200).

Al Assam, Mukhtar (n.d.), *Decentralization in the Sudan*. Ministry of Culture and Information, Khartoum.

Al Fasher, 1989, Proceeding of Reconciliation Conference 1989. Al Fasher, Sudan.

Alier, Abel, 1990, *Southern Sudan: Too Many Agreements Dishonoured*. Ithaca Press, Exeter.

Asher, Michael, 1984, *In the Search of the Forty Days Road*. Longman Groups Ltd.

Barth, F., 1967, "Economic Spheres in Dar Fur", in Firth, R. (ed.), *Themes in Economic Anthropology*. London, Tavistok: 149-174.

Barth, F. (ed.), 1969, *Ethnic Groups and Boundaries: The Social Organization of Culture Difference*. Universitetsforlaget, Bergen.

Barth, F., 1988, *Human Resources: Social and Cultural Features of Jebel Marra Project Area*. Bergen Studies in Social Anthropology, No. 42.

Delaco, Samuel, 1980, "Regionalism, Decay and Civil Strife in Chad", *The Journal of Modern African Studies*, 18, 1, (pp. 23-56).

Doual, Tassoum-Lydie, 1991, "Chad: Civil War and Development Prospects", *Voices from Africa*, No. 3, March 1991:27-75.
El Mahdi, Saeed M.A., 1971, *A Guide to Land Settlement and Registration*. Khartoum.
Harir, Sharif, 1987, *"Politics of Numbers": Mediatory Leadership and the Political Process among the Beri Zaghawa of the Sudan*. Ph.D. Thesis, Department of Anthropology, University of Bergen.
Håland, G., 1969, "Economic Determinants in Ethnic Processes", in F. Barth (ed.), *Ethnic Groups and Boundaries*, 53-73.
Håland, G., 1972, "Nomadism as an Economic Career among the Sedentaries of Sudan Savannah Belt", in:I. Cunnison & W. James, (eds.), *Essays in Sudan Ethnography presented to Sir E. Evans-Pritchard*. Hurst, London.
Håland, G., 1991, "Systems of Agriculture in Western Sudan", in G.M. Craig (ed.), *The Agriculture of the Sudan*. Oxford University Press (pp. 230-251).
Ibrahim, A.A., 1989, "Uneven Development and the Genesis of the Sudan Crisis", in El Tereifi (ed.), 1989, *Decentralized Rule in the Sudan* (in Arabic), pp.36-48, Khartoum University Press, Khartoum.
Ibrahim, A.A., 1985, "Regional Inequalities and Underdevelopment in Western Sudan". Unpublished Ph.D. Thesis, University of Sussex.
Ibrahim, F.N., 1978, *The Problem of Desertification in the Republic of the Sudan with Special Reference to Northern Dar Fur Province*. Development Research and Studies Centre (DRSC) Monographs No. 8, University of Khartoum.
Ibrahim, F.N., 1984, *Ecological Imbalance in the Republic of the Sudan with Reference to Desertification in Dar Fur*. Druckhaus Bayreuth, Verlagsgesellschaft mbH.
Khalid, Mansur, 1990, *The Government They Deserve: The Role of the Elite in Sudan's Evolution*. Kegan Paul International, London.
May, Roy, 1989, "Internal Dimensions of Warfare in Chad", *Cambridge Anthropology*, Vol. 13, No. 2: 17-27.
Musa Al-Mubarak, 1964, *Tarikh Dar Fur Alsiyasi (A Political History of Dar Fur 1882-98)*. Khartoum University Press.
O'Fahey, R.S., 1980, *State and Society in Dar Fur*. C. Hurst, London.
Salih Kamal Osman, 1990, "The Sudan 1985–89: The Fading Democracy", *The Journal of Modern African Studies*, Vol. 25, 2.
Theobald, A.B., 1956, *Ali Dinar: The Last Sultan of Dar Fur 1898–1916*. Longmans, London.

Other periodicals and journals

Africa Confidential, 1980, Vol. 29, No. 2, 9, 11; 1986, Vol. 27, No. 12, 19; 1987, Vol. 28, No. 4.
Sudan Update, 1991, Vol. 3, No. 7 and 8.

Tribal Militias

The Genesis of National Disintegration[1]

M.A. Mohamed Salih and Sharif Harir

The emergence of tribal militias in the Sudan can be linked to the beginning of the second civil war in 1983 which split the public opinion between support for SPLA/SPLM and the Government of Sudan. The actual number of militias is unknown, but it is a common knowledge that there are militias operating among the Baggara (Missiriya and Rezaigat) of Southern Kordofan and Southern Dar Fur, the Fur of Southern Dar Fur, Rufa'a of the White Nile, Fertit and the Nuer (*Anya Nya* II) of Bahr El Ghazal and the Mandari and the Toposa of Equatoria Region.[2]

The actual endorsement of some of these militias by the Government could be traced to the Gardud massacre of 1985 when groups of armed Dinka attacked a Baggara village in South Kordofan. There were, of course, several versions of the events. The Government accused the SPLA/SPLM and condoned the retaliation by the Baggara, while the SPLA/SPLM accused renegade tribesmen of exacting vengeance for earlier cattle raids by the Baggara of El-Gardud. A second incident, of greater national significance, was the notorious massacre of 1987 which was described by Baldu and Mahmound in *The Diein Massacre and Slavery in the Sudan*.[3] The Diein massacre was carried out by armed Baggara (Rizegat) militias who killed and burnt to death hundreds of Dinka and took many others into captivity. Government and independent reports conflicted on the issue of how many Dinka lost their lives. However, the subsequent detention of those who con-

---

[1] We are most grateful to Professor Martin Daly, Memphis State University, for commenting on the first draft of this paper and for his invaluable suggestions.

[2] Some of these militias are sponsored by the government such as those called *Murhalin* (Arabic) among the Baggara, others are less openly endorsed though accepted tacitly by the Government such as the *janjawid* (Arabic) hordes of the Beni Helba Arabs and yet others are actively combated by the Government such as those of the Fur.

[3] In this incident unarmed Dinka tribesmen were attacked and massacred by armed and horse-mounted Rezaigat Baggara tribesmen in the town of el-Diein in Southern Dar Fur. As this town is the centre of the Rezaigat *Nazirate* (Arabic for tribal paramount chief), this incident draws special significance not only because of that but also because of the fact that active protection by Government forces, i.e. police and security, of the Dinka tribesmen was completely lacking. Furthermore, the Government of Sadig al-Mahdi did not undertake any steps towards the criminal prosecution of the perpetrators. This is significant especially in the light of the fact that the Rezaigat constituted one of the firmest constituencies of the Umma party; a party of which the prime minister was the president and spiritual leader.

fronted Sadiq Al-Mahdi's Government with first-hand evidence of this brutal massacre created a national outcry.

A similar episode of mass killings took place in 1989 when about 214 Shilluk were massacred and over 2,000 displaced by Rufa'a militias in Al-Jabalyin in the border area between the White Nile and Upper Nile provinces. It was also reported that 90 of the Shilluk who fled for safety to the local policy station were killed in cold blood, a pattern similar to what had happened in the Gardud and the Diein massacre.[4] Although we have mentioned a few episodes, there were, of course, hundreds if not thousands of incidents involving the militias which cannot be reported here. What we have intended to emphasize is the fact that tribal militias have imposed themselves on Sudanese politics because they were now endorsed by the Government in power. When the Prime Minister Sadiq Al Mahdi was confronted by the army about the existence of tribal militias in 1989, he "told the army that those para-military forces were only to defend democracy" (Khalid, 1990:357). However, posterity shows that the Prime Minister could not be more mistaken as was testified by the successful army coup of June 1989 in which the army did not fire as much as one bullet. Later, those militias were elevated and given legal status by the Popular Defence Act of 1989 as enacted by the new military regime.

During the early period of the present civil war some Southern ethnic groups, mainly Toposa, Mundari, Fertit and Nuer (Anya Nya II), were also engulfed in activities seen by the army as friendly. These ethnic groups were against the SPLA/SPLM because of old enmities with the Dinka who constituted the majority of the SPLA/SPLM leadership. Anya Nya II shifted allegiance between the Government and the SPLA/SPLM but mostly worked side by side with the army. We presume that the present split in the leadership of the SPLA/SPLM is alongside the Anya Nya II/SPLA—or Dinka/Nuer lines. With the beginning of the war in 1983, Anya Nya II dug out its hidden weapons from the first war (1955–1972). Most Southern militias received training and arms from the National Army or from defecting soldiers who volunteered to protect their ethnic groups against the SPLA/SPLM troops. Other Southern tribes supported the SPLA/SPLM and received arms from it or from defecting Government troops.

Both Southern and Northern tribal militias have direct or indirect links with the National Army, and, in many cases, fought alongside it. However there is no reason to suggest that they were all under the full control of the Government, a fact which prompted the Government to promulgate, in

---

[4] The discernible pattern in all these incidences is one in which unarmed Southern tribesmen take refuge in a police station after surviving the initial assult by armed Baggara tribesmen. As soon as the pursuit party arrives at the police station, the police withdraw, ostensibly because they are out-gunned by the militias that carry unlicensed assault rifles. The refugees are then massacred, ironicaly they were supposed to be protected by the sanctity of law!

1989, the Popular Defence Act, to bring militias in the war zone under the control of professional and ideologically committed army officers of its choice.

This paper deals with the proliferation of tribal militias in Southern Kordofan, with the prime objective of delineating the relationship between the militias and the Sudanese state. Three interrelated ideas will be explored; competing perceptions of the present war and their political meanings at the local and national levels, the emergence of the tribal militias as an extension of the state's repressive arm thus weakening its monopoly over the use of violence and coercion, and the impact of these on the process of national integration in the Sudan. It is argued that tribal militias negate two principal attributes of the state. First, they render futile any notion of the state as an integrating factor of diverse and conflicting ethnic interests. This is so mainly because the militias owe their allegiance to an ethnic group, or a 'nationality' which perceives its political and physical security independent of the state. Second, resort by civilians to violence to protect life and property reveals a loss of faith in state institutions, such as the police and the army, which are supposed to be entrusted with the duty of defending citizens and maintaining peace and order. Hence, once the state's role as an ultimate arbiter of political affairs is challenged and its function as the overriding social institution within which individuals and groups invest their loyalties is subdued, its legitimacy is in jeopardy. Militias take the law in their own hands, an act which signals political anarchy, wherein decentralized violence becomes the rule (Mazrui, 1986:11–18).

The challenge of tribal militias to national integration is compounded by the ethno-religious nature of some sectors of the apparatus of Government. Ethnicity and religion intrude into several interdependent socio-political spheres. The ethnic dimension of the present war can be seen more clearly at the level of local politics than in a larger synthesis of South *versus* North or Muslims *versus* Christians. Resistance to state policy and personnel in the least-developed regions of the Sudan is conducted on a societal basis spreading out politically and spatially to use local social and cultural values to enhance protest against the centre. Hence, even though the national political arena is dominated by debate over the values and ideology of the state, Islam and Christianity have never entered the realm of local politics nor have they provided the main source of antagonism at the village level, simply because they are not issues of political concern to the majority of the rural population. However, once an Islamic ideology captured the state apparatus, as is advocated by some sectors of the Sudanese political elites as the only means of expressing national identity or strengthening their grip on power (which actually is the case after the coup of June 1989), the rural populace used the war to pursue objectives that are different from those of the political elite, for instance, to square old enmities with neighbouring ethnic groups or to rustle cattle, seize women and plunder crops under the camouflage of religious wars. This ethnic dimension of the war negates claims of both sides. The claim that the war is for national unity is contradicted since tribal militias threaten the very basis of that unity. The claim that the war is for liberation from Western ideology denies the political reality which has led to popular involvements, i.e. fears of internal colonization.

It is therefore not possible to associate the emergence of tribal militias indirectly with the upsurge of strong Islamic sentiments within certain political elites in the North. Islamic fundamentalists have seen in Northern tribal militias and their Muslim background a guardian of the current ethno-religious character of the state. As such Islam is used by these elites to galvanize the nationality of the riverain and Arabic north (El Affendi, 1992).

A weak state striving to survive underdevelopment and unprecedented economic crises, has misconceived tribal militias as an inexpensive defence force. Legalization of the tribal militias in 1989 was a vindication for the prevalence of that notion. Moreover, the militias were considered by some factions within the state apparatus as an extension of the state's monopoly over the use of coercive power; a contradiction in terms! It is important to emphasize that the political implications of the tribal militias are grave, considering the fragility of the post-colonial states and their inability to overcome the age-old ethnic sentiments and their accompanying political values.

THE PERIPHERY/CENTRE PERCEPTION OF THE WAR

Wars usually have an ideological justification to motivate the fighters and those who support them morally and materially. Such ideological referents are broad and often perceived differently by the fighting groups at the periphery as compared to those at the centres of power. Such perceptions do not need to constitute a coherent ideology since there are conflicting ideas as to what the war is all about, even within one side.

Considering itself representative of the periphery (the South, the East, the West and Nuba Mountains), the Sudan People's Liberation Army (SPLA) and its political wing the Sudan People's Liberation Movement (SPLM) saw the war as a struggle for liberation built on a populist, but nonetheless socialist, ideological base. The struggle against oppression and domination represented the main theme of SPLA/SPLM ideology. In this respect the SPLM 'manifesto' declares that

> ... the main task of the SPLA/SPLM is to transform the Southern Movement from a reactionary Movement led by reactionaries and concerned with the South, jobs and self interest to a progressive movement led by revolutionaries and dedicated to the socialist transformation of the whole country. It must be reiterated that the principal objective of the SPLA/SPLM is not separation for the South. The South is an integral and inseparable part of the Sudan. Africa

has been fragmented sufficiently enough by colonialism and neocolonialism and its further fragmentation can only be in the interests of her enemies.[5]

According to the SPLA/SPLM manifesto, the present war is, therefore, intended to liberate the whole Sudan from its main enemies, represented by Northern and Southern Sudanese bourgeoisie and bureaucratic elites, religious fundamentalism and the reactionary commanders of the Anya Nya II. Liberation has assumed the wider meaning of a socialist transformation by which the enslavement of the masses by a local-sectarian-based aristocracy acting in collusion with rapacious foreign business interests will be brought to an end. These objectives gave the SPLA/SPLM programme a national character different from that of the original Anya Nya which fought for separation from the North between 1955 and 1972.[6] The original ideological base of the SPLA/SPLM encompassed features common to guerrilla warfare in Africa and other parts of the world. It is nonetheless premature to connect extension of the war to Southern Kordofan with the grand ideological pretensions of the SPLA/SPLM, although its political programme has appealed to many Nuba and Dinka inhabitants of the province. As will be explained in the next section of this chapter, Southern Kordofan has a long history of inter-ethnic conflict; this has found an outlet for open expression in the present war. On the whole, the war in South Kordofan was fought by tribal militias rather than by soldiers in uniform until 1992 when the Sudanese army extended its campaign into the Nuba mountains in a genocidal manner.

Reinforcement of a hostile enemy image is usually deployed to justify the need to liquidate the 'enemy' and to eliminate the threat he poses. Of all the SPLA/SPLM stated enemies, Islamic fundamentalism has dominated the political scene because all the peace initiatives foundered on the fundamentalists insistence on the continuing Islamic *sharia* laws. The SPLA/SPLM sees liberation as involving the separation of religion from the state. But the ethno-religious make-up of the Sudan does not offer much hope in that direction, and has instead produced a strong counter-productive ideology. In practice, this is ultimately linked with a strategic SPLA/SPLM attempt to create a 'new Sudan', a concept appealing to those on the periphery. For example, the SPLA/SPLM declared that

> ... the new Sudan as a concept strives to establish a new cultural order in the country. It takes as its point of departure the notion that human beings, in any given society, have equal rights and obligations regardless of colour, etc. The establishment of the new cultural order demands of necessity a radical restruc-

---

[5] SPLM, manifesto especially article 7/21. However, one should note that this position, i.e. on unity, underwent a dramatic revision *de facto* after the August 1991 split in the SPLA command.

[6] C.B. Eprile (1974) brings out these aspects in a clear manner.

turing of state power to establish genuine democracy and to follow a path of development that will lead to far-reaching social changes.[7]

Ideally, the SPLA/SPLM is fighting for the dismantling of the old regime with its unjust mechanism for distributing economic and political power. Although the SPLA/SPLM claims that it is an all-embracing movement dedicated to all the Sudanese people regardless of their racial origin or religious denominations, it is evidently too early to discern a level of popular political awareness that is sufficient to relegate the traditional values of political expression to these secular objectives. The perception gap between the populace and the ideologies perpetuated by the educated political elite is confronted with harsh realities when they are to be put into practice. Evidently, this is the stone at which the unity of the SPLA foundered in August 1991.

Since the majority of SPLA/SPLM fighters are unaware of the political implications of concepts such as "liberation" and "socialism", one must question whether they are fighting to realize the same political ideology as their leadership. The unifying factors in any liberation movement are a shared sense of attachment to a given territory, and a greater sense of identity among its members than between them and others. But the war has been seen by some in the South, Southern Kordofan and southern parts of the Blue Nile as a struggle against Northern domination on the one hand, and as a fight against immediate enemies among neighbouring ethnic groups, on the other. An indirect result of the genuine, modern and 'non-tribalistic' objectives of the SPLA/SPLM is that these have been redefined among ethnic groups in the South to fit into a traditional ideology that structured war and peace. This is especially understandable in societies in which high rates of illiteracy limit exposure to modern political values. The recent advocacy of "separate existence" by the Nasir/SPLA and the self-determination compromise by the Torit/SPLA vindicates the above assertions.

The Sudanese state has maintained a certain degree of persistence in its policy towards the SPLA/SPLM and the war in the South, Southern Kordofan and the southern parts of the Blue Nile. Declarations by various Sudanese politicians and parties, claimed that the state has resorted to the use of force to subdue rebellion and to maintain national unity; thus signalling their suspicion that the SPLA/SPLM may have objectives other than those which it declared. The main line of thought in the state establishment is that states cannot give in to pressure from rebellious civilians carrying arms to pursue their political aspirations. Nevertheless, in its failure to live up to its obligations to sustain peace and order, the Sudanese state has itself bowed to pressure from the sources of its political support. In this sense, local politics echoed in the corridors of national institutions the most indecorous signal

---

[7] SPLM/SPLA views on "The New Sudan" were presented in an information bulletin issued on February 1989.

that the state is so weak and incapacitated that some ethnic groups must assume the responsibility of protecting themselves.

Islamicists saw in Numeiri's *Sharia* laws[8] a golden opportunity to install their long awaited Islamic state. Moreover, a combination of strong Islamic sentiments and a hostile attitude against socialism has culminated in outright rejection of the political programme put forward by the SPLA/SPLM among some sectors of the Sudanese population in the North, the South and the Nuba Mountains. The SPLA/SPLM political programme has identified the holders of power and the Northern sectarian political organizations as the "belligerent" enemy. It is no wonder that a strong group of Islamic activists with hostile attitudes to the SPLA/SPLM has been prominent in the Sudanese political arena from the beginning. Some Islamic ideologues have gone as far as to describe the present genocide as a holy war against the enemies of Islam.

The lack of a uniform Northern or Southern political attitude towards the war has delayed its end. A number of political activists in the North opposed the war and the Government's insistence on imposing *sharia* laws created a new stalemate. Likewise, many Southerners, notably Equatorians who suffered greatly during the 1955–1972 war opposed the SPLA/SPLM political programme. In fact many Equatorians would prefer to fight for separation from the North rather than for what they call the idealistic objective of liberating the whole Sudan. Again some Southern ethnic groups have fought the war for reasons completely different from those of the SPLA/SPLM. A concept of pan-Dinka nationalism came to the surface since 1983 (see, for example, C. Gurdon, 1984:60–4) when the South was redivided by Numeiri into three regional Governments. While the Dinka saw re-division as an attempt to diminish their political role in a unified South, Equatorians saw it as an opportunity to govern themselves and control their own affairs. Hostility between the SPLA/SPLM and the Equatorians remained high, with suspicions that paralleled those between the South and the North. A similar situation of involution of conflict within similar resistance groups is reported by Pirouet (1977:211) who argues that

> ... it seems correct to conclude that the greatest danger to those committed to resistance comes, not from the regime, but from the tendency to disunity among themselves. It is sometimes argued that for this reason those involved in resistance need to be united by an ideology. On the evidence so far available from Africa, the adoption of an ideology is likely to intensify conflicts among the resisters as it is to overcome them. People struggling to win freedom from oppression are not likely to appreciate having an ideology forced upon them. (M.L. Pirouet, 1977:211)

---

[8] The Presidential decree of September 1983 imposed *Sharia* law upon the Sudan in contravention to the then operative 1973-constitution of the Sudan. For the Islamists who have argued always that Allah's *Sharia* is not subject to human choice; i.e. the Ballot box, this was more than a golden chance which they have defended ever since.

The present war revealed that both the South and North have failed to unite the populace with a common ideology, whether Islamic or socialist. On the contrary, neither the SPLA/SPLM nor the Sudanese state has succeeded in securing mass support for its political programme either on the periphery or at the centre. Consequently, some enclaves within the Southern Sudan have supported the SPLA/SPLM while, at an early stage of the war, others supported the National Army—including the Mandari, Bari and some of the Nuer. Meanwhile small sectors of the Northern educated political elite have supported the political programme of the SPLA/SPLM, i.e. the so-called modern forces. In both cases the Southern masses have suffered most.

The split of the SPLA/SPLM leadership in terms of unionists (Garang faction) and separatists (Machar faction) threatens with the involution of war and the revival of some of the militias which were subsumed under the SPLA/SPLM. There is also the distinct likelihood that the SPLA/SPLM might disintegrate into smaller tribal militias which would drive the prospects of peace even further off.

PRELUDE TO THE TRIBAL MILITIAS

The presence of tribal militias in Southern Kordofan pre-dated the colonial period. A detailed account of this history cannot be undertaken here and we confine our analysis to recent inter-ethnic warfare and factors which have contributed to the emergence of tribal militias during the present war. It is important now to record the events taking place in parts of the war-zone and to explain their implications for national integration in the Sudan; a dream which seems more remote than ever. Therefore we begin by describing these events and their socio-political background and then exploring the links between these and the national political environment.

Southern Kordofan province is an interesting one since it borders two Southern provinces and the loyalty of its population is divided between the South and the North. It is located in the northernmost part of the South and borders the regions of Upper Nile and Bar El Ghazal. The total population of the province is about 1.2 million who belong to four main ethnic groups: the Nuba, the Arabic speaking Baggara conglomerate, Jallaba traders and Nilotic Ngok Dinka. The Nuba claim to be the original inhabitants of the Nuba Mountains which dominate the central and southern parts of the province (for social history see S.F. Nadel, 1947). The Ngok Dinka live in the southern parts of the province along side their Dinka fellows in the Upper Nile and Bar El Ghazal regions (see P. Howell, 1955). The conglomeration of the Baggara Arabs whose main constituents are the Missiriya, Humr and Hawazma tribes have migrated to the province in two waves during the seventeenth century (see K.D.D. Henderson, 1939) and after the collapse of the Mahdist state in 1898. The Jallaba of Northern and Central Sudan, first came to the Nuba Mountains as slave-raiders during the eighteenth century,

but settled in the 1920s and during the cotton boom in the late 1940s which
opened up vast opportunities for trade and cash crop production. Since then
the Jallaba have dominated trade and business in South Kordofan. The distribution of the population does not suggest any form of ethnic segregation,
even though some areas are dominated by certain ethnic groups and present
a less heterogeneous appearance than others. There are, of course, enclaves
of homogeneous ethnic groups occupying smaller territories and with less interaction with neighbouring ethnic groups.

Sources as early as 1920s reveal that contacts between these ethnic groups
were not common except for trade or cattle and slave raiding. Laws banning
slavery in South Kordofan were enacted only in 1927 when a special decree
declared all the inhabitants of the Nuba Mountains free citizens.[9] The period
between 1922 and independence, in 1956, was one of great stability. The
various ethnic groups mixed freely as Native Administration was introduced
in two phases; Powers of Nomadic Shaikhs in 1922 and its amendment in
1927. Cotton was introduced as a cash crop, market-places were established,
and health, education and veterinary services were introduced. Most roads
remained seasonal, operational only during the dry season which offered the
possibility for long-distance movement and migration to towns and urban
centres.

The outbreak of the first civil war (1955–1972), affected Southern
Kordofan in two main ways: first, many Jallaba traders fled from the South
after the Torit massacre and established themselves in the Nuba Mountains;
second, the Dinka in the southern parts of the province identified with the
South and demanded separation from Kordofan province in order to join Bar
El Ghazal province.

The Ngok Dinka's demand to join the South gained impetus after the
failure of the Round Table Conference in 1965 and an explosion of violence
continued between the Humr Baggara and the Ngok Dinka in Babanusa and
Ragaba Zargha.[10] This conflict continued but could not be described as an
organized campaign of genocide. Nor was it supported by the government of
the time. Fighting between youths over pasture and water points was a routine feature of Ngok Dinka/Humr relations. When the Addis Ababa
Agreement was enacted in 1972, the Ngok were successful in securing a
clause which could grant them the right to separate from the North
(Southern Kordofan) and join the new Southern region.[11] The new mood

[9] See, for example, the document entitled: "Devolution in the Nuba Mountains
Province", in the National Records Office (NRO), Khartoum.
[10] In fact, in 1965, a large number of Dinka men, women and children who took
refuge in the Babanusa police station were also burned to death by a mob of horse-
mounted Humr Baggara; a forerunner to the ed-Diein and El Jebelyan incidents referred to above.
[11] Even if it did not effect separation, the clause gave the Ngok-Dinka the right to
choose between being, administratively, a part of Southern Kordofan or becoming a
part of the Southern Region of the Sudan.

which followed the Addis Ababa Agreement delayed the Ngok quest for separation and they remained within South Kordofan despite continuing traditional warfare between them and their Humr neighbours.

Notwithstanding the consent by the Ngok Dinka to remain within the hostile political environment of South Kordofan, they soon began to resent the slow pace of development and became increasingly disillusioned by the local repercussions of decades of animosity between North and South. Such grievances had often found their way into regional politics in the southern fringes of Southern Kordofan. But optimism and a few jobs created by the discovery of oil gave new hope for eradicating the problems of underdevelopment. Various tribal conferences were held to settle disputes between the Ngok Dinka and the Humr. This situation prevailed until the current war started in 1983.

The Nuba Mountains had been quiet during the first civil war (1955–1972). The Nuba feared exchanging Northern domination for Southern domination because the North is more developed and had more to offer educated Nuba than the South. There was, however, some secret Nuba political support to the Anya Nya movement, specially among Christian Nuba communities such as Heiban, Catcha and Moro of the southern hills. In general, the Baggara and the Nuba enjoyed a relatively peaceful co-existence, with no serious incidents of inter-ethnic warfare.

The emergence of the Nuba General Union (NMGU) in 1965 was a direct response to the Southern struggle for autonomy and equal rights of citizenship. The NMGU was led by educated Nuba who were using political means to achieve political objectives. In 1966, they succeeded in winning the abolition of poll tax which had been a constant reminder of their domination by the Northern Sudanese who operated the administrative structure and controlled local and regional trade. The NMGU also gained recognition as a pressure group representing the Nuba and striving to secure development funds and projects for their region. Inter-marriages between Nuba and Baggara, especially the Hawazma were already common and it seemed the region was destined to become a "melting pot" for the various ethnic groups which inhabited it. Peaceful co-existence between the Nuba and other migrant ethnic groups continued and was somehow strengthened by the Addis Ababa Agreement of 1972 which brought greater security for life and property in the borderlands between the Nuba Mountains and the South.

Mohamed Salih has argued elsewhere (Mohamed Salih, 1989) that the Regional Government Act of 1980 was counter-productive in that it resorted to a traditional balancing of power at the regional level between competing tribal elites. It soon became clear that some Nuba were secretly lobbying for a separate region (the 1918–1927 Nuba Mountains province) in order to escape domination by the Jallaba and other Northern Sudanese in Northern Kordofan. There were also strong feelings between the Nuba, on the one hand, and the Hawazma and the Missiriya Baggara, on the other. Tension culminated in 1983 in the dissatisfaction of some Nuba politicians who felt that their share of power under the Regional Government Act was insufficient. Infuriated Nuba members of the Sudanese Socialist Union (SSU), Committee of Kordofan Region including the Speaker of the Regional Assembly, Yusuf Kua Meki later joined the SPLA/SPLM. Yusuf Kua Meki is now a member of the High Command of the SPLA/SPLM and Commander in Chief of its military operations in South Kordofan. The Nuba Mountains was by then fully incorporated into the war-zone.

TRIBAL MILITIA AND THE POLARIZATION OF SOCIETY

The 1983 war denied the population of Southern Kordofan (Nuba, Baggara, Dinka and Jallaba) the opportunity to form a solid basis for national integration. Although the SPLA/SPLM opposed tribalism, the present war has created its own momentum which had resulted in the retribalization of local politics. Attacks on Baggara or Nuba villages and cattle camps is interpreted as Dinka (or Southerners) strikes against a real or potential enemy. Attacks on Dinka villages and cattle camps by the Government troops are likewise perceived as 'tribal' strikes by Baggara (or Northern) Arabic-speaking groups on the Dinka. The line between an attack by a tribal group and the Government troops was so faint that unarmed civilians, inherently suspicious, would not discern the differences. It is natural that at times of great distress and fear people become so confused about who to blame for their misery and why. Once an enemy image is perceived, it would always be used to justify aggression as means of self-defence.

The NMGU and Southern Sudan Political Association (SSPA) were the first to raise the issue of disarming the tribal militias with the Transitional Military Council (TMC) in 1985. There were also Dinka delegations from Southern Kordofan who demanded state intervention to protect lives and property against the Baggara militias which were ravaging the villages and devastating cattle, crops and even burning grazing lands. However, Dinka and Nuba leaders accused the Government of arming the Baggara against them. Public opinion was divided and many Dinka and Nuba tribesmen believed that the Government was taking the side of the Baggara, who formed the majority of the army personnel in Kordofan and Dar Fur, and frequently refrained from protecting the Dinka from attacks by members of their own tribal groups. The Diein massacre was drawn as a glaring example of how the Government troops could stand idly by while hundreds of Dinka were massacred in cold blood.

In 1988 the forces of SPLA/SPLM attacked large garrison towns in the Nuba Mountains such as Liri and Talodi, and large market and administrative centres such as Umdorein and El-Azrag. Many people were displaced and the population of Kadugli, the capital of South Kordofan had tripled between 1983 and 1986. Since 1988, there have been frequent attacks by the

Nuba, especially in Heiban and Buram on the farms and shops of Jallaba. It had become impossible for Baggara to travel in small bands because they increasingly feared attacks by the Nuba or renegade SPLA/SPLM fighters. Umdorein town, the capital of the Moro which is located about 40 kilometres from Kadugli was again under heavy shelling by the SPLA/SPLM forces (between 22 and 26 January 1990). Several Government soldiers were ambushed on the road from Kadugli to Umdorein and killed.[12] The war had now been brought to within kilometres south of Kadugli, and the sounds of artillery fire could sometimes be heard in the town.

Meanwhile, the political elite in the centre were more preoccupied with what share they would acquire from the spoils of Numeiri's regime than with issues of security on the periphery. Even though the war was widely discussed and contacts were intensified among the SPLA/SPLM, the National Alliance for National Salvation (NANS) and the Transitional Military Council (TMC), unfortunately, all were attempting the maintenance of the *status quo* which gave rise to the war in the first place. It did not take the SPLA/SPLM long to discover that many Northern politicians were not yet ready to exchange the promise of power for national reconciliation or redeem the common man from the devastation of war and famine. This gloomy political atmosphere was intensified by some of the resolutions of the TMC revealed by John Garang, the leader of the SPLA/ SPLM. Of most relevance at this juncture is the second resolution which reads as follows

> ... it was reaffirmed that the question of arming Northern tribesmen had become most urgent and of paramount importance now. The armed natives will fight along and side by side with the Sudan army. These tribes will be encouraged to harass their neighbouring tribes with a view to destabilizing and impoverishing them by destroying their properties and looting their belongings and animals with the overall aim of eventually depopulating the Northern Bahr El Ghazal and Benieu areas and creating a buffer zone between the North and the South.[13]

These revelations naturally caused great concern within the Sudanese military establishment, not because of their shocking content, but because they raised the possibility of infiltration of their meetings by Southerners or Northerners sympathetic to the SPLA/SPLM. The notion of a *taboor khamis* (Arabic) or 'fifth column' was in wide circulation and demands were made to alienate anyone openly supporting the SPLA/SPLM. Hence public condemnation of tribal militias became synonymous with *taboor khamis*, especially in areas with mounting inter-ethnic tension or previous incidents of tribal warfare.

---

[12] BBC monitoring summary of world broadcasts confirmed this on 29 January 1990.

[13] John Garang, the C-N-C of the SPLA revealed this in a statement he made at the opening session of the preliminary dialogue between the SPLA/SPLM and the National Alliance for National Salvation (NANS) in Koka Dam, Ethiopia, 20th March 1986.

It was by then widely evident that greater cooperation between the army and armed tribesmen had become organized. Mohamed Salih witnessed the return of an army column to the Kadugli army garrison from the southern parts of South Kordofan in 1987, almost half of the fighters were volunteer Baggara tribesmen either defending their lives and property against possible counter-attacks or interested merely in the spoils of war. Cooperation between the army and tribal militias continued, contrary to the stated Government policy which denied any form of cooperation between the army and tribal militias or their involvement in arming civilians in the war zone. A report by Ryle suggests that

> ... for strategic reasons, the Government of the Sudan has sponsored the extermination of a segment of its own civilian population. Many thousands of the people have been killed by the Government militias; thousands more died as a result of their raids; and thousands, probably, have been disenfranchised, held in servitude by the members of these militias hand-in-glove with Government forces. (J. Ryle, 1988)

Though appears exaggerated, the fact remains that tribal militias have devastated the lives of thousands in the Southern Sudan.

By 1988 the population of the principal towns along the border between Southern Kordofan and the Southern regions of Bar El Ghazal and Upper Nile was tripled by steady waves of Southern refugees fleeing the war zone. Famine which has been caused by instability and displacement of large numbers from the farming communities, claimed the lives of thousands of those who escaped extermination by the army or the militias.

The tribal militias had become an open secret when in February 1989, Sadiq El-Mahdi, the then Prime Minister, proposed a motion in Parliament to legalize their establishment under the overall command of the army. It was further proposed that tribal militias should be renamed to become popular defence forces. Some political commentators saw in this a desire to establish strong militias in the regions of his party's support (Kordofan and Dar Fur) as a safeguard against military coups. In fact the motion was proposed not long after a military ultimatum which had forced Sadiq El-Mahdi to accept the November 1988 peace agreement between the SPLA/SPLM and the Democratic Unionist Party (DUP). By November 1989, however, the new military Government of Lt. General Omer El-Bashir had promulgated the National Popular Defence Act (NPD) as a paramilitary force to operate in collaboration with the army and to assist in counter-insurgency operations in the buffer-zone between the South and the North. The Defence Act (6 November, 1989) and the appointment of Brig. Babiker Abd El-Mahmoud Hassan to head the Popular Defence Forces (19 November, 1989)[14] were clear indications that the state had now legalized war by proxy, i.e. civilians to act on its behalf.

---

[14] *Africa Watch*, 6th December 1989:3–5

In brief, the population of Southern Kordofan which seemed to be heading for ethnic integration is now caught in the war and has become a party to it. The populace have defined their loyalties according to long-held enemy images. The end result is polarization of society in tribal militias whose objectives are incongruous with the notion of a 'nation-state' and closer to a situation of 'war of all against all'. One of the main tasks of any Government is to disarm these militias and bring power home to those institutions of the state (the police and the army) which are entrusted with the maintenance of peace and order.

THE SOCIAL ORGANIZATION OF THE MILITIAS

Tribal military organizations were common among African societies and existed both in 'state' and 'stateless' societies long before the European conquest. In the Sudan, the greatest assault on paramilitary tribal organizations occurred under Anglo-Egyptian rule (1898-1956). But, the colonial policy of "divide and rule" created suspicion between diverse ethnic groups. Peace which the tribal groups enjoyed during the colonial rule did not last long after the colonialists left the country. Some old enmities were resurrected and in the face of weak national Governments unable to offer citizens the minimum conditions of individual security, tribesmen resorted to ways familiar to their social organizations and value systems in order to protect their lives and property. The warrior tradition which is described by Mazrui as

> ... that sub-system of values and institutionalized expectations which define the military role of the individual in the defence of his society, the material criteria of adulthood and the symbolic obligations of manhood in time of political and military stress. At one level, the warrior tradition is a major link between the individual and society. At another level the warrior tradition links each household with the wider community. (Ali Mazrui, 1977:2)

In defending his own cattle, and his own women (the two most important resources in the reproduction of the group) from external raiders, the warrior is often fulfilling a military obligation just as participating in a regular army has been reconstituted to serve the interests of the tribal and educated elites, both at the local and national level. In the general case of East African pastoral tradition to whom the fighting tribesmen of the Sudan belong, Baxter reminds us in his widely quoted statement that

> ... for a man ... to be a warrior is simply a routine feature of late youth and early manhood, it is not a specialized occupation simply because it is one which every male follows for the specially marked period of life when he is an active herder. During warriorhood, features of male role such as valour and aggressive virility, are accentuated and others, such as oratorical skills, wisdom and gentleness are subdued because they are appropriate to elderhood. (P.T.W. Baxter, 1977:77–8)

This answers two questions which confronted us in addressing a Western audience. First tribal fighters were not specialized in the sense of modern armies. Secondly, they were neither recruited on a permanent basis nor conscripted professional warriors. Becoming a tribal warrior was a routine feature of late youth and early manhood; a rite of passage all able-bodied males should pass through.

The social organization of the Dinka, for example, is based on an elaborate age-set system. The military aspect of the Dinka social organization is described by Deng, as follows

> Among the symbols a man receives when released from the status of an initiate are gifts of well designed spears. These are objects of beautification, and songs are composed in praise of those who make the gifts. But they are really symbols of the military function of youth. This function is not limited to war even though that is the central point; it covers those aspects of culture which require youth, vigour and valour. These may be directed against humans or beasts, but may also be extended to activities that invest physical strength in construction and production. In fact, the military distinction of youth is largely a matter of show, for every Dinka male is a soldier. Once war erupts, the ideal fighters are those adults who have the strength to fight and children to survive them should they die: they are still unmarried youth. (Francis M. Deng, 1971:73)

If a warrior is an able-bodied man of a certain age-group as argued by Baxter, then it is only logical that in societies with clearly demarcated age-groups such as the Dinka, every man is a soldier since males routinely pass through the warrior age-group to adulthood and elderhood. Social values which glorify the military role of youth also exist among the Baggara, the main political rivals of the Dinka through the years. It is therefore, worthwhile to explore what social values enhance the transformation of tribal social organization into a military organization, i.e. in tribal militia.

The Dinka mostly live in hamlets built on the high ground away from the swampy areas near rivers and insects. Cattle-herding and watering are carried out by youths who also form a military group responsible for defending cattle against intruders and aliens. While intra-lineage disputes can be solved by elders or local courts, inter-ethnic conflicts are always difficult to contain. It is therefore possible that a fight between two youths over pasture or watering points might erupt into a larger fight which may include the whole tribal or sub-tribal group.

The same applies to Baggara pastoralists who move in larger groups of six to thirteen households called *khashim-bait* (or extended family), a number of *khashim-baits* makes *ial-rajil* (or lineage) a number of which makes *omodiya* (sub-tribe) and a number of *omodiyas* makes *gabila* (or tribe). The *omodiya* pays *dia* (blood compensation) consisting of cattle collected from each *ial-rajil* and paid for any major damages inflicted by its members on individuals or groups from other *omodiyas*. Militarily they defend each other against attackers. In common with the Dinka, disputes between two or more youths may evolve into major warfare between *ial-rajils* or whole *omodiyas*. Disputes between individual Baggara and non-Baggara (Dinka and Nuba) may also involve whole *omodiyas* (I. Cunnison, 1966).

It is argued elsewhere (Mohamed Salih, 1989:71) that tribal military values are associated with self-defence and can easily be transformed from traditional to modern military combat, albeit with considerable modification. Many tribal groups (or what we refer to as tribal militias) in both the South and the North have resorted to such values and spontaneously formed groups of armed men to defend themselves. Both the SPLA/SPLM and the Sudanese state have found in these tribal military values a ready institutional framework for recruitment and morale-raising among their respective fighters.

CONCLUSION

The participation of the Sudanese political elite, via the state, in the present genocide is outrageous by all standards. The political objectives of the state have been manipulated and ethnic interests reinforced in order to keep in power a leadership which failed to secure political gains through modern political institutions. Hence, ethnic claims have pre-empted national interests and the available power resources seem not to have transcended the values inherent in local politics. This paradoxical situation has created divergent ideological expressions consciously geared towards political survival. Both Islamic ideology, which is mainly propagated by the ethno-religious nature of some sectors of the Sudanese state, and the socialist ideology as advocated by the SPLA/SPLM have so far failed to redeem the masses from exploitation and oppression. Both ideologies seem irrelevant to the populace and their immediate needs and concerns. However, available evidence suggests that the war has given impetus to traditionalist political values, mistrust and fear among all Sudanese "nationalities". In this situation which is marred by serious confusion between the 'state' policies with its ethno-religious character, tribal militias are erroneously seen as an extension of the state's monopoly over the use of force. The result is destruction of the meagre public amenities and infrastructure of the South and its reduction to a pre-colonial situation, or even worse. The problem remains unsolved as long as the ethno-religious nature of the state is the over-riding concept for the expression of national political objectives and aspirations. The suffering caused by these crises is inflicted mainly upon the politically and economically deprived sectors of the population for whom neither socialist nor Islamic ideology mattered, even though the educated political elite likes to believe the contrary.

The war in the Sudan is a war between educated political elites in which they have mercilessly amassed and destroyed vast human and economic resources. The perception gap between the elite and the populace reveals that the masses in the North and South have been brutally manipulated to fight for their own genocide. Traditional tribal values and systems of self-defence have been modernized and incorporated into the state's monopoly over violence and coercion, a process which will preclude national integration.

REFERENCES

Albino, O., 1971, *Anya Nya Periodical Publications*. London, 1971–1972.
Amnesty International, 1989, *Sudan: Human Rights Violations in the Context of Civil War*.
Baldu, S.A. and Mahmoud, U.A., 1987, *The Diein Massacre: Slavery in the Sudan*. No publisher.
Baxter, P.T.W., 1977, "Boran Age-Set and Warfare", in D. Turton and K. Fukui (eds.), 1977, *Warfare among East African Pastoralists*. Osaka, Japan.
Colin Legum, 1990, "Stalinist Terror in Ethiopia, Sudan and Somalia", *Third World Reports*. London, 17 January 1990.
Cunnison, I., 1966, *Baggara Arabs*. Oxford.
Deng, F.M., 1973, *Dynamics of Identification: A Basis for National Integration*. Khartoum University Press, Khartoum.
El Affendi, A., 1992, "Discovering Southern Sudan: Sudanese Dilemmas for Islam in Africa", *African Post Newsletter*, Vol. 1, No. 4, June 1992:9–10.
Eprile, C.B., 1974, *War and Peace in the Sudan*. London.
Gurdon, C., 1984, *Sudan at the Cross Roads*. Kent.
Henderson, K.D.D., 1939, "The Migration of the Missirya into Southwest Kordofan", *Sudan Notes and Records*, XXII.
Howell, P., 1955, "Notes on the Ngok Dinka", *Sudan Notes and Records*, XXXII.
Khalid, M., 1985, *Nimeiri and the Revolution of Dis-May*. KPI (Ltd.), London.
Khalid, M., 1987, *Garang Speaks*. London and New York.
Khalid, M., 1990, *The Government They Deserve: The Role of the Elite in Sudan's Political Evolution*. Kegan Paul International, London.
Mazrui, A.A. (ed.), 1977, *The Warrior Tradition in Modern Africa*. Leiden.
Mazrui, A.A., 1986, *The Africans: A Triple Heritage*. BBC Publications.
Mohamed Salih, M.A., 1979, *Inter-tribal Conflicts in Southern Kordofan*. An unpublished M.Sc. Thesis, University of Khartoum.
Mohamed Salih, M.A., 1989, "Tribal Militias, the SPLA/SPLM and the Sudanese State", in A.M. Ahmed and G. Sørbø (eds.), *Management of the Crisis in the Sudan*. Centre for Development Studies, Bergen.
Nadel, S.F. 1947, *The Nuba*. Oxford.
National Records Office, Khartoum, *Devolution in the Nuba Mountains Province*, 44–106–IF–13, 48–126–127–IF–14A, 49–IF–129–23.
Pirouet, M.L., 1977, "Armed Resistance and Counter-insurgency: Reflections on the Anya Nya and the Maumau Experiences", in A.A. Mazrui (ed.), *The Warrior Tradition in Modern Africa*.
Ryle, J., 1988, *The Road to Abyei*. Granta, London.
SPLA/SPLM, 1989, "New Sudan", in A.M. Ahmed and G. Sørbø (eds.), 1989, *Management of the Crisis in the Sudan*. Bergen.
SPLM, *Manifesto*, 1983, Chapter 7, article 21, pp. 16–7. No publisher.
Sørbø, G. and Ahmed A.M. (eds.), 1989, *Management of the Crisis in the Sudan*. Proceeding of the Bergen Forum, 23–24 February 1989.

Wai, D.M. (ed.), 1973, *The Southern Sudan and the Problem of National Integration.* London.

Welch, C.E., 1977, "Warrior, Rebel, Guerilla, and the Putschist: Four Aspects of Political Violence", in A.A. Mazrui (ed.), 1977, *The Warrior Tadition in Africa.* Leiden.

Alternative Economic Strategies for the Sudan

Karl Wohlmuth

SUDAN'S CRISIS

Sudan is in a deep economic, social, political and ecological crisis manifest in the large-scale human rights violations, the mass displacement of people and the increasing poverty and starvation in the country.

The economic crisis escalated at the end of the 1970s when the country abandoned its Six Year Plan and negotiated a stabilization programme with the IMF (International Monetary Fund). However, the crisis emerged earlier and has to do with the development path chosen since independence. From the end of the 1970s onwards one observes a decline of the industrial output and of industrial capacity use, a deterioration of overall growth performance and productivity, a high instability of agricultural output, a decreasing saving capacity and declining investment rates. One notes an increase of regional economic imbalances within the country, a worsening of income and wealth distribution especially in the rural areas, a fast decline of real wages and a high informal sector growth in the urban areas, a sharp decline of payments and of productivity in the public sector and the civil service, and a weakening of the overall capacity of the government to manage the economic crises. One can also observe a decline of the international competitiveness even of traditional export crops (like cotton, sesame, gum Arabic and groundnuts), and a reduction of aid commitments from the side of the donors. Even commodity aid is not forthcoming at sufficient levels. Many other negative socio-economic trend figures may be mentioned but the main issue is that all these tendencies are reinforcing each other, thereby leading to shrinking market levels and productivity growth rates, declining saving and investment rates, a deteriorating performance on the world market, and increasing imbalances with regard to income, wealth and the regions.

The economic record of the new regime (in power since June 1989) is so far extremely poor (see Table 1). The figures do not give any indication of change to the better.

Table 1. *Sudan's economic decline*

Forecast Summary	1989	1990	1991a	1992b
Real GDP growth (%)	7.4	-6.0	-12.0	-5.0
Consumer price inflation (%)	64	80	150	175
Exports fob ($ mn)	545	555	425	500
Imports fob ($ mn)	1,051	1,216	1,325	1,450
Current A/c balance ($ mn)	-152	-390	-500	-475
Total external debt ($ bn)	13.0	13.2	13.4	13.6

a = Estimates, b = forecasts
Source: *Sudan Studies*, January 1992:6

The negative growth rates over the years mean that less and less product is available for the subsistence needs of the growing population. Inflation is escalating thereby impoverishing the poorest segments of the population. Trade deficit is still increasing and imports are now three times the level of the export values. The current account deficit, including also services and remittances, is deteriorating as well because Sudanese Nationals Working Abroad (SNWA) are unwilling to remit income earned in foreign countries, and because of too late and uncoordinated devaluation, import control and debt policies. Agricultural policies of the new regime are highly politicised and concentrated on irrigated agriculture first, and on mechanized farming second (with preference for wheat cultivation in irrigated areas at the expense of cotton). These agricultural policies also have a bias against the traditional agricultural sub-sector and small farmers. The loss of traditional export markets, high dependency on import with regard to so many investment and consumer goods as well as intermediate goods and the increasing reluctance of the donors to commit and supply commodity aid culminated in unsustainable balance of payments' positions.

The above figures give only an impression of the tensions and the climate surrounding the Sudanese economy now. Alternative economic scenarios give a much gloomier picture of the situation (*Sudan Studies*, 1992:4–6). For the years 1976–1989, the Sudanese economy has experienced a decrease of income (Gross National Product) on a per capita basis of 18 per cent; the exports showed a negative trend rate of -0.3 per cent annually. Much higher negative rates in income and in exports were recorded for the 1980s (see World Bank, 1987b, 1990). Sudan's world share of merchandise exports fell by 46 per cent in this period and this reveals the tremendous decline of international competitiveness. Therefore one observes an acceleration of the negative trend since the 1970s with an escalation in the 1980s and in the early 1990s.

The human costs of this crisis are extremely high. According to World Bank estimates, in some areas of Northern Sudan around 50 per cent of the population live under conditions of chronic or transitory food insecurity or are threatened by food insecurity (World Bank, 1990:ii). The decrease of the access to and of the quality of education, health, water and sanitation systems as well as of the overall physical infrastructure since the 1970s is well evidenced (ILO, 1987; World Bank, 1988).

Parallel to this escalating economic crisis the political crisis started to gain momentum in 1983 when the Addis Ababa Agreement was abandoned by President Numeiri. An annual burden of up to 1 billion dollars for meeting the direct costs of the war in the South has since impeded any attempt to consolidate the reform and stabilization efforts of the country. The lost economic chances of oil exploration/production and of the Jonglei Canal have to be added to these war-related direct costs. Region-wide destruction, proliferation of tribal militia, increasing tensions between Arab and non-Arab

Muslims, between the North and the South, between Southern tribes, between Western tribes, the unprecedented misuse of ethnicity for political reasons and the extent of displacements throughout the country have disrupted the social fabric and have destroyed the basis for maintaining human rights in the country.

Large-scale displacements of people (4–6 million people) led to the crowding of suburban regions of Khartoum and of other towns; meanwhile the pressure has increased for forced return to the original areas (up to 1 million people are affected so far). The policy of forced return in an environment of political and food insecurity implies that problems are transferred to the relocation areas. The policies leading to displacement and forced relocation have an impact on the sending and on the receiving areas. Affected are the state of the environment and the quality of the natural resources. The breakdown of basic infrastructure, of the governmental control of economic activities, of tax collecting, and basic support and survival systems has intensified the ecological destruction.

The ecological crisis of Sudan is not independent from these economic and political crises as people have to adjust to these harsh conditions in order to survive in periods of war, destruction, drought and economic recession. The ecological crisis is also a result of the political destructions and the large-scale displacements. A new wave of rural to rural and rural to urban migration has set in in the 1980s and has led to a new population pressure in various regions so that the already weak administrative and infrastructural base has further deteriorated. The loss of governmental control over the ecological situation and the natural resource base implies that even the rudimentary environmental policy guidelines established since Sudan's independence have lost their real importance for environmental protection of sectoral activities as agriculture, livestock-raising, forestry, transport and industry.

The deterioration of the environment poses a real problem as there is virtually no disaster management capacity in Sudan as experiences have shown during the floods in 1988 (see Parker, 1991 on the lack of crisis management during flooding).

The ecological situation has changed dramatically in the 1980s because of the extent of urbanization in the country to which the resource use systems have had to adapt in fundamental ways (see Abu Sin, 1991). The combination of natural disasters, civil war, economic recession and urban population concentration left their mark on the environmental situation; it is a necessity to control the effects of the large-scale damage to the environment on the basis of a new long-term oriented management strategy. Regrettably, no such policy approach is visible now or has a chance to develop in the present environment.

Structural adjustment policies since the 1970s also have affected the state of the environment in Sudan. Critics of the IMF and World Bank policies (Wohlmuth and Hansohm, 1984; Wohlmuth and Hansohm, 1987; Hansohm, 1989; Prendergast, 1989) have continuously warned against the negative effects of "typical" structural adjustment programmes on the environment, especially with regard to the impact of new agricultural policies and the lack of accompanying poverty alleviation policies. Specifically it was argued that the Agricultural Rehabilitation Programmes of the World Bank for Sudan which have focused mainly on irrigated agriculture have been a further cause of environmental degradation (Prendergast, 1989:44–46). This has mainly to do with the extremely poor ecological management of these programmes but also with the lack of clear environmental objectives in structural adjustment programmes (see Wohlmuth, 1992). The shortcomings in the first generation of structural adjustment programmes have even contributed to problems in countries with a more favourable position with regard to economic, political and external factors.

Large-scale population movements and the economic recession have affected the social networks especially in rural areas and have thereby destroyed the existing ecological balance. With regard to Eastern Sudan it can be shown that established and successful ecological adjustments between farming and pastoral societies have changed dramatically because of the aggravating economic and social situation (Sørbø, 1991). The more recent government policies (since 1989) may have contributed to the deterioration of the situation by specific government interventions on behalf of vested commercial interest groups (middle- and large-scale mechanized farmers). Thereby the formerly successful systems of ecological adaptation have broken up. Governmental interventions at all levels with regard to land allocation, credit allocation and price control are important when designing new policies which aim at preserving or regaining ecological balance (Sørbø, 1991). Land rights policies and land allocation policies are especially important to this argument; one can observe that the new regime uses these instruments politically to sustain the regime, disregarding completely the social and ecological balance. The policy to expand further the areas for mechanized farming and the allocation of credit to middle-scale and large-scale farmers are elements of this policy. However, land degradation and ecological imbalance are not inescapable tendencies as Sørbø (1991) and many other observers have demonstrated.

Sudan's crisis is also a social crisis and a crisis of the social production relations. One could observe in Sudan a steep increase of rural-urban migration in spite of declining real incomes in urban areas for the last two decades. The growing social costs of large-scale dislocation and relocation, a worsening of income and wealth distribution situation especially in rural areas, and an increasing awareness that the limit of the capacity of the informal sector to absorb more labour has already been reached further aggravates the employment crisis in the country. All these tendencies imply higher levels of open unemployment in the towns, increasing levels of poverty and food insecurity in the rural areas, and a sharp decline or even virtual breakdown of social and physical infrastructural services, thereby affecting mostly the poorest people in society. The breakdown of the basic physical infrastructure (transport, energy supply, water, housing, telecommunication) places an additional burden on the people in their fight for survival, but also leads to an erosion of the future capacity and viability of Sudan's capital stock (see on transport the study by Bush, 1991 and on energy Wohlmuth, 1993). The material as well as the immaterial capital stock of Sudan is deteriorating very fast. Low and declining investment rates and decreasing per capita expenditures on education and health are affecting the overall viability and productivity of the capital stock. Neither public nor private investment is forthcoming at minimum sustainable levels so as to bring the process of destruction to a halt.

The interaction of these crises (economic, political, environmental and social) is responsible for the extent of stagnation and recession and for the degradation of the resources' base. Any alternative economic development programme has to start with an explanation of the real causes of the economic crisis of Sudan.

EXPLAINING SUDAN'S ECONOMIC CRISIS

The real causes of Sudan's economic crisis

What are the causes of Sudan's economic decline since the 1970s? One view, mainly held in IMF/World Bank circles, looks at the economic crisis from the viewpoint of distorted economic incentives for productive activities. The economic crisis is related to misplaced interventions from the side of the government. Poor economic policies in Sudan are considered as the prime cause besides natural disasters and the civil war (World Bank, 1990:ii–iii). Indeed, there is some validity in this type of reasoning. The war issue is very much related to the cause of poor economic policies as extra-budgetary expenditures over the years disrupted the system of budget planning and the monetary policies of the Central Bank. The overall economy suffered from these uncontrolled expenditures by the respective transmission channels of deficit financing, inflation and crowding out the private sector from credit allocation. Another transmission channel but related to deficit financing and inflation is the impact on the international value of the currency. Sudan became caught in a permanent state of overvaluation of the currency whatever the government had done in terms of devaluation measures. The international competitiveness declined as complementary policies were not pursued to support the devaluations and to compensate the export sector for the overvaluation of the Sudanese Pound (£S). Even the natural disasters in Sudan (the drought of the period 1982 to 1985 and the floods of 1988) may be related to policy failures as there was no anticipatory policy approach to cope with the disasters. Government policy did not prepare for the states of emergency; it failed to react to the crises by adequate instruments to secure food supplies and to prevent the breakdown of infrastructure and of public services.

The IMF/World Bank view relates the extent of Sudan's economic crisis to the inappropriate economic policies over a long time, to the constancy of policy failure (World Bank, 1990:iii). However, it is not sufficiently explained why there is a 'constancy of policy failure' in Sudan. The explanation of the 'why' is not very deep in its analytical content. According to the IMF and the World Bank the government of Sudan has mistrusted the private sector so that a web of regulations was built around the economy and all its sectors. Another aspect related to this is the urban bias of the government policies, protecting the urban people from the mechanics of the price mechanism by subsidizing consumer goods and giving generously and far below cost public services and other privileges to them. This may be considered as another element of a government policy mistrusting the private sector and the market. These beliefs have so far led to an overemphasis of public sector activities and public sector companies. Disincentives for private businesses were then the result of the incentives for the public sector and the public companies. From this point of view, "Sudan's economic history presents an archetypical case of distortionary government policies, ..." (World Bank, 1990:iii).

More concretely, a dilemma resulted from this policy approach: the price controls applied by the government were effective at the producer level only (because of the small number of firms involved) and ineffective at the wholesale/retail level (because of the great number of traders and consumers involved). This dilemma of price controls never could be solved, thereby taxing the producers first of all with the consequence of cumulative disincentives for them.

New investment was discouraged by these anti-private sector policies/anti-market economy policies/anti-small business policies. The whole system of regulations by licences, price controls, credit allocation and taxation procedures were then responsible for the negative effect on new investment and the whole production system. Also exports became negatively affected by this type of policy as overregulation, inappropriate prices for exporters, inappropriate exchange rate policies and even export bans reduced incentives to export (World Bank, 1990:iv). The crucial role of exchange rates as a price signal and as a tool for inducing development and structural change was never recognised by Sudanese governments.

Related to these overregulation and price control policies is the anti-developmental character of the tax system and the structure of expenditures leading to an increasing fiscal gap. The fiscal gap led to a siphoning off of credit to the central government and the public corporations at the expense of private businesses and companies and the regions and provinces (as these entities were not financially autonomous). The perverse result was a share of the public sector in credit allocation of more than 80 per cent so that not much more than 10 per cent was left for the private sector (World Bank, 1990:iv).

According to this view a circle of inappropriate policies led to the long-term stagnation of the Sudanese economy. In this situation the governments had two ways to respond: firstly, by introducing even more regulation and foreign exchange controls so that the private sector was even more harshly controlled than before, or secondly, by liberalizing the whole economic system completely. No government of Sudan has really made a clear decision between the two options but changed from one position to the other. This is true also for the years of the new regime. The lack of policy consistency affected the private sector development, first of all because of the lack of clear and unambiguous decisions. Table 1 reveals the extent of imbalances after a period of harsh controls since June 1989 and later a period of a proclaimed liberalization policy since 1991/92.

Since 1977 the IMF and the World Bank have negotiated various funding agreements with the Government of Sudan covering the macro-economy and some economic sectors, especially agriculture and industry. Various policy prescriptions from the side of the IMF (see IMF, 1986) and from the World Bank (1986, 1987a,b,c, 1988, 1990) laid the foundations for the envisaged policy reforms to be implemented from the side of the Government of Sudan. The recommended policies of price decontrol, elimination of overregulation, revision of the tax structure, and reform of the parastatals were emphasized all over the years from the side of the international organizations. However, critical evaluations of the policies reveal that neither design nor implementation were appropriate and successful (see Wohlmuth and Hansohm, 1987; Hansohm, 1989; Prendergast, 1989; Awad, 1986 and Abdel Gadir Ali, 1985). Some of the critics emphasize the inappropriate design of the IMF/World Bank model, others more the implementation problems or the issue of the adequate time horizon for intended policy reforms. All of the critics argue that the agenda and the conditionality of the IMF and the World Bank are insufficient for countries like Sudan, that the implementation of reforms is expected in a too short period, that the issues of structural malformation and of vested interests are not covered, and that the social aspects of adjustment were not considered at all or too late (as revealed by the fact that a programme to mitigate the social costs of adjustment had to wait for not less than 10 years since the first adjustment programmes for Sudan; see World Bank, 1988).

However, the alternatives presented by the critics are not at all conclusive, convincing and operational (see Part 4 of this paper). Also this factor explains why Sudan remained caught in a situation of increasingly complex and inappropriate conditionalities, applied from the involved international organizations over years without having any significant effect on the macro-economic and sectoral situation. The inappropriateness of the IMF and World Bank policies and the lack of any consistent alternative from the side of the

Table 2. *The decline of the productive economic sectors in the Sudan*

THE CASE OF AGRICULTURE	THE CASE OF INDUSTRY
1. *Pre-independence period* Development of export crops, but very limited agricultural development (colonial agricultural policy).	1. *Pre-independence period* Destruction of cottage industries; colonial-type processing of exported primary products.
2. *Period 1956–1969* Continuation of colonial-type agricultural policy, neglecting traditional rain-fed agriculture; development of mechanized farming; monetization of the livestock economy; parallel emphasis on large-scale irrigated agriculture and (largely uncontrolled) expansion of mechanized farming.	2. *Pre-independence period* Indirect public intervention towards industry by the Investment Act of 1956 and start of modern manufacturing; the state became active in large-scale agricultural and infrastructural projects, and the private sector in light industries; the regional concentration of industry was already pronounced; small industries were neglected. 3. *Period 1960–1969* Direct public intervention in industry, especially in agro-industries, and parallel to this governmental support of private industrial investments; state is active in large-scale and raw materials-based industries, and the private sector is more and more active in the production of non-essential goods; no interest in small industries promotion.
3. *Period 1969–1977/78* Continuation of the colonial bias against traditional rain-fed agriculture; unplanned expansion of mechanized agriculture is continued; productivity decline by nationalization of private pump schemes; strategy of import substitution of food by horizontal agricultural expansion and the promotion of agroindustries ('Breadbasket Strategy'); parallel development of modern and traditional subsectors was recommended by ILO and became part of the Six Year Plan, but the recommendations were never followed up, and the Six Year Plan was abandoned after one year.	4. *Period 1969–1973* Nationalization and confiscation of private industries in 1970, but soon (1971) a policy reversal took place, though unsuccessful because of lack of domestic and foreign investors' interest; no policy focus on small industries. 5. *Period 1973–1977/78* Huge agro-industrial investments (sugar, textiles, meat, etc.) were started by public sector; some Arab support was granted under the label of 'Sudan: the breadbasket of Arab countries'; external and internal factors led already 1977/78 to an abrupt end of this offensive (expansionist) attempt of structural adjustment; no policy on small industries.
4. *Period 1977/78 until now* Negative effects of stabilization policies on the agroindustrial expansion programme; Export Action and Agricultural Rehabilitation Programmes are basically oriented towards irrigated agriculture; neglect of traditional rain-fed agriculture; no control of mechanized farming; elaboration of a detailed Strategy for the Development of Rain-fed Agriculture, but rejected at the political level; lack of political interest, of foreign exchange and domestic finance; the effects of drought cycles and the civil war led to a renewed interest in 'safe' irrigated agriculture; since the national Salvation Revolution (NSR) slogans of food security and self-reliance ('we eat what we produce'); lack of an integrated and coherent strategy to bring forth the intended 'agricultural revolution'; lack of a coherent export promotion policy.	6. *Period 1977/78 until now* Decline of public industries because of lack of inputs, markets and management; continued disinterest at the policy levels in small and informal industries (of traditional as well as modern small industries); industry sector rehabilitation strategy for sugar and textile factories with meagre results, so that the long overdue self-sufficiency even in sugar is out of reach; incredibly low capacity utilization in industry; since National Salvation Revolution (NSR) chaotic privatization policies and new Investment Act of 1990, unsupported by other policies; no consistent export promotion policy with regard to manufactures.

Source: Wohlmuth, 1989, 1991

government and/or other social/political groups in Sudan are important factors for explaining the rapidity and the character of Sudan's economic
decline and the extent of its economic crisis.

An alternative explanation of the economic crisis is presented by those authors who look at the crisis from a historical and structural perspective
(Wohlmuth and Hansohm, 1984, 1987; Hansohm, 1989; Prendergast, 1989;
Wohlmuth, 1989, 1991; and also ILO, 1986a, 1987) rather than from an
economic management and price-theoretic ("getting the prices right") point
of view. These authors have in common that they refer first of all to the
causes of the declining performance of the productive sectors (agriculture
and industry) relative to the situation of other sectors (trade, services, civil
service) when explaining the serious state of the macro-economy. Table 2
(based on Wohlmuth, 1989 and 1991) summarizes for the various periods of
Sudanese economic development the structural impediments and the central
issues for structural adjustment policies at the sectoral level. Another explanation of Sudan's economic crisis emerges from this periodization and the
related analysis of Sudan's structural constraints. It is obvious that the governments and the vested interest groups in Sudan are responsible for the imbalance between agricultural sub-sectors and between industrial subsectors,
the lack of integration and linkages between sectors, the imbalances between
private and public, small and large industries, the outgrowth of the civil service and other structural impediments which have built up in Sudan since independence (see ILO, 1987).

Even more important, the development of the two productive sectors was
never synchronized in the planning process which led to such perverse results
as raw materials shortages in industry in an agriculture-based country like
Sudan, a lack of growth of markets despite huge potential markets in rural
and urban areas, a lack of linkages between agriculture and industry despite
the high potential forward, backward and final demand linkages in a country
such as Sudan, and an overdependence of both sectors via exports and imports from the world market despite a significant internal production and
processing potential. An important implication of this type of planning was
that the growth, productivity and employment potential of neither sector
could be exploited and that the balance of payments position has continuously worsened. Therefore, the 'constancy of policy failure' argument has to
be replaced by the 'constancy of structural malformation' argument.

Consequences of this type of development were increasing poverty in rural areas, increasing unemployment in the urban areas, limited employment
prospects in industry, even in informal activities, and also in rural areas with
regard to off-farm activities, a low capacity utilization in industry, a deterioration of the production base of rural and urban small industries, a lack of
domestic and foreign investment, the non-development of input and intermediate goods industries, and, most destructive, a decline of the productive
potential of traditional rain-fed agriculture with repercussions on food se-

curity and the export potential of Sudan (see Wohlmuth, 1991). All this took place under the umbrella of a growing public sector and civil service and the funding of a huge machinery for national planning and aid administration.

Structural malformation and dislinked development over all relevant periods of Sudan's economic development are important elements for the explanation of the depth of the crisis in Sudan; ways out of the crisis can be found on the basis of this explanation.

A most serious consequence of the lack of market development and the lack of political and economic stability was the decline of the investment rates since the 1970s parallel to the inappropriate structure of investment within and between subsectors (see Wohlmuth and Hansohm, 1984, 1987; Wohlmuth, 1989, 1991). Investment in neither sector took place at a sufficient level and in an adequate structure. The decline of private investment was never compensated for by higher public investments. Incredible and rapidly changing macro-economic policies did their part to impede investment activity over the years. The steep decline and the low level of investment especially since 1983 (see World Bank, 1990:8) imply a drastic and dramatic deterioration of the capital stock and will cause—if not corrected soon—a further weakening of the international competitiveness of Sudan. The new Investment Act of 1990 (to replace the one of 1980) cannot itself compensate for the lack of credible macro-economic and sectoral policies.

There is a lack of integrated sectoral policies since independence. Integrated sectoral policies comprise not only incentives policies (e.g. prices, exchange rates, tariffs, charges, duties), but also institutional reforms (of extension services, investment and export promotion agencies and financial institutions), policies on innovations (reform of research and development centres, improved transfer of technologies to agriculture and industry), policies on input supplies (with regard to raw materials, fuels, skills, foreign exchange, intermediate goods and spare parts), policies on information and coordination (by a better cooperation of public and private actors, administrative and commercial institutions, at horizontal and vertical levels), and infrastructural policies (with regard to physical and social infrastructure). Integrated programmes in Sudan were limited to some few integrated rural development programmes which could not be sustained because of lack of national support and non-synchronized sectoral planning in Sudan (see ILO, 1987; Wohlmuth, 1991).

It can therefore be argued that the structural adjustment and stabilization policies since 1977/78 have not addressed the fundamental problems of the productive sectors, neither at the intra-sectoral level nor at the inter-sectoral level. The message is that there is much more than mistrust of the private business from the side of the government that led to the current state of economic disaster. An alternative development path has to encounter the deeply rooted structural impediments in Sudan; especially it has to be made clear that the development path chosen since independence was accepting a very high degree of capital- and import-intensity in its projects and programmes.

IMPLICATIONS FOR SOUTHERN SUDAN

The structural malformation in Northern Sudan had serious implications for the development of Southern Sudan (see Yongo-Bure, 1989; Bwolo, 1991). What happened in the economy of Southern Sudan during the crucial periods of its development? Four periods have to be distinguished in order to understand the current situation.

1. During the pre-independence period (up to 1956) there was only a very limited interest in socio-economic development of Southern Sudan. The beginning of some interest is marked by the proposed Ten Year Plan of Development presented in 1938. The proposal for the Zande Area Development Programme in 1943 and the inclusion of the proposal in 1945 as a part of a package of projects and programmes including also the Equatoria Agricultural Projects Board encouraged some producers to grow cotton, other cash and food crops, and led also to some fisheries development. Nevertheless, the impact of these first programmes related to the development of productive sectors was rather limited.

   In the political field, the Juba Conference of 1947 was very important as it ended with an agreement on future federalism in Sudan (although the open confrontation since 1955 and the formal abandonment of the conference results in 1958, led to the civil war).

   From an economic point of view, the period between 1953 and 1956 was crucial. A study published in 1955 and called 'National Resources and Development Potential in the Southern Provinces of Sudan' highlighted already the role of Southern Sudan as a supplier of various goods (sugar, coffee, tea, meat and fish) to Northern Sudan, thereby prescribing for Southern Sudan the role to substitute imports of the North from third countries. However, the political conflicts since 1955 surrounding the earlier commitment to federalism in independent Sudan overshadowed more and more the positive impulses to exploit the chances and opportunities of economic development in Southern Sudan.

2. The period after independence of Sudan until the Addis Ababa Agreement (1956 to 1972) witnessed some limited Northern Sudanese interest in the development of Southern Sudan's agriculture. However, the projects identified for Southern Sudan in the 1955 Study never were implemented. But the intensification of hostilities after 1963 witnessed a complete halt of all development effort.

   The May 25, 1969 *coup d'état* brought a turning point leading directly to the Addis Ababa Agreement of 1972 by granting regional autonomy to the South. Since then, some economic instruments were used to integrate the Southern Sudan into the planning and development process of Sudan.

Between 1969 and 1972 annual Special Development Budgets were designed for the South. Also a Regional Co-ordination Council and a
Regional Planning Council were set up in 1970 to integrate a development
plan for the South into the then relevant Five Year Plan for Sudan
(1970/71 to 1974/75). However, it was too late from an operational point
of view to include the Southern parts of the plan document in the Plan for
Sudan so that only some projects could be included between March and
May 1970 in the overall Plan document (in the form of priority projects,
resettlement projects, and some development projects). The idea of incorporating a plan for the South into the National Plan was then abandoned
and preference was given to annual Special Development Budgets on
grounds of flexibility (Yongo-Bure, 1989:11).

3. The period in which the Addis Ababa Agreement was working (March
   1972 to June 1983) saw first of all some repatriation, resettlement and rehabilitation programmes for Southern Sudan. Development objectives for
   Southern Sudan's reconstruction and development were the provision of
   support for food and cash crop production, integrated rural development
   and human resources development. The periods since 1972/73 saw annual
   Special Development Budgets, but soon it became obvious that there was
   a continuous decline of actual spending relative to scheduled spending
   (from 40 per cent in 1972/73 to 20 per cent in the fifth annual budget in
   1976/77). This tendency of a deteriorating ratio of actual to scheduled expenditures (see Yongo-Bure, 1989:13) soon led to discussions about the
   constraints to absorption of funds for projects and development in
   Southern Sudan. Various constraints were cited in this context: finance
   problems, shortage of skills, scarcity of materials, fuels and inputs, transport problems, but the overriding factors seemed to be finance and foreign
   exchange.

   The vagueness and arbitrariness of central government finance commitments and allocations to the South, the high degree of variability of
   Southern access to Sudan's external assistance, and the variability and
   uncertainty about the level of regional taxes led to growing problems with
   regard to timely availability of funds for projects and programmes, and
   reduced the potential for detailed planning on the basis of expected revenues. All three sources of Southern finance (direct transfers from the
   central government; shares of Sudan's external assistance; and regional
   taxes) showed some arbitrariness, uncertainty and variability. These factors hampered first of all the execution of development projects and of
   long-term planning for Southern Sudan. But other factors were also important: lack of public accountability for funds, excessive public sector
   growth in the South, lack of co-ordination of projects and finance, and the
   lack of any integration of projects and programmes into long-term planning. The last point is important when discussing the issues of why it was
   not possible to overcome the constraints to development in the South.

Then, in July 1977, the Regional Plan for the South was finally integrated into the new Six Year Plan of 1977/78 to 1982/83. However, this
inclusion never became operational as the Plan was discontinued in
1978/79 and was replaced by three year public investment programmes
until 1984/85, and then by one year development expenditure budgets and
three or four year development programmes. All these planning exercises
were more or less confined to central government budgets, not including
regional and provincial budgets. Long-term planning was abandoned as
well as the inclusion of the South and other regions into central development budgeting.

4. The period of the Six Year Plan one can observe that the actual investments in the South relative to the envisaged investments reached only 25
   per cent (and only 45 per cent if the much lower revised figures of the
   later three year programmes after the abandonment of the Six Year Plan
   are taken as the basis). The problems of the lack of integration of the
   South into overall planning in the Sudan and of the reduction of the financial base for Southern Sudan were compounded by a further diversion
   of public funds which occurred because of excessive growth of expenditures for government administration. All this affected the execution of
   larger development projects which never became finalized (this was especially so for the sugar industry projects). However, it is important to
   mention that the most important projects identified for the Southern
   Sudan already before independence were abandoned prior to or during
   implementation, because of the abrogation of the Addis Ababa Agreement
   in 1983.

   The ongoing civil war halted all agricultural and industrial development in the South, caused the loss of an estimated USD 3 billion in terms
   of revenue from oil exploration and the close down of the Jonglei canal
   construction after having completed more than half of the canal and after
   having invested already more than 300 million dollars up to February
   1983. However, most disruptive for the whole economy of Sudan was the
   daily cost of the war which is estimated at 11 million British Pounds (see
   Bwolo, 1991:40).

   In this period the growing fiscal crisis, the economic recession, the failure of structural adjustment policies, and the lack of any long-term planning perspective for Sudan made dysfunctional the system of financing
   Southern development by direct transfers and/or shares of external assistance (the regional tax revenues became meanwhile irrelevant as a source
   of finance) completely. Therefore, the few ongoing development projects
   have also collapsed.

It is obvious that the structural malformation in Sudan was reinforced by the
North-South conflict, by the failures to negotiate a resolution to the conflict,
and also by the lack of any integration by planning and budgeting of

Southern Sudan's economic potential into the Sudanese national economy. Economic and political crises in the Northern and Southern Sudan therefore reinforced each other. The huge potential for the development of the productive sectors in the South was neither fully identified nor utilized, but continuously neglected and devastated. The economic foundation for a political unity of Sudan was never laid. A functioning mechanism for financing an autonomous Southern Sudan was never constructed after 1972, although there were, from time to time, proposals to solve the financial issues by appropriate revenue and burden—sharing formulae to be applied between the regions and the central government and between the regions and the provinces (see especially Due, 1984). Elements of a new strategy for Southern Sudan to lay the foundations for economic and political unity of the whole Sudan have been proposed more recently (see Yongo-Bure, 1989, 1990, 1991); new economic policies, financial autonomy and agriculture-based small industrial development are some of the guiding principles.

Altogether, we find the explanation of Sudan's economic crisis on the basis of the argument of a constancy of structural malformation more convincing than the argument of a constancy of policy failures. The non-resolution of the North-South conflict and the non-integration of the Southern economy into planning and budgeting for Sudan since independence were additional factors reinforcing the overall decline. The development of productive sectors in Northern and Southern Sudan was seriously affected by this combination of adverse factors; this was the case in all periods of development identified for Northern and for Southern Sudan.

THE ECONOMIC POLICIES OF THE NEW REGIME AND THE IMPACT ON THE PRODUCTIVE SECTORS

The political and economic doctrines of the new regime

The new regime in Sudan since the *coup d'état* of 30 June 1989 has argued in favour of a radically different economic philosophy. (According to the Statement made by the New regime on the National Conference for Economic Salvation (1989)), a new economic philosophy should be based on the cultural values of the country and should be focused on environmental, materialistic and spiritual dimensions and the aspirations of the Sudanese citizens. As socio-economic objectives the following were mentioned: first, maintaining individual and national dignity; second, realizing regionally integrated development; third, promoting material and human resources development; fourth, preserving the environment; fifth, fair distribution of wealth; and sixth, handling properly the production and infrastructural deterioration of the country (Statement, 1989).

It was repeatedly argued by the proponents of the new regime that the main cause of Sudan's political and economic decline and its instability is the absence of an authentic political and socio-economic philosophy. Such a new economic philosophy has to guide all economic policies and programmes as outlined in the programme of the National Conference for Economic Salvation of 1989 (see United Nations, 1990:22–27).

The following economic guidelines were mentioned as well: organizing for a mobilization of the productive sectors of the economy; concentration on production and investment; improvement of the role of the banking and finance system; and adoption of planning at all levels under the consideration of the principle of self-reliance. The National Conference for Economic Salvation called also for integrated economic policies; overall administrative reforms and a reform of public institutions; a greater emphasis on direct taxes and on combatting tax evasion; and measures to consolidate the fiscal situation and to reach monetary and exchange rate stability (see United Nations, 1990:23). Regarding foreign trade, some issues mentioned were: finding ways of combatting smuggling activities, organizing border trade, rationalization of importation by more selective import policies, and diversification of exports. Credit policy was also considered as an important issue, and a better mobilization of savings for productive sectors was envisaged. Food security/self-sufficiency policies and related infrastructural policies were also recommended; they should be based on a more balanced agricultural policy and a better allocation of public investment funds. The small farmers should benefit from such policies first. Administrative reform, public accountability and increasing the performance of the public sector were mentioned as other important areas of concern. On the whole, no important area of economic policy reform is left out of the agenda.

All these policy measures should be guided by ten principles (or doctrines)

1. The overriding objective is self-reliance/self-sufficiency/self-dependence/ real independence and complete liberation from Western economic, political and cultural domination; self-reliance is considered as a strategy to be applied nation-wide, sector-wide and region-wide, especially with regard to regional fiscal autonomy and regional food self-sufficiency.

2. Related to this principle is the doctrine of independent decision-making in all international affairs and also at the regional African level, implying a specific attitude towards international organizations like IMF and World Bank; this implies a complete rejection of all conditionalities as applied from the side of donor organizations.

3. Another principle refers to an economy based on a new system of democracy, federalism and popular participation, involving 'masses', 'forces' and sectoral interests (such as trade unions and employers' organizations being in one group bundled together so as to channel interest groups' activities in the national interest).

4. An important element of the economic doctrine refers to macro-economic and exchange rate stability, having in mind a strict control of monetary

circulation (enforced by a currency reform), of exchange rate changes and credit allocations.

5. Crucial is the sectoral complementarity between agriculture and industry, with agriculture being the backbone of the economy, as the leading sector of the economy; the slogan 'we eat what we produce' is related to all spheres of production and to all regions; implied is a call for an 'agricultural revolution' and the support of agro-based industries, especially of small and rural industries; to some extent the idea of Sudan as a breadbasket of the region and of the Arab world is brought up again.

6. Refers to the mobilization and use of local resources, especially of local savings, and to the production of goods for the local demand; all this implies an educational, manpower and human resources development revolution in the country, as well as a broad-based cultural revolution (based on Arabicisation, Islamization and Sudan's 'folk values'); higher education therefore has to be adapted to the local needs/resources/advantages.

7. A new social security contract is propagated based on Islamic and governmental Social Security Funds and a strict control of foreign NGOs/GROs/VDOs which have activities in social and humanitarian areas; the new social contract should allow for a fair distribution of goods as long as scarcity of goods exists and a gradual replacement of relief support by production—related support, especially for the displaced and the refugees.

8. A further principle refers to the prudent use of public money and the restoration of public accountability at all levels of administration and public corporations; this involves a complete administrative and civil service reform.

9. Later (since 1990/91) the principle of liberalization, deregulation and privatization gained importance, and is replacing more and more other principles so far upheld in crucial policy areas.

10. Rehabilitation of the Southern Sudan is mentioned as another principle (but obviously understood as a reconstruction based on a new system of values (Islamization and Arabicisation).

These 10 principles altogether would involve a complete reversal of society and economy if applied, and they are meant to guide all programmes of reform. However, there is no clear and unambiguous definition and interpretation of any of these principles, so that the policymakers are free to decide and to adapt according to political tactics and political pressures. It is clear since the proclamation of these principles that the meaning of these principles will remain vague and that there are contradictions and trade-offs between them, especially now between principles of self-reliance and those of liberalization, deregulation and privatization.

However, much more important are the contradictions between the principles and the real policies of the regime. Table 3 gives an impression of what these guiding principles of the new regime imply for the macro-economic policies, the sectoral development policies, the international economic relations and the organization of the developmental state in Sudan.

A look at the more recent macro-economic developments (see Table 1) does not give the impression that any of these 10 principles is taken seriously in day to day politics, if we look at the increasing import dependence, the lack of monetary control, the lack of exchange rate stability and the absence of sectoral complementarity. Self-reliance, mobilization of domestic resources, prudent use of public funds and other principles do not seem to have any real meaning with regard to practical politics. It is therefore necessary to look first of all at the specific policies pursued by the new government sector by sector of the economy and area by area of macro-economic policies. This will help to assess the policies with regard to the characteristics of Sudan's economic crisis.

THE REAL POLITICS AND ECONOMICS OF THE NEW REGIME
Agriculture

The new government claims to revive agriculture, first of all the traditional rain-fed sub-sector, and to improve the production conditions of the small farmers and especially the agricultural credit system so as to support them more directly. In reality however the policy of the new government did not follow this course at all. Land was allocated toward wheat production at the expense of cotton in irrigated agriculture, and toward sorghum production in mechanized farming; there is a clear bias towards middle-scale farmers rather than small farmers; the same is true with regard to credit allocation. The traditional rain-fed agricultural sub-sector and the small farmers were not targeted by sectoral policy measures.

Table 3. *Views of the new regime on Sudan's economic development*

1. *Stimulating productive sectors*
1.1. Re-orientation of economic policies towards the mobilization of productive sectors (new credit and fiscal policies);
1.2. Agricultural revolution; import substitution of strategic crops like wheat; Small Farmers Programme; promotion of agricultural finance on the basis of Islamic principles;
1.3. Food Security Programmes based on self-reliance/self-sufficiency principles (strategic stocks of grain);
1.4. Mobilization of resources in the region (regional self-reliance);
1.5. Revitalization of large-scale industries; small industry development; implementation of the new Investment Act of 1990;
1.6. Educational and cultural revolution to support productive development (revolution of higher education); Islamization and Arabicisation;

1.7. Development of appropriate technologies and control of imported technology.

2. *Macro-economic stabilization and market reform*
2.1. Fiscal consolidation by production-orientation; public accountability and prudence with regard to the use of public funds; higher direct taxation and avoidance of tax evasion;
2.2. Stabilizing monetary circulation and currency reform;
2.3. Orientation of credit allocation towards productive enterprises; re-orientation of the finance system on the basis of Islamic finance principles;
2.4. Privatization/deregulation/liberalization of the economy to create favourable and competitive market conditions;
2.5. Re-orientation of public and Islamic social security funds from relief towards support of production;
2.6. Regional financial autonomy and fiscal self-reliance;
2.7. Creation of an appropriate legal framework for macro-economic stabilization.

3. *New foundations for international economic relations*
3.1. New commercial policies to support the productive sectors; organization and control of border trade;
3.2. New bilateralism in trade and payments relations;
3.3. Stabilizing the exchange rate; generation of remittances from SNWA;
3.4. Stimulation of South-South trade and of cooperation/integration agreements on a bilateral, regional and multilateral basis;
3.5. Rejecting any conditionality from multilateral/bilateral donors;
3.6. Control of foreign NGOs;
3.7. Diversification of exports and rationalization of imports.

4. *Revitalizing the developmental state*
4.1. New foundations for democratic development;
4.2. New modalities of federalism;
4.3. Controlled participation of sectoral interest groups in the political process, especially of employers' organizations and of trade unions;
4.4. Strict control of basic organizations (mass organizations) and of foreign interests;
4.5. Laying the foundations for a new political and economic philosophy;
4.6. Reform of administration and national planning;
4.7. Re-establishing long-term planning.

Sources: United Nations 1990; *Sudanow*, various issues; *Sudan Democratic Gazette*, various issues; *Sudan Update*, various issues; other sources.

The self-sufficiency strategy in wheat (see on this story the various issues of *Sudanow* since 1989/90) at the expense of cotton is propagated and implemented without any consideration of cost and environmental considerations. Wheat is considered by the new regime as a strategic crop for urban people and so all relevant production and distribution issues are handled by a National Committee for Wheat. Although this committee has the task to formulate an integrated policy, neither a strategy nor tactics are observable so far. Also the special High Committee for the Harvest lacks any clear and

Karl Wohlmuth

coherent strategy for food self-sufficiency and food security issues. Typical of the approach of the government is the campaign style of actions, so as to mobilize scarce means of transport and other resources for harvest, and also labour. The economic mechanism of production, marketing and distribution does not matter, despite the often repeated references to liberalized and deregulated markets. The necessary services related to agricultural production (seeds provision, transport, extension services and research) are still extremely unreliable and deficient. Private investors are reluctant to invest in these areas as the public services are so insufficient.

There seems to be a fundamental contradiction between the proclaimed support for traditional agriculture and the small farmers by the expressed strategy of promoting local cereals and other crops and the practice of following an urban-biased import substitution policy with regard to such strategic crops as rice, wheat, lentils and maize. As is the case with all classical-type import-substitution policies, cost and comparative advantage do not matter.

It is not observable that the new regime has a consistent policy with regard to production, provision of services, investment promotion, natural resources conservation, storage systems, and research and extension services. The credit policy, especially of the Agricultural Bank of Sudan, does not differ from the policy of former years in its bias against small farmers. But even the declared policy of priority for wheat is not conclusive as there are not adequate price incentives in place for the producers, first of all because of very low procurement prices. High cost production makes the production of wheat a rather unattractive production option. It can be concluded that the wheat import substitution policy is more motivated by the interest of the new regime to stabilize its political base by observing the interest of urban elites; equity and self-reliance considerations do not seem to matter at all.

The so-called Small Farmers Programme of the government seems to be oriented explicitly towards middle-scale farmers if one observes the extent of importation and sale of tractors and the pattern of allocation of credit. The programme is much more related to mechanized farming than to traditional rain-fed agriculture. Up to now it is not clear whether the Islamic banking principles have had any beneficial effects on the small farmers with regard to agricultural credit and the finance of seeds and services. There have been so many initiatives and experiments in Sudan to build up institutions for the agricultural sectors based on Islamic finance principles, but there is no clear evidence on the impact so far. Still the access of small farmers to credit is a major problem (see Sudanow since 1989/90, various issues).

The policies followed so far by the new regime do not give the impression that the intentions of the Strategy for the Development of Rain-fed Agriculture in Sudan (see Wohlmuth, 1991) and of other plans and recommendations for the development of traditional rain-fed agriculture are really taken up seriously. The increasing rural-urban and rural-rural migration in recent years despite the vanishing rural-urban (average) income gap points to the fact that the regime's pro-agricultural sector policy remained biased against and ineffective with regard to traditional agriculture. A new role for the Agricultural Bank of Sudan was envisaged by focusing on higher productivity, food self-sufficiency and export promotion, but its bias against the small farmer in the traditional rain-fed sub-sector still prevails.

The situation is even becoming more serious in some regions, especially in Kordofan and Dar Fur. One cannot expect them to meet subsistence needs from the output of rain-fed crops, despite a higher harvest in 1991/92 compared to the previous year. Cereal stocks are insufficient although strategic stocks of grain were an integral part of the new agricultural policy. Liberalization, privatization and deregulation policies seem to be in conflict now with the doctrine of holding strategic grain reserves. It is now argued by the government that such strategic stocks may lead to undue intervention in the grain market. On the other hand, in spite of increasing grain shortages, barter deals of sorghum against fuel from Libya are regularly undertaken. To a large extent, however, the proclaimed liberalization, deregulation and privatization polices in agriculture remained symbolic so far. The Public Agricultural Corporations do not seem to be affected so far.

There are some efforts to improve the situation of the livestock sub-sector by introducing new institutions—the Bank for Animal Production and the Sudanese Animal Wealth Company. However, deliberate policies to exploit the potential of this sector for foreign exchange generation, basic needs provision and a balancing of agricultural development are not observable.

Forestry development is also considered as an important activity, and a new National Forest Company was established under the 1989 Forestry Act to consider simultaneously the issues of environmental control, fuel wood supply and satisfying agricultural and industrial demands. But, again, besides the introduction of these activities in institution-building not much has happened in terms of investment and public control; the lack of finance remains a decisive constraint. The regional coverage of the forestry programme is still extremely limited. A Sudan Forestry Conservation Programme aims at integrating all relevant institutions and services in the sub-sector, but neither a co-ordination with the Ministries of Finance and Planning and Agriculture nor with the National Energy Administration has taken place so far.

Taken together, there is some institution-building going on in the country but neither a coherent programme emerges nor are investments undertaken at sufficient levels in the various subsectors.

INDUSTRY

The new regime's policy on industry centres first of all on privatization policies and secondly on the implementation of the New Investment Act of 1990.

The privatization policies can be considered as highly chaotic and spontaneous in Sudan as there is no clear-cut procedure or guidance to the process.
Privatization is based on ad hoc measures but not on objectives and targets
as efficiency, equity, employment creation and foreign exchange generation.
Privatization policies obviously are not guided by the proclaimed doctrines of
the new regime (like self-reliance, mobilization of local resources, independent decision-making or prudent use of public funds). Neither is the privatization policy based on a coherent strategy to mobilize foreign exchange, employment, savings and investment. Even the efficiency criterion is not met as
there is no guarantee involved in the process so that privatization will enhance efficiency in the companies. As analysed elsewhere, inefficiencies in
public and private industries in Sudan have often similar causes (see Wohlmuth, 1989).

The new Investment Act of 1990 can therefore only be effective if it is
based on coherent trade, foreign investment, tax, competition, banking and
finance, land allocation and infrastructure policies, and if there is a supportive macro-economic environment based on effective stabilization policies and
an appropriate legal framework. However, the new Investment Act does not
give encouragement to the small and informal ventures; they are excluded
from benefits, guarantees and privileges as was the case with the Investment
Act of 1980. The Small Industries Programme proposed by the government is
not yet elaborated but only discussed, so that the new Investment Act is only
beneficial to a small number of already privatized companies.

The extremely low level of investment in industry can only be redressed
on the basis of comprehensive and credible structural adjustment policies (see
Rodrik, 1990 and Wohlmuth, 1992).

The New Investment Act is a cornerstone of the regeneration/rehabilita-
tion/ economic salvation strategy of the new regime, but investments depend
on markets, credible policies, stable political conditions and an adequate financing mechanism. All these preconditions are not met in the case of Sudan.
However, an innovation of the new Act is the possibility to also include investments that envisage rehabilitation, modernization and extension of existing ventures.

The greatest weakness of the Act is its limited relevance; the new Act is
relevant only for a few large companies, but not for the great number of
smaller ventures. This implies that the Act has no impact on the most important segment of industry as the smaller industrial ventures produce more than
50 per cent of the industrial value added in Sudan (see ILO, 1987;
Wohlmuth, 1989 and Hansohm, 1992). Another fundamental weakness of
the new Act is the fact that too many development objectives are mentioned
so as to qualify for the benefits, exemptions, guarantees and privileges: regional dispersion, self-sufficiency in food, export promotion, integrated rural
development, equitable income distribution, employment creation and import substitution of basic goods. A third issue regarding weaknesses of the

Act, is that there is a protection clause in the new Act to protect the domestic production of goods from foreign competition; this implies that there are limits to the proclaimed policy of an open, liberalized and competitive environment. There is no reference whatsoever to a policy of only temporary or infant industry protection. A fourth weakness has to be added; the Act is not embedded in an industrial policy framework, covering trade, competition, tax and financing issues.

A new Public Investment Corporation is in charge of creating a more favourable environment for investors by encouraging investments more directly under the umbrella of the new Investment Act. The new institution is now alongside other institutions having similar objectives, as for example the Sudan Development Corporation or the Industrial Bank of Sudan. New institutions are entrusted with the task of revitalizing the investment activity in the country without analysing the reasons why already existing institutions have failed so far (such as the Sudan Development Corporation and the Industrial Bank of Sudan). One can also observe that the proclaimed policies of liberalization, deregulation and privatization are not taken that seriously by these corporations and banks in the industrial sector, and by the new governmental committees and councils in place now (Ministerial Committee and Ministerial Investment Council). All these corporations and committees are heavily involved in activities of price regulation, credit rationing, foreign exchange regulation, and raw materials, fuel and land allocation. In this regard the overall picture remains one of over-regulation, arbitrariness of decisions, and insecurity and time-lags in the administrative process affecting the potential investor who is dependent on so many licenses for action.

Still completely untouched by these policies is the area of necessary support for informal, traditional and modern small industries and off-farm activities in the rural areas. These actors are neither covered by the Investment Act nor by elaborated Small Industries Programmes nor by appropriate industrial policies. Regional institutions for investment identification, selection and promotion and similar channels at the provincial level are necessary but are not in place.

There is some activity going on with regard to the development of cooperatives and family-based production activities, and there is some emphasis on self-help organizations, but neither the regulatory nor the finance and supply problems have been solved. Recent evidence reveals how deeply rooted the anti-small industry lobby in Sudan still is (see especially Hansohm, 1992).

Foreign investments and bilateral inter-Arab investments are also targeted by the government but the overvaluation of the currency, despite a number of devaluations, and the lack of a supportive policy environment make it unprofitable even for the Sudanese Nationals Working Abroad (SNWA) to invest in Sudan (although from time to time some special incentives are granted to them). Most problematic is the fact that the actual remittances from the

SNWA have decreased sharply so that a huge potential of foreign exchange earnings (there are estimates of up to 40 billion dollars held by SNWA) cannot be exploited for Sudan's development. All attempts to mobilize the funds have failed (approaches relying on force as well as more liberal approaches). The deadlock in the negotiations with the IMF because of the inability to pay arrears and to meet obligations from re-scheduling agreements also inhibits foreign investment (despite some symbolic actions from the side of the government to act in conformity with IMF policies).

There is always some talk about new Arab investments in Sudan's economy but at the moment only the Sudan-Libyan integration programme seems to be active; however this agreement is not much more than a bilateral trade agreement.

The self-sufficiency rhetoric comprises also sectors like textiles, sugar, shoes, soap, chemicals and pharmaceutical products. However, the situation of the textile industry is still disastrous with a capacity utilization of not more than 15 per cent. The self-reliance slogan has no real meaning with regard to this sector as well as other sectors because in the absence of new investments, alternative technological choices (with lower capital and import content) cannot be incorporated in the capital stock. The textile industry in Sudan remains, even after some funding for rehabilitation, a typical example of an unbalanced industrial development as production is not synchronized with raw material supplies from agriculture and the location of markets for end products. The sector is still working in the context of inappropriate incentives structures (prices, taxes, protection rates) and is affected by the lack of integrated trade, production, competition, tax and investment policies. There are talks about future export markets in the African region (as in the countries of the Preferential Trade Area—PTA) and about international assistance in privatization of the textile industry, but there is no real evidence about any progress in the sector. Sudan still expects something from the PTA zone and from bilateral trading agreements. In fact, the experiences with bilateral trading in post-independence history were not unfavourable for Sudan (see Hansohm and Wohlmuth, 1989).

The situation of the sugar industry is not much better. Even the most modern and large-scale Kenana sugar plant has problems because of the lack of foreign currency to maintain the capital stock and because of increasing problems in getting sufficient inputs and even raw materials (sugar cane). The employment performance is low as are the regional dispersion effects and the impact on the generation of government revenues. The sugar price paid by the government is too low to maintain production standards. The supply of cane has become a major bottleneck and this is caused by factors related to the scarcity of land, environmental problems, problems with supplies of inputs for cane production, but also labour shortages. Land scarcity has led, over the years, to an exhaustion of the natural resources and to decreasing yields per *feddan*; and the lack of fertilizers has led to a non-optimal agricultural cycle for cane growth.

Although Sudan has made very high investments in the sugar industry since the 1970s, it is still struggling for self-reliance with regard to this strategic commodity. Up to 1990 considerable sugar imports were necessary; the situation today does not seem to be very different. Nevertheless the official ideology of making Sudan the supplier of two or three strategic commodities to the Arab region and to the world market (of grain, sugar and in the future also petroleum) is upheld. However, the prospects for the realization of this perspective seem not to be much better today than in the 1970s when the Sudan intended to become the 'breadbasket' of the Arab World (see on this period Oesterdiekhoff and Wohlmuth, 1983).

Even the food, leather and soap industries have enormous problems now, especially with regard to raw materials supply. The declared strategy 'we eat what we produce', 'we wear what we produce' and 'we use what we produce' is more and more becoming an irrelevant slogan. These industries are further examples of sectors with a still high level of regulation, input and output rationing, import protection and administrative control by a multitude of governmental authorities and institutions besides the Ministry of Industry. Concerning raw materials and input supplies, these industries depend heavily on barter deals. The 'new bilateralism' in trade relations is a result of the debt dilemma of Sudan and its unviable balance of payments position; the Sudan is caught in this dilemma because neither regulation nor liberalization of the economy seem to show a way out of the foreign exchange scarcity.

Another observable tendency today is the propagation of large-scale infrastructural, mining and energy projects despite of the savings and foreign exchange gaps. This resembles previous planning attitudes in the Sudan: to start with new large-scale projects instead of maintaining existing ones by appropriate investment and incentives policies.

LINKAGES BETWEEN PRODUCTIVE SECTORS AND RURAL-URBAN INTERACTIONS

The stimulation of the productive sectors depends on appropriate mechanisms to develop agro-industrial and rural-urban linkages, and on policies that create the required physical and social infrastructure to foster such linkages. The most serious failure of Sudanese development since independence has been the neglect of laying the foundations for such linkages between agriculture and industry and the neglect of creating dynamic rural-urban interactions that could lead to a regional equalization of development levels. The potential backward, forward and final demand linkages of agricultural development in Africa and in Sudan are important but are not exploited (see Adelman and Vogel, 1992). This policy failure has had severe repercussions.

The processing of local agricultural raw materials and the use of local industrial inputs and of intermediate goods in agricultural production remained insignificant (see Wohlmuth, 1989, 1991). Hence, the market potential of rural development was neither exploited for industrial development nor for the stimulation of rural off-farm activities.

The economic interaction between regions was confined largely to migration of labour in various forms. All this is the result of a systematic neglect of traditional agriculture for decades (see Wohlmuth, 1991), and of an industrial development path confined mostly to the needs of urban consumers (Wohlmuth, 1989). Results of this stagnation in rural market development have been the emergence of gaps in investments and in employment, and an increasing trend of migration to the towns in spite of the decreasing rural-urban (average) income gap (as observed during the 1980s). In addition to the huge number of people displaced by civil war, drought and floods (4–6 million), the number of migrants of a more permanent type was rising sharply through the 1980s. The increasing of poverty and the worsening of the income distribution in rural areas are push factors explaining this new type of migration (see Jamal, 1992 on this Africa-wide phenomenon).

It is however obvious that the impoverishment of the people in Sudan started long before the drought cycles and the civil war. There is evidence that the poorest 40 per cent of the population earned 16 per cent of total income in 1967/68 and only 12 per cent in 1978/79 (World Bank, 1990:10). As the poorest people in Sudan had to bear a much higher fall of their real income in the 1976-1989 period than the average income earner whose relative income position declined by 18 per cent, it is not unreasonable to assume a further real income decline of the poorest by 40 to 50 per cent since 1978/79. In this context it is also necessary to consider the dramatic decline of the per capita social expenditures in Sudan. Government expenditures on health fell in the 1980s in nominal terms by 60 per cent, but much more than that in real terms (World Bank, 1990:10). An estimated nine million people in the Northern Sudan suffer from chronic hunger or food insecurity, from transitory food insecurity or are threatened by the prospects of falling into transitory food insecurity (World Bank, 1990:11).

It is therefore very necessary to differentiate carefully between causes and forms of displacement and migration and to consider specifically the various forms of migration (according to motivations, duration and regions affected). Hence, the problem of displaced people should not be confused with the more lasting problems of poverty and food insecurity as these are the result of unsound macro-economic, social, sectoral and regional policies. Migration has first of all to do with the extreme decline of the real incomes of the poorest people in rural Sudan, and only this extreme decline makes it possible to understand why people migrate to Khartoum and to other towns where real income declines were accelerating sharply since the 1970s (on urban poverty in Khartoum, see World Bank, 1988). Although some return migration (either forced or voluntarily) also takes place, the fact of continuing large-scale net migration to the towns is undisputed.

How has the new regime reacted to these developments? Instead of building new foundations for the economic sectors and the whole economy in order to address these problems, only some relief and self-help initiatives were supported. A new Islamic social welfare system (based on Islamic funding principles) was propagated and some self-help and relief institutions were being supported, but coverage and impact have been insignificant. The new regime also argues for a national population policy and a return migration/relocation policy so as to balance in a better way the distribution of the population over the regions. However, the main causes of the maldistribution of the population are not attacked thereby.

There are some discussions going on about a new production strategy (based on smaller projects) and a new environmental protection policy (to cope better in future with impacts of natural disasters and drought cycles), but a coherent programme has not emerged so far. Solutions for these problems are envisaged in the context of a new federal structure of Sudan, especially by referring to the necessity of regional food self-sufficiency programmes and local relief and production initiatives.

The new wave of migration to the towns implies also that open unemployment is increasing sharply as the informal sector has already reached its limits to absorb labour (while modern sector employment is even shrinking). This dilemma of unfavourable urban employment prospects can only be solved in the context of a new strategy directed to the productive sectors (promotion of small industries, services and of exports), but the new regime has not so far given such policy directions. The new regime argues more in favour of a new population policy. However, such a new population policy makes sense only as a complementary policy because of the millions of migrants and the 4–6 million displaced people in the country. Therefore, any population policy has to be related to production increases.

The new regime favours in principle the strategy to substitute relief measures by production-oriented measures, but this policy orientation has to be planned carefully in order to avoid new damage to people and to nature in the areas where the displaced/the migrants are to be relocated. The relocation policy can only make sense in the context of long-term sectoral and regional plans and policies. It is doubtful whether the government's Relief and Rehabilitation Commission is equipped to implement such a long-term and production-oriented population redistribution strategy. Also the Commission for the Displaced which has been operating since 1988 is too weak an institution to work out such a long-term programme of relocation. Especially the financial means for the promotion of productive employment schemes and relocation schemes are scarce, and foreign aid components for such programmes are rather negligible. Only test integration schemes and small scale relocation programmes are under implementation so far.

The governments of Sudan have not so far distinguished in their policies the various causes and forms of population movements in the country, neither with regard to migration (temporary, permanent, return migration, seasonal and non-seasonal migration, rural-rural migration and rural-urban migration), nor with regard to the displaced and the refugees. Such a distinction is necessary so as to develop a long-term and production-centred strategy which is adapted to the local resources and is ecologically viable.

Co-ordination of policies in this regard is so necessary as the causes of displacement and of migration overlap and as their various impacts cumulate. According to one source 63 per cent of the displaced are in this situation because of political instability and a further 23 per cent because of food insecurity. Food insecurity and poverty are also reasons for the new type of rural-to-urban migration. A co-ordination between labour sending and labour receiving areas never took place in Sudan. This created additional pressure on basic needs provision and affected access to infrastructural services, land, credit and the quality of the natural resources. In an economy which has been rationing basic goods over many years, this situation disrupts not only production and the environment but also the distribution of scarce basic goods.

Co-ordination is also necessary with regard to international donors. The government's Relief and Rehabilitation Commission is guiding local and also foreign NGOs on the basis of the Foreign Voluntary Activities Act; this guidance refers in principle to creation of projects of productive employment, rehabilitation programmes in origin areas, permanent settlement schemes, and the provision of basic goods for the displaced. However, in reality the work is biased by the political interest of the new regime to consolidate its power base by avoiding uncontrolled population movements and is inhibited by the fiscal situation of the country. International support for such programmes is therefore limited.

A comprehensive strategy would require that the programmes for the productive sectors and the development of regions are coherent and integrated, that public investments for such programmes are forthcoming, that self-help initiatives, cooperatives and small industry programmes are better coordinated and continuously supported, that income generation and public works programmes are initiated on a larger scale and that better equipped early warning systems help in assessing the food and water situation in remote areas. Poverty alleviation programmes and policies to protect the social expenditures from a further decline have to complement these measures. National planning has to take up the issues of population distribution and redistribution, of migration and large-scale displacement, of urban population growth and rapid labour market change.

It can only be hoped that the population census of 1990 may lay some statistical foundations for such a new policy. The Population Policy Statement of 1990 addresses only some issues: the necessity to redress policies at the village level, especially to initiate basic and social services, and to stimulate growth-related programmes as well as women initiatives to enhance their position in production and in households. However, so far concrete policies and programmes have not followed from this Policy Statement.

The problem is that neither the government nor the National Democratic Alliance (NDA) (as the opposition movement) have coherent and detailed programmes to cope with these problems. The ideas of the NDA (see *Sudan Democratic Gazette*, February and March 1992) centre on the revitalization of the rural economy, but the economic programme remains vague. There is no discussion about what should be done when, how, by whom and for whom?

ALTERNATIVE ECONOMIC STRATEGIES FOR SUDAN
Approaches in the formulation of alternative economic strategies

Many suggestions and proposals have been made for reforming economic policies in Sudan. However, no concept emerged from these ideas and proposals and no action was taken on behalf of the successive governments of Sudan (Mustafa, 1985 lists some causes for inaction). These proposals relate to four areas

1. Stimulating productive economic sectors;
2. Macro-economic stabilization and market reform;
3. New foundations for international economic relations; and
4. Revitalizing the developmental state.

Area 1. There have been proposals to lay the foundations for new agricultural and industrial policies and to link effectively the two sectors. The report by the ILO (ILO, 1976) has emphasized a strategy of parallel development of modern and traditional agricultural subsectors, whereas the second ILO report (1987) emphasized as well a new industrial policy and a strategy to link the agricultural and industrial subsectors in a more productive way. Kursany (1983) has argued in favour of a strategy to overcome the underdevelopment of 'precapitalist parts' of agriculture. Contributions in a study edited by Awad (1983) refer to institutional constraints of modernization in agriculture and how to overcome them. A long-term strategy for the agricultural sector is presented by Eltom (1986).

Wohlmuth (1991) has emphasized the necessity of a new development model for Sudan by referring to an industrialization strategy based on agricultural development (as proposed under the label ADLI-Agricultural Demand Led Industrialization—by Adelman and Vogel, 1992 and Hansohm and Wohlmuth, 1987, 1990). Hansohm (1992) has considered various strategic elements of small industry development with regard to structural adjustment and development. Yongo-Bure (1989, 1991) has emphasized the role of small industry development for Southern Sudan as related to new agricultural policies. Sudanese economists (ILO, 1986a; Abdel Gadir Ali, 1985) have emphasized a 'real economy approach' of stabilization for Sudan rather than following IMF policies.

IMF/World Bank prescriptions for Sudan have argued implicitly since 1977/78 for radically reforming the functioning of productive sectors by changing the incentives structure, by pursuing effective stabilization policies and by reforming the parastatals. Programmes for industrial sector reform (World Bank, 1987c) as well as programmes for export promotion were also presented by the World Bank.

The governments of Sudan have however not made clear, in their documents on development planning and development budgeting, what their orientation is and whose advice is accepted.

Area 2. Macro-economic policy reforms and market reforms have been the central issues of all relevant World Bank economic memoranda for Sudan (World Bank, 1987a, 1987b, 1990). Sudanese economists from the Ministry of Finance and Economic Planning have developed a programme for the restoration of credible macro-economic policies based on a revenue-led fiscal strategy and a new policy for credit allocation to productive sectors (Attaelmannan Taha et al., 1990). Wohlmuth and Hansohm (1984, 1987) and the World Bank (1987a) have presented action plans for structural adjustment policies including a sequencing and timing for the most important areas for action. Whereas the World Bank developed its action programme on the basis of its specific agenda (eliminating the public sector bias, reducing the rural-urban income gap and correcting for the distorted price and allocation systems), the proposals by Wohlmuth and Hansohm refer also to historical and structural factors and impediments as well as to the vested interests having an impact on development in Sudan.

Sudanese economists (see Abdel Gadir Ali, 1985; ILO, 1986a) have presented alternative views on the exchange rate, fiscal, banking and monetary policies arguing for a stricter control of the banking system and a more effective taxation system. Crucial in their alternative macro-economic package is the control of the foreign exchange market, since Sudan is considered to be too weak structurally for implementing liberal economic policies. Awad (1986) has proposed a more expansionist approach to structural adjustment policies ("reflation" of the Sudanese economy), as the production capacity of the country is, to a large extent, unused.

It is not clear to what extent governments of Sudan have taken up such proposals at all.

Area 3. Various proposals relate to the issues of exchange rate reform and the stimulation of the export sector. Authors being critical on the extent and form of liberalization and the opening of the Sudanese economy to the world market have raised time and again the question of whether the Sudan economy is not structurally too weak and too disintegrated to pursue open door policies (Abdel Gadir Ali, 1985; ILO, 1986a) as well as issues related to the extent to which comparative costs and world market prices can be considered as a guide to trade, foreign exchange and finance policies.

The discussion about the required/necessary/feasible degree of opening the Sudanese economy and about the timing and sequencing of this process is still going on. Most of the concrete proposals for reform came from the World Bank by emphasizing more uniform and lower levels of protection, an elimination of disincentives to agriculture by a more balanced trade protection policy and by eliminating quantitative restrictions so as to make the price system (and especially the adjustments to world market prices) more effective.

Much fewer proposals were made with regard to export promotion (although export action programmes were propagated by the Government in the early 1980s at the advice of the World Bank). Policies to improve the export marketing system and policies for appropriate export pricing were never coordinated. However, various programmes have been submitted to emphasize Sudan's role as a supplier of agricultural goods to the Arab region (see Oesterdiekhoff and Wohlmuth, 1983) and to consolidate bilateral trading and payments arrangements (see Hansohm and Wohlmuth, 1989).

However, the governments of Sudan never have initiated coherent reforms in this area of policies.

Area 4. Various proposals have been made to lay the foundations for a new social contract between the social partners (see Mustafa et al., 1988; ILO, 1987, Chapter 7.4), to lay the foundations for financing a new federal structure of Sudan (see Due, 1986), and to revitalize long-term planning (Wohlmuth and Hansohm 1984, 1987).

According to Aguda (1973) a great problem in Sudan's development since independence has been the indecisiveness of the governments with regard to the role of the state in the economy. It was never made clear whether there should be limits to the role of the state in the economy. This has affected negatively development of the private sector since independence. Kursany (1986) and others however argue that a much stronger and deeper involvement of the state would have been necessary to overcome the obstacles of underdevelopment.

Although the new regime has brought up some ideas about popular participation, new democracy, new federalism and a revival of long-term national planning, the programmes submitted so far are neither consistent nor implementable. The same can be said about the programmatic ideas submitted by the NDA; the implications for finance and implementation remain unclear.

Alternative strategies for Sudan have to integrate programmes and plans for these four areas simultaneously in order to be relevant. *Priority areas and guidelines for reform* have to be integrated and interlinked (see the synopsis in Table 4) so as to give the basis for a consistent and coherent strategy. Such a strategy for Sudan has to be sustained in the implementation process on the basis of political commitment for a long period of time. It is necessary to show the interrelation of these four areas by referring to objectives, constraints and policy measures.

Table 4. *Priority areas and guidelines for alternative economic strategies*

1. *Stimulating productive economic sectors*
1.1. Sub-sectoral balance between irrigated, mechanized and traditional rain-fed agricultural subsectors is important, as costs and benefits of subsectors to the whole economy/society have changed drastically since independence;
2.2. Sub-sectoral balance between large/small, private/public, modern/ traditional, small traditional/small modern, and formal/informal industries is necessary as the concentration on large public industries has become increasingly inappropriate with regard to relevant development objectives;
1.3. Exploiting the linkages between the rural and the urban economies and between agriculture and industry is crucial, especially because of the increasing interrelation of rural and urban labour markets and the huge economic potential of exploiting linkages;
1.4. Developing the social and physical infrastructure and the systems of environmental protection are urgent tasks as the degradation of infrastructure and of environmental resources endangers the survival and the productivity of all actors in the productive economic sectors.

2. *Macro-economic stabilization and market reform*
2.1. Reforming the Fiscal System and the Administrative System is important because the structure of public revenues and expenditures is inappropriate and the ways of financing the deficit are disrupting the economic process;
2.2. Implementing effective monetary and credit policies is necessary because neither the control of liquidity nor the efficient allocation of required credit to productive sectors are possible in the currently practised system;
2.3. More balance between private and public sectors is required, especially with regard to private and public investments; neither the investments of the 'public sector' nor of the 'private sector' are at a minimum level to prevent a further erosion of Sudan's capital stock;
2.4. More balance between productive and social expenditures is required as well as a cut of unproductive expenditures; resource mobilization and additional international finance are required as sustainable structural adjustments necessitate productive investments but also social programmes to mitigate the costs of adjustment and structural change.

3. *New foundations for international economic relations*
3.1. New Policies for Export Promotion, Export Diversification and Import Rationalization are required as the international competitiveness of traditional exports is still declining and essential imports are more difficult to procure than ever in Sudan's history;
3.2. Sustainable exchange rate policies are crucial for revitalizing Sudan's economy that requires a support by credible fiscal, monetary, credit and supply-side policies to enhance the productive capacity;

3.3. New integration and cooperation policies have to be based on long-term assessments of the comparative advantage of Sudan's export products; the new bilateralism cannot be a substitute for an open international trade policy;

3.4. New approaches towards the Brettonwood institutions (IMF, World Bank) are necessary as the long term costs of a break with these institutions may be extremely high; access to international credit is necessary for revitalizing trade and new investment.

4. *Revitalizing the developmental state*

4.1. Moves towards effective popular participation are important as the lack of participation at all levels (horizontally as well as vertically) has led to a fast decline of motivation, mobilization, accountability, information, awareness and responsibility;

4.2. Approaching a new federal structure for Sudan requires not only that a system of real power sharing is established; a sharing of national financial resources, commitments and debts is necessary at the horizontal and vertical levels; control and accountability at all levels are important elements for successful governance in such a system;

4.3. A strengthened system of labour administration and a Social Contract could support more equitable structural adjustment policies; the social effects of liberalization policies can be mitigated only if trade unions, employers' organizations and the labour administration take on the new tasks evolving from liberalized/deregulated markets;

4.4. Revival of long-term planning is important as ad hoc decisions have overshadowed serious planning and budgeting; this has led to unrealistic vested interest group demands, corruption and short-sightedness in politics.

Implications of a broader package of alternative economic policies stimulating productive economic sectors

Since independence Sudan has promoted the productive economic sectors on the basis of long-term planning (the Ten Year Plan, the Five Year Plan and the (then abandoned) Six Year Plan, and has given emphasis to irrigated and mechanized agriculture only. An imbalance emerged between the three agricultural subsectors (irrigated, mechanized and traditional). The serious neglect of the traditional sub-sector became already the focus of the ILO report in the 1970s (ILO, 1976) and in the 1980s of the Strategy for the Development of Rain-fed Agriculture (see Wohlmuth, 1991). However, none of these strategy documents for revitalizing traditional agriculture were taken up seriously by the successive governments of Sudan. The traditional sector (especially also the livestock sector) was the looser in development policy since independence, with little access to credit, basic services, public investment, government protection, foreign exchange and subsidies. The second ILO Report to the Government of Sudan (ILO, 1987) then stressed the necessity of a policy reversal again and argued that irrigated agriculture is no longer an important net foreign exchange earner to the country relative to rain-fed agriculture. However, this report also did not have any real policy impact. A related imbalance—between agriculture and the livestock economy—gained momentum over the years with repercussions on the environ-mental resources of Sudan.

Another source of imbalance has been the neglect of rural and urban small industries and of traditional industries (based on simple technologies) relative to the highly protected and subsidized public and private large-scale industries as they were built up after independence with an ever-increasing scale of public intervention (see Table 2). All policy instruments for industrial development, as the successive Investment Acts indicated, have benefitted only some few large-scale and capital-intensive public, private and foreign ventures. All relevant economic policies had an implicit bias against smaller industries which have however distinctive advantages (e.g. in terms of sec-toral complementarities, employment generation, saving capital and foreign exchange and supplying goods to local markets at reasonable prices). Even the new Investment Act of 1990 does not bring a fundamental change to this situation. A new policy for small industries is therefore required and can complement a new agricultural policy which is supportive of a more bal-anced development of agricultural subsectors.

The insufficient linkages between agriculture and industry are not caused only by the neglect of traditional agriculture and of small industries, but also by the extent of unequal trade protection granted to industry relative to agri-culture, thereby discriminating against agriculture. The claim of the new government to pursue a pro-agricultural policy has to be substantiated by policy reforms on this basis. This requires more balance between subsectors, a credible stabilization programme, a programme of public investments ori-ented towards agriculture, a small industry development programme, a new orientation of foreign trade and exchange rate policies, and genuine pro-grammes for the support of small agriculturalists and industrialists.

Neither a small farmers programme nor a programme for the support of rural industrialists exist at the moment in Sudan. Credible rural development policies imply action in the areas of agricultural institutions, inputs, infras-tructure, prices and other incentives, research and extension; all these policy components are in design and implementation much more long-term and complex than envisaged by past and present governments. Integrated rural development schemes in Sudan so far have not fulfilled their promises. However, relocation programmes for the displaced people as planned now can only be executed on the basis of integrated rural development pro-grammes.

Most important for productive sector development is that infrastructure development plans are designed as soon as possible, for social as well as for physical infrastructure; this has also to include an environment protection plan. Productive sector development is possible only if further destruction of infrastructure is ended and if new investments take place. The serious degra-dation of physical infrastructure (especially of transport, telecommunication, water development) and of social infrastructure (especially of education and health) can only be stopped by government commitments to long-term infrastructure development plans. However, Sudan now has neither an education development plan nor a health sector plan, nor are there plans and programmes for the rebuilding of its physical infrastructure. There is no co-ordination with budget planning so as to ensure the provision of minimum levels of development expenditures and social expenditures for such purposes. Core budgeting is required to formulate minimalist programmes as soon as possible. However, the complete loss of control of government's expenditures (because of the increasing reliance on extra-budgetary finance and the extent of use of deficit financing) leaves no room for such core budgets and minimum commitments for infrastructural development.

A National Infrastructure Plan is therefore urgently required to end the erosion of the capital stock. This policy is consistent with new financing strategies based on cost recovery and taxing the wealthier segments of the society on equity grounds, but inconsistent with current deficit financing practices.

Macro-economic stabilization and market reform

Central to stabilization policies in Sudan is a fundamental fiscal reform. Neither the structure of revenues, nor the structure of expenditures or the structure of financing the fiscal deficit are sustainable (see Attaelmannan Taha et al. 1990). The structure of expenditures (mainly consisting of direct transfers to the regions, salaries and security-related expenditures) leaves less and less scope for productive sector-related development expenditures. The misuse of funds and the lack of accountability with regard to the ever-increasing extra-budgetary expenditures are elements of those policies that lead to a complete loss of macro-economic control. The revenue structure (mainly based on indirect taxes, a low share and a declining contribution of direct taxes, and a serious lack of non-tax incomes) is also unsustainable, so that a revenue - led strategy has to be followed, based on the revival of productive sectors (see Attaelmannan Taha et al. 1990). Such a strategy for fiscal consolidation has to rely much more on direct taxes, real estate and land taxes. The structure of financing the deficits (relying on central bank credit for deficit financing and also on counterpart funds of commodity aid) is disrupting the financial and monetary systems. No currency reform (as undertaken recently by the new regime) can have lasting effects unless the government itself is willing to control its fiscal deficit and to restructure revenues and expenditures.

It is obvious that all this can only be achieved in conditions where a minimum level of autonomy of the Bank of Sudan (BOS) relative to the government can be taken for granted. The BOS has become more and more a vehicle to finance extra-budgetary expenditures and ever-increasing fiscal deficits. In such a situation neither fiscal nor monetary or credit policies can

work; savings and investments will not come forth and remittances by
SNWA will not add to the local savings. The savings can only be stimulated
by a consistent policy of stabilization and a policy of financial deepening and
widening, including also the Islamic banks and finance institutions in the
country (as they work up to now more or less uncontrolled). An extension of
the coverage of credit institutions to all regions and a re-orientation towards
more productive and long-term lending are necessary steps. Credit allocation
on an administrative basis according to BOS rules and procedures has so far
been neither effective nor developmental. Credit was not allocated for long-
term and productive projects but for short-term and speculative purposes.
The government itself was not following the BOS credit allocation policy. A
new and more flexible credit allocation policy is an important complement of
a fiscal consolidation policy (see Attaelmannan Taha et al., 1990; Wohlmuth
and Hansohm 1987).

The fiscal implications of a new federal structure for Sudan have yet to be
elaborated. Up to now principles and formulae for sharing public revenues
between the federation, the states (regions) and the provinces were not outlined. Revenue-sharing formulae , debt and credit guarantees, commitments
for minimum revenues and expenditures for all levels of the federation, and
appropriate control procedures are extremely important for any revival of
federalism in Sudan. The idea of a system of regional self-reliance is up to
now not more than a slogan; the fiscal implications of new taxes and duties
for the regions and the provinces should therefore be considered carefully (as
well as potentially detrimental effects of local and regional taxes, e.g. on the
environment).

The imbalance between private and public sector development has to be
redressed urgently. Privatization policy is on the agenda of the new regime.
However, privatization in an economically meaningful way requires a co-ordination with competition policy, market deregulation policy, exchange rate
policy, industry and trade policy, and capital markets promotion policy.
Otherwise, a spontaneous and even chaotic type of privatization emerges,
leading to windfall gains for some businessmen without beneficial impacts on
the productive system. Such a type of privatization could even disrupt further
the industries remaining in the public sector. Up to now such a deliberate
privatization strategy has not been followed in Sudan.

Privatization also implies that the value of company shares has to be
assessed by finance and capital market institutions. However, the finance institutions and the capital market cannot develop in a situation of unsustainable macro-economic policies and inconsistent micro-economic interventions
from the side of the government. Privatization makes sense only in a situation where access to foreign exchange, credit and inputs can be taken for
granted so that private ownership leads immediately to new investments.
None of these conditions exist in Sudan now.

Privatization can never be a substitute for fiscal consolidation as it seems to be the case now in Sudan, by the way of generating non-tax revenues through large-scale sales of companies and company shares. Privatization is therefore meaningful and useful only in the context of sustainable fiscal reforms. In the case of Sudan, commercialization and consolidation of public sector companies should therefore be the first priority; commercialization means first of all restoration of a functional autonomy of the company so that responsible decision-making and public accountability can be established. Clear rules and procedures for the guidance of public enterprises are important, as are new investments in the companies remaining in the public sector. However, selection and evaluation procedures for public sector investments have also to be improved in Sudan.

Mitigation of the social costs of stabilization and structural adjustment policies is another important area of policies to accompany macro-economic and market reforms. Privatization implies retrenchment of employees; liberalization and deregulation of markets have social effects because of price adjustments; budget consolidation has social implications because of the necessity to reduce budget deficits. This may also imply a further cut of subsidies and of social expenditures and the use of cost recovery measures. The employment effects can be mitigated partially by Employment and Training Funds and by Vocational Training and Guidance Funds; other effects can be mitigated by Social Development Funds. The price effects can be mitigated by selective and targeted subsidies; the effects on the social expenditures can be mitigated by core expenditure programmes which have to be related to comprehensive poverty alleviation strategies. All this requires that Social Development Funds and Social Welfare Funds are coordinated and executed by effective social welfare institutions. Such programmes have been discussed for Sudan since the late 1980s (see World Bank, 1988), but no action has followed. Such programmes to mitigate the effects of structural adjustment can and should be integrated with food security policies (e.g. strategic stocks), commodity aid programmes, public and specific employment programmes and other measures that have an impact on poverty and social welfare.

New foundations for international economic relations

New foundations for Sudan's international economic relations are extremely important because growth depends also on successes in this area. Many crucial issues in this area were not officiently addressed by successive Sudanese governments. A new trade policy should improve the international competitiveness of exports and should enable the country to produce efficient substitutes for imported goods and services.

The loss of international competitiveness of traditional export crops and the inability to produce efficient import substitutes are factors that create tensions in the foreign exchange market, limit the access of productive sectors to foreign exchange and retard development because of a lack of imported inputs. The non-exploitation of Sudan's huge agricultural export potential (as calculated again by the authors of the Strategy for the Development of Rain-fed Agriculture) is an important aspect; however, the non-exploitation of the export potential in such areas as crafts, manufacturing and tourism is also an issue to be discussed in the context of suitable policies to improve the export supply capacity.

Sudan has never developed an export promotion policy (comprising export marketing, pricing, financing, market awareness and product development policies), and has never succeeded in implementing an export supply management strategy (by providing appropriate infrastructure, inputs supply, and a sound regulatory framework). More than this, the failure to use actively foreign exchange rate policies as a developmental tool has to be added to this long list of shortcomings. Export promotion has to envisage a comprehensive long-term strategy, comprising also international marketing support, selective subsidization of export production, and granting some special incentives to companies that have a good record as exporters. On the contrary, the Sudan has consistently taxed the export sector directly (by export taxes and duties) and indirectly (by import protection affecting the producers of exportable goods).

Sudan has never followed a consistent export supply management policy. Periods of export bans, neglect of traditional export crops, deterioration of infrastructure (irrigation, livestock amenities, transport facilities, health systems, research and extension services), inappropriate mechanisms and policies on export pricing, distribution and marketing, and on exchange rates and export taxes have virtually destroyed the export capacity of the country. Often changing taxes, tariffs and pricing formulae , an overall lack or weakness of export sector institutions (especially in the fields of quality controls and health standards), and widespread infrastructural and administrative deficiencies prevented the use of the (abundant) resources for export.

Most serious in its consequences was the neglect of the role of foreign exchange rate policies for development purposes. Sudan has experienced so many devaluations since 1978 but no devaluation so far was really supported by consistent monetary, fiscal and supply-side policies so as to stabilize the exchange rate whenever an 'equilibrium rate' was reached. The 'battles' among Sudanese economists around the devaluation policy (see especially Abdel Gadir Ali, 1985) too often tended to ignore the main issue: that only a stable real exchange rate (reflecting the domestic inflation rate relative to inflation rates of trading partners) can be a sound basis for decisions of producers, exporters, capital owners and of SNWA. The core elements of profitable international economic relations (export promotion, export supply management and stabilization of the real exchange rate) were not considered at all (see on relevant export marketing issues Oesterdiekhoff, 1991).

Sudan is now moving towards a new era of bilateral trade and payments agreements. This is a consequence of the deterioration of the balance of payments and of the debt situation. Extreme scarcities (e.g. of fuel, food, and pharmacy products) lead to these new (old) arrangements. The experiences with former bilateral agreements should be carefully studied in this context. Bilateral transactions can only be useful temporarily and sector-wise; they cannot be a substitute for a sound trade and payments policy on a multilateral basis. Bilateral trade transactions imply low prices for exported goods, a non-exploitation of domestic capabilities, a loss of cost and price consciousness, a politicization of trade and an erosion of commercial trade relations (as based on economic incentives).

Some new bilateral trade/payments/integration/cooperation agreements (as with Libya, other Arab countries, Asian Islamic countries, India and China) are very limited in scope. These agreements lead to bilateral trade and payments but are rarely extended to the establishment of joint ventures, to production cooperation and to private investment activity; the potential for expansion is therefore limited. Such agreements should be used mainly for short-term actions to procure scarce goods and inputs so as to rehabilitate important sectors and strategic industries (e.g. sugar, textile industries), and in cases of extreme scarcities of basic goods (fuel, pharmacy, food). Even in these cases these deals should be arranged in a dynamic and developmental form (with regard to prices, volumes and partners).

In the longer run, these approaches cannot be a substitute for a realistic evaluation of international trade options based on comparative advantage as calculated for Sudan since the 1980s (on the methodology see Nashashibi 1980). Such comparative cost calculations had been undertaken as the basis for Sudan's Export Action Programmes in the early 1980s. However, the implications in terms of export promotion policies were never taken up seriously.

New policies on international economic relations therefore imply that the state involves itself in a more rational way in export promotion, exchange rate policies, industry and trade policies, public and private investment policies, and that, a stable and credible macro-economic environment is established. This also requires that a new working relation with the IMF is established as access to new international credit is otherwise extremely difficult and costly. Tactical measures and symbolic actions (devaluations, moves of liberalization, deregulation and privatization, or even currency reforms) as practised by the new regime cannot be substitutes for a sound policy framework. The real situation (see Table 1) is so serious that tactical measures and symbolic actions can never convince the international financial community that a real policy change is intended in Sudan.

From time to time a renewed attention is given to the idea of developing Sudan so as to become the breadbasket of the Arab world. Neither the experiences of the 1970s (see Oesterdiekhoff and Wohlmuth, 1983; Wohlmuth and Hansohm, 1984) nor the developments of the Arab World after the Gulf War give any support for pursuing such ideas: Sudan is still an importer of food and has never realised the self-sufficiency targets in important food crops (as for example sugar).

Revitalizing the development state

The present regime has experimented with some new forms and modalities of popular participation. According to the intentions of this regime, popular participation should be based on people's congresses at the local, provincial, state (regional) and national (federal) level. The People's Congress should, however, be complemented by organizations expressing sectoral interests; sectoral committees should be formed for Economy, another one for military/defence, and a third one for legal affairs.

This system—if operative—will have far-reaching implications for the society as, for example, the Committee on the Economy will comprise all organizations dealing with labour issues (trade unions and employers' organizations). These organizations will be bound together in one Committee so as to reconcile sectoral interests; which would mean that conflicts of interest cannot be expressed freely and that negotiations about wages, labour conditions and employment issues cannot take place in an open way. This may lead to a structural immobilization at the level of institutions and procedures; which may also impede structural adjustments as structural adjustment policies imply by their very nature a system of free negotiations between the social partners in the labour market. The state would have much more than a facilitating and mediating role in this system of organizing labour relations; this could complicate also price and wage adjustments. A strengthening of trade unions and employers' organizations is however necessary for effective structural adjustment and development policies.

It is therefore most important that the government supports the functioning of the labour market and the design of appropriate employment policies by an effective labour administration (and the Sudan has a history of an efficient labour administration to build on). An effective labour administration has to deal with the repercussions of structural adjustment policies, especially with the effects of liberalization, privatization, stabilization and deregulation, and with problems associated with the increasing level of urban unemployment, real wage declines and increasing poverty. A revitalization of the developmental state in Sudan has therefore implications for the mandate and the organization of trade unions, employers' organizations and a strengthened national labour administration.

A new social contract was proposed in the 1980s by the Ministry of Labour in Sudan (see Mustafa et al., 1988) and also by the ILO (see ILO, 1987). The tripartite structure proposed as the basis of the social central (government, trade unions and employers) might prove to be an important instrument to lay the foundations for a strengthened democracy and a revitalization of the developmental state. However, such a social contract has to include all those issues and policy areas that are now central to the activities of labour administration and the other partners—to mention especially the support of informal sector workers and entrepreneurs, rural plantation workers, petty traders, the old and the new poverty groups and the openly unemployed persons in urban areas. Productive sector development has to be based on a new mode of cooperation between these three partners. This new attitude can support structural change and ease conflicts which arise especially in the context of recession, economic crisis and structural adjustment.

On the basis of a social contract inappropriate decisions from the side of the government can be more easily corrected, and policies can be broader based. This is relevant especially for investment and employment policies. Investment Acts can be made much more relevant for investors by bringing in the experiences of the various partners. New employment and social policies can be better designed, as well as more appropriate vocational training and labour market guidance strategies. Strong and broader based economic organizations such as trade unions and the employers' organizations can help to reach informal sector entrepreneurs and workers. Public employment schemes and private employment initiatives can be supported effectively by the social partners, especially the programmes for women and the poorest in society (see especially ILO, 1986 and Mustafa et al., 1988, 1989).

Secondly, revitalization of the developmental state also implies that new foundations for financing the federal structure are built. The failures of decentralization, regionalization and of earlier attempts to build a federal structure in Sudan have to do with the fact that clear rules for revenue-sharing and for expenditure commitments, and rules on debt accumulation and budgeting at federal, regional and provincial levels, were not properly designed. This is still the case now.

Clear commitments on direct transfers, on shares of taxes to be allocated to regions (states) and provinces, and on other rules and procedures do not exist. Direct transfers have to be based on principles such as the equalization of income levels, and on quantitative targets (e.g. investment and employment targets, indicators of regional resources development and the regional population base). Control and accountability procedures also matter in such a federal finance system and no such procedures exist so far. This has implications for peace in Sudan as fiscal autonomy and regional finance have never worked. Ad hocism in financial relations and large-scale deviations between commitments and disbursements led to so many problems and not only for the Southern Region. But concrete proposals for adequate federal finance systems are scarce (see on some views Ahmed and Sørbø, 1989). The new regime has so far not developed any firm rules and procedures for the proclaimed new federalism. It is vaguely argued that regional self-reliance is the solution to these problems.

A third important element for a revitalization of the developmental state is the revival of long-term planning (already emphasized at the Erkowit Conference in 1988). With the abandonment of long-term planning in 1978 Sudan has had experiences with three to four year rolling plans or annual development expenditure budgets; all these plans lacked a long-term perspective. It is obvious that this practice was due to the external and internal shocks affecting the economy, but the consequences were a loss of perspective and vision and the generation of contradictory and non-sustainable policies and programmes.

Revitalization of long-term planning is so important because Environmental Action Plans, Infrastructure Plans, Social Development Plans, new generation Structural Adjustment Programmes, Public Investment Programmes, and Poverty Alleviation and Rural Development Programmes need to be supported by long-term planning on the basis of agreed development objectives, investment allocations and appropriate consistency checks. Most of these plans have a time horizon of more than 10 years. This implies that long-term planning has to be linked with development expenditure budgets and sectoral plans. Planning was substituted more and more by merely issuing action programmes stating only some objectives and policy measures (for instance, the programme emanating from the National Conference for Economic Salvation in 1989).

REFERENCES

Abdalla, I.H., 1991, "Structural Impediments to Democratic Experiments in the Sudan", contribution to the Second International Sudan Studies Conference, Sudan. Environment and People, University of Durham, 8–11 April 1991, Vol. I of the Conference Papers.
Abdel Gadir Ali, A., 1985, *The Sudan Economy in Disarray. Essays on the IMF Model.* Khartoum and Ithaca Press, London.
Abu Sin, M.E., 1991, "Urban Process and Resources Conservation and Management in Sudan", contribution to the Second International Sudan Studies Conference, Sudan. Environment and People, University of Durham, 8–11 April 1991, Vol. II of the Conference Papers.
Adelman I. and St.J. Vogel, 1992, "The Relevance of ADLI for Sub-Saharan Africa", pp.258–279, *African Development Perspectives Yearbook, 1990/91.* Münster/Hamburg, LIT.
Aguda, O., 1973, "The State and the Economy in the Sudan: From a political Scientist's Point of View", pp. 431–448, *The Journal of Developing Areas, 7,* April.
Ahmed, G.M.and G.M. Sørbø (eds.), 1989, "Management of The Crisis in the Sudan". Proceedings of the Bergen Forum 23–24 February 1989. Bergen, Centre of Development Studies.

Attaelmannan Taha, E. et.al., 1990, "Towards Alternative Economic Policies For Sudan". University of Bremen, Sudan Economy Research Group Discussion Papers, No. 20.

Awad, M.E. (ed.), 1983, *Socio-economic change in the Sudan*. University of Khartoum, Graduate College Publications, Selected Essays, Monograph No. 6.

Awad, M.H., 1986, *Sudan, A Zero-Option Approach*. Unpublished paper.

Bush, S., 1991, "Transport in the Sudan: A System in Crisis", contribution to the Second International Sudan Studies Conference Sudan. Environment and People, University of Durham, 8–11 April 1991, Vol. I of the Conference Papers.

Bwolo, A.D., 1991, "The Impact of Armed Conflict on the Development of Sudan", pp. 37-44, *Voices From Africa*, Issue Number 3, War, Armed Conflict, Destabilisation. Edited by UNGLS (United Nations Non-Governmental Liaison Service), March 1991.

Due, J.F., 1984, "A New Approach to the Financing of an Autonomous South Sudan", September 1984, for US AID Sudan, Khartoum.

Eltom, A., 1986, "Towards a Long-Term Agricultural Development Strategy and Related Policies", study for Sudan First National Economic Conference, Agricultural Sector Conference, Khartoum, 18–20 February 1986.

Erkowit Conference, 1988, *Final Report, 11th Erkowit Conference*, 19–24 November 1988, Khartoum. English translation from the Arabic original.

Hansohm, D., 1989, "IMF/World Bank Policies in Sudan and its Critics", pp. 259–280, in K. Wohlmuth (ed.), *Structural Adjustment in the World Economy and East-West-South Economic Cooperation*. Institute for World Economics and International Management, University of Bremen.

Hansohm, D., 1992, *Small Industry Promotion in Africa—Lessons from Sudan*. Bremer Afrika-Studien Bd. 2. Münster/Hamburg, LIT.

Hansohm, D. and K. Wohlmuth, 1987, "Promotion of Rural Handicrafts as a Means of Structural Adjustment in Sudan", pp. 170–190, *Scandinavian Journal of Development Alternatives*, June–September, Vol. VI, No. 2 & 3.

Hansohm, D. and K. Wohlmuth, 1989, "Sudan's East-South and South-South Economic Cooperation", p. 481–513, in K. Wohlmuth (ed.), *Structural Adjustment in the World Economy and East-West-South Economic Cooperation*. Institute for World Economics and International Management, University of Bremen.

Hansohm, D. and K. Wohlmuth, 1990, "Sudan's Small Industry Development: Structures, Failures and Perspectives", pp. 146-165, in Meine Pieter van Dijk and H.S. Marcussen (eds.), *Industrialization in the Third World: The Need for Alternative Strategies*. London, Frank Cass.

ILO (International Labour Office) 1976, *Growth, Employment and Equity. A Comprehensive Strategy for the Sudan*. Geneva, ILO.

ILO 1986, *After the Famine. A Programme of Action to Strengthen the Survival Strategies of Affected Populations*. Report of the ILO Identification and Programming Mission to the Republic of the Sudan, September 1985. Geneva, ILO.

ILO 1986, *Employment and Economic Reform*. Background Papers by Sudanese Economists for the ILO Mission to Sudan 1986. Khartoum, ILO.

ILO 1987, *Employment and Economic Reforms: Toward a Strategy for the Sudan*. Geneva, ILO.

IMF 1986, *The Current Economic Situation in Sudan*. Washington D.C., June 25, 1986.

Jamal, V., 1992, "Wages and Implications for Structural Adjustment—How to survive in Africa?", pp. 247–257, *African Development Perspectives Yearbook* 1990/91, Vol. II. Münster/Hamburg, LIT.

Kursany, I., 1983, "A Strategy for the Transformation of the Precapitalist Part of the Sudanese Society", pp. 167–189, *Development and Peace*, Vol. 4, No. 1, Spring.

Kursany, I., 1986, *The State, Class and Development*. Unpublished research report. Khartoum

Mustafa, El-Murtada, 1985, *A Development Strategy for the Sudan*. Khartoum, National Defence Faculty.

Mustafa, El-Murtada et.al., 1988, *A Social Contract—Bridge from Confrontation to Partnership*. Unpublished. Khartoum.

Mustafa, El-Murtada et.al., 1988, Dimensions of Employment Generation and Productivity Enhancement in the Sudan. Unpublished report. Khartoum, February 1988.

Mustafa, El-Murtada et.al., 1989, *Strategy Document on Income Generation and Employment in Refugee—Affected Areas of the Sudan*. Unpublished Mission Report. Khartoum, March 1989.

Nashashibi, K., 1980, "A Supply Framework for Exchange Reform in Developing Countries: The Experience of Sudan", *IFM Staff Papers*, Vol. 27, No. 1.

Oesterdiekhoff, P., 1991, "Agricultural Marketing and Pricing: A Synopsis of Current Problems", pp. 365–394, in G.M. Craig (ed.), *The Agriculture of the Sudan*. Oxford, Oxford University Press.

Oesterdiekhoff, Peter and K. Wohlmuth (eds.), 1983, *The Development Perspectives of the Democratic Republic of Sudan. The Limits of the Breadbasket Strategy*. München/Köln/London, Weltforum Verlag.

Parker, R. St., 1991, *Mobilizing International Donors for Reconstruction: The Sudan Emergency Flood Reconstruction Program. Environment and Natural Disaster Management*. EDI Working Papers, Economic Development Institute of The World Bank, Washington D.C.

Prendergast, J. 1989, "Blood Money for Sudan. World Bank and IMF to the 'Rescue'", *Africa Today*, Vol. 36, Nos. 3 & 4, pp. 43–53.

Rodrik, D., 1990, "How Should Structural Adjustment Programmes Be Designed?", *World Development*, Vol. 18, No. 7., pp. 933–947.

Sørbø, G.M., 1991, "Resource Management and the Problems of Scale Examples from Eastern Sudan", contribution to the Second International Sudan Studies Conference, Sudan. Environment and People, University of Durham, 8–11 April 1991, Vol. II of the Conference Papers.

Statement, 1989 (on behalf of the National Conference for Economic Salvation in Khartoum, November 1989).

Sudan Studies, 1992, Current Affairs in Sudan, pp. 4-6, Bremen.

United Nations 1990, *Sudan*. Country Presentation to the Second United Nations Conference on the Least Developed Countries, UNCLDC II/CP. 32, Paris, 3–14 September 1990.

Wohlmuth, K., 1989, "Sudan's Industrialisation after Independence: A Case of Africa's Crisis of Industrialisation", pp. 357–379, in Nurul Islam (ed.), *The Balance between Industry and Agriculture in Economic Development*, Vol. 5, Factors Influencing Change. Houndmills, Basingstoke and London: Macmillan.

Wohlmuth, K., 1991, "National Policies for Agriculture", pp. 436–454, in G.M. Craig (ed.), *The Agriculture of The Sudan*. Oxford, Oxford University Press.

Wohlmuth, K. 1992, "Towards a New Generation of Structural Adjustment Programmes for Sub-Saharan African—An Introduction", pp. 166–192, in *African Development Perspectives Yearbook* 1990/91, Vol. II. Münster/Hamburg, LIT.

Wohlmuth, K., 1993, "Policy Reforms and Energy Adjustments in Sub-Saharan Africa", contribution to Vol. III of *African Development Perspectives Yearbook* 1992/93. Münster/Hamburg, LIT.
Wohlmuth, K. and D. Hansohm, 1984, "Economic Policy Changes in the Democratic Republic of Sudan". Research report. Bremen, University of Bremen.
Wohlmuth, K. and D. Hansohm, 1987, "Sudan: A Case for Structural Adjustment Policies", pp. 206–225, in *Development And Peace*, Vol. 8, No. 2, Autumn 1987.
World Bank 1986, *Sudan. A Comprehensive Approach to Sudan's Economic Problems*. Washington D.C., May 19, 1986.
World Bank 1987A, *Sudan. Problems of Economic Adjustment.* Vol I, Summary Report. Washington D.C., World Bank, June 19, 1987.
World Bank 1987B, *Sudan. Problems of Economic Adjustment.* Vol. II, Main Report. Washington D.C., Report No. 6491–SU, February 11.
World Bank 1987C, *Sudan. The Manufacturing Sector: Setting the Stage for Restructuring.* Vol. I and II. Washington D.C., World Bank, June 30, 1987.
World Bank 1988, *Program to Alleviate Social Costs of Adjustment in the Sudan.* Unpublished report. Washington D.C., April 1988.
World Bank 1990, *Sudan. Reversing the Economic Decline. Country Economic Memorandum.* Washington D.C., July 1990.
Yongo-Bure, B., 1989, *Economic Development of the Southern Sudan: An Overview and a Strategy.* Sudan Economy Research Group Discussion, Paper No. 16. Bremen, SERG, University of Bremen.
Yongo-Bure, B., 1990, *The Nationalities Question and National Unity or Disintegration in Sudan.* Sudan Economy Research Group, Discussion Paper No. 19. Bremen, SERG, University of Bremen.
Yongo-Bure, B., 1991, *The Role of Small Scale Rural Industries in the Recovery and Development of the Southern Sudan.* Sudan Economy Research Group, Discussion Paper No. 22. Bremen, SERG, University of Bremen.

Other periodicals and journals

Africa Watch, Reports on Sudan, especially 1990, 1991, 1992 issues.
Amnesty International, Reports on Sudan, 1990, 1991, and 1992 issues.
Sudan Democratic Gazette, 1991 and 1992 issues.
Sudanow, 1990, 1991, 1992 issues.
Sudan Update, 1990, 1991 and 1992 issues.

Constitutional Framework for Peace and Stability

Peter Woodward

One only has to mention the Weimar Republic to remind students of politics that constitutions alone solve few problems. Sudan has not been short of constitutional discussion, nor constitutional experiments: what it has lacked has been stable constitutional government. I do not wish to prolong a critique of past constitutional shortcomings that I have offered before, yet reference to it is salutary not just for Sudan but in the heady atmosphere of Africa's (and the world's) new embrace of liberal democracy (Woodward, 1987). There are many reasons for being universally cautious: liberal democracy is an attractive and desirable form of government, especially when various alternatives appear to have failed signally, but it is not a panacea. Many of the underlying problems of democracy in Africa will be, at least, as apparent in the 1990s as they were in the heady days of independence (Decalo, 1992). In Sudan the problems are particularly clear since it has had three spells of liberal democracy under the same simple Westminster-style constitution into which it drifted for want of anything better at independence in 1956.

Institutionally I have suggested two outstanding weaknesses of those three periods. First the party balance thrown up by successive elections has been such as to prevent a clear winner with an undoubted capacity to govern (always an alleged virtue of the Westminster model). As a result elections always produced coalition governments that proved weak and unstable. At the same time the capacity for building political participation through parties with a share of the system has been limited to northern Sudan (and not all of that) with the result that the south in particular, but also other geographically peripheral areas, have felt alienated from the political process. There have also been three military regimes and they too have had problems. All have fallen back on flexible clientilism. This has included dependence on the major 'ideological' movements—once the Sudanese Communist Party (SCP), more recently the Muslim Brotherhood in the guise of the National Islamic Front (NIF)—but the capacity of such narrow-based movements to affect the different 'revolutions' they proclaim has always been in doubt (though both have made their own contribution to constitutional debate) (Woodward, 1990).

Thus the need for new constitutional thought with regard to Sudan has not been in doubt ever since independence, and there has been recognition too that 'democracy' is not enough, but needs further definition if it is to prove stable and effective.

Some African states have also recognised this, most notably South Africa as it struggles to find a new constitutional form, but everywhere it requires not only a sophistication that extends beyond simply 'democracy', but also a route to the constitutional goal. For much of Africa (including South Africa) this has meant in the early 1990s a national conference of some kind. This in turn poses the proceeding questions of who should attend and on what terms. In much of Africa this has meant essentially those in power, whose legitimacy (being almost everywhere undemocratic) is under attack, together with their critics in various organised groups and parties who have been denied power for years.

In the Sudan the situation is clearly rather more complex. In one sense the present regime has endeavoured to carry out two such exercises: first in 1989 the Dialogue Conference, and then in 1991, the Conference on Comprehensive National Strategy. However, both consisted of invitees of the regime in power, and other political groupings were either not invited or have declined to attend. Thus at present there appears to be a reluctance by both the regime and its opponents to engage in the kind of 'level playing field' discussions being undertaken elsewhere in Africa.

Instead the two sides have staked out their own positions and use them in an attack on one another. The regime in Khartoum has evolved from the above mentioned meetings as a political system based on what are called congresses (see Figure 1). This congress system combined local communities, functional groupings ('youth and students' etc.) and geographical constituencies in a system which it is alleged will see active participation at the grass roots and an upward flow of power and authority. (The system is on top of the federal system already introduced, but although the new system refers to state congresses, there is surprisingly not the special reference to this level that one might expect of a federal system.) The system will, it claims, be a non-party one since it is said that the multi-party and one-party systems of the past signally failed to develop the country. The grass roots congresses will permit the true expression of the people's aspirations and will not require any further refinement since these aspirations will flow upwards through the congress hierarchy.

One hesitates to criticise that which is not yet fully operational, but a basic comparative awareness points to potential problems with the new arrangements. The most obvious parallel is with the Libyan system (from which at least part of the inspiration for the congresses was drawn). The Libyan experience was generally seen as less than dynamic at the grass roots with localities largely able to manoeuvre to relative advantage (as appeared to happen when Sudan was ruled by the Sudan Socialist Union during Nimeiri's regime) (Bearman, 1986). At the same time the several branches and levels of the congress system makes it hard to imagine the free flow of the many different expressions at the bottom into some form of policy without an aggregating mechanism. Thus for all the apparent openness of the

Peter Woodward

Figure 1. *A new political system. Congresses system*

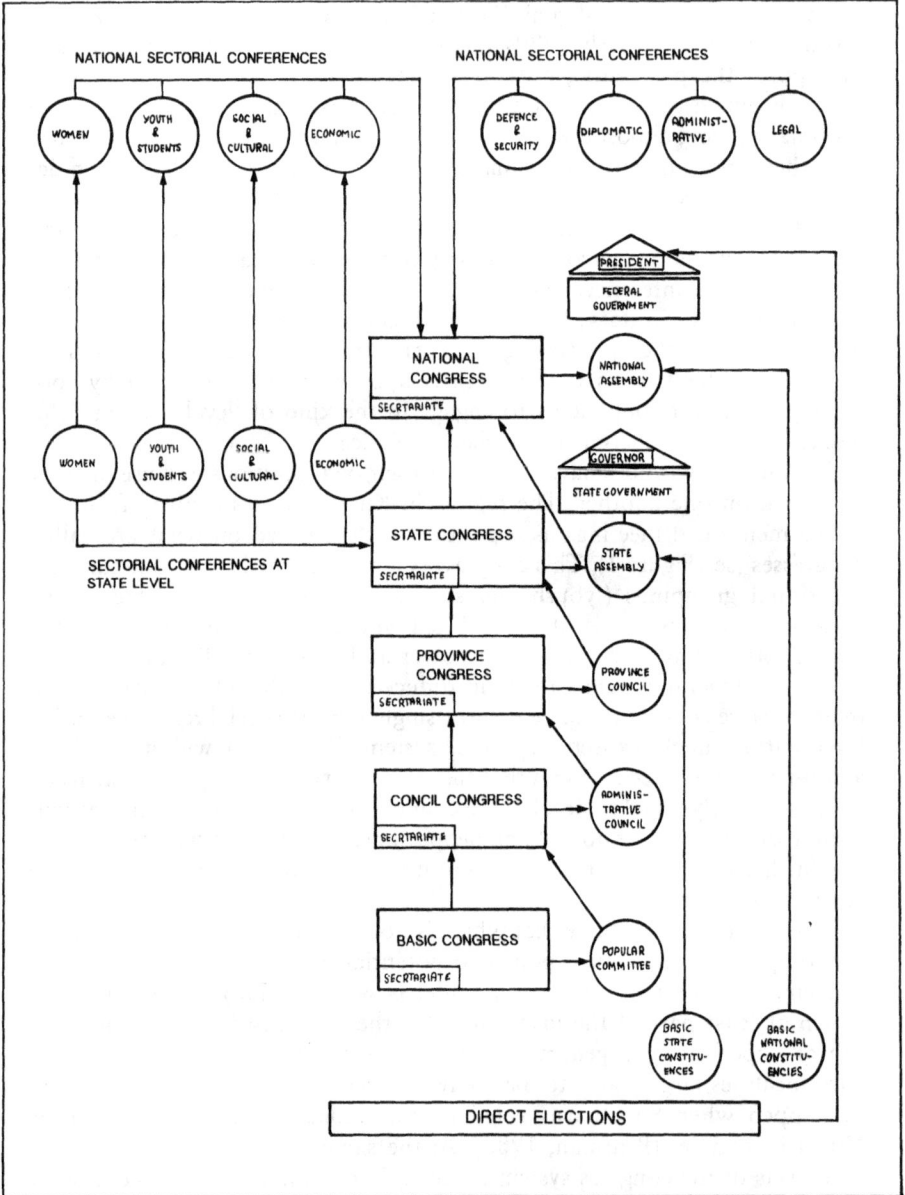

NATIONAL SECTORIAL CONFERENCES

NATIONAL SECTORIAL CONFERENCES

WOMEN · YOUTH & STUDENTS · SOCIAL & CULTURAL · ECONOMIC

DEFENCE & SECURITY · DIPLOMATIC · ADMINISTRATIVE · LEGAL

PRESIDENT
FEDERAL GOVERNMENT

NATIONAL CONGRESS
SECRTARIATE

NATIONAL ASSEMBLY

WOMEN · YOUTH & STUDENTS · SOCIAL & CULTURAL · ECONOMIC

SECTORIAL CONFERENCES AT STATE LEVEL

GOVERNOR
STATE GOVERNMENT

STATE CONGRESS
SECRTARIATE

STATE ASSEMBLY

PROVINCE CONGRESS
SECRTARIATE

PROVINCE COUNCIL

CONCIL CONGRESS
SECRTARIATE

ADMINISTRATIVE COUNCIL

BASIC CONGRESS
SECRTARIATE

POPULAR COMMITTEE

BASIC STATE CONSTITUENCES · BASIC NATIONAL CONSTITUENCIES

DIRECT ELECTIONS

Source: *Sudanow*, February 1992

system there is a case for critics to argue that it is likely in practice to perpet-uate and possibly develop the power of the National Islamic Front (NIF).

Meanwhile on the other side a broad grouping of opposition calling itself the National Democratic Alliance (NDA) met in London to hammer out an alternative (National Democratic Alliance, 1992). Central to this was of course the illegitimacy of the NIF regime, whose involvement in human rights abuses rules it out of even a future multi-party democracy in Sudan. However, on other constitutional issues the final declaration was less specific since it was concerned to outline the agreed principles of a transitional gov-ernment to last for up to five years, which after six months would convene a National Constitutional Conference (NCC). Until that constitution is imple-mented the transitional government would rule through a 'Supreme Council, National Legislative Council and the Council of Ministers'. (The issue of *sharia* was to be left to the constitutional conference, whereas in the present regime's system it has been in operation since 1991.)

Given these competing groupings and positions, and their apparent un-willingness at the time of writing to engage in dialogue, it is difficult to con-ceive of exactly who would participate in broader constitutional discussions in the Sudan and on what conditions? The most extreme example of that has been the conflict within the Sudan Peoples' Liberation Army (SPLA) with fac-tions fighting over issues that appear to include basic differences of political aims as well as personal and allegedly ethnic tensions. On a less dramatic level a number of different groups and politicians now in opposition had been publishing their views which expressed a considerable range of opinion in advance of the January 1992 meeting of the National Democratic Alliance.[1] With or without the present regime (and the readiness of different persons or groups to talk with it or not is far from clear) there would clearly be considerable problems in agreeing who would represent who in a national constitutional conference; and with differences of opinion expressed once there (with the old parties not yet very critical of the old democratic system which they operated to some party advantage).

Sudan's past record of peace-making and constitution-making (related but not synonymous processes) has not been good. The Addis Ababa agreement of 1972 that ended the first civil war in the south has been seen as the excep-tion to this generalisation. For all the complaints about its content (notably from the SPLA) the Addis Ababa agreement was an achievement (not just in Sudanese but Third World terms) in being a negotiated end to a conflict. It appeared to be facilitated by the crystallisation of power into two main hands, the regime in Khartoum and a relatively united Anya Nya leadership in the south. It also separated the ending of the war from a fully fledged con-stitutional discussion. (Regional autonomy for the south was agreed at Addis

---

[1] Recent ones across my desk include the Alexandria Declaration of the Unionist Party, the Adare Declaration by a group of southern politicians, and views on federalism from Ahmed Diraige, the former governor of Darfur.

Ababa, the permanent constitution was only introduced one year later—and both were subsequently undermined.) On other occasions the Sudan has been less successful. In peace-making efforts, the Round Table Conference of 1965 was in retrospect naive, throwing too many views and interests into one pot (though the subsequent working group paved the way for the Addis Ababa agreement). In the second civil war (1983 onwards) there have been a catalogue of endeavours (including that in Bergen in 1989) but to little effect: you can lead a horse to water but you cannot make him drink (Ahmed and Sørbø, 1989). Likewise constitutional talks at intervals, ever since independence, have generally floundered, and major changes have come not from negotiation and consensus but from regime dictate, as in the Permanent Constitution of 1973, the introduction of regional government in 1980, the introduction of *sharia* in 1983 and the establishment of federal government in 1990. The lack of consensus for such developments makes acceptance limited and a change of regime is immediately accompanied by the re-opening of the constitutional debate.

At present peace-making and constitutional issues appear inextricably linked—as evidenced by the pressing of the issue of an Islamic state—and in consequence the processes appear more difficult. The resulting polarisation has been one factor putting the survival of the state itself in question with more political actors speaking of secession than hitherto.

At the time of writing (March 1992) both factions have the door slightly open referring to future self determination, though hitherto the SPLA (Torit faction) had opposed all talk of secession, while the splinter Nasir group of August 1991 appeared to favour it. In addition to the intractability of the problem, events in eastern Europe, and the Horn of Africa, suggest that the international community is more amenable to the prospect of new states. The international context will be significant for whatever end is pursued in terms of a united or divided Sudan; as will a limited number of participants in any peace-making and/or constitutional discussion, and a higher ambition than factional, ideological or regional advantage (an ambition which does not necessarily exclude secession).

Given the problems of the process of peace-making and constitution-making, it seems almost a project of wild optimism to begin talking about issues in a future agreed constitution. It would certainly be both inappropriate and a waste of time for an outsider to be propounding a constitutional blueprint. Perhaps the most that can or should be done is to consider some of the alternative ingredients in a constitution to those the Sudan has had hitherto. My objections to Sudan's past democratic practice have been seen; while the 1973 Permanent Constitution emphasised an executive presidency that degenerated into 'personal rule'—as so often in Africa (Jackson and Rosberg, 1982).

The next divisive issue (perhaps literally) is that of an Islamic state. It may be the rock on which any hope of constitutional discussion founders, leading to the division of the state. If that is to happen, then it is perhaps better that it is done first in order that the two separate constitutional debates can then be held, presumably for North and South under whatever titles they choose to adopt. If, however, there is consensus that the maintenance of Sudan has higher priority than the issue of an Islamic or secular state (where the constitutional differences may actually be of less significance than the ideological principle) then it may be that *sharia* should come later in order that some area of agreement has been established for a new national constitution which participants would be reluctant to see lost as a result of a breakdown on the issue of *sharia*.

If it is possible to agree on the principle of one or two states fairly early on, then it may be possible to proceed towards transitional government(s). If the issues of unity or division can only be decided as negotiations develop (in effect a mutual veto of both sides in the negotiations) then it will be harder to establish the confidence from which to proceed. Nevertheless, whether as one or two states, there is much to be said for the prospect of a transitional government(s). The essence of it would be that it is unelected, since immediate elections could destroy the whole process of movement towards a sustainable future by once more producing a reversion to the past failed system. Yet in being unelected it must be a representative transitional government i.e. one that seeks a broader consensus on which to engage in constitutional discussion than the constitution by dictate of Nimeiri's military regime or the present one. Sudan has had experience of transitional government before, in 1964–65 and 1985–86 and could draw on this experience in establishing a new one to oversee the process of constitution-making and implementation (the current situation in South Africa is indicative of the potential significance of a broadly based transitional government as a step towards a new constitution).

Proceeding towards the content of a constitution (and assuming the outcome of the *sharia* issue was either agreed or deferred, as mentioned above), then a major question hitherto which will arise again will be federalism. I think this will (rightly) be an issue in one or two states of a future Sudan. Federalism has been under debate in Sudan since independence, essentially for reasons of heterogeneity and size. There will clearly be an issue of the federal map, and much here must depend on the extent to which the debate can be conducted in administrative terms and not simply that of the political advantage of state proliferation, largely for the purposes of ethno-regional representation and clientilistic acquisition of resources from the centre, both of which motives should be treated with considerable care if not cynicism (Suberu, 1991).

Ethno-regionalism can become an endless division and lead ultimately to a morass of ethno-political rivalries. At the same time the continuing financial dependence on the centre must be avoided since it can perpetuate 'federal clientilism'. However since most of the Sudan's regions are very poor, while the centre is disproportionately advantaged, that will call for some system of direct and entrenched transfer from central government to the regions. Federalism is not then a panacea any more than democracy: on occasions it has not effectively lessened the political authority of the centre; it may only open up new arenas for argument between federal states and the centre; and it can be a more costly and inefficient form of government and thereby be a hinder rather than a stimulant to economic development. In putting forward the principle for the Sudan I am probably pushing at an open door, but the point I am seeking to emphasise is that the detail of federalism is as important as the principle if it is to become an effective system. It might also be worth considering the Nigerian example of writing a third layer of government -local government—into the constitution to give greater guarantee of grass roots involvement.

Discussion of federalism leads on to thoughts of confederation, the looser linking of two or more entities that seem more distinct than the states of a federation. Confederalism may be an alternative to total separation of North and South for Sudan; and confederalism is not necessarily an alternative to federalism *within* North and South.

Federalism and/or confederalism may also be of relevance to another old and difficult subject, namely that of the multi-party competition so regularly regarded as an essential freedom of liberal democracy. In Sudan it has proved divisive in ways mentioned at the start of this paper, and if returned to under a Westminster model would probably be just as flawed again. What are the alternatives? One is to pursue some kind of one-party state as Nimeiri did with the Sudanese Socialist Union (SSU), and the present regime's moves may be interpreted as attempting that. Though the Sudan never in reality went far down this road (for the SSU was little more than an appendage of the military regime). Both the theory and practice of such regimes are now much out of favour internationally and with good reason which there is no need or space to rehearse here. An alternative is some half-way house of the kind on which Nigeria is trying to embark (and for which there are other precedents), a kind of controlled party system (in Nigeria's case two parties, one right of centre the other left of centre, referred to by cynics as the 'yes' party and the 'yes sir' party). While there might be some appeal, simply establishing the party number and parameters (non-racial etc.) might be difficult to effect and could be seen only as a guise for the divisions (north-south, as has often been maintained of the two-party system imposed in Nigeria). Another alternative is to leave the party-system but to so devolve power under a federal constitution that the significance of national parties would be much reduced. That would have the merit of liberal politics without the distortion of past national party competition, but it does involve an effective constitutional breakdown of the power which has remained in Khartoum under successive regimes and constitutional arrangements. A vital element of any such achievement is the re-thinking of Sudan's economy, the structures of which have been so complementary to the accumulation of power in the capital.

Attempts to break the grip of sectarian party politics, hitherto, have also involved non-geographical representation. It began with the graduates' constituencies, but later developed into the issue of special representation of the 'modern forces'—professional groups, trade unions, the army etc. 'Developmentally' the case can be seen especially when the 'modern forces' were concentrated in the main cities and outweighed in the legislature by those elected in seats that were in practice bastions of 'rural traditionalism'. Yet any such system which seeks to distort 'one man one vote' is in some sense arbitrary: federalism which succeeds in pushing decision-making outward and downward may contribute to the reduction of the significance of this past dimension of the battle for the centre.

Functional representation could though go some way towards giving the armed forces a political voice which might be important in reducing the propensity towards coups, which is now well-established in Sudan and will be a continuing threat unless some transcending institutional development can be fostered.

Another difficult issue in central government will be the presidency. Sudan has experienced executive presidency, especially under Nimeiri, and it developed into personal rule. On the other hand attempts to create a non-executive presidency have had too much wrangling over the membership of Five-man Supreme Councils and the like, and have not always stopped political interference as under Ismail El-Azhari's presidency. Perhaps a combination of federalism, fixed period in office, and central checks and balances could be one way to make executive presidency acceptable, along American lines.

The issues discussed hitherto are all old chestnuts in Sudanese politics, but still unavoidable for all that. Consideration of democracy in heterogeneous societies has also had a number of other areas of thinking under the general heading of consociational democracy that are not as well known in a Sudanese context (Lijphart, 1977). A number of these have been considered or adopted in Africa and could be worth considering.

I have referred already to the controlled two-party system being attempted in Nigeria for 1992. And the idea considered has been that of sharing federal government offices between regions, and alternation of office-holding on a regional basis. At the same time there can be a staggered re-introduction of elections to build from the bottom up. Thus in Nigeria (as in Ghana) local elections have preceded state elections which have in turn preceded the scheduled national elections. As well as seeking to practice democracy from the bottom up in this way (and enhance the perceived importance of sub-national elections) a staggered timetable for different levels of government could provide the overlap of institutions which might enhance institutional stability at all levels. At the same time there could be staged elections for particular institutions for similar effect, as with the American senate. A delay in permitting the freedom of political parties to operate until after the initial steps in institution-building have taken place is another possible way of contributing to the enhancing of the positions of institutions.

A further possible area of experimentation lies in elected national positions requiring cross-regional political support. As an idea the first reference to this I know in Africa was the system proposed for the Ugandan elections in 1971 whereby candidates for the national legislature would have to stand not in one electoral constituency but in two in different regions of the country and achieve a particular level of support in both in order to be elected. A comparable idea arose in Nigeria with the president under the constitution of the Second Republic requiring not only an overall majority, but a minimum of 25 per cent support in two-thirds of the states (in fact President Shagari only just scraped in after a favourable interpretation by the courts of an ambiguous electoral outcome).

Another important issue that must be addressed in any future constitution is that of a bill of rights. Sudan's human rights record has always been somewhat mixed. Back in the 1960s there was some atrocious abuse of civilians in the south during the course of the first civil war (1955–72), and since 1983 in particular there has been a worsening of the civil rights situation throughout the country. However, the situation has grown significantly more repressive since the present regime took power in 1989 (*Africa Watch*, 1990). Civil rights though is not just about the application of universally accepted standards in the Sudan, the question of *sharia* itself represents an area in which there can be a fundamental clash over the essential nature of such rights. As a result the bill of rights could be in principle one of the most contentious areas, and one which could be central to a failure to agree on a constitution. A less considered aspect hitherto would be the developmental possibilities of a bill of rights. Human rights could be represented in a way not only to emphasise the individuals freedom from the state, but the responsibilities of the state towards individuals. These could include social and educational provisions.

A bill of rights is of little use without an independent judiciary. The present regime in the Sudan, in particular, has dismantled much of the machinery of what had been hitherto a judiciary with at least a degree of independence including a number of significant past political interventions such as the courts' protection of the right of the Sudanese Communist Party in the 1960s. Though dismantled now, the tradition has not died but rather gone into exile, and could be resuscitated in the future.[2]

---

[2] The Sudan Human Rights Organization (SHRO) re-launched itself in London in October 1991 claiming that it was no longer possible for an independent body to function in Sudan.

This paper has been no more than a brief discussion of certain aspects of Sudan's constitutional debate past and present and some issues for the future. But perhaps the most that should be done at this stage is to promote consideration of broad outlines for a future constitution, whether for one or two states. As a matter of procedure it may be better to avoid trying to decide on a blue print: and procedure is going to be as vital as constitutional substance in deciding whether or not one or two Sudans are going to have any form of peaceful future. Even if there is some agreement on constitutional principle it may need to remain as a framework initially allowing for a good deal of flexibility and pragmatism in implementation. Many areas of the country are, at least, in such a condition of decay and violence that to draw up a constitutional blueprint to improve on such a situation seems probably inappropriate at present.

The situation is clearly going to be difficult for the development of constitutional government. In addition to the hostile circumstances themselves is the problem of developing a sense of constitutionalism, of seeing the state as a constitutionally ruled social structure and conducting political life in a way that recognises the centrality of that relationship. The present Sudanese state was not built that way: it was the product of imperial state formation beginning early in the last century and that will remain as true if it now breaks in two as it has been as a single state hitherto. The respect for the Westminster-style constitution in the period after independence was itself not that great. Personal, factional and party advantage generally appeared to take precedence over constitutional consideration, and contributed to the making of opportunities for military intervention in consequence.

If that makes the outlook appear bleak, political life is not unchanging. Few states in the world were founded on democratic constitutional principles and have continued to run on them without problems. Some have evolved towards liberal democracy; others are now seeking liberal democracy because of the failings of alternatives. Sudan has experienced one form of liberal democracy; military rule; a one-party state; and attempts to implement ideological programmes of extreme left and right. Perhaps the weakness of all forms of government hitherto will enhance the appreciation of the need to seek a consensus for a more effective constitutional structure than hitherto (whether in one country or two). It has to be the hope, for without it the future appears bleak.

REFERENCES

Africa Watch Report, 1990, *"Denying the Honour of Living'. Sudan a Human Rights Disaster*. London.
Ahmed, A. and G. Sørbø (eds.), 1989, *Management of the Crisis in the Sudan*. Bergen, Centre for Development Studies.

Al-Teraifi, A., 1991, "Regionalisation in the Sudan", in P. Woodward (ed.), *Sudan after Nimeiri*. Routledge, London.

Bearman, J., 1986, *Qadhafi's Libya*. London, Zed Press.

Decalo, S., 1992, "The Process, Prospects and Constraints of Democratization in Africa", *African Affairs* 91, 362:7–35.

Hamid, M. B., 1986, "Devolution and National Integration in the Southern Sudan", in M. Al-Rahim et.al. (eds.), *Sudan since Independence*. Gower, Aldershot.

Jackson, R. and C. Rosberg, 1982, *Personal Rule in Black Africa*. Berkley, University of California Press.

Lijphart, A., 1977, *Democracy in Plural Societies*. London, Yale University Press.

Suberu, R. T., 1991, "The Struggle for New States in Nigeria 1976–1990", *African Affairs* 90, 36.

Woodward, P., 1987, "Is Sudan Governable? Some Thoughts on the Experiences of Liberal Democracy and Military Rule", *Bulletin*. 13,2:137–149. British Society of Middle Eastern Studies.

Woodward, P., 1990, *Sudan 1898–1989: The Unstable State*. Boulder, Lynn Rienner.

A Chronology of the Sudan 1972–1992

Sharif Harir, Kjell Hødnebø and Terje Tvedt

1972

Addis Ababa conference, 16–17 February. The Sudan government sent a 9 man delegation, headed by Vice-President and Minister for Southern Affairs, Abel Alier.
The Southern Sudan Liberation Movement (SSLM), sent a delegation of 8 men,
headed by Ezboni Mindiri. The General Secretary of All Africa Conference of
Churches, Canon Burgess Carr, was acting as chairman at the conference.

President Nimeiri ratified the Addis Ababa agreement through a presidential decree
on 3 May. "The Southern Provinces Regional Self-Government Act 1972" became part of the Sudanese constitution in 1973.

A High Executive Council was appointed for the south, Vice-President Abel Alier became President. Joseph Lagu, the former commander of the Anya Nya forces, was
appointed major general in the Sudanese army and commanding officer for the
Southern Command in Juba.

This new regional government stated that its 3 main objectives in its 18 month transitional period were:
1. Integration of the former Anya Nya soldiers (6,000) into the Sudanese armed
forces.
2. Relief and resettlement of the southern refugees in collaboration with the
Sudanese government, different UN organizations and NGOs.
3. Establishment of a constituent and legal local government through elections,
and the preparations for such elections the following year.

Foreign relations: Ugandan soldiers supporting ex-president Milton Obote were
training in camps in Equatoria, and in March were transported via Khartoum to
Dar es Salaam to join Obote. Tense relations with Ugandan president Idi Amin
and also his ally Gadaffi of Libya. Diplomatic rapprochement towards China and
North Korea in September and October.

A re-orientation of the foreign policy: after the unsuccessful coup attempt by the
communist party in 1971, diplomatic relations were broken with the Soviet
Union. Diplomatic relations were restored with the USA during the spring of
1972.

1973

The People' s Assembly in Khartoum ratified the first "Permanent Constitution"
since independence in April. Approved by President Nimeiri on 8 May.

Nimeiri announced on 8 May. the release of the remaining political detainees, i.e.
leaders of the Communist party and Sadiq el Mahdi, former Prime Minister and
leader of the Umma party and head of the Ansar section.

Nimeiri dismissed the old cabinet and appointed a new one on 10 May.Of 14 members only one member was new. The president became also Prime Minister and
Minister of Defence. No Southerners appointed.

The UN High Commissioner for Refugees announced a programme for the repatriation of 180,000 southern refugees from the neighbouring countries into the
south.

Foreign investments start flowing into the Sudan. Western and Arab funds started
coming in after the crushing of the Communist party' s coup attempt in 1971,

banning of the labour unions, the break with the Soviet Union, compensation for the companies which were nationalized in 1970 and the Addis Ababa agreement. The Sudan was envisaged as a future "bread-basket" of the Middle East.

Large scale emigration to the oil-rich Arab states started. Remittances became a major source of foreign currency earning.

Clashes between students and the police and army and strikes ended in a declaration of a state of emergency in August and September.

Elections to the Southern Regional Assembly (October) and the establishment of the first legally elected government in the South with Abel Alier as the first President. Regional ministries were established in Juba.

Food shortages and famine conditions were reported from Dar Fur, western Sudan. Dar Fur students in higher educational institutions in Khartoum demonstrated in front of the people's assembly. The Sudan Government denied these reports and no relief action was undertaken.

1974

Signing of an agreement for "political and economic integration" between Sudan and Egypt, by presidents Nimeiri and Sadat on 12 February. A Joint Supreme Political Committee, consisting of members from the Sudanese Socialist Union (SSU) and Arab Socialist Union (ASU), was set up to coordinate political and ideological issues. The Egypt-Sudan agreement included the utilization of the Nile waters, food production and co-ordination of policies.

Plans to attract Arab funds, especially from Saudi Arabia. King Faisal personally promised aid for 2,000 million dollars. The food production planned to be increased 20 times with more water and irrigation, partly by the digging of the Jenglei Canal from Bor to the Sobal junction.

Demonstrations took place both in Khartoum and Juba in March–April. In Khartoum students with sympathies for the Moslem Brotherhood, Communist party and Umma party demonstrated against Nimeiri. In the south demonstrations were directed against plans for the Jonglei scheme.

General elections to the Peoples' s Assembly in Khartoum in May. Of 250 seats 125 were elected on a geographical basis, of which about 40 were Southerners.

Allegations of anti-government plots put forward in May and October. President Nimeiri claimed a Libyan conspiracy against his person. Leaders of the opposition abroad, "The National Front", had established headquarters in Tripoli. Allegations were put forward that Khartoum students, especially the Moslem Brotherhood, were financially backed by Libya.

Kuwait contributed to the funding of irrigation schemes in El Rahad and sugar cane scheme in Sennar. The Sudanese government states that it will be the world' s largest sugar cane producer by 1985.

A heavy drought in the Sahel countries, especially Mauritania and Chad, led to a heavy influx of refugees to the western Sudan; Dar Fur. The UN Secretary General Kurt Waldheim, visited the Sudan to discuss the matter in June.

A policy of "balance" between Arab countries and black Africa was formulated by Nimeiri. State visits by the two presidents Kenneth Kaunda of Zambia and Julius Nyerere of Tanzania followed at the end of the year.

1975

A major cabinet reshuffle took place in January: Foreign Minister Mansour Khalid, Finance Minister Ibrahim Moneim Mansour and two others were shifted to minor posts or removed. Loyalist members of the SSU were appointed to the cabinet. President Nimeiri took over as Minister of Foreign Affairs himself.

A mutiny by Anya Nya soldiers took place in Akobo in March. More than 200 persons were reported killed, and 150 soldiers executed, and 48 mutineers were sentenced to imprisonment for 1–15 years. Statements were given accounting for "a growing frustration at the slow pace of economic investment and development" in the south.

At the six years' celebration for the May revolution the president of Libya, Gadaffi, was surprisingly taking part, both in Khartoum and Wau. A joint statement was issued towards "strengthened unity" between the two countries. A committee was formed to study the integration between Sudan' s Dar Fur province and Libya' s Kufra district. Joint control of movement, trade and customs was the stated aim.

A military coup attempt by the "National Front" was suppressed on 5 September. Both communists and religious groups (Moslem Brotherhood) participated. The leader was supposed to be Lieut.-Colonel Hassan Hussein Osman. President Nimeiri accused Gadhafi and Libya of backing the plot.

Constitutional amendments were adopted by the People's Assembly on 16 September. and by the president on 17 September, granting the government emergency powers, including the detaining of persons suspected of subversive activities for an indefinite period without previous trial (suspension of Habeas Corpus).

A State Security Amendment Bill was approved by the Peoples' s Assembly on 10 November. Two state security courts were established to conduct trials against people accused of violating state security.

Chevron Oil starts prospecting at the northern fringe of Bahr el Ghazal at Bentiu.

1976

Lieutenant Colonel Hassan Hussein Osman and 15 other ranks were executed in January and February. A total of 142 persons were accused of taking part in the coup attempt of September 1975.

Nimeiri announced a major cabinet reshuffle and reorganization of the Sudanese Socialist Union (SSU) on 11 February. Twelve ministers were dismissed and replaced by officers from the May revolution command Council. The new Minister for Information and Culture was a Southerner; Bona Malwal Madut Ring.

An army company, mostly previous Anya Nya secessionists, defected from Wau, killing high ranking officers in February; the start of what has later been called the Anya Nya II movement. 45,000 southern refugees were reported to live in 4 camps near Cambela in Ethiopia.

Former Minister of Labour, Joseph Oduho; deputy speaker in the Regional Assembly, Benjamin Bol, Eziboni Mindiri and several other southern politicians were arrested in March, accused of conspiracy aiming at a military rebellion in the south with secession as its aim.

In May the Sudanese press was put under state control by President Nimeiri. (Officially under control by the SSU, the only legal party in the country).

"Sudanow" was started in June, with the new Minister for Information, Bona Malwal, as its first editor.

Attempted *coup d' état* on 2 July. Libya was accused of plotting against the Sudan. The case was brought to the United Nations Security Council, described as a "foreign invasion with 1,000 mercenaries coming from training camps in Libya". The Sudanese national opposition movement in exile (Umma party, Moslem Brotherhood, DUP) was the force behind the incursion from Libya.

Defence agreement with Egypt was concluded in July. Egypt placed 12,000 troops in Sudan.

1977

12 Air Force members allegedly seized the airport of Juba in a coup attempt on 3 February. Twenty-eight officers and soldiers were arrested on 6 February. Abel Alier stated that "Israeli elements" were behind the scheme.

Nimeiri, as the sole candidate, was re-elected as president for a new term of six new years on 3 April by a vote of 99,1 per cent, according to official announcements.

About 100 Soviet embassy personnel/military experts were asked to leave within a week on 29 May. Nimeiri confirmed that Egypt and Sudan agreed on checking the Soviet "neo-colonialist" influence in Africa and the Arab world.

After several meetings, ending at Port Sudan on 6–7 July between the president and Sadiq el Mahdi, an agreement was reached for a policy of national reconciliation and a general amnesty to all Sudanese opposition abroad. A special list of 13 persons, including Sadiq el Mahdi and El Sharif Hussein el Sharif el Hindi, both condemned to death in 1976, was issued, with a grant of full amnesty.

About 900 political prisoners were released in July, and the government claimed that there were no more political prisoners in the Sudan.

The Juba university was established, together with four teacher' s training institutes in other southern towns.

The foreign debt, at the end of 1977 reached 2 billion dollars. Problems of servicing the debt were already apparent at this very early stage.

1978

General elections to both the National Assembly and the Southern Regional Assembly in Juba took place on 2 February. Total number of seats was increased to 304 in National Assembly. Almost all ministers from the HEC (High Executive Council) of 1972 were not re-elected in the south. Nimeiri nominated Joseph Lagu as the new president of the HEC of the southern region. Among the new ministers were Benjamin Bol and Joseph Oduho (imprisoned in 1976 and released in 1977 under the amnesty).

Nimeiri appointed some leaders of the former opposition to the central committee of the SSU in March: Sadiq el Mahdi, Abdul Hamed Saleh, Omer Nur el Dayem (Umma), Hassan el Turabi (Moslem Brother), Abdin Ismail (left wing) and Ali el Mirghani (DUP and Khatmiyya), although the ban on other political parties was still in force.

Conclusion of "National Reconciliation" agreement between the political opposition (National Front) and the Sudan government was signed on 12 April. Main points:

– Dissolution of the National Front, especially its military units.

– Abolition of Ansar military training camps.

– Re-affirmation of the 1973 constitution and the Addis Ababa agreement.

– Freedom of expression and repeal of emergency laws.

– Freedom of religion, both for the Ansar and Moslem Brothers.

Negotiations between the Sudan and the United States for US supply of combat aircraft and other military support (F-5 fighters).

Normalization of relations with Ethiopia and Libya and restoration of diplomatic relations.

Agreement with China on mutual technical and economic cooperation. Nimeiri visits China in June.

Nimeiri supports the Egyptian–Israeli peace agreement signed at Camp David in September. Sadiq el Mahdi resigns in protest from the SSU Political Bureau and leaves the country in December.

1979

General Joseph Lagu, the president of High Executive Council (HEC) and three regional ministers (including Joseph Oduho) and the governors of Upper Nile and
Jonglei provinces were removed from office on 12 July. Lawrence Wol Wol had
been dismissed in February from the southern High Executive Council (HEC). On
26 July. Clement Mboro, Speaker of the Southern Regional Assembly was also
dismissed.

Civil unrest: workers strike and student riots break out in Khartoum and other
towns on 7–8 August. The railway workers, striking for 5 days, demanded higher
salaries and lower cost of living. Students demanded political changes:
– Restoration of press freedom.
– Liquidation of the SSU as the sole political party.

Diplomatic sources reported the presence of Egyptian troops in the Sudan, most of
them arriving the second week of August, controlling all major strategic places in
larger towns.

On 17 August. Major Abul Gassim Mohammed Ibrahim was dismissed as First Vice-
President and Secretary General of SSU. He was replaced by Lt.General Abdel
Magid H. Khalil, appointed Minister of Defence, Commander in Chief of People'
s Armed Forces and First Vice-President of the Republic. Nimeiri took over as
Secretary General of SSU. Dismissal of eight ministers and two advisers, and the
appointment of six new ministers and three Ministers of State. Hassan el Turabi
(the leader of the Muslim Brotherhood) was appointed as attorney general.

On 18 August Nimeiri announced a far reaching reorganization, involving changes in
the structure of the leadership and a reduction of the political bureau of the SSU
from 27 to 17 members. Among members removed were:Bona Malwal, Ahmad
Ali al Mirghani, Joseph Oduho, Sadiq al Mahdi, Clement Mboro.

Works on the Jonglei canal started, implemented by the French firm Compagnie de
Construction International (CCI).

The International Monetary Fund (IMF) approved further credit to the Sudan as a
result of the agreement of 1978–79, and a 40 million USD worth credit was
purchased as a compensatory financing facility in November.

The Arab Monetary Fund (AMF) agreed on 17 October to provide Sudan with an
extended fund facility of 44 million USD as a balance of payments assistance,
following similar subscriptions of September and August 1978 to the AMF.

1980

Regional reorganization of the Sudan, first proposed at the SSU congress in January–
February. On 6 March new governors were appointed for 5 regions (in the
north), with regional assemblies and local cabinets similar to those already existing in the south. On 11 November these five governors were replaced by five
others by a presidential decree.

Following allegations of misappropriation of funds and unconstitutional conduct the
Vice-President and President of the HEC of the Southern Region, Joseph Lagu,
had to resign in February.

New elections to both the Southern Regional Assembly and the National People' s
Assembly were decreed on 1 February, Abel Alier was re-elected as a President in
the HEC of the Southern Region (Peter Gatkuoth Vice-President). On 6 June,
Abel Alier was re-appointed by Nimeiri as national Vice-President.

Negotiations took place in November 1979 and April 1980 between the Sudan
Government and Sudan' s principal creditor countries with the World Bank as
chairman. Results: the West German government decided on the cancellation of
Sudanese debt valued at 200 million USD, other commercial bank loans were re-

scheduled with a 3 year grace period followed by a 7 year maturity and possibly new loans.

Several development projects attracted international financial assistance: the Juba-Lodwar (Kenya) highway (EEC,US,Norway), expansion of Sudan' s electricity generating capacity (IDA, ODA-UK, German Ministry of Economic Cooperation and others), institutional reforms and imports to improve irrigation of cotton for export (co-financed by EEC), rehabilitation of the New Halfa irrigation scheme, 105 million USD worth programme co-financed by IFAD and ADF (African Development Fund), a 10 year health programme against schistosomiasis, malaria and diarrhoea in the Gezira, and Rahad and Managil irrigation schemes (WHO, total cost: 155 million USD).

The US based Chevron Oil Company announced that oil reserves around Bentiu in Upper Nile province were extensive and experts stated that this could meet a major proportion of Sudan' s oil requirements. Southern politicians demanded the refinery be built in Bentiu.

The National People' s Assembly in late 1980 passed a bill on regional reorganization, attaching a map where the border between north and south in the Sudan was moved southwards to include the areas with possible large oil reserves in the north, which led to widespread protests among the Southern Sudanese.

1981

Following Libya' s intervention in Chad in December 1980 the Sudanese government called for a Libyan expulsion from the Arab League. An estimated 2 million Chadian refugees and nomads were reported to have trekked into Dar Fur. Nimeiri, on 31 March called for an international action to "overthrow or kill" Kaddafi.

Serious violence occurred in El Fasher in January where 10–20 people were killed in demonstrations against the government' s appointment of a non-Darfuri governor. The appointment was rescinded on 19 January. This was what came to be known as the Dar Fur upheaval, i.e. *Intifadha*, as a result of which Ahmed Ibrahim Diraige was appointed governor. For the first time since 1916 a Dar Furi person ruled Dar Fur.

In March Nimeiri announced that the government had foiled a military coup plot, led by Brig. General Saad Bahar. Eleven people were arrested, alleged to be backed by foreign powers: Syria, the Soviet Union and Libya.

IMF extends further credits under the Compensatory Financing Facility to cover running state expenditure, re-scheduling and augmenting the foreign debt in April.

Sudan normalized political relations with Egypt and called for US military aid, especially mutual aircraft activity. Reagan announced in March 100 million USD worth of military aid and further economic aid. Sudan, as the only Arab League member, re-established diplomatic relations with Egypt in May.

Decision was taken to build the oil refinery at Kosti. A pipeline was to be built from Bentiu to Kosti jointly with Chevron Oil and the International Finance Corporation (IFC).

Industrial unrest and a national strike by railway and river-transport workers in June. Nimeiri on 21 June invoked death penalty for the strike organizers and imprisonment for life for participants.

Both the National People' s Assembly (NPA) and the Southern Regional Assembly were dissolved by presidential decree on 5 October and new elections were held. The NPA was to be reduced in size from 366 representatives to 151 following the devolution of powers to regional assemblies.

Presidential decree of 5 October appointing a new interim President for the Southern Regional HEC. A southern Moslem: General Gismallah Abdullah Rassas was appointed to the post.

Presidential announcement on 9 November of dismissal of Sudanese cabinet and introduction of an economic austerity programme. Following negotiations in October, an 18 point plan was agreed with the IMF, including devaluation of the Sudanese pound, tax raising, withdrawal of public subsidies and reduction of public expenditure. As a response the IMF and other credit institutions would once again re-schedule debt payments. The foreign debt stood at 3 billion USD.

1982

Internal security problems and student riots followed the rise in food prices caused by withdrawal of subsidies (December–January). Student demonstrations started in Khartoum and spread to other cities. A demonstration in Khartoum was broken up by tear gas on 6 January and reports stated that five students were shot dead in Wad Medani by anti-riot police. Other clashes followed.

Arrest of 21 leading politicians in Juba on 4 January. Charged with forming an illegal political party: The Council for Unity of Southern Sudan (Chairman, Clement Mboro, Deputy Chairman, Samuel Aru Bol, Foreign Affairs, Michael Wal, Assistant Secretary Martin Magi).

Nimeiri announced on 25 January the dismissal of Lt. General Abdul Magid Hamid Khalil from his posts as First Vice-President, Minister of Defence and Commander in Chief of the Armed Forces as well as Secretary of the SSU. Colonel Awad Malik was appointed as new Secretary and the President took over the military leadership. The political bureau of SSU and Central Committee was also dissolved. A 41 member committee formed instead, with Nimeiri as chairman. The President held the following posts: President of the republic, Prime Minister, Minister of Defence, Minister of Agriculture and Irrigation, Field Marshal and Commander in Chief of the People' s Armed Forces and Chairman of the SSU.

Elections to Southern Regional Assembly in April. Of 115 seats, 29 of 36 from Equatoria were Divisionist, but the majority from the 4 other provinces were Unionists. Joseph James Tembura was elected as President of the Southern region HEC on June 29, and approved by Nimeiri. Joseph Lagu was on June 29. sworn in as the new Vice-President of the Republic.

In October Egypt and Sudan signed a Pact of Unity which called for further economic, political and military cooperation and a joint "Nile Valley Parliament" to deal with all mutual matters.

Devaluation of the Sudanese pound, 15 November from 90 piastres to 1 USD to 130 piastres to 1 USD. New negotiations with the IMF over further re-scheduling of foreign debt were started.

1983

The southern garrison in Bor refused to relocate to the north in February. and further fighting escalated in March and April ending in the mutiny by the 105th Battalion of the First Division, led by Lt. Colonel William Nyuan Bani.

In March two leading opponents of redivision were arrested: Vice-President of the Southern Region, Dahl Acuil Aleu and Speaker of the Southern Regional Assembly, Matthew Obur.

Nimeiri was re-elected as President of the republic in a national plebiscite in April with a vote of 99.6 per cent.

Inauguration of the Nile Valley Parliament in the end of May.

Nimeiri announced on 5 June the redivision of the Southern Region into three separate regions: Equatoria, Bahr el Ghazal and Upper Nile. As governors were appointed: Lawrence Wol Wol, Joseph James Tombura and Daniel Kout Matthews for Bahr el Ghazal, Equatoria and Upper Nile respectively.

On 8 September Nimeiri announced a revision of the penal code to link it "organically and spiritually" with Islamic law. Theft, adultery, murder and related offences would be judged according to the Sharia. Alcohol use and gambling were prohibited. Non-Moslems would be exempted, except when convicted of murder or theft. The inauguration of the new code was marked by a ceremony in Khartoum on 23 September presided over by Nimeiri, where stocks of alcohol were destroyed and dumped into the river.

Anya Nya II besieged Nasir in December. The Sudan People' s Liberation Army (SPLA) was formed, and attacked foreign firms involved in two development projects; Chevron Oil drilling in Bentiu and the French construction consortium, Compagnie de Construction International, working on the Jonglei canal.

1984

SPLA takes responsibility for an attack on a Nile steamer in February. 150 out of 800 passengers were reported to have been killed. All river and rail transport to the south halted as a result.

Air raid on Omdurman by a single aircraft, identified as a Tupolev 22 bomber on 14 March. Five people killed and Omdurman radio damaged. Senior Egyptian officers arrived in Khartoum. Libya was accused of the attack, which was denied by Libya, saying that "revolutionary elements" of the Sudanese Air Force were responsible. On request the US sent an AWACS surveillance aircraft to monitor the Sudanese-Libyan aerospace.

The leadership and political aims of the Sudan People's Liberation Army Movement (SPLAM) were announced: Leader: Joseph Oduho; Commander in Chief: John Garang; other military leaders: Kerbino Kuanyin, William Nyuan Bani, Gordon Kong.

29 April Nimeiri proclaimed a state of emergency because the "enemies of the government were active both within Sudan and abroad". Emergency regulations included: suspension of constitutional articles, special powers to the army and police, e.g. to enter private houses, detention of suspects, censorship on personal mail, special state courts with no appeal headed by one civilian judge and two members from the armed forces, etc.

The Cabinet or Council of Ministers was replaced by a "Presidential Council" on 23 May. It comprised the Chief Justice, First and Second Vice-Presidents, Speaker of the National People' s Assembly, presidential advisers, the First Secretary of the SSU, governors of the regions, the mayor of Kharthoum, the controller general, ministers of central ministries, ministers of state, the secretaries of the SSU committees, the Governor of the Bank of Sudan, chairmen of special councils and the Secretary-General of the Alms and Taxation Office.

The Wahdah (Unity) province with its capital at Bentiu was created on 12 June. Wahdah Province would be part of the northern administration. The capital of the Jonglei Province moved from Bor to Ayod.

Pressure by Southern politicians led to the postponement of debate on amendments to the 1973 Constitution in July.

The release of Sadiq el Mahdi and 14 of his followers, arrested in September 1983, on 18 December.

1985

The founder and leader of the Republican Brothers, the 76 year old Mr. Mahmoud Mohamed Taha, was arrested together with 52 members of his group on June 1983 for criticizing the decision on the Sharia laws. Mr. Taha and four leaders were, on 8 January, convicted and sentenced to penalty, but only Mr. Taha was executed. Hanged on 18 January.

Massive influx of refugees from the south into Ethiopia in February. An estimated 120,000 refugees had arrived in Gambela and other south-western towns.

On 3 March the President declared a unilateral cease-fire in the south, amnesty for the rebel forces and the formation of a 30 man committee, led by Sir el Khatim Khalifa, to establish peace and reconciliation in the south.

On 10 March Nimeiri removed leading figures of the Moslem Brotherhood from governmental posts, including Hassan el Turabi, several advisers and three leading judges. 200 members of the Muslim Brotherhood were arrested in the following week as a "preventive measure".

A severe economic decline occurred during 1984 and spring 1985, resulting in shortage of foreign currency and suspension of the IMF and World Bank agreements for re-scheduling of the foreign debt, now estimated to 9 billion USD. Petrol shortage and increases of prices on bread, sugar and petrol by 30 to 60 per cent in February. New price increases were announced on 27 March, the day Nimeiri left for a private visit to the USA. Riots broke out in major cities the same day.

Demonstrations and a general strike broke out at the end of March, leading to the army take-over by General Abdel Rahman Swar el Dahab, the Commander in Chief of the Armed Forces. But the strike was led by a group of medical doctors, headed by El Gizouli Dafalla.

The Transitional Military Council (TMC) formed on 9 April, by General Swar el Dahab, deputy: General Tag el-Din Abdulla Fadul with 13 other officers as members. After negotiations a civilian interim Cabinet was appointed, with El Gizouli Dafalla as Prime Minister and Samuel Aru Bol as his deputy.

Southern Regional Cabinet comprised of the governors of the three regions and four other members was established.

From April to June a number of decisions were taken: multi-party system was allowed and the SSU abolished; the Islamic courts closed; the Sharia penalty code remained in force, but with a re-examination of its more severe applications; all other laws of the former regime would be revised; a non-aligned foreign policy, including good relations to the West combined with resumption of diplomatic relations with Libya and a continuation of the cooperation with Egypt. Diplomatic relations with Ethiopia were not resumed.

General Swar el Dahab, on 20 April, appealed to foreign donors for additional food aid. Both western, eastern and southern Sudan were declared disaster zones. The UN, EEC, USA and other countries started their transport of food aid in June–July. Garang stated that there had been good harvests in the south and that this was only a "military tactic" by the northern government to transport military equipment to the south.

Relations with the United States deteriorated as a result of the Sudanese–Libyan rapprochement. Sudan did not participate in the joint USA-led military exercise called "Bright Star" in the Middle East in August. In November US citizens were advised to avoid Khartoum following the increased presence by Libyan personnel. In 1985 Sudan received 500 million USD in aid. This was reduced to 33 million USD in 1986.

The integration process with Egypt, started by Nimeiri, was "frozen temporarily" in October. Egypt refused to comply with the Sudanese request for extradition of

former President Nimeiri. Regular "high-level political meetings" ceded and the "Nile Valley Parliament" stopped functioning (formally decided in March 1986).
The new leader of Ana Nya II, William Abdullah Chuol, was killed by the SPLA in August.
An interim constitution was approved by the TMC and the Interim Cabinet on 10 October providing a legal framework for the coming elections.
The official name of the Sudan was revised on 15 December. The new name: "The Republic of Sudan" was to replace the previous one; "The Democratic Republic of the Sudan".

1986

Economic problems—resignation of Minister of Finance and relations with the IMF deteriorated (December 1985–March 1986). Mr. Awad A. Majeed, the Minister of Finance in the Interim Council, resigned in December 1985 when the cabinet rejected his proposals for economic reforms drawn up in conjunction with the IMF. The new Minister of Finance, Mr. Sidahmed Taifour Osman, presented an alternative austerity package on 29 January. This plan was not accepted by the IMF, which on 4 February declared the Sudan "no longer eligible for further loans". New austerity measures were announced in February and March, including a 22.4 per cent devaluation of the Sudanese pound.
In the Ethiopian town Koka Dam, 20–24 March, as a result of a series of meetings between representatives of the SPLA and NAS (national alliance of professional organizations and labour unions) a joint declaration was agreed upon for a coming national constitutional conference in Khartoum.
General elections held on 1–12 April, the first multi-party elections since 1968. Only 27 of 68 constituencies in the south arranged voting. Results:

Umma Party (UP)	99
Democratic Unionist Party (DUP)	63
National Islamic Front (NIF)	51
South Sudan Political Alliance (SSPA)	9
Sudanese National Party (SNP)	8
Progressive People' s Party (PPP)	5
Sudanese African People' s Congress (SAPC)	5
Sudanese Communist Party (SCP)	3
Sudanese African Congress (SAC)	2
Others	19

The new assembly first met on 26 April. On 6 May, Swar el Dahab, ceded his power to a five member Supreme Council and the newly elected Prime Minister, Sadiq el Mahdi. Negotiations for a coalition government started. 27 southern representatives walked out of the assembly as a protest against a "southern under-representation" in the council.
A broad-based coalition formed the basis of the new cabinet of 20 ministers: 9 members of the UP, 6 DUP, 1 SSPA, 1 SFP (Sudanese Federal Party), 1 NAS, 1 PPP and 1 SAC. The NIF was not represented, nor was the SPLA. Dr. Khalid Yagi, former head of the NAS delegation to the Koka Dam negotiations, was appointed Minister of Peace and Unity.
Meeting between Sadiq el Mahdi and Col. John Garang in Addis Ababa in April ending in separate press conferences.
SPLA shot down a civilian aircraft over Malakal on 16 August. 60 passengers and crew were killed.
Several international organizations gave alarming reports of a coming famine in the south (August). SPLA claimed military control of the entire southern Sudan and

urged international aid agencies to channel their food and emergency through the humanitarian wing of the SPLA: the Southern Sudan Relief and Rehabilitation Association (SRRA). Serious food shortages were reported by September and 2–3 million people were at risk of starvation. After closer contact between the UN organization World Food Organization (FAO) and the SPLA, an operation called "Operation Rainbow" was launched in October.

On 21 August The prime minister Saddig el Mahdi announced that the "September Laws" would be abrogated.

Social unrest in the north (September–November). Clashes between civilians and the police took place as a result of price increases and shortages of other commodities. Riots in Nyala in south Dar Fur two people were shot on 13 September. The Governor of Dar Fur was attacked by an angry crowd, burning shops and government buildings. Massive demonstrations in Port Sudan and student-led demonstrations continued in Khartoum in October and November.

The Sudanese ambassador to Ethiopia, Mr. Osman Nafi, recalled to Khartoum "for consultations" on 23 November. The measure was followed by strong accusations by Sadiq of Ethiopian assistance to the SPLA.

1987

Agreement reached on 31 January on the establishment of an interim Council in the South until a national constitutional conference could be held. The council composed of representatives from six southern parties and the governors from the three regions. The chairman was Mr. Mattew Obur with Peter Gatkouth Gwal as deputy.

1,000 Libyan troops reported to have entered Dar Fur in February. By March an agreement had been reached to withdraw the troops.

On 18 February, a "Charter of Brotherhood" was signed by Mubarak and Sadiq.

The chairman of the Supreme Council, Mr. Ahmed el Mirghani, dissolved the Council of Ministers on 13 May and asked Sadiq el Mahdi to form a new government. The Deputy Prime Minister and Minister of Foreign Affairs and Secretary General of the DUP, Sharif Zayn el Abidin el Hindi, resigned.

Tribal units in the north-south borderland were armed by the government, and started operating as militias against the SPLA-controlled areas. These included the Messiriya, the Fertit, the Murle, the Toposa and the Mundari. In March a group of northern Dinka were massacred by members of the Rezigat.

State of emergency for one year was declared by the government on 2 July. Approved by the Assembly in September after several articles being rejected for violating important civil liberties. Several groups called "Guardians of May" (Nimeiri supporters) were arrested.

Several senior DUP members in the Cabinet resigned in June. On 22 August the DUP announced its withdrawal from the government. A compromise agreement reached on 7 October, followed by new appointments of DUP ministers in December.

After several meetings in Addis Ababa, Kampala and Nairobi between the six southern based parties and the SPLM/A and the Anya Nya II, an agreement was reached in Nairobi on 22 September on a joint appeal to the government for convening of a national constitutional conference.

During autumn the SPLA gained support from the Mundari, Toposa and Kakwa. Several towns were captured during the year: Kurmuk, Nasir, Mundri, Jokaw and others.

The Sudanese pound devalued by 37.5 per cent in early October. Other measures also taken: debt re-scheduling, fresh loans and a continuation of the structural adjustment programme requested by the IMF. The government was also to present an economic recovery programme to a consultative meeting of donors to be held in Paris in May. The foreign debt was estimated in February to 10.3 billion USD.

Serious inter-ethnic conflicts in Dar Fur coupled with a rapidly deteriorating security problem led to the convening of the first Dar Fur security conference in El Fasher in November this year.

1988

A transitional charter was signed by representatives of the government and 17 political parties, except SPLA/SPLM, on 10 January. It was intended to act as an interim measure defining Sudan's political structures until the holding of a national constitutional conference during 1988.

Sadiq el Mahdi was re-elected Prime Minister by the Constituent Assembly by a vote of 196 out of 222. Sadiq was supported by NIF, following an agreement between the UP, DUP and NIF in early April. The new cabinet was extended by 20 new members, with Hassan el Turabi as Attorney General and Justice Minister.

On 16 December 1987, the Prime Minister reiterated his intention of repealing the Sharia penal code, declaring that "the barbaric aspects of the laws have been repealed and we are now preparing to abrogate the rest".

Floods seriously affected northern Sudan after catastrophic storms on 4 August. 8 inches of rain—the yearly norm—fell in 13 hours. A state of emergency was declared and an appeal for international assistance was made.

An Islamic code of justice was tabled by the government to the Constituent Assemby on 19 September. 22 members of the southern opposition walked out. The new code introduced by Turabi included flogging, stoning and amputations for different offences. It was to be applied to all members of the society in northern Sudan. On 4 October it was decided to refer the issue to a legislative committee for "further studies".

DUP and SPLA held a series of meetings from August to November and an agreement was reached in Addis Ababa on 14 November. The SPLA would implement a cease-fire after the ratification of the agreement by the Constituent Assembly. The Council of Ministers did not endorse the agreement. DUP resigned from the government in late December.

Serious inter-ethnic warfare continued in Dar Fur leading to a very explosive security situation exasperated by the easy supply of modern arms through the various Chadian factions using Sudan as their staging ground.

1989

Several strategic towns were captured by SPLA late January and February: Nasir, Liria, Torit and others. Several Western agencies reportedly supplied aid directly to SPLA-held areas.

In a memorandum on 20 February military leaders demanded major changes in the government and its policies within one week. On 21 February the Defence Minister, General Abdel Majid Hamid Khalil, resigned from the council in protest.

Western creditors demanded in February that the government should allow transport of famine relief to southern areas.

Sadiq appointed a new Council of Ministers in March with the stated aim of reviving the peace process. NIF refused to participate, and went into opposition.

On 1 May SPLA announced a one month cease-fire in order to start peace negotiations and to assist famine relief operations. On 6 May Sadiq lifted the state of emergency and sent a delegation to Addis Ababa for talks with the SPLA.

Reports of ethnic clashes in Dar Fur between the Fur and nomadic Arab groups near the Chadian border in April, with hundreds of people killed and villages burned. Massive displacement and loss of life occurred as a result.

On 27 May Sadiq announced talks to take place in Addis Ababa on 10 June about ways to implement the November 1988 DUP-SPLA agreement.

On 10 June SPLA and government delegations opened negotiations. An agreement was reached the first day: continued cease-fire, lifting of state of emergency, freezing the implementation of Islamic laws and abrogation of military agreements with Egypt and Libya.

On 30 June Sadiq' s government was overthrown in a bloodless coup by a group of army officers led by Brig. Gen. Omar Hassan Ahmad al Bashir in what came to be known as the "Revolution of National Salvation".

A 15 member Command Council for "the Revolution of National Salvation" was appointed; El Bashir as Prime Minister, Defence Minister and Commander in Chief. Suspension of the constitution, dissolution of parliament and all political parties, banning of strikes, trade unions and all newspapers except the Army newspaper were taken as measures to curb opposition.

Sadiq was arrested on 6 July together with other officials of the former regime.

On 7 July El Bashir stated the revolution' s opposition to the November peace agreements of DUP-SPLA which was later approved by the Mahdi government in March.

A national conference for dialogue and peace took place in Khartoum from 9 September to 10 October without SPLA being present.

In October the former political parties in the dissolved Constituent Assembly and professional organisations had formed an umbrella organization called the "National Democratic Alliance" (NDA) to oppose the new regime in power.

On 1 December the Carter Centre in Atlanta initiated a new round of peace talks between the military government and the SPLA in Nairobi. The talks ended with no result on 5 December.

On 7 December Col. Mohammad el Amin Khalifa, regarded as the third strong man in the regime stated that the Sharia laws would be implemented fully for the whole country, including the penal codes of amputation etc.

1990

In January SPLA claimed several victories in Equatoria: the Kaya garrison fell on 14 January, Yei on 28 January and the Kajo-Kaji plateau came under SPLA control. Juba was put under siege, and 100 foreign aid-workers were evacuated during a cease-fire. The SPLA appealed to the government to allow 300,000 civilians to flee the town, which was rejected by the government.

In March USA stopped all further military and economic aid to the Sudan, announced "in accordance with a policy that military regimes which acceded to power via coup would be denied aid unless it improves the situation of the country".

28 army and police officers executed after being accused of a coup attempt on 23 April.

A new coup attempt was crushed on 12 September.

IMF declared the Sudan "non-cooperative" in September. The Saudi Arabian government voted against Sudan in the IMF council.

A joint charter between Lybia and Sudan was signed in October to link Dar Fur with
the neighbouring province of Kufra in Libya to promote trade and control immigration.

In mid-November railway workers and students at the Khartoum University rioted.

The Sudanese government was isolated internationally as a result of its support of
Sadam Hussein in the Gulf War.

The "Hilat Shouk" camp in the Khartoum area was bulldozed in late October and
some 30,000 occupants were moved to Jebel Aulia, 40 km south of Khartoum.

International relief agencies stated at the end of the year that 8 million people on the
Horn faced starvation, and that Sudan would need 1.5 million tonnes of food the
coming year.The gravity of the situation was officially denied by Gen. Bashir,
saying that "The Sudan will be self-sufficient with food and grain within a year
or two".

1991

On 8 February Bashir signed a decree which divided the Sudan into 9 "states", sub-
divided into 66 provinces and 281 local government areas. These new states
would be responsible for local administrations and some tax collection, while the
central government retained control over foreign policy, military affairs, trade,
the economy and other key sectors. The new states were: Khartoum, Central,
Kordofan, Dar Fur, Northern, Eastern, Bahr el Ghazal, Upper Nile and
Equatoria. The Islamic penal code, introduced on 1 February 1991 being an
amendment of the Sharia law, was not to be applied in the three southern states,
which could decide upon this issue later themselves.

SPLA denounced these measures on 18 February. They said: "The NIF' s meaning of
federalism is very clear: it is to promote Arabism and Islam in the south".

A conference on new ways of organizing the political system in Sudan was held in
Khartoum from 29 April to 2 May "popular committees" on local basis were
proposed, on the lines of the Libyan model, as the "Western-style, multi-party
parliamentarism" was rejected as not suitable for Africa and the Sudan.

Sadiq el Mahdi, Mohammed Ibrahim Nugud (the general secretary of the Sudanese
communist party) and other political prisoners were released under an amnesty
announced at the opening of the above mentioned Conference.

A coup attempt was reported by Egyptian newspaper El Wafd on 20 April and the
execution of 20 army officers allegedly involved in the coup. The report was
denied by Sudanese officials.

The overthrow of President Mengistu' s regime in Ethiopia by different guerilla
armies in May was followed by expulsion of the political and military bases of
SPLA and several hundred thousand southern Sudanese refugees from Ethiopia.
The Ethiopian regime had supported SPLA and perhaps been its most important
foreign ally. The take-over organizations of EPRDF, EPLF and TPLF in Ethiopia
had been backed by the Sudanese government and by May destroyed SPLA' s
main foreign bases. This was celebrated as a decisive victory in Khartoum, and
the SPLA subsequently had to move its headquarters to Equatoria.

Intensified diplomatic activity by SPLA and the military government in June and
July. Intensified diplomatic activity on both sides from mid-June raised new
hopes for peace negotiations. The US Assistant Secretary for Africa, Herman
Cohen, acted as mediator. The Chairman of the OAU, the Nigerian President
Babangida, brought in as mediator, but by July the government backed out. The
initiative by the Nigerian president was called Abuja I.

1,300 political prisoners released as the famous Kobar prison was demolished, as
part of a public demonstration shown on the Sudanese television. On 26 July the

Sudanese government presented a report to the UN Human Rights Commission in Geneva in response to the UN allegations of human rights violations in the Sudan later considered by the committee as insufficient.

A statement published in Nairobi on 28 August and signed by three of the thirteen SPLA field commanders: Riek Mashar, Lam Akol and Gordon Koang, announced that Col. Garang was removed from the SPLA leadership, and that the three commanders had taken over the command. Col. Garang was accused of being dictatorial and of "war lordship". The group had its base in Nasir, and issued a policy statement, with the following main points: stop the war, immediate negotiations for cession of the south, implementation of democracy in the liberation movement and a greater emphasis on relief efforts.

Strained relations to the IMF, Sudanese currency devaluation in October by 70 per cent and cuts in subsidies on basic commodities. Although not excluded from IMF, Sudan still regarded as "non-co-operative" in November by the fund. The world's financial markets were *de facto* closed for Sudan by the end of the year.

Clashes between the "Nasir" (Machar) and "Torit" (Garang) factions of the SPLA in November around Bor and Kongor led to numerous civilian casualties, and a heavy stream of refugees southwards into Equatoria. The attack was according to NGO reports a combined attack by the Government-backed Anya Nya ll, SPLA-Nasir and Nuer tribesmen on a rival Dinka group, the home village of Col. Garang. As a result of mediation by the National Council of Churches in Kenya in Nairobi, a 12 point peace plan was reached on 18 December by representatives of the two factions.

Fighting in Dar Fur. Fighting between government troops and SPLA forces led by an ex-NIF member, exploded in December around Jebel Marra area. After heavy losses on both sides the SPLA force led by Dauod Bolad was beaten back and Bolad himself was arrested and shown on the Sudanese TV.

A 157 member delegation headed by the Iranian president Rafsanjani, visited Sudan 13–15 December. A cooperation agreement was signed, including Iranian support on oil deliveries, trade exchanges and the "training of technical cadres" by Iranian personnel. According to Arab and US press reports, 2,000 Iranian Revolutionary Guards were training Sudanese recruits in desert camps. Iran was also to be funding the purchase of Chinese weaponry to Sudan.

Africa Watch on 10 December reported on a government campaign in the Nuba mountains as a result of Nuba support of the SPLA. Described as a "steady war of attrition" where Sudanese authorities sought to eliminate community leaders and the educated classes among the Nuba. On 29 December it was announced that a *Jihad*, had been declared in the province of Southern Kordofan.

1992

Austerity measures and economic reforms were announced by the Minister of Finance, Abdul Rahim Mahmoud Hamdi, on 3 February, including devaluation of currency, privatization, cuts in commodity subsidies and other measures. The Sudanese pound was floated, and *de facto* devalued from USD 1 = £S 15.15 to USD 1 = £S 90 (mid-February) The privatization included the sale of the national airline, telecommunications, shipping line, and industrial complexes to local and foreign investors.

A Transitional National Assembly formed on 13 February, appointed by the military government, met for the first time on 24 February under the chairmanship of Mohammed el Amin Khalifa.

A dry season offensive by the military government was launched in February against SPLA, "Torit faction", starting from several places in the south: from Wau,

Malakal and Juba, as well as up the Bahr el Jebel towards Shambe and also from Gambella. The border town, Pochala captured by March. Ethiopian and Iranian troops reported to have participated in the offensive, but denied by Sudan government.

Government forces captured several southern towns in its dry-season offensive. In April; Bor, Yirol, Pibor, Mongalla. In May; Liria, Kapoeta and "the biggest rebel camp in the Bahr el Ghazal".

A new round of talks between the two parties started in Abuja on 27 May, but this time with two SPLA factions. Broke down after a few days on major issues as Sharia laws and the political system of the new Sudan. This round of talks was called Abuja II.

The Council of Minister on 17 May announced a new currency, the Dinar, worth 10 Sudanese pounds, to gradually replace the pound.

Contributors

Raphael Badal
(Ph.D.), Political Sientist, Universiy of Khartoum, Sudan.

Sharif Harir
(Dr.Philos.), Social Anthropologist, Center for Development Studies,
University of Bergen, Norway.

Kjell Hødnebø
(Cand.Philol.), Historian, University of Bergen, Norway.

Douglas H. Johnson
(Ph.D.) Historian, St. Anthony's College, Oxford University, England.

M. A. Mohamed Salih
(Ph.D.), Social Anthropologist, Institute of Social Studies, The Hague,
Netherlands.

Terje Tvedt
(Dr.Philos.), Historian, Center for Development Studies, University of
Bergen, Norway.

Karl Wohlmuth
(Dr.Philos.), Economist, University of Bremen, Germany.

Peter Woodward
(Ph.D.), Political Scientist, University of Reading, England.